TRANSFORMING

Fear

INTO Gold

To Andrew Snyder,

Thank you for your courage
to face the darkness + bring
more Light to this planet!

Love, peace, + Joy,

Barbara Stone, PhD

Also by Barbara Stone:

Invisible Roots: How Healing Past Life Trauma Can Liberate Your Present (2008)

Foreword by Bernie Siegel, MD

Case histories and Soul Detective Protocols for healing past life trauma and earthbound spirit attachments.

Cancer As Initiation: Surviving the Fire (1994)

The popular form of Dr. Stone's doctoral dissertation in clinical psychology on the emotional factors influencing cancer survival.

TRANSFORMING

Fear
INTO *Gold*

How Facing What Frightens You the Most
Can Heal and Light Up Your Heart.

BARBARA STONE, PhD

Library of Congress Control Number: 2012918037

Names and identifying details in the descriptions of clients and situations in this book have been changed to protect client confidentiality.

The term Soul Detective was trademarked in 2010 by Barbara Stone. For convenience and clarity, the superscript registration mark will not be used in the text of this book.

Cover design by Karen Kane

Published by The Indigo Connection, LLC
Strongsville, OH

Paperback ISBN 978-0-9883898-0-9
ePub ISBN 978-0-9883898-1-6
ebook/pdf file ISBN 978-0-9883898-2-3

To send correspondence to the author, visit her website at
www.SoulDetective.net

Printed in the United States of America

First Printing: 2012

Dedication

I dedicate this book to my sister in heaven,
Johanna Mary Stone, for being the impetus
to jump headlong into the spirit world,
to my clients and Soul Detectives,
who have been my teachers,
and most of all to the Beings of Light
who guide our way back to wholeness.

Disclaimer

The information contained in this book, including ideas, suggestions, remedies, approaches, techniques, protocols, methods, and other materials, is provided only as general information, is solely intended for educational purposes, is not meant to be a substitute for medical or psychological treatment, and does not replace the services of health care professionals. If you experience any emotional distress or physical discomfort using any of the suggestions, remedies, approaches, techniques, protocols, or methods contained in this book, you are advised to stop and to seek professional care, if appropriate.

Publishing of the information contained in this book is not intended to create a client-therapist or any other type of professional relationship between the reader and the author. The author does not make any warranty, guarantee, or prediction regarding the outcome for an individual using this book for any particular issue.

You agree to assume and accept full responsibility for any and all risks associated with using any of the suggestions, remedies, approaches, techniques, protocols, and methods described in this book and agree to accept full and complete responsibility for applying what you may learn from reading this book. By continuing to read this book you agree to the terms of the Disclaimer and to fully release, indemnify, and hold harmless, the author and others associated with the publication of this book from any claim or liability and for any damage or injury of whatsoever kind or nature that you may incur arising at any time out of or in relation to your use of the information presented in this book. If any court of law rules that any part of the Disclaimer is invalid, the Disclaimer stands as if those parts were struck out.

Contents

SECTION THREE: Hope for Humanity

Foreword

If you want to awaken all of humanity, then awaken yourself.
If you want to eliminate the suffering in the world,
then eliminate all that is dark and negative in yourself.
Truly, the greatest gift you have to give is that of
your own self-transformation.
—Lao Tzu

Transforming Fear into Gold: How Facing What Frightens You the Most Can Heal and Light Up Your Heart is an amalgamation of Barbara Stone's brilliant mind, her creative spirit, and her desire to facilitate bringing peace and light into each human heart. Gold is the most valued metal on the planet. Finding the light and love in our hearts is the most valued goal of human life and is the *gold* that brings us to inner peacefulness and connectedness with the Divine. Just as the therapeutic use of energy psychology is beginning to radically change the speed and depth of mental health therapy, Soul Detective work, utilizing Dr. Roger Callahan's Diagnostic Thought Field Therapy, is offering the mental health profession an adjunctive treatment for deep-seated mental and emotional discomfort and illness. Many of the chronic issues that have been medicated into submission and undiagnosable conditions that have caused emotional-mental disintegration can now be ameliorated by finding the underlying cause, the Invisible Roots that feed and maintain chronic, internal dysfunction.

Transforming Fear into Gold brings new information into mainstream awareness about our human origins. For many years, the consensus of thought regarding Earth's history was that humankind started from very primitive beginnings and steadily progressed upward in the development of culture and science. However, anomalies such as the unearthing of "out-of-place arti-facts," the knowledge ancient people had about astronomy, and astonishing feats of engineering such as the Pyramids of ancient Egypt do not fit the es-tablished pattern of prehistory. Evidence points to the existence of advanced civilizations on planet Earth before any of the known ancient cultures came into being. Indeed, all over the world, cultures refer to ancient references about extraterrestrial visitors imparting either their knowledge or technology. The unparalleled rate of technological advances and scientific discoveries in the last century relative to advances over the previous 2000 years and the increas-ing numbers of reliable sightings of UFOs (many times by trained military personnel, astronauts, and airplane pilots) point to the possibility that we may not be alone in the universe.

Obviously, something is missing from the history of life on this planet. This book shares information uncovered from the translation of ancient Sume-rian tablets found in modern-day Iraq, site of the civilization of ancient Sumer in the fourth millennium BC. It includes the significance of gold and an expla-nation of the real origins of *Homo sapiens*. As you read through this book and perhaps dig into the writing of Zecharia Sitchin and his scholarly translations of the Sumerian tablets, you begin to learn that humanity has been taught many "truths" that may not be true at all. As you trace the history outlined by Sitchin and others and learn about planet Nibiru and the Anunnaki civilization there and on Earth, you'll be able to recognize the Anunnaki as part of the Christian Old Testament, in which they were called the Nephilim, and this recognition may begin to open your awareness, challenging you to understand and accept.

The Anunnaki, Nibiru, and Gold

The Anunnaki were an advanced civilization facing the demise of their planet Nibiru because of a breach in their atmosphere. They needed gold to repair their atmosphere and came to Earth to mine this metal. Human beings have long been enslaved by gold: first, as workers in the Anunnaki gold mines, and second, by the need to be adorned with gold as the Anunnaki gods were adorned. Author Michael Tellinger[1] postulates that the Anunnaki drank mona-

---

1 *Slaves Species of god.*

tomic gold, "water gold," or water enhanced by gold, in the belief that it extended life, prevented illness, and repaired DNA. Unfortunately, this use of gold may have also kept their crown chakras closed, causing them to depend on themselves for their survival and separating them individually and culturally from the Divine.

Today, research has shown that gold does have healing properties, and when used wisely, it can be beneficial. "In patients with inflammatory arthritis, such as adult and juvenile rheumatoid arthritis, gold salts decrease the inflammation of the joint lining and also prevent the inflammation from destroying the bone and cartilage surrounding the joint."[2] Current research is showing some positive results using gold in the treatment of cancer. Various medications containing gold are marketed and used throughout the world: auranofin (UK and US), aurothioglucose (gold thioglucose; US), disodium aurothiomalate, sodium aurothiosulfate (gold sodium thiosulfate), and sodium aurothiomalate (gold sodium thiomalate; UK). As with most medications, they do have side effects.

For the Anunnaki, a side effect of their use of monatomic gold was blocking their emotional capacity for compassion and love. They unintentionally shared with humanity their fears, jealousies, and tendency to solve their issues with violence instead of with love. But as intellectually gifted beings, they also introduced the positive elements of their culture, including advanced healing techniques, geometry, sacred geometry, astronomy, genetics and cell research, and engineering and building technology. *Transforming Fear into Gold* presents a well-studied theory regarding their early contact with this planet, the way they influenced our origins, and the importance of understanding their culture to heal our lives and the Earth.

Soul Therapy

Life is a miracle! The essence of who we are, the part that came into being at the moment of our soul's birth, exists forever. Most of us have minimal insight and understanding into the life of our own soul. The knowledge we gain helps us heal our life today, benefitting the totality of who we are. The lessons

---

2   Medicinenet.com: "Gold sodium thiomalate; aurothiomalate, Myochrysine." http://www.medicinenet.com/aurothiomalate/article.htm

we learn enrich our existence individually, culturally, and universally. Working at the intuitive level has been linked to the occult, and spiritual work is left to religion and pastoral care. These traditions are the primary reasons professional psychological and psychiatric organizations are reluctant to fully accept and endorse energy psychology and its emphasis on clearing and balancing the human energy field by correcting the energetic flow of the meridians of traditional Chinese medicine and the chakras of ancient Ayurvedic medicine. However, many of our mental and emotional issues originate within our intuitive and spiritual energy bodies, often causing feelings and thoughts we don't readily understand, accompanied by symptoms conventional approaches often diagnose as serious mental illness.

Some of what we perceive as our day-to-day reality is an illusion. What we perceive as reality is based on what we perceive through our five senses, or six senses if we include the kinesthetic sense that helps us relate to the world through our body wisdom. Yet much of what goes on around us exists behind a spiritual veil and out of our conscious awareness. While some of us are able to sense the spiritual beings around us, many of us go through life completely unaware of their presence and their importance. Sometimes we have questions about isolated experiences that seem to have no logical explanation. For instance, one of my clients has a little dog who constantly barks at the same empty chair as if someone is sitting there or runs into her office and barks angrily as if to warn that someone is present. Some of us report dreams so authentic they can hardly be distinguished from reality, and some of us experience déjà vu episodes and visions.

The Soul Detective protocols developed by Dr. Stone and the insights they facilitate help us answer our questions and heal the emotional and spiritual pain that lies deep within our being. The Soul Detective protocols are uniquely helpful tools for mental health professionals. They naturally and routinely allow access to the innate higher wisdom we all possess and to information and memories stored at levels beneath our conscious awareness. The various protocols provide hope to individuals with chronic, difficult to diagnose issues: releasing negativity; facilitating insight, self-awareness, and self-empowerment; and providing clients the emotional freedom needed to build a happier, richer, more satisfying life.

Knowing Who I Am

My Soul Detective training, which included sessions with Barbara Stone, has changed my life in profound ways. Most important, I know who I am, and I am comfortable in my physical body and with the life I've chosen. Our work has expanded my emotional-spiritual awareness, my intuition, my inner knowing, and it has allowed me to experience the profound love that formed the Universe. I now understand that you and I have absolutely no limitations in our life other than the ones we create for ourselves. Our life book is wide open, just waiting for us to fill the blank pages. I have glimpsed the meaning of Unity Consciousness, the network of people and experiences that God creates for us in order to share love and support us and to provide opportunities for growth and increased understanding. I've gained wisdom that allows me to understand that we are all one, sharing the same vital life-force energy, birthed by the same omnipotent primary source. All forms of life on Earth and throughout the Universe and Creation originated from the energy the Anunnaki called the Creator of All. It is the same loving energy that Taoism and the Integral Way understood and taught about in 550 BC, that Buddha shared with his followers approximately 400 BC, that Christ brought into the world during his lifetime, and the same universal being some Native American cultures call Gitche Manitou.

I used to identify myself as daughter, wife, mother, grandmother, student, teacher, therapist, and author. Now I understand how limited these definitions are. I've accepted and internalized the fact that my life didn't begin on the day of my physical birth, but began with the birth of my soul many thousands of years ago. While my current life history is important, it is just a moment in time. There were many moments in my soul life before my birth as Janet, and there will be many moments of my soul life after the death of Janet. My soul history may be the most important part of who I am, as it holds the awareness of every single experience it has encountered and survived since its birth.

When we investigate the realities of being alive, is it any wonder we have dreams that seem like reality, recognize deep mental-emotional-spiritual responses to certain individuals when we meet them for the first time, are able to talk in detail about a place we've never been, possess inner wisdom that doesn't stem from current education or religious training, or experience a driving need to travel to some obscure part of the world that wouldn't interest us at all if it weren't for the mysterious obsession?

Soul Detective Listening

Today when I hear a client mention unusual or frightening symptoms, I listen with my Soul Detective ears. I'll probably still recommend a good physical exam, or if emotional symptoms are significant, recommend an orthomolecular psychiatrist for an evaluation of neurotransmitter levels so the individual can come into emotional balance naturally with nutrients, supplementing with medication only as much as is necessary. As soon as a trusting rapport is established, I'll mention energy psychology and the life-changing possibilities of Soul Detective work. For example, a prospective Soul Detective client might have a story similar to the one I heard years ago before Soul Detective work came into being. My artist friend said something like this: "I stood in front of a painting hanging on the wall in the museum, and I knew instinctively and instantly that I'd painted that magnificent piece of art in a former lifetime. I just stood there, very emotional, recognizing the art, feeling it resonate within my being. I knew I was meeting evidence of and experiencing a bit of another life, another existence."

If the same incident happened today, I'd have two Soul Detective Protocols to offer her: one for Past Life Trauma and one for a Positive Past Life. If the artist lifetime had trauma, she could sort through her memories, heal the issues of that life, apply the lessons learned, and help any part of her that painted the masterpiece that might still be stuck between the worlds to go home to the Light. If she had no trauma in that lifetime, we could do the Positive Past Life protocol to bring the gifts of her artistic talent and mastery into this present lifetime.

Other potential Soul Detective alerts: repeated dreams or nightmares, recognition and emotional response to an individual you have never met before, an issue that keeps coming up over and over in various situations, anxiety or depression with no apparent cause, inability to accomplish minor tasks or a particular kind of task, a diagnosis that does not respond to appropriate medications, voices heard mentally, and visions or déjà vu experiences that seem to be informational, containing important information to move your life forward.

Therapists and their clients do not have to believe in past lives, dark energies, or extraterrestrials in order to achieve a positive result. The language of the various Soul Detective protocols allows the clients, through imagery and intuition, to tap into their unconscious memory bank. Because the language of the protocols is uniquely and expertly written, therapy savvy clients can't anticipate the therapist's next words, comments, or questions and, in so doing, find a way around the memories and limiting beliefs that reside deep within them. Whether the story that evolves is true or not, the client is guided to the root of a soul issue and given an acceptable way to heal the pain. Then, through multiplying the benefits, a technique originated by Gary Craig, the father of Emotional Freedom Techniques (EFT), which he called "borrowing benefits," we can invite others who have had similar experiences to come into the protected space we have established and obtain their own healing. Thousands of souls are healing and finding peace through the work of Soul Detectives, EFT practitioners, and many other energy healing techniques. As mentioned earlier, my own soul has found healing, a new level of self-acceptance, and new insights that positively enhance every aspect of my life.

Morphic Resonance

My soul part that has healed and grown is somehow connected in resonance to Ea, the son of Anu, the ruler of Nibiru. Ea, or Enki as he is sometimes called, came to earth more than 400,000 years ago in search of the gold the Anunnaki needed to heal their planet's atmosphere. My story and my relationship with Ea are detailed later in the book. You'll find Ea to be a very interesting being: on one hand a brilliant, caring, and responsible son, father, and brother; and on the other hand, a strong, powerful, assertive, maybe even dominating, free-thinking leader who went to extraordinary lengths to preserve his planet and his civilization.

Thank you, Barbara Stone, for the *Invisible Roots* Soul Detective Protocols, for developing the Soul Detective Certification classes, and for writing *Transforming Fear into Gold: How Facing What Frightens You the Most Can Heal and Light Up Your Heart*! Thank you for opening our hearts and minds to a new way of approaching mental health symptoms and the distress they create. Many lives have been enriched through individual Soul Detective sessions, and thousands more will reach out for this deep, transformational healing work now available. Each Soul Detective who has studied with you and each client who has experienced the benefits of Soul Detective work is grateful. Our world is shifting to a more positive reality, in part because this work exists. Thank you for your tireless efforts on behalf of humanity and all beings that might exist throughout Creation. Your work, and the work of a growing number of Certified Soul Detectives, is creating peacefulness within, opening hearts, and changing the world for the better. Soul Detective work amplifies real, tangible, hope for peace on Earth.

—Janet Nestor, author of *Pathways to Wellness*

Acknowledgments

I am so grateful to my parents for bringing me into this world when my work could blossom at this monumental time in history, the 2012 Shift of the Ages. They gave me a platform to grow and launch my Soul Detective work, a part of the tremendous wave of healing going on in the Universe right now.

I am grateful to all of my family for their loving support of my work, which goes way outside the box of our former belief systems. I thank them for listening to me as my ideas were forming and for all the ways they have brought healing information into my awareness. I especially thank them for letting me practice new methods on them first before using them with my clients! I thank my long-time dear friend and colleague Bert Fellows for his spiritual insights and his love and support which includes my whole family.

I am deeply grateful to my clients, who have been my teachers and have given me glimpses into other worlds and other times and places on Earth. I thank all of my clients who have given me permission to share their stories in this book, with identifying details changed to protect their privacy.

I am grateful to all of the energy psychology teachers who have contributed to the toolbox of therapeutic interventions I have learned. I thank Roger Callahan, PhD, for developing the power tool I use the most, Thought Field Therapy (TFT), and his wife, Joanne, for her support in using TFT in humanitarian trauma relief work in Africa. I thank my colleague Lori Leyden, PhD, for providing the chance to travel with her to Rwanda and to support her humanitarian work through Project LIGHT Rwanda, online at www.createglobalhealing.org. I thank my colleague Dr. Iwowarri Berian

James for giving me a chance to teach with him in his humanitarian work in Nigeria. Special thanks go to Greg Nicosia, PhD, who first taught me TFT and mentored me through the process of becoming a teacher.

I thank my dear friends and colleagues—too numerous to list them all—for their dialogue with me and helping me see deeper truths. You know who you are! I am especially grateful for the expansion and support that has come from my colleague Robert Alcorn, MD, a holistic psychiatrist. I also thank intuitive counselor Karen Rollins for helping me see how big the vision of this work really is.

I am incredibly grateful to my students as we learn together and expand each other's understanding of how to heal the human soul. I am especially grateful to my students who have completed Soul Detective Certification and are listed on my website under practitioners: in the United States, Mary Anderson, Margaret Clench, Dianna Costa, Debra Brown-Gordy, Jennifer Closshey, Janet Nestor, Phyllis Robinson, Tom Searcy, Karen Turner, and Diane Winn; in Bulgaria, Irena Kostadinova, Georgieva, Maria Kirova, Georgi Dimitrov Krastev, Evgeniya Ventsislavova Pekova, Rositsa Mitkova Stakeva, Emilia Tsvetkova, and Veselina Tsvetkova.

I thank Karen Kane for creating a dynamite cover for the book! I thank my daughter for her careful proofreading and suggestions for clarity and all the others who have helped shape this material. I am grateful to my editor, Stephanie Marohn, for taking on this challenging material.

Most of all, I thank my spiritual guidance team, which includes my beloved Yeshua, Archangels, and hosts of other angels, for their love and support and all the work they have done behind the scenes to guide and protect me. I am deeply grateful to the power and strength of Archangel Michael's presence as I bring this message of how to transform fear into the golden Light of love.

SECTION ONE:

Transforming the Dark Side

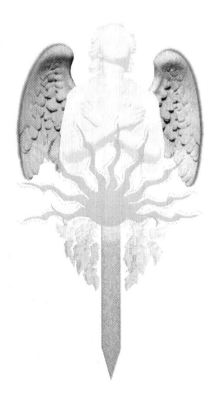

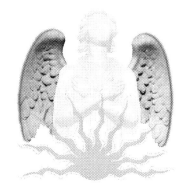

CHAPTER 1

Dark Force Mechanics

Look all around thee, O man.
See thine own light reflected.
Aye, even in the darkness around thee,
Thine own Light pours forth through the veil.[1]

*T*his book is for healers everywhere who have felt pulled into the underworld by extremely traumatic case material their clients have presented and whose hearts have been broken by seeing the depths of depravity that humans are capable of perpetrating upon each other. It is for everyone who wonders how people could be so blind as to abuse someone else when the action damages the soul of the perpetrator.

The goal of this book is to understand the belief systems that run detrimental mental and emotional patterns and programming, to shine light on how they have gotten into our thinking and influence our behavior, and to provide a step-by-step Soul Detective protocol to transform the distortions into the golden light of truth.

---

1   Doreal, *The Emerald Tablets of Thoth the Atlantean*, 49.

My own heart was broken by listening to the memories of a client I call Paula who reported being sadistically abused by the satanic cult to which her father belonged. She told me unspeakable horrors and then asked me to write her story. This book reports her case in detail in Section Two: I Want This Nightmare to End. When Paula was not allowed verbal expression of her pain, she could tell her story through sketching what happened. A talented artist, her drawings and poetry included in her narrative amplify the emotional impact of her story.

Paula, Self-Portrait

Whether everything Paula told me was literally true, fabricated to get attention, or metaphorical, her account was always consistent. I had trouble keeping the ages straight of the thirty-four dissociated parts of Paula that we met, and when I mistakenly thought a twelve-year-old part was ten years old, that part was adamant that I had her age wrong!

Sacrifice of the Firstborn

Paula said that every cult member had to sacrifice their firstborn child and remembered ceremonies where these children were killed and burned, including her own firstborn, even though she never joined the cult. I knew that in the Bible, God had asked Abraham to sacrifice Isaac, his firstborn son, as a burnt offering to the Lord, but I was shocked that such a barbaric practice might still be happening in modern times. I searched to understand the distorted belief system that in order to show loyalty to a god, a person had to give as a burnt offering their very best, most precious thing in the entire world—their firstborn child. That search led me to another truly shocking body of knowledge about the ancient origins of our race that comes from translations of cuneiform tablets found in Iraq, the location of ancient Sumer, the oldest civilization on Earth that has left a recorded history. The translations reveal that Sumer had a very advanced culture in 4000 BC, with knowledge about the origins and makeup of our solar system and the placement of the planets revolving around our sun that is hard to explain, given the technology available during that time period. The Sumerian tablets report that ancient astronauts came to Earth in search of gold and gene spliced a slave race of gold miners by crossing their genes with a primitive hominid species already walking on the planet, probably *Homo erectus*, to produce *Homo sapiens*. While this idea flies against everything science believes about human evolution being a gradual process of one species evolving from another, it might explain the quantum jump in civilizations that suddenly sprang up out of nowhere about 10,000 years ago on both sides of the Atlantic Ocean.

> They went, almost overnight historically speaking, from being hunter-gatherers to sophisticated farmers. They sowed crops, the crops we still grow today, which seemed to appear from nowhere and whose original wild variants we have still not identified. They started reading, writing, mathematics, astronomy, and science.[2]

It might also explain why authors such as Erich von Däniken,[3] Sir Frances Crick (molecular biologist and co-discoverer of the structure of DNA), and Zecharia Sitchin, author of the seven-volume *Earth Chronicles* series,[4] all came to the conclusion that our civilization was seeded by ancient astronauts who gene spliced our race, brought us grains and livestock, and taught us the arts of civilization.

God's Regrets

I grew up in a Christian home in the Bible Belt and was taught that God is love. As I read the whole Bible through several times as a teenager, I was

---

2   Stuart Miller commenting on an article by Will Hart at www.World-Mysteries.com

3   *Chariots of the Gods.*

4   Sitchin, *The Twelfth Planet, The Stairway to Heaven, The Wars of Gods and Men, The Lost Realms, When Time Began, The Cosmic Code,* and *The End of Days.*

puzzled by reading about how fickle, vicious, and vengeful God was with his people in the Old Testament. First God created them. But the humans did not behave well, so God wanted to kill them all and also wipe out all other land creatures. Then Noah found his favor, and God saved a few humans and animals in the ark. Church sermons preached that God is all-powerful. I wondered how an omnipotent Creator could make such a defective product. I felt something was missing from this story!

> The LORD saw how great the wickedness of the human race had become on the earth, and that every inclination of the thoughts of the human heart was only evil all the time. The LORD regretted that he had made human beings on the earth, and his heart was deeply troubled. So the LORD said, "I will wipe from the face of the earth the human race I have created—and with them the animals, the birds and the creatures that move along the ground—for I regret that I have made them." But Noah found favor in the eyes of the LORD. (Genesis 6:5-8 NIV [New International Version])

The Bible does not say why the Lord suddenly changed his mind and saved the race.

Fear Imprints

Fear seems to be imprinted into the matrix of the human energy system. If a political leader can make people afraid, the leader gains power over them. Fear operates differently in the animal kingdom. Animals in nature become frightened when danger approaches. For example, if a gazelle grazing on the plain sees a lioness approaching, a fight-or-flight sympathetic nervous system response launches, and the gazelle runs as fast as she can. If the gazelle survives the attack, afterward her whole body shakes to clear the adrenaline created by the chase. Then the gazelle goes back to calmly grazing in the field. She does not develop posttraumatic stress disorder (PTSD) or live in mortal fear that the lioness is going to attack again. With people, however, we hold on to past trauma and are fearful that it might recur. I sense the fear of annihilation

4

present in the collective consciousness of our times, reflected in movie previews of the threat of the world coming to an end. As a child, my greatest fear was that planet Earth would be blown up in a nuclear war. A house I bought had a bomb shelter, which was a big selling point in the 1970s. Have you ever wondered why we humans seem to be so vulnerable to fear?

Translations of the Sumerian tablets reveal that the ancient astronauts came to Earth because their planet was dying. Earlier, there was a war between the north and the south on their planet, which escalated to the use of nuclear weapons. Then their atmosphere developed a breach, and their summers got hotter and their winters got colder. The rains did not come, winds blew, and the crops failed.[5] Does this scenario sound familiar? Our planet has a hole in its ozone layer, which is causing disruption in our weather patterns; as I write this book, the summer of 2012 has had record heat and drought. The home planet of the astronauts and every living thing on it were all going to die if they did not do something. This primal fear of annihilation was behind every desperate decision they made, and thus the genes they would have spliced into *Homo sapiens*, if the story is true, would carry severe ancestral fears of world annihilation, which would have imprinted into our emotional bodies.

The Role of Gold

Gold was the antidote to the fear of the ancient astronauts because, according to the tablets, they found that powdered gold (gold heated to break its atomic bonds, resulting in a white powder that is its monatomic form) was light enough that they could jettison it into the area of the atmospheric breach. The powdered gold would stay in suspension around their planet and shield them from rays of the sun in summer and would retain the planet's heat when they were in the winter part of their cycle.[6] In modern times on Earth, cotton farmer David Radius Hudson rediscovered this process of creating monatomic gold and presented his work at the International Forum on New Science in Fort Collins, Colorado, in 1995. Gold was salvation for the astronauts and they needed lots of it. They wanted the humans they created to fear them so we would obey

---

5   Sitchin, *The Lost Book of Enki.*
6   Ibid.

them and keep helping them get the gold they needed to ensure survival of their planet and their race. As a teen, I could never figure out why the Bible kept saying, "The fear of the LORD is the beginning of wisdom." Love and fear are opposites, and how could a God of love want me to fear Him?

> The fear of the LORD is the beginning of wisdom; all who follow his precepts have good understanding. To him belongs eternal praise. (Psalms 111:10 NIV)

> The fear of the LORD is the beginning of knowledge, but fools despise wisdom and instruction. (Proverbs 1:7 NIV)

The Pyramids

The Sumerian tablets say that these ancient astronauts built the Great Pyramid of Giza in Egypt as a control tower for landing their spacecraft.[7] The technological expertise needed to build this pyramid is truly amazing. For example, covering a base of thirteen acres, the peak is only one-quarter of an inch off of true center. In addition to the colossal outer structure one sees, the pyramid has an intricate system of inner rooms lined by huge slabs of stone that show engineering feats we cannot replicate today.[8] How could humans 12,000 years ago have been capable of this kind of precision? What we do know is that the Pyramids are an ancient marvel dating from a time when life on this planet was supposed to be very primitive.

Molech

The Sumerian tablets include all of Old Testament history but in an expanded form that explains why there were so many competing gods and how the wars between them involved the humans they had created. Remember, the first commandment the Lord gave his people was "Thou shalt have no other gods before me." If the Israelite God was the Creator of All, why would he have created competition with his lordship? In the Old Testament, one of the

---

7 Ibid.

8 Hancock, *Fingerprints of the Gods.*

rival gods to the Israelite God Yahweh was Molech, who required that each of his humans give their firstborn child to him as a burnt offering. Yahweh commanded the Israelites not to participate in this practice.

> Do not give any of your children to be sacrificed to Molech,
> for you must not profane the name of your God. I am the
> LORD. (Leviticus 18:21 NIV)

Whether the Sumerian account of our history is literally true—and mounting archeological evidence supports the information in the tablets—or whether it is mythology to explain the psychological structures behind human behavior, either way, the archetypes behind the practice of human sacrifice are still running the belief system of the cult activity that Paula reported.

New Tools

The work that Paula and I did together was like a guided tour of hell, and I had to find new therapeutic tools to avoid being swallowed by the terror of the underworld and my own rage at the ways she had been hurt. Energy therapies were the key to helping me get through my vicarious traumatization and to understand the unique challenges presented with satanic ritual abuse. The whole case was shrouded in fear and dark energy. Over time I developed Soul Detective protocols using energy therapy to systematically find and resolve the multifaceted disturbances in Paula's emotional and mental system. Chapter 2 presents the Detrimental Energy Protocol I developed, based on the pioneering work of William Baldwin, to transform fear and negative life beliefs.

One of the most extraordinary findings we discovered is that Paula's mind had been programmed by the cult with two important destructive features:

1. If she started to recover her memories, she would self-destruct. She became highly suicidal and had multiple suicide attempts during our work together. By the Grace of God, she made it through that programming and has lived to tell her story.
2. Anything that should help her and would help most clients would be reversed and have the opposite effect on her system. At the time, I had never heard of the concept of polarity reversal or a person having a

hardwired program that would make every attempt to heal deepen her wounds. This programming is as frustrating to the client who wants to get well as it is to the therapist who is wondering why the interventions that should make the client feel better instead make the client feel worse.

Soul Detective work is like finding and eliminating the viruses in the computer programming of the mind. In the process of searching for the origins of the negative life beliefs and the darkness that run satanic cults and the practice of human sacrifice, my worldview expanded from global (Earth only) to universal, looking at the ancient astronaut theory. As radical as this idea is, I found it explained some features about history, archeology, and psychology that I could not account for otherwise. A comparison of the Old Testament account of creation with the much more detailed Sumerian account of how life started on the Earth shows that the Bible was not the first account and left out some very important details that did not suit its political and spiritual purpose.

The Darkness

The darkness was first. It is primal and undifferentiated, the way the world was before the active principle of Light entered the picture. The account of creation in the Bible starts out in the book of Genesis:

> In the beginning God created the heavens and the earth. The earth was without form, and void; and darkness was on the face of the deep. And the Spirit of God was hovering over the face of the waters. Then God said, "Let there be light"; and there was light. (Genesis 1:1-3 NIV)

Scientists estimate that the universe is about fourteen billion years old, and our solar system is only about four and a half billion years old. We might say that the moment when God said, "Let there be light" was the moment when the glob of primordial material on the edge of the Milky Way galaxy that was forming from clouds of dust, gasses, and dark matter coalesced and was ignited by nuclear fusion, birthing our sun. This process in which two atomic

8

nuclei join together to produce a single heavier nucleus releases some of the mass of the nuclei as energy and is the process that powers all active stars.

The account in Genesis says that God divided the light from the darkness, calling the light "day" and the darkness "night." Darkness has its place in creation. Plants need a time of darkness to rest, or they become exhausted. Likewise, the human body needs to alternate between rest and activity, recharging our energy fields during sleep so we can function during our waking hours. Deep rest for the human body is easier in a dark place, where the stimulation of light does not come to the eyes. But this physical darkness that everything on the planet needs in our day-night cycles is different from the emotional, mental, and spiritual darkness that can pull a person into despair.

Parts of our souls—each person's individual soul as well as the collective soul of humanity—remain in the dark about who we really are, the infinite potential we each have, and the true power of the light of love that resides at the core of our being and connects everything in the Universe as one.

> Without the realization of oneness, differences are perceived as a cause for alarm, fear, hostility and violence. The history of human experience over the millennia is proof…As the Buddha said, you can not do violence to another when you realize oneness.[9]

Beings of Light

No darkness is in the next world, in the higher planes of being. Everything is imbued with the radiant Light of the creator. Metaphysical teacher Drunvalo Melchizedek[10] says that in the higher planes, everything glows with golden light, making those who have had a glimpse of "heaven" say that the streets are paved with gold. Revelations 21:21 (NIV) reports that, in the author's vision of heaven, "The great street of the city was of gold, as pure as transparent

---

9   Greer, *Hidden Truth*, 35.

10   Melchizedek, *The Ancient Secret of the Flower of Life*.

glass." Facing and transforming our fears gets us out of the lower realms of self-created hell and into the gold of the higher planes.

In the heavens, God created Beings of Light to help carry out creation's plan. Stories of magical little interdimensional Beings of Light called fairies abound in literature, and these Light Beings are starting to show up in photographs. At the Universal Light Expo in Columbus, Ohio in 2010, I met Laura Walthers, who has published a book of photographs she took of "faeries, gnomes, and elves."[11] Her photographs resemble the one shown here, of tiny Beings of Light. The fairies are thought to attend to flowers, opening each new blossom and each new leaf, as in the lyrics to "Shine" from the soundtrack of the movie about a fairy called Tinkerbell.

Photograph by Inky of a tiny Being of Light attending to a poppy

Shine

What makes a river flow?
Open the leaves of trees as they grow

It's the wings of the world that's just out of you

Wonder is all around
Raising each breeze
Each seed in the ground...[12]

---

11   Walthers, *Life in Nature Revealed*.
12   Lyrics by Tiffany Giardina, verse 1.

The creator made bigger and more differentiated Beings of Light called angels to help more complex forms of creation such as humans. The biblical story of Job points to a reference that indicates the angelic realm was created long before Earth was formed. God lectures Job, asking,

> "Where were you when I laid the earth's foundation?
> Tell me, if you understand.
> Who marked off its dimensions? Surely you know!
> Who stretched a measuring line across it?
> On what were its footings set,
> or who laid its cornerstone—
> while the morning stars sang together
> and all the angels shouted for joy?" (Job 38:4-7 NIV)

The creator gives each created being consciousness and free will. One of the Beings of Light that God created was not happy with his position.

The Lucifer Rebellion

According to *The Urantia Book*, "Lucifer was a magnificent being, a brilliant personality; he stood next to the Most High Fathers of the constellations in the direct line of universe authority."[13] The name Lucifer means "light." He became enthralled with his own beauty and perfection and wanted to become the ruler of the universe. According to *Urantia*, Satan is not the same as Lucifer but was Lucifer's first lieutenant, assigned to promote Lucifer's agenda on planet Earth.

The book of Revelation in the Bible speaks about a woman appearing in heaven "clothed with the sun, with the moon under her feet and a crown of twelve stars on her head" (Revelations 12:1 NIV). She was pregnant with a child that was to rule all nations with an iron scepter. A dragon stood before her to devour her child the moment it was born. But God snatched up the male child to his throne, and the woman fled.

---

13   Urantia Foundation, *The Urantia Book*, 601.

11

And there was war in heaven. Michael and his angels fought against the dragon, and the dragon and his angels fought back. But he was not strong enough, and they lost their place in heaven. The great dragon was hurled down—that ancient serpent called the devil or Satan, who leads the whole world astray. He was hurled to the earth, and his angels with him. (Revelations 12:7-9 NIV)

Revelations continues to say that Archangel Michael and his angels overcame the dragon "by the blood of the Lamb" (12:7), referring to the power of what Christ did on the cross. The dragon pursued the woman and made war "against the rest of her offspring—those who obey God's commandments and hold to the testimony of Jesus" (12:17). This war seems to be going on still.

Working for Lucifer

Lucifer created an alternate reality where he was in charge of everything, so everything is reversed in his reality. Light is bad and darkness is good. Many clients who have felt attacked by these dark forces report that Satan rules his fallen angelic servants with fear, threatening severe punishment if they disobey his orders. Psychiatrist Shakuntala Modi reports that her patients are able to dialogue with these Dark Force Entities, who say they work for Satan as their master and that they have never been in human form. They express fear when they have been discovered because they think they will be in trouble with their boss, Satan, who considers their discovery a failure.

> They do not want to fail at any cost. They are afraid that the punishment by Satan will be worse than before.[14]

They are terrified of Satan's wrath and report that in the past, Satan has cut them into pieces, beaten them with a belt with nails on it, and stripped off their skin. One reported it was "tortured to extreme pain, choked by thorns, burned

---

14   Modi, *Remarkable Healings*, 302.

in a fire, left in a cold, dark pit for a long time."[15] The Dark Force Entities then project the pain inflicted on them into humans. They believe the distortions of truth their master has taught them. In their worldview, the creator cannot be trusted, and the highest values are power and control over others. They believe that light is dangerous and would destroy them. They are fighting for their own survival by attacking people who carry a great deal of spiritual Light. They try to stop these people by finding their vulnerabilities and attacking them through their emotional wounds.

This belief system that light is dangerous to the dark forces holds a half-truth—that light can indeed penetrate into and eliminate darkness. Just flip on a light in a dark room. Where does the darkness go? It disappears. The Dark Force Entities are like dark rooms, and when the light comes on, the darkness disappears. They are not the darkness in the empty space in the room, however; they are the room itself, and turning on the light in this room that was formerly dark can show them who they really are. Everything in creation, including each Dark Force Entity, has a spark of light within it, the consciousness given to it by the creator, and that light expands when it finds out the truth. Soul Detective work helps rehabilitate these fallen angels and bring them back into harmony with the Creator and back to working in service of the Light.

Viewpoint of Thoth

Another perspective of the conflict between darkness and light comes from the viewpoint of Thoth, acclaimed in Sumerian mythology as the designer of the Great Pyramid of Giza, also known as Quetzalcoatl in South America. Thoth says that warfare between the darkness and light began long, long ago in the first days of man.

> Men, then as now,
> Were filled with both darkness and light;
> And while in some darkness held sway,
> In others light filled the soul.[16]

---

15   Ibid.

16   Doreal, *The Emerald Tablets of Thoth the Atlantean*, 31.

The forces of darkness have always worked for destruction and have tried to draw others into their darkness. They have fought to tighten the fetters of the chains binding man to darkness by using dark magic to shroud the soul.

According to Thoth, the dark brotherhood tries to ensnare Lightworkers who have made more progress on their pathway of Light because they know these Lightworkers have more power and would therefore be more valuable to the dark side. "They [the dark brotherhood] help men to gain certain things and powers until they have them in their toils. Then when there is no escape, they clamp down. They have certain specific powers developed such as opening the seventh dimension and calling in elementals to fulfill their purposes."[17]

Thoth encourages all to strive hard on the pathway of wisdom and light.

> Follow ye not the Dark Brothers ever.
> Always be a child of the Light.
> For know ye, O man,
> In the end Light must conquer
> And darkness and night be banished from Light.[18]

Thoth also names the unseen guardians who walk beside us to help us as the Children of Light, who have never been divided from the Oneness eternal. These helpers aid us to conquer "the phantom of fear." Thoth gives a formula for conquering darkness. The first step is to go inside and find out whether the disturbance originates from within or without. If the origin is within, he gives a protocol of cleansing by sending out waves of energy from the pineal gland. If the origin is outside, he gives a protocol for calling in spiritual helpers with an incantation to fill one with Light.[19] I had not yet read Thoth's material when I developed my Soul Detective protocols by trial and error to find what worked. The process of diagnosis is the same in my work: first I find out whether a problem has originated from inside or outside of a client. When the problem originates within, I investigate further to see where a negative life belief became entrenched in the client's thought patterns and use energy therapies to

17   Ibid., 32.
18   Ibid., 33.
19   Ibid., 34-35.

eliminate the negative idea and to reprogram the client with a counteracting positive life belief. When the problem comes in from outside, I call in guardian angels to help reform the Dark Force Entities and fill them with Light.

Similarity to Cancer

Darkness works a bit like cancer. The genetic information in a single cell can become distorted through exposure to radioactivity or other toxins, erasing its telomeres, the genetic "bookends" that mark how many replications of itself a cell can make before it is time for the natural death of the cell. Cancer cells lose this ability to regulate their own life span and will go on reproducing into infinity if given the nutrients they need to sustain their cellular metabolism. MCF-7 breast cancer cells harvested from a nun named Sister Catherine Frances who died in 1970 are still dividing away and being used in cancer research.[20]

Our thoughts create the reality we live in, and one distorted thought is like one cancer cell. If a person believes that humankind's core is sinful and depraved, then giving in to jealousy and rage will feel congruent with this belief system, and these emotional states may grow just like a cancer cell until they take on a life of their own. At first, a cancer cell just divides, replicating itself at a faster rate than a normal cell. Most chemotherapeutic drugs target any cell that is dividing, usually repeating the process a number of times, with several weeks between each treatment, to try to kill cells that are dividing faster than normal. This process is similar to the scatter pattern of a shotgun's tiny lead pellets rather than the consolidated bullet of a rifle aimed at one specific target. When a tumor has grown to sufficient size, it sets up an independent blood supply so it can grow even faster. This process is called vascularization. Then it takes on a life of its own. Likewise, a dysfunctional thought can grow into a negative life belief, which can eventually take on a life of its own like an advanced malignant tumor. I do not personally know whether dark forces would have any reality or power of their own if the fears of humankind did not ener-

---

20   "Achieving Immortality: The Breasts of Sister Francis Catherine Mallon." Breast Cancer Action Newsletter Issue #66, July-August 2001.
http://archive.bcaction.org/index.php?page=newsletter-66i

gize and feed them. I do know that our fears can definitely produce the boogie man under the bed, the monster hiding in the closet, and demons after our soul.

Cancer cells are less stable than healthy, normal cells. Part of the strategy of chemotherapy is to stress the total system to a point where the less stable malignant cells will give up and die, but the stronger normal cells will be able to survive. Likewise, lies are less stable than the truth. Muscle testing is built on this law of nature and the ability to distinguish truth from non-truth, light from darkness, and helpful from not helpful. Muscle testing gives us a key to finding and eliminating the dysfunctional thought patterns on which the dark hierarchy builds. Cancer does not consider the good of the whole physical system. Its only focus is on its own growth, and it sends out missionary cells to start new cancer colonies in other parts of the body. The end result of the cancer plan is that, in its egocentrism, it winds up killing its host. Thus, cancer's growth plan is not sustainable because it winds up killing itself as well. Likewise, the ultimate effect of unchecked dark energy in a person leads to that person's destruction, often through suicide.

Conversion Rather Than Exorcism

Rather than battling cancer with chemotherapy, trying to kill all of the cancer cells, a more gentle approach would be to set up communication with each individual cell that has mutated, let it know of the flaws in its plan to take over the system (self-destruction being a major design flaw), and offer each cell the energy it needs to replace its telomeres and revert to being a healthy, normal cell. The Soul Detective approach to working with Detrimental Energy sets up communication with the dysfunctional thought patterns, finds the specific goal in each case, points out the flaws in the dark force belief systems, helps the darkness find the light that is in its core, and then offers it a chance to upgrade its belief systems and join the forces of Light.

This process is entirely different from exorcism, which labels the energy as bad and seeks to destroy it or cut it off from the person. The psychological equivalent of exorcism is repression or dissociation—and neither plan works well in the long run! Charismatic groups that cast out demons use a model of direct combat for exorcism. When a member has been attacked by what they label as demon possession, the subject may writhe on the ground, yelling obscenities and cursing God. The group then joins forces in prayer and commands the demon to leave. In the short run, the process is successful, and dark energy leaves the subject. However, the demon seems then to run around the block, return, and attach to the most emotionally vulnerable member of the group, continuing the drama.

The martial art Aikido takes a very different approach to dealing with a direct attack. An exercise we practiced in Jon Kabat-Zinn's Stress Reduction and Relaxation Program,[21] which I used to teach, was stepping sideways at the moment of being attacked, putting an arm around the attacker, and first moving with the attacker along his or her trajectory. (The psychological equivalent in communication is first trying to see a situation from the point of view of one's adversary.) Then we used the arm we had around the attacker to steer the attacker gently around a half circle so the person was making an about-face, able to see our point of view. The beauty of this approach is that the momentum of the attacker is harnessed and used for transformation. Likewise, the Soul Detective approach addresses the destructive energy, gives it a chance to find the flaws in its own belief system, and then offers it a better job working for the Light! Details of the protocol are in Chapter 2.

Darkness and Sexuality

One of the ways that dark energy can get into a person is through a sexual wound. When a child is sexually abused, as happened repeatedly to Paula, that pain provides a chink in the emotional armor through which negativity can enter. Later in life, a person can become contaminated with detrimental energy by having sexual contact with a partner who is infected with Dark Force Entities.

Eckhart Tolle calls the contents of the shadow "the pain body" and illuminates how it interferes in relationships. When we refuse to face and move through our own pain, we seek an escape in an addiction. For a time, the high from a new love relationship covers up the pain, but eventually "your partner behaves in ways that fail to meet your needs, or rather those of your ego. The

---

21   Developed by Dr. Jon Kabat-Zinn, who researched the results through the University of Massachusetts Medical Center. I was a teacher in this program from 1993 to 1995.

feelings of fear, pain, and lack that are an intrinsic part of egoic consciousness but had been covered up by the 'love relationship' now surface."[22] Furthermore, Tolle continues, you then perceive your partner as the cause of this pain and launch a savage attack to try to change the partner's behavior to keep using that person to cover up your own pain. Of course, this plan never works. Here are some principles of Tolle's relationship theory:

1. Our most intimate relationships give us the perfect opportunity for spiritual growth because they are where our shadow erupts: all of our unconscious guilt, anger, self-criticism, and low self-esteem.
2. However we most deeply feel about ourselves, we will treat our partner that way. We just can't help it! When we carry an introjection of a critical parent, we find this voice not only criticizing everything we do, but also everything our lover does!
3. We want our partners to take away our pain by loving us unconditionally—but this plan never works. After the initial euphoria of falling in love wears off, the partner winds up adding to our pain.

Most clients with severe sexual trauma need not only to heal the original wound, but also to heal the negative life beliefs around what happened. Sometimes a survivor of this kind of trauma seems to be infected with an autonomous energy, like a Dark Force Entity, promoting ideas that people cannot be trusted, that opening up the heart to love is not safe, or that staying angry is the only way to have power.

Reversing Torsion Spin

The essence of the subtle energy that healers use has a force based on particle spin that is separate from either electricity or magnetism. Russian astrophysicist Dr. Nikolai Kozyrev (1908–1983) researched this force he called "torsion" and its effects on time. "Since every elementary particle, such as electrons and protons, have spin, this means that torsion is a universal force which has been overlooked by Western physics."[23] Torsion has some unusual

---

22   Tolle, *Practicing the Power of Now*, 88.

23   Swanson, *Life Force, the Scientific Basis*, 273.

properties, travelling much faster than light, penetrating barriers, and appearing to go both forward and backward in time simultaneously. Torsion fields spin either to the right or to the left. Right-handed torsion spin (clockwise, as viewed from above) causes objects to repel each other, and dark energy has right-handed torsion. The dark energy in the universe makes the objects in it fly apart from each other, perhaps a safety mechanism so that galaxies do not accidentally collide with each other. What a mess that would be! Scientists calculate that about 7.5 billion years ago in the history of our universe, which started about fourteen billion years ago, the acceleration of objects in the universe flying apart from each other started increasing, and this acceleration has continued to increase.[24] Part of the unease of our times may be the subconscious fear that everything seems to be speeding up, and at some point our ecosystem might not be able to adjust to all the changes on our planet, resulting in another global disaster, as has happened many times before on Earth.[25] *Transforming Fear into Gold* shows an alternative way of looking at the issue that can calm these fears.

Left-handed torsion spin attracts things together, and the dark matter in the universe has left-handed torsion spin. If we take these principles of physics and apply them to psychology, we might say that some forces split people apart and other forces unite people. On a psychological level, right-handed torsion spin (dark energy) splits people apart: both inside themselves, causing internal conflicts; and separating a person from others, from the primordial unity of the Universe. Psychological programs of dark energy generally aim at destroying a person's social network, especially primary relationships, and trying to separate the spirit from the body, a process commonly called death. The opposite pulling together energy, left-handed torsion, can help a person on the individual level to retrieve soul fragments and can help on the societal level by drawing people together to work for the common good.

The process of reversing a torsion spin from one direction to the other is extremely simple. As a spinning table tennis ball bounces off the table, its spin reverses. Likewise, the torsion spin of a particle reverses when it hits a mirror.

---

24   "Dark Energy, Dark Matter." NASA Science Astrophysics.
http://science.nasa.gov/astrophysics/focus-areas/what-is-dark-energy/

25   Hancock, *Fingerprints of the Gods.*

Holding up the mirror of consciousness is transformative. The key to working with detrimental forces is reflection, calling them to reflect on what they are doing, the belief systems running their behavior, and what is at their own core. This process seems to reverse their right-handed torsion spin of split-off dark energy into left-handed torsion spin of reconnecting with the unity of the whole.

Everything in the universe has a spark of light in its center, a fact of sacred geometry. Once dark programs see their inner light for themselves, the whole charade of deception perpetrated upon them crumbles, and they change their spin from working for the detriment of humankind to working for the betterment of humanity. This book provides a road map to change the directional flow of energies that pull us down and redirect that energy into avenues that uplift the spirit. This book is an open invitation for Dark Force Entities and Fallen Angels to transform through knowing the truth. The Soul Detective Detrimental Energy Protocol presented in the next chapter is a step-by-step procedure to guide this process.

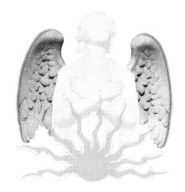

CHAPTER 2:

Soul Detective Detrimental

Energy Protocol

*I*n his preface to *The Screwtape Letters*, C. S. Lewis says that there are two equal and opposite errors into which we can fall concerning the topic of devils:

> One is to disbelieve in their existence. The other is to believe, and to feel an excessive and unhealthy interest in them. They themselves are equally pleased by both errors and hail a materialist or a magician with the same delight.[1]

William Baldwin, DDS, PhD, wrote the first technique manual on regression therapy. He left his dental practice in 1982 and was also an ordained

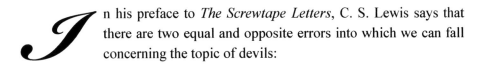

1   Lewis, *The Screwtape Letters*, ix.

minister, pastoral counselor, hypnotherapist, past lives therapist, international lecturer, and seminar facilitator. During his hypnotherapy sessions, he ran into what he called Dark Force Entities and had to figure out how to deal with them. He states:

> Whether it is imagination, archetype, collective hallucinations, mass hypnosis, a projection of the beliefs of the therapist, or something else again, dark forces seem to exist in some form and are capable of intruding on living individuals in this reality.[2]

How do dark forces get into people? Think of what happens with a deep physical flesh wound. If one does not treat the wound by washing out the dirt, stitching it up, and applying ointment for it to heal, the wound can become infected by bacteria and get worse. Likewise, with an emotional wound, if we do not face the pain, rebalance the disruptions in the energy field, and heal the emotional injury, dark forces can invade through the portal of the open wound and aggravate the situation. Dark forces seem to be hanging around just looking for an opportunity to steal a wounded person's power and energy. If we want to be free from dark influences, then we need to face and work through our emotional pain. Baldwin points out additional ways that Dark Force Entities can gain entry into the psyche and interfere with people:

1. Mental distortion caused by alcohol or drugs.
2. Sexual interaction with someone infested with Dark Force Entities.
3. Feelings of intense anger, hatred, rage, and vengeance.
4. Greed and desire for power and control over others.
5. Calling on the forces of darkness for protection when going into battle.[3]

---

2 Baldwin, *Healing Lost Souls*, 74.
3 Ibid., 74-75.

A Remarkable Healing

Shakuntala Modi, MD, is a psychiatrist who uses hypnotherapy to find the origins of her patients' issues. In her book *Remarkable Healings: A Psychiatrist Discovers Unsuspected Roots of Mental and Physical Illness*, she tells the story of a thirty-five-year-old patient she calls Nick who came for long-standing migraine headaches that had started when he was a teenager. Also suffering from depression and chronic fatigue, Nick was willing to try hypnotherapy. As she asked Nick to look inside his head and let her know what he saw, first Nick could only see darkness. Then that darkness became a black blob moving around. Dr. Modi was already familiar with working with earthbound spirits and thought the black blob might be the spirit of a deceased person who had attached to Nick. As she dialogued with the black blob, to her surprise, it said it was a demon that had easily entered when Nick had been using drugs in his teens. The demon was there to torture Nick and claimed it had been causing all of Nick's problems. Nick's headache became worse, and then the angels did an intervention of filling the whole room with brilliant white Light.

> He [Nick] saw the angelic beings surrounding this black being, the so-called demon in his head, with the Light. The being was reacting very violently to the Light and screaming, "Take this Light away from me. It will destroy me; it will kill me."[4]

Dr. Modi was totally amazed at watching this intervention. Nick was experiencing a severe splitting headache and described the dark being looking like a fish struggling to get out of a net of Light. The demon believed the Light would kill it and that if the Light did not do it in, Satan would annihilate it because being discovered was a failure. The angels were asking the entity to look inside and pressing and squeezing the black entity with the Light.

---

4   Modi, *Remarkable Healings*, 28.

> The entity, still struggling with the Light and squirming around
> in a helpless way, started to look inside itself and screamed,
> "What is it?"[5]

The entity saw a diamond of Light within itself that made its darkness disappear. Then it looked like the angels and was very surprised that it was not dead. It felt good. Nick was amazed and could see the total transformation of the entity into Light.

Both Dr. Modi and Nick were shocked that Nick's headache vanished completely after the transformation of the entity. The transformed demon was filled with peace and joy and was lovingly accepted back into the Light. It apologized to Nick for all the trouble it had caused and thanked Dr. Modi for helping it. The angels then healed and cleansed the space in Nick's head where the demon had been. The following week, Nick was free of both his depression and headaches and felt more energetic.

Dr. Modi had many questions about why this intervention had worked when traditional psychotherapy and medication had not given him relief. She thought that possibly his subconscious mind had fabricated this story to avoid responsibility for his problems.

> But if it was just his fantasy or a figment of his imagination,
> how could this session totally cure his longstanding crippling
> headaches and depression? But then I realized that it did not
> matter. What really mattered was that Nick was free of his
> problems.[6]

Over the years, Dr. Modi found that other therapists were using similar techniques, which proved to be extremely effective. She also found that the formal induction of hypnosis was not necessary to find and release the spirits.

---

5   Ibid., 29.
6   Ibid., 30.

Angelic Authors

My Soul Detective protocol for transforming Detrimental Energy is remarkably like the process in Dr. Modi's case, which I did not read until after I had already developed the protocol. Now I think that the angels are the real authors of this system of healing! Rather than exorcise a dark entity, this protocol goes into the heart of the belief systems running the dark forces, helps them see the true nature of reality, and offers them the opportunity of transformation, to quit their old jobs and accept job promotions to join Archangel Michael's angels, called the "Band of Mercy" by Doreen Virtue,[7] and the special division of the Band of Mercy that I call the "New Lightworkers," former dark spirits who quit their old jobs and decided to work for the Light.

> **Disclaimer:** This is an advanced protocol, requiring background skills and competence in mental health counseling, energy therapy, trauma treatment methods, and the ability to keep one's own energy system organized and centered under duress. Presentation of this protocol is for informational and educational purposes only, and the reader agrees not to use it with clients or others unless fully qualified to do so. The major risk factor I have observed is that if a practitioner uses this advanced protocol with a chink in the practitioner's self-confidence, the detrimental energy will hone in on that specific vulnerability and try to stop the process. Working with the dark side will inevitably bring up shadow material in the therapist. To do this work successfully, a person needs to commit to ongoing emotional and spiritual growth. The reader agrees to assume and accept full responsibility for any and all risks associated with using the Detrimental Energy Protocol.

> **Soul Detective Advisory:** Even if you are trained and certified in Soul Detective work, if you get stuck at any point along the way, working with a Dark Force Entity that refuses

---

7   Virtue, *Angel Therapy*, 209.

to cooperate, please turn the whole issue over to Archangel Michael and ask his band of New Lightworkers to work with the dark force and invite it to join them and to do whatever is necessary to free the client from this invasion.

Detrimental Energy Protocol—what to do when you muscle test that the origin of the problem is detrimental energy: Dark Force Entity/Fallen Angel/ Dark Angel/dark energy/dark spirit/evil spirit/suffering being.

Credits: In this twenty-four step protocol, steps six through thirteen are based on William Baldwin's book *Healing Lost Souls: Releasing Unwanted Spirits from your Energy Body.* Sue McKenney, originator of Ultimate Energy Healing,[8] also gave special input.

By definition, dark spirits are entities that never were in human form. In some cases, however, the dark side may conscript an earthbound spirit who has extreme emotional damage to cause suffering in someone who is still living. Addressing the gamut from fallen angels to entrenched negative thought forms, the following protocol corrects cognitive distortions and offers these detrimental forces the opportunity to see truth and raise their level of consciousness.

Detrimental Energy Protocol Checklist

1. Getting centered
2. Getting spiritual help
3. Getting permission to proceed to step 4
4. Classifying type and number of detrimental energies:
    a. One or more negative thoughts
    b. One or more pervasive negative thought patterns or negative life beliefs
    c. One or more Dark Force Entities/Fallen Angels
    d. One or more Dark Devices
    e. One or more Minions (servants of the Dark Force Entities)
    f. One or more Bound Spirits (an earthbound spirit conscripted by the dark side)

---

8 Ultimate Energy Healing blogsite: http://suemckenney.wordpress.com/

    g. Higher ranking Dark Force Entities/Dark Angels

    h. One or more Impostor Spirits

5. Getting permission for each item of the inventory
6. Interviewing for purpose
7. Employer: "Who do you work for, the darkness or the Light?"
8. Cognitive Distortions: "What did your employer tell you about the Light?"
9. Going to center: "What is in your center? Look inside yourself to see what is present at your core."
10. Focusing on the Light
11. Pointing out the deception
12. Working for a liar
13. A chance to quit
14. Checking for energetic cords
15. Inventory of the damage
16. New job assignment (optional)
17. Additional inventory items
18. Multiplying the benefits
19. Giving thanks
20. Tracing the origin
21. Repairing the energy field
22. Checking for other wounds
23. Giving thanks again and closing the octahedron
24. Final grounding

Detrimental Energy Protocol Expanded with Case Examples

1. *GETTING CENTERED: Do whatever corrective exercises are necessary to get your energy field organized and flowing properly so you have an equal amount of energy on all sides and above and below your body.*

I made a series of YouTube videos demonstrating a set of centering tests and corrections.[9] Many other centering techniques from many disciplines also organize and balance the energy system. Prayer is another excellent way to center the energy field.

2. *SPIRITUAL HELP: Call in your spiritual help FIRST! If you have a favorite way of setting sacred space that helps you feel protected, feel free to use your method, but please include a request for the protection of Archangel Michael. I use octahedrons of golden Light (a pyramid above the earth and an inverted pyramid below it going down into the earth) because of the strength of this sacred geometrical figure. The angelic realm calibrates at a very high vibrational energy, and I need to have their energy around me so that I feel safe working to raise the dimensional consciousness of the darkness. Here is the invocation I use:*

Soul Detective/Archangel Invocation

"I call an octahedron of golden Light around my client, me, and anyone else involved in this issue. I ask the Archangels Raphael, Gabriel, Ariel, and Uriel to stand in the center of each of the four sides of the pyramid that is above the earth. I ask Archangel Michael to stand at the apex of the pyramid and Archangels Metatron and Zadkiel to stand at the point beneath the earth. I call the guardians, including the body protectors and essence protectors, and guardian angels for the client, for me, and for anyone and everyone else involved and ask that *only what is in the highest good for everyone and everything* (this includes the detrimental forces) would come to pass."

---

9   Seven Centering Corrections: http://www.youtube.com/watch?v=ClplrezFWgg
Muscle Testing Tips: http://www.youtube.com/watch?v=1BnOZdefNM0
Proper Energy Flow Up-Down: http://www.youtube.com/watch?v=6KuqiP4y_CY
Non-Polarization and Corrections: http://www.youtube.com/watch?v=64qc8THwLtA
Proper Energy Flow Front-Back: http://www.youtube.com/watch?v=cED982CQrvA
Proper Energy Flow Left-Right: http://www.youtube.com/watch?v=y1FTr24KY0I
Heart-Brain Integration: http://www.youtube.com/watch?v=p6XLeby90qg

Levels of Angels

Angels are beings of Light created by God to be intermediaries between the higher spiritual realms and the world of matter. According to medieval Christian theologians, God created nine ranks of angels. The highest level, the Seraphim, circle God's throne constantly, singing praises to the Divine. These are the nine levels:

Seraphim
Cherubim
Thrones
Dominions
Virtues
Powers
Principalities
Archangels
Angels

Only the bottom two levels, the Archangels and Angels, interact with people on Earth. Some authors and people who channel metaphysical material also say that, just as humans are in a constant process of evolution, the angels also are constantly studying and learning how to handle new issues.

Everyone on earth has at least one guardian angel assigned to them from birth through death and the transition into the next world. Guardians can include deceased ancestors or other spiritual figures outside of the angelic realm. Call in *all* of the client's guardians and all of your guardians. If your client has a special spiritual figure that brings a feeling of protection, include that being in your sacred space.

3. *ASKING PERMISSION: Muscle test whether or not you have spiritual permission to proceed to step 4 of the protocol, an inventory of the detrimental energy present. If you do not get permission to proceed, ask Archangel Michael, the angel of protection, to do "whatever is necessary to resolve the problem and free the client from this detrimental energy."*

In the following case, we did not have permission to work directly with the dark force.

Five-Generation Curse

This case demonstrates the energy dynamics of two people locked into a negative pattern that prevented both of them from going into the Light when they died. Because they were both still earthbound, the hate they felt for each other kept sending out a stream of negative energy, which contaminated all of their descendants.

Outrageous Behavior

Jewel was a gifted and talented energy worker herself, but the turmoil in her family of origin agitated her so much that when she spent time with them, she would occasionally override her intuitive sense of right action and use outrageous behaviors to lash back at the venom unjustly heaped onto her.

A clairvoyant saw that her family had a curse on it from five generations back, from someone who had been wounded by a mean action and had cursed the whole family. The pattern that resulted was an unwritten rule, *"Nobody in this family is allowed to be happy!"* Jewel noticed that whenever she started a new pattern to take better care of herself, as soon as the positive change started to register, she would self-sabotage and revert back to her former dysfunctional patterns.

Jewel was able to clear 90 percent of this curse, which opened up her family to more possibilities of true connection, but she asked for a Soul Detective session to get the last 10 percent for complete freedom from this negative pattern.

Disaster Difficulties

We traced the origin back to a great-great-grandfather who had been wealthy. After a natural disaster hit, a friend and business colleague came to him asking for money to rebuild. Grandfather refused, thinking that he had worked hard for that money and it was his. He was not in a place of kindness, and he feared he might need the money for his own family. The man he refused to help was filled with rage and put a curse on Grandfather and all of his descendants.

Both men had remained earthbound, infected by the dark energy of this interaction. When we connected with Grandfather, the emotions that came were fear, anger, and a desire for vengeance toward the man who had put this curse on him. We muscle tested that dark energy was involved, but we also tested that we did not have permission to go ahead with step 4 of the protocol and find out the specifics of the dark energy. So instead, we turned the situation over to Archangel Michael with the prayer: "Please do whatever is necessary for the highest good of everyone and everything to free this ancestor from the influence of the dark energy."

Peace at Last

Right away, peace came to Grandfather's heart. Jewel then visualized her Grandfather bringing a little wooden box with money in it to the man who had requested his help, with the message, "Here, let me help you."

The man accepted the gift, and they made peace with each other. Grandfather had not noticed that his spirit had left his body and was stunned when Jewel informed him we were in the year 2011 AD. We did a group treatment for both Grandfather and the other man and all of their family members who had been infected with this negative program of fear of not having enough resources. Then they both crossed into the Light together, and we multiplied the benefits for any other family members who were still earthbound.

Next we did a clearing for Jewel for all the trauma she had experienced from her family's nastiness. We prayed for emotional freedom for her and all of the ways the curse had affected her life, asking for a miracle of healing. We asked to open her to receive God's dream for her and all of His blessings in her personal life and in her mission as a Lightworker and an energy worker, to bring her gifts out into the world. She also asked to release the feeling that asking for abundance is a sin. She affirmed the belief that God intends a paradise for us on Earth and does not intend for us to struggle. From her heart, she set the intention to believe in the dream of her life mission and to open to the possibility that God hears her requests.

We closed the session with adding Matrix Energetics Frequency 8, Integration,[10] to assimilate these new patterns, and Frequency 21, Exploring Inner Space, to retrieve any of her soul fragments that had been lost in the ruckus of the turbulence of this family curse.

This next case brought up another aspect of the issue of permission, as the subjects were not clients of mine, but rather were health care providers for my parents.

Dr. Gabriele

The following is a true story of events that happened to my mother's ophthalmologist. Mom needed eye surgery but was unable to get a timely appointment with providers in her area. Then she found an advertisement for a new ophthalmologist just starting his practice, Dr. Philip Gabriele, and got a cornea

---

10   Bartlett, *The Matrix Energetics Experience* audiobook.

transplant on September 11, 2001—a historical day! She loved Dr. Gabriele and his extraordinarily beautiful and charismatic wife, Marcella, who was also his office manager. My parents said, "Marcy made you feel like she was really taking care of you." Philip and Marcella were each other's best friends, and their devotion to each other was outstanding. A beautiful couple, they were an accomplished ballroom dance team and won the Indiana State Amateur American Smooth Championship. Once, while Mom was waiting for her appointment, Marcella showed her a set of their ballroom dancing photographs and let her choose one to take home. Not having any children, Philip and Marcella adored the three Persian cats they had adopted from the animal shelter.

I accompanied Mom to one of her eye checkups and met her beloved Dr. Gabriele, a charming redhead with sparkling, clear eyes. According to the website for their Gabriele Eye Institute, Philip graduated summa cum laude from the Thomas Jefferson University Medical School and ranked in the top 0.1 percent on his medical boards. He served nationally as a cataract and glaucoma surgery instructor, pioneered the "Hydro-Lift" LASIK enhancement technique, and was the only surgeon in his geographical area trained to perform several special techniques. They operated three clinics in neighboring cities and wanted to open a fourth clinic.

The Charges

In May 2007, investigators executed search warrants at the couple's home as well as all three of their offices on charges of health care fraud. They seized many boxes of client records, which created problems for treatment, not having the charts for patient histories. The couple stopped ballroom dancing when the investigation started.

Friday, June 13, 2009, a federal grand jury indicted them on multiple counts of health care fraud, wire fraud and criminal conspiracy. According to a news release from the U.S. Attorney's Office in Hammond, the indictment alleged that Dr. Gabriele, who was a medical doctor and eye surgeon, falsely diagnosed cataracts and other disorders and performed unnecessary surgeries, then billed Medicare, Medicaid, and insurance companies for the work. They were accused of later altering patient charts and records to make the diagnoses seem correct.[11] The government sought forfeiture of their home and all three of their offices to repay funds allegedly received fraudulently.

Their Response

The Gabrieles responded with a written statement saying they were "deeply saddened and dismayed by the government's decision to proceed with an indictment." They said they would maintain their business.

J. P. Hanlon, one of the attorneys representing the couple, said, "This case should have never been prosecuted. It is an attempt to criminalize medical judgments. The allegations merely demonstrate that government officials do not understand the practice of good medicine, the workings of a medical office, and particularly complex issues involving eyesight."[12]

According to their close friend Susan Manuszak, the Gabrieles were extremely upset by the indictment. She also reported that both of them had major heart problems and were hanging on "by a thread."[13] Their legal bills were topping $2.5

---

11 www.Etruth.com, June 13, 2009.
12 Ibid.

13 Jesse Davis, "Dr. Philip J. Gabriele and his wife found dead in clinic, "*Goshen News*, June 15, 2009.

million, and the government froze their assets on the day of the indictment so that they had no way to pay the staff in their three clinics. Marcella's brother visited them that Saturday and said, "The happiness was all gone. The sparkle in their eyes was gone."[14]

The Gabrieles were scheduled to turn themselves in to court on Monday afternoon, June 16. They knew they would be taken into custody and jailed separately.

Shots

On Monday morning, June 16, police received a call about gunshots heard at the Gabriele Eye Institute. When the officers arrived to investigate, they heard another gunshot. When they entered the building, they found Marcella Gabriele dead of nine gunshot wounds to the chest[15] and Philip dead from a self-inflicted gunshot wound to the head. Their deaths were ruled as homicide and suicide. Their friend Susan found a suicide note in their home asking that their three cats not be separated and not returned to the animal shelter.

Permission

My mother felt extremely upset by these shocking deaths and was grieving deeply, as she had loved and trusted the Gabrieles. She said Marcella always had a smile for everyone, and that they were so dedicated that they would take calls from their patients anytime of the day or night. She told me that they did many operations for free for people who did not have health insurance and could not afford the cost of restoring their eyesight. She said the Gabrieles had written a letter to the local TV station saying that sometimes when a person man-

---

14 www.cbsnews.com, June 17, 2009.
15 www.wsbt.com, March 11, 2009.

ages to be cleared of charges, there is still an inability to be restored to one's work area. Mom felt that life would not have been worth living for Dr. Gabriele if he would have lost his freedom to work in local hospitals without going through the tremendous amount of red tape that would have come from the investigation, even if cleared. The damage to his reputation from the allegations hurt him terribly. Mom also felt that they were unable to handle being separated from each other.

Talking with Mom, I pondered, "I don't know whether I should do some Soul Detective work with them or not." I felt her agitation about the tragedy, but normally I only work when someone asks me for help—and being out of their bodies, they could not ask me for help and sign my consent form! Mom suggested I muscle test whether or not I had permission.

That afternoon, I took a shower, set up a pyramid of Light with guardians and guardian angels for everyone, and then muscle tested whether or not I had permission to work with the Gabrieles. Clearly, I did. I called into the pyramid the spirits of Marcella and Philip Gabriele, and sent a telepathic message, "Hello. I'm Rosa Stone's daughter." Immediately, I was flooded with extremely intense heart-wrenching sobs.

Treatment

Confused, neither of them realized that they were dead. I explained the situation and asked them to do a heart massage, repeating, "Even though we were indicted by the grand jury, we love and accept ourselves. Even though we chose not to go through the trial and to end our lives, we deeply and completely love and accept ourselves."

They calmed down greatly with this heart massage, and I felt that they then understood what had happened. I asked Philip to take the lead and do an energy treatment and for Marcella to copy what he did. I muscle tested for the exact points they needed to treat, and the points that emerged released shame, rage, anger, guilt, and fear.

Dark Force Energy

Philip communicated to me, "We made some mistakes, but we are not guilty of all the charges."

Muscle testing indicated that one dark force was behind the indictment. I muscle tested that I did not have permission to work with this dark energy, so I asked Archangel Michael to do whatever was necessary to extricate the Gabrieles from it. I saw Archangel Michael wrapping the tail of the serpent into itself.

The dark force had suggested the homicide-suicide plan as a way to avoid being separated from each other. Marcella chose to be shot in the heart, as she did not want her face messed up. Philip communicated to me that he had so much emotion around ending the life of the woman he loved with his whole heart that he could not aim well. With the first shot, she cried out and wrenched, so he shot again and again. Very shaken, he had to wait to steady himself before taking his own life so he could aim correctly and leave with his wife. If he had missed his target on himself, he might not have been capable of firing another shot to finish the job.

The dark force plan was to keep their souls caught between the worlds in torment forever, like they were at the beginning of this session.

I heard the telepathic message, "It's over now." I asked Spirit to put them both under a healing waterfall and watched it wash off all the effects of the dark energy. Then they stepped into

37

the fullness of their soul energy, and they appeared to me to be about nine feet tall. They were ready to cross into the Light.

Greeting Committee

I asked who wanted to be on their welcoming committee and a whole crowd appeared—relatives and former patients, all cheering and welcoming them.

Soul Lesson

They communicated that their soul lesson for this incarnation was, "Only love matters."

Multiplying the Benefits

When we invited any others with similar issues to step into the resonance of healing established by the work Philip and Marcella just did, I muscle tested that over three thousand other people who had committed suicide while caught in the grips of dark forces were able to realize what happened, get free, and move into the Light.

Spirit told me, "The dark forces sometimes go after the brightest lights."

I called Mom, who was already feeling at greater ease. The intensity of her grief had lifted during the time I was doing this surrogate work, and the anguish she had felt in the pit of her stomach was released, leaving her at peace.

I cannot say for sure whether this surrogate work I did with the Gabrieles was accurate or was simply a figment of my imagination, but the strength of the emotional response I felt in my heart while working with them is a guideline to me indicating it was real, and the emotional relief my mother experienced is another indication that the work had a beneficial effect. It also brought great joy to my own heart!

In the following case, the trauma was set in a very ancient time, 13,000 BC. I muscle tested that I did not have permission to work with this extremely traumatic material. Then I realized that I had fallen into fear and gotten reversed. Once I straightened out my own polarity, we could proceed and I did get permission to work with the Detrimental Energy.

He Whose Name I Know

Jane, a psychotherapist in her early fifties, was dedicated to healing her own trauma. She had felt emotionally raped by her mother's unprovoked vicious verbal attacks on her, which felt like they also carried distorted sexual energy. As an adult, sexuality had been shrouded with the emotion of shame. Her goal was to be able to relax into her own sexual energy. We found an ancient trauma interfering with her ability to reach this goal.

13,000 BC

We tested that Jane's soul had an incarnation over 15,000 years ago in the area that is now on the eastern coast of Canada. The tribe was primitive, and Jane could tell that they thought differently. She had great difficulty establishing communication with the earthbound spirit of this primitive man. She could see his face looking at her, but he did not understand who she was. We tried to explain that she was a future incarnation of his soul, but that idea was totally incomprehensible to him. He did not trust her and feared that she was a bad spirit. Before her previous incarnation could accept Jane, the shaman needed to approve of her. The shaman let us know that the way the tribe integrated things was by killing and eating them. We realized this plan would not work for us in this situation. We asked for their totem animals to help, but that idea did not work either. The tribe believed in the healing energy of plants, and finally the shaman was able to accept her as a healing plant spirit. We asked the angels to give her previous incarnation the plants he knew for healing, and Jane saw him munching on lots of green leaves, opening up to trusting her.

He Whose Name I Know

He communicated telepathically rather than with words. He asked Jane to call him "He Whose Name I Know," because he felt she knew him on the inside. He then revealed to Jane the traumatic memory of his falling into enemy hands at age twenty and being raped and murdered. At first he wanted to deal with his sexual trauma by cutting off his penis and leaving that part of his body behind, but that solution did not eliminate his trauma. We offered him the possibility of wrapping his penis in some leaves, but that idea would not have solved the issue for him either. He Whose Name I Know explained that he could no longer be a man from the deep mental and emotional wound left by his sexual violation. Like scalping, his enemies had purposely abused and killed him in this way to harm him as much as possible.

Five Dark Angels

We muscle tested that dark energy was keeping him in the trauma, but we felt helpless to communicate to him the intricacies of the Dark Force Protocol. I muscle tested we did not have permission to address the dark energy directly. Jane reported that He Whose Name I Know fully understood the concept of dark forces and was eager to do whatever we could to resolve this problem. He was jumping up and down, excited by the possibility of finally getting some real help! Realizing that my fear had reversed my ability to test clearly on this issue, I did a heart massage on myself to correct my polarity, and then I tested that we did have permission for the Dark Energy Protocol—a surprise to me!

Dark Force Protocol

Purpose: The purpose of the dark energy was to conquer and destroy He Whose Name I Know, to enslave him so his energy could be used on an ongoing basis by the enemy tribe.

Employer: The dark energy claimed it was working for the Light, but I pointed out that the job of destruction and energy theft could not possibly be something the Light would ever do. I pointed out that they had been deceived.

Cognitive Distortions (CDs): Another distortion the dark forces carried is that the more power they would bring to their boss, the more their dark employer would protect them. However, when I asked if they were afraid of their boss, they admitted they feared their boss would turn on them, reporting, "We can't talk about it."

Center: I asked to speak with the most powerful of the five Dark Angels present, letting him know that better job opportunities were available for him. In his center, he found a terrible hellish fire. When we asked him to find what was present when he was created, he perceived a weird feeling of light, but felt he was separate from it and could not merge with it. We asked him to request of Archangel Michael to be freed from this distortion of the truth about his own light. A strange shift came about as he was able to connect with his own light. We offered him a better job, but this angel did not want to go to work. He just wanted to be a baby! He wanted to be like a little pilot fish, just attaching to and cruising with Archangel Michael. Of course, we assured him he could have as much time as he needed in the Spiritual Nursery (a concept we made

41

up on the spot to meet his needs), until he wanted to grow up and do something else.

We asked this angel to call in all four of the other Dark Angels who had been working with He Whose Name I Know and all of their servants, all the little bits of negative programs running that involved sexuality and violation and to reprogram them all for better jobs, free from the cords of deception from their dark boss. We had these angels call back all of their own power that had been taken from them while they themselves had been enslaved. With the help of Jane's spiritual mentor Osho, we did a reprogramming for the soul of He Whose Name I Know to fully restore his sexual value and worth.

Soul Lesson

Jane saw that her soul had a choice, even while being hurt, to be one with the experience rather than fighting it. No matter what was happening, the soul could choose to be in the Light. She then applied this lesson to the ways she had felt raped by her mother. She realized that splitting was not the path and reported, "I need to transform my vision, to see what my mother is producing as just energy. It is my choice whether to perceive her as toxic, or as being radiant. In a group encounter while I was in India, a man was yelling at another woman, but she just perceived him as giving her energy and was grateful he was sharing. I see I am the one who had been making it bad!"

We cleared limiting beliefs around her mother's violation and then tapped on points to release the cellular imprints of trauma and rage from the system so that Jane could integrate the experience rather than fighting it. At the end of this tapping sequence, Jane's vision of her mother was shimmery, as if her mother herself could see light.

Jane expressed amazement at her experience of entering into a primitive mindset, finding a way to establish communication, and healing this very ancient wound in her soul. We multiplied the benefits of this treatment for other dark spirits and others enslaved by the chains of the negative emotions of their sexual violations. We muscle tested that an additional seven Dark Angels got better jobs, and thousands of earthbound spirits coupled to this healing!

4. *CLASSIFYING TYPE AND NUMBER OF DETRIMENTAL ENERGIES:*
   a. *One or more negative thoughts*

In the following case, the person doing the Soul Detective work carried a negative thought that she had done something wrong that resulted in harm to her people.

Disaster Preparedness

Andra was a highly intuitive, powerful healer in her own right, 99 percent of the time. During the other 1 percent of the time, she got frustrated, and then her energy ran backward through her system (counterflow chi).

Angelica Michelle

We traced the origin of this pattern to a lifetime where she was born along the coast of India in 127 AD. This woman asked us to call her Angelica Michelle. Her happiest time was sitting in a grassy pasture on a hill overlooking the ocean, feeling totally unencumbered by fear. She was so closely connected to Source energy that her body radiated light, and she felt etheric, almost translucent. People came to her for the light, love, guidance, and healing her presence imparted.

Trouble began one day when she was thirteen years old. She sensed from Spirit that a natural disaster was coming to the island and tried to warn people. They did not want to hear what she had to say and turned away from her, thinking she was betraying them. This abandonment by her people broke her heart. We paused the story to do energy tapping to release her anxiety and shame around feeling that she had done something wrong and had not properly prepared the village.

Tidal Wave

Then the tidal wave came. She was on top of the hill, where she had tried to call the villagers to the safety of its height. But the tsunami wave was monstrous, bigger than she could ever have imagined, and swept her to her death from the top of the hill, destroying the entire island, all the animals, and every inhabitant. Andra suddenly understood why she feared big waves in her current life, and also why she feared saying or not saying the correct thing.

Saddled with sadness, rage at the situation, and shame, Angelica's spirit remained earthbound. Once we made a customized tapping sequence to treat these emotions, Angelica realized that she had no control over the people or the disaster. Nothing she could have said or done, or hadn't said or done, would have made any difference or saved anyone. This insight released her soul from its shackles, and Angelica Michelle was ready to go to the Light. First, however, she needed to call out to others in the village that died in terror and had also remained earthbound. We sent out Angelic search parties to find them. Andra saw people standing on top of the dark water and angels like helicopters with searchlights in the dark rescuing them. Then Andra and thousands of others crossed to the Light together. At last, she had fulfilled her mission of showing her people the Way.

Soul Lesson

From the other side, Angelica's soul realized that, as a carrier of the Light, she was simply to impart Light in the form of possibilities and understanding. Her soul council was laughing as she realized she was not in control of anything or anybody. The tidal wave was part of a greater plan not understood on Earth at that time.

Application for Andra

Andra reported that the lesson for her current incarnation is: "When I feel frustrated and out of control, instead of hanging on, I just need to let go and simply allow the light to flow." Andra felt a tremendous burden lift from her shoulders after this work. Gone was the feeling that she had failed her people, because she had finally helped them get to safety. Peacefulness came to her heart as she realized her proper place and that many events of the world are simply beyond our control. After this work, she was better able to hold her center through the ups and downs of daily life.

b. *One or more pervasive negative thought patterns or negative life beliefs (for example, "anger makes you powerful")*

Craniotomy

Gretchen's family had been marked by tragedy. She was the only one of four children who survived to adulthood. Her mother lost her first child when the baby was only a few days old. After Gretchen's birth, her mother had a stillborn baby girl. Her mother was eight months' pregnant with a son when Gretchen's father, Hubert, killed himself. When this last child was ten years old, he died in an accidental drowning. Gretchen's mother died of widespread cancer one day after the anniversary of her husband's suicide, forty-five years later, at the exact same time in the morning.

Gretchen was a high-functioning executive, but her life gradually fell apart in her fifth decade. She gained sixty pounds, lost interest in keeping her house in order, felt loss of interest in everything, started drinking a little too much alcohol, and could not see a future for herself. She had headaches and considered killing herself. Her friends noticed something was not right and insisted she consult a physician, who sent her for neurological testing. When asked to draw a clock, Gretchen put all the numbers bunched up into one place. Because she could not properly organize information, she was sent for an MRI, which detected a large, slow-growing tumor on the left side of her brain.

Craniotomy

An operation removed the tumor with no short-term or long-term memory loss, and Gretchen felt she had a new lease on life. She lost the weight she had gained, stopped drinking, and attended to her other physical problems to bring her body back to a state of balance. She came for a "tune-up" to find the next step in her soul's mission. Soul Detective work muscle tested that she had been carrying the earthbound spirit of her older sister, who had died a few days after her birth. We helped her sister cross to the Light, and then tested that her sister had been attached to Gretchen through Gretchen's brain!

Zeus and Athena

This situation touches on the mythology of Zeus and his daughter Athena, who sprang fully grown from his forehead, dressed in battle armor. Like Zeus, Gretchen also had something growing in her head. Normally, the immune system attacks anything in the body that is growing too fast. The one exception is a fetus, which grows very fast but is a normal occurrence and is supposed to grow rapidly. *Tumors hide from the immune system by mimicking the chemistry of a fetus.* Metaphorically, the tumor in Gretchen's brain was like a child who was trying to be incubated—just like Athena! In this case, however, the child did not spring out fully grown; rather, we treated her sister's earthbound spirit for her trauma and then called the spirit of their mother to come get her baby!

The Other Sister

The stillborn baby girl's spirit had been attached to their father. When Hubert killed himself, the child's spirit was blown out of his system and had been wandering, alone and unattached to anyone. We treated her for the shame she had been carrying and then called their mother and the other sister to come get this baby, too! Their brother, who had already crossed into the Light, also came for this family reunion.

Negative Life Belief: I have sinned.

We had to wonder whether Hubert might also have had a tumor growing in his brain. Gretchen sensed he might have had an organic problem that he could not figure out. As the pressure of the tumor grew and her father felt mood changes and rising rage, he thought the only way to stop the monster growing within him from hurting someone else was to kill himself. Since he was Catholic, he believed he was violating the commandment "Thou shalt not kill" and because of this sin, he was condemned to a long stay in purgatory. He did not realize that he had been successful in his suicide, as his emotional pain was still fully present when we began our session.

After treating his rage and helping Hubert to forgive himself for not knowing what else to do, Hubert was ready to move into the Light. Over fifty years in purgatory had been enough!

He wanted all of his family already in Heaven, Divine Mother, Jesus, and all of his angels to help him make this crossing. What a joyful moment when Hubert was finally released from his suffering!

We multiplied the benefits of these healings for any others who had taken their own lives and any other earthbound children, calling their angels and their parents to come get them and to couple to this healing process!

Soul Lesson

Gretchen's soul lesson was about transformation: life can be transformed. Now she has the opportunity to help other people transform their lives as well. Her spiritual path is about connecting directly to Divine energy through nourishing the Light within her own soul.

c. *One or more Dark Force Entities, which could be called Fallen Angels, Unharmonized Entities, Suffering Beings, or Dark Angels. Ask your client what name for addressing this level of detrimental energy sounds the best. If more than one entity is present, ask to work the highest-ranking leader or the most powerful one. Later, invite the others to multiply the benefits of the work the leader does.*

Cockroaches on you!

Rachel, a highly spiritual woman, was very aware of what was happening in her energy field. As a child she had suffered physical and sexual abuse from her grandfather, mother, and brothers. This abuse generated feelings of rage and self-hatred. The goal of our session was to restore proper function to her throat chakra. She sensed a hole in the back of her throat where a chakra funnel should have been. We muscle tested that the problem was due to one Dark Force Entity. When we asked its purpose, it gave us an uncooperative attitude, saying, "I read the script. You can't fool me." It was not going to tell its purpose, saying, "You know." Rachel sensed its purpose was to cause trouble and pull her down.

The entity worked for the darkness and believed the Light would kill it. When we asked it to look inside, it retorted, "I'm not going there." It was following orders not to listen. When it did finally look inside and saw its light, the entity was very shocked and hopping mad. It believed there was no God and that it had no choice and would be punished if it quit its job of causing trouble for Rachel. The New Lightworkers told it that those beliefs were not true.

Curse on Barbara

The Dark Force Entity was not buying the story and tried to put a curse on me, saying, "Cockroaches on you!" It continued, saying, "None of it is true. It's all lies." Then we asked Archangel Michael to show it the truth, cutting away all lies, including the issue of whether or not there is a God. The entity had a change of heart and said, "Let's go to the beach!" We multiplied the benefits, inviting any other Dark Force Entities with similar jobs and fears to come get better jobs working for the Light.

Origin of the Wound

Rachel experienced that the wound that allowed this dark entity to attach was from her most recent past lifetime. Her soul had an incarnation as a Jewish child named Carl who was killed at age three in a gas chamber in 1940 in World War II in the area that is now the Czech Republic. The happiest moment of that lifetime was the birth process, making it out of the tunnel. At the time of Carl's death, his parents and big brother were also killed. We worked with Carl's mother, who was still earthbound, to release her sadness, trauma, and guilt.

Soul Lesson

Rachel felt that Carl's lifetime had the dual purpose of paying off a karmic debt and also learning the lesson of loving others unconditionally, a contrast to the hate for those doing the gassing. She reflected that in comparison to the huge traumas that were incurred in the war, many of the interpersonal problems she sees in this lifetime feel like "small potatoes." Rachel reported that the Nazis doing the gassing provoked hate with their body language, looks, spoken words, and how they handled people. In multiplying the benefits, we saw a big crowd come forward, "beyond counting." Then Rachel saw Carl as a little boy, filled with love, beckoning with his hand and arm, and most of the souls who had coupled to the healing headed over the bridge of Light. One little seven-year-old boy who had been involved in the war was angry with his father, who was one of the Nazis. He shouted, "Why, why, why?"

We worked with his father, who was begging forgiveness for his mistakes. He had raped four women. They all had crossed, and we asked them to stand before him and let him ask forgiveness individually for all the pain he had caused them. They forgave him, and then we treated him for his own guilt and grief and his feeling that he could never be forgiven. At last he was willing to accept and release his guilt and rage against himself. We called spiritual ambulances to come get this man and the other Nazis who accepted our invitation to multiply the benefits.

Vengeance

Still, the son was angry and wanted to hold onto vengeance. We asked him who was paying for his father's mistakes. He

50

said he was, and added, "I've always paid." When we asked Archangel Michael to open his eyes to his father's suffering, we saw that dark energy had been attached to the little boy and invited the dark energy to cross into the Light. Next Rachel saw the boy on his deathbed with his father kneeling and praying for him. Then they were hugging, and the father carried him over the bridge. An area that had been a big flat paved surface now had grass and trees growing.

We ended the session with clearing Rachel's Gallbladder meridian from the accumulated violations of her abusive childhood. Rachel understood that hating herself for the first forty-eight years of her life was futile, and holding onto her rage was also futile. As we tapped on the release points for rage, which were on the bones around her eyes, Rachel felt she was finally able to finish releasing her rage. It was quite a session!

d. *One or more Dark Devices, inert machinelike devices inserted by the dark side to cause problems such as irritation of nerves, prongs or screws to cause pain, displacement devices to throw the body out of alignment, or devices to receive thoughts broadcast to the client by Dark Forces.*

e. *One or more Minions, servile creatures of lesser consciousness that simply take orders and do the will of their master. I think of them a bit like R2D2 robots. They are smaller in stature than the angels.*

f. *One or more Bound Spirits, the earthbound spirit of a human who is so damaged emotionally that the dark side has been able to bind the spirit into doing a dark job to cause suffering in someone else. Sorcerers and demons can call on them. They forget who they are, and it is very healing and liberating for the human to remember how he turned to the darkness and to feel forgiveness and love.*

Minion Conscription

Margee presented with the issue of a rash on her hand that had been unresponsive to the various treatments she had been trying on it over the past year. Two Dark Angels, one minion, and one bound spirit were involved in this issue. I do not usually ask the Dark Force Entities what name they would like us to call them, as giving something a name gives it more power. But in this case, the entity identified itself with the name Bart.

Head Honcho Bart

Bart, the most powerful of the two Dark Angels, was like a head honcho military commander who carried out the orders he was given. Bart's purpose with Margee was twofold:

1. My purpose is to stop you from claiming your true self.
2. We do not want you to love yourself and others. Your capacity for love frightens us.

Bart disclosed that they were actually very afraid. The second Dark Angel was like a teenager who wanted us to call him Allister. Neither of them had ever thought about whether they were working for the darkness or the Light. They just took orders.

They had come on board with Margee fifteen years earlier when she had visited her very ill father in the veterans' hospital. She had come away with the strong negative feeling, "I'm not a good enough daughter because I can't help him." Margee remembered getting very sick for two days after that visit and wondering what she had picked up at the hospital. She tried an Epsom salt bath, but it did not give her relief. The Dark Angels disclosed that they attacked those whose hearts were vulnerable.

Center

Bart found some cobwebs and mucus in his center, and also a tiny speck of light. Allister's light was brighter than Bart's. We treated them both for their fear, and Bart's color improved. Allister got more confused.

We asked Archangel Michael to offer Bart a job promotion. Bart was unsure, overwhelmed by the power he felt in Michael's energy. Bart was afraid of getting in trouble with his old boss, but after talking with some New Lightworkers, he decided he wanted to work for the most powerful one. But he wanted to know the exact details of what his new job would involve.

The New Lightworkers told him, "We are actually freer than you are." Margee noticed Bart's black armor cracking and crumbling.

Allister had many questions for Archangel Michael: "Will I be totally free of the dark? Can I travel at will with these wonderful energies around me now?" He took a couple of steps closer to Michael. When he asked to have his cords of deception removed, he burst right into the Light! Allister stood on the periphery with the angels and called to his servant, his minion, who was confused. The concept of freedom and having free will was totally foreign to him. He wanted us to call him Renee, and he just took orders from Allister. Archangel Michael showed him that without the black cords attached to him, he could fly and move about very fast. As Renee's light was getting stronger, we turned our attention back to Bart, whose light was also brighter.

One Last Cord

Archangel Michael showed Bart his sword, and Bart was really impressed with its power! Michael was dressed like a warrior, which Bart liked. As they talked over the terms of the job upgrade, one cord was still attached to Bart. The minion serving Bart was full of anger and rage. He was an earthbound spirit who had been conscripted by Bart to help with his mission of shutting down Margee's ability to love. This bound spirit had never gotten any love from anyone and had been repeatedly beaten as a child in India, so he did not want others to have what he did not get. We offered him a treatment for the trauma of his childhood physical abuse. He flat out did not think that getting over his trauma was possible. We knew this limiting belief could be cleared, so we had him tap the energy point under his lips and say, "Even though I do not believe it is possible to get over my trauma, I accept all of my feelings about it." The spirit softened, and then we called in Divine Mother to give him real love. Mother Mary embraced and caressed him, enveloping him in her love. She was so beautiful and gentle! He allowed her to hold his hand. He wanted to know, "Will you love me as a mother and protect me from beatings?" Mary assured him that he would never get another beating when he went into the Light with her. They went together, with him holding her hand.

Minion Renee

Next we went back to Allister's minion Renee, who was excited and filled with anticipation. Could it be true he could get this job upgrade? He talked with other minions who had chosen the Light, and he was in awe of the possibilities. Allister was calling to him. We did energy tapping with Renee for his rage about having his free will taken away and his fear of what might lie ahead. He made a happy, dramatic shift to a new level of calm. Margee told him, "See Michael's power and love and walk into it. You have free will." Renee was right at "the line," the crossover point into the Light, but afraid to go any further. I asked him to stick one toe over the line to see how it felt. Zloop! As soon as he put his toe over and felt the wonderful power of the Light for himself, he was drawn right into it.

New Uniform

Bart was still conversing with Michael. He wanted a warrior outfit and a sword. He was negotiating the uniform he would get in his job promotion. Michael said, "A sword for God." Michael showed Bart a beautiful warrior outfit in a blue metallic color with a metal breastplate and a sword. Bart took the sword and cut that last cord to his old employer himself! He was tired of the old darkness job, which we muscle tested he had been doing for over a million years. Bart disclosed that during the time of the Romans, he helped make Roman soldiers more vicious.

Past Life Involvement

I inquired whether Bart had been involved with Margee's immediate past life, in which she had been a Jewish physician named Yoseph killed by the Nazis in Poland. Margee covered her face with her hands, weeping. Bart showed her that he had been inside of the man who tortured Yoseph, taking pleasure in breaking all of his fingers so he could never again work as a surgeon. Then another Nazi shot Yoseph.

We asked Jesus Christ, the great healer, to heal all of those broken bones for Yoseph. Bart communicated, "I'm so sorry! I was filled with evil. You are a healer, and I didn't want you to heal anyone, because I did not feel I could be helped." Bart needed to ask Margee's forgiveness for this pain he had

caused her, a true sign that his soul had grown in consciousness. Margee looked at Bart's essence when he asked for forgiveness and saw that his light had brightened dramatically.
Her heart softened toward him, and she forgave him with the
strong intention of helping him go into the Light.

When Yoseph died, he had stayed earthbound because he felt
such shame that he was not able to help his son, who had been
sick. Yoseph came out of hiding to get medical supplies for his
little boy, as he would have died without medical intervention.
But during this process, Yoseph was captured and therefore
was unable to help his son. We muscle tested that both of his
children from that life had been killed, and both were earthbound. His wife had also been murdered, but she had made it
home to the Light.

We asked Yoseph to help his children *right now*, and Margee
again covered her face and wept. We called the earthbound
spirits of his son and daughter to come to him. Yoseph told
them they would have all the food they wanted, that they
would not be hungry anymore, and that where they were going, they would be whole, healthy, and happy. They trusted him and were close to crossing into the Light but still
not ready.

Multiplying the Benefits

We asked Yoseph to put out a call to all others who had been
tortured and murdered in this or any other war to come into
our octahedron of Light, couple to his healing, and move together into the next world. Margee felt a huge whoosh! We
muscle tested that over eight thousand others, and maybe
more, had made that crossing along with Yoseph and his children. Bart got swept away in the crowd and also moved fully
into the Light.

Soul Lesson

Margee reported her soul lesson was "To continue to keep my heart open with love to all, no matter what the circumstances. Believe in myself and my integrity, and keep my heart open!" She noticed that in this lifetime, she had become overly responsible, taking on caretaking roles out of her shame of not feeling good enough.

She added, "I am to trust and slow down. I go too fast, which distracts me from being present. I am to know I come from a place of integrity *and believe in myself.*"

This last statement corrected the former dark program of trying to keep her from loving herself and others and claiming her true self. After this two-hour Soul Detective session, Margee felt lighter, and the itching decreased on the rash on her hand. The open wound on her hand took about three weeks to heal completely and had not returned when I checked in thirteen months later.

g. *Higher ranking Dark Force Entities. If you encounter anything above the rank of a Fallen Angel, for your own protection, please immediately turn the matter over to Archangel Michael. Otherwise the situation would be like a person with a bucket trying to drain Lake Erie. Ask the higher echelons of the angelic realm to deal with the situation, and remember the protection of your octahedron of Light around you.*

Fatima and Alima

Fatima struggled with depression, especially after the holidays. She wondered what was behind her periodic downward mood slides. At a dinner party that included Fatima and her husband, me, two other Soul Detectives, and a woman named Alima who was trained to work as an intuitive reader, Fatima inquired, "Do I have any angels around me?" Alima responded that she could look but seeing the spirit world took focus, and we were all eating supper right then. Alima did take a quick peek, saw an angel, and promised to continue after the meal.

After dessert, Alima focused on Fatima and saw two angels: one female with long blonde hair and a male angel, right beside each other. These two angels reported they were working with Fatima all the time. The female angel did most of the talking. Fatima asked, "Is her name Ariel? I've been calling on her." Fatima had taken an Integrated Energy Therapy (IET)[16] class which works with the healing energy of Archangel Ariel and generally sees her as feminine, although Archangel Ariel can also be seen as male. Alima responded that Archangel Ariel was off to the right side and was available whenever Fatima called, but she was not the ever-present female personal guardian angel.

Then Fatima and Alima and I worked together to find the origin of Fatima's mood swings. I muscle tested that two dark energies were present. One was a Fallen Angel and the other was its minion, defined as "a servile follower or subordinate of a person in power." Whatever the dark entity did, the minion followed suit.

Detrimental Energy Protocol

I asked Fatima to attune to the Fallen Angel and to ask its purpose for being with her. She could not make any kind of connection with this energy. Alima said that the Fallen Angel was not cooperating with us and was resisting our efforts to communicate. He was quite put out that he had been discov-

---

16   IET website: www.LearnIET.com

ered. He was wearing a cape, perhaps trying to cloak himself from detection.

Fatima's husband noted that she had gotten depressed when she was working on her book about her life experience as a Muslim female who had served in the U.S. Army. She could see both sides of the issues between the Muslims and the Americans. When her husband mentioned the book, Alima saw the Fallen Angel turn to him and shout, "Shut up!" He did not want us connecting to the importance of Fatima writing this book. I sensed that he had been assigned to Fatima because her light was so bright.

I proceeded with the protocol, asking for whom the Fallen Angel worked. Again, no response came forth—more resistance. I told him we assumed that since he was trying to decrease Fatima's light, he was working for the darkness. Alima continued to report the activity of this Fallen Angel, saying she saw him make menacing faces at me and raise his hands as if he were clawing me.

I inquired what his employer had told him about the light. The Fallen Angel shouted three times in rapid succession, "Don't go there!" The light felt dangerous, and the Fallen Angel thought he would be annihilated if he got too close to the Light.

I asked him to look inside to see what was in his center. Alima heard the Fallen Angel say something like, "Humph!" and turn his back on me in open defiance. When he turned around, however, he saw Fatima's two angels standing there. Slowly, the reality of the Light seeped in, and the Fallen Angel found a spark of light within himself. His resistance broke up, and he began to transform. His inner light grew and felt good. The minion just followed along, doing whatever the Fallen Angel did without thinking for itself.

I pointed out that the Light was not like his employer had portrayed it and pointed out that the Fallen Angel had been deceived. I inquired how he felt working for a liar. The Fallen Angel did not like this situation at all. We offered him a chance to quit his old job and to come work for the Light. He accepted, and I told him I would call him "Angel" in the future instead of "Fallen Angel."

The Cord

He still had a cord connecting him to his employer. I asked whether Angel wanted to ask Archangel Michael to cut this cord or invite his employer to also find his own light and get a better job. No answer came, so I muscle tested and got the answer that we should invite the employer. When I made the offer to the employer, I met with a shield of stony silence. Alima saw the employer standing off to the left, and that one was really big, larger than I feel comfortable working with! Since it was a higher-ranking Dark Force Angel, I asked Archangel Michael to deal with the employer directly and explain the new job offer to him. Alima said the employer had no personal connection to Fatima like the Fallen Angel and its minion had. She saw the employer going off with Archangel Michael and his band of angels.

Unplugging the Cord

Alima saw Angel put his hands around the cord connecting just above his navel area to his employer. It was thick, about three inches in diameter, and very heavy. Angel popped this cord out himself, dropped it, and then ran and hid between Fatima's two angels for protection! Alima added, "He ditched the cape!" His whole countenance had changed from dark (literally!), intense, aggressive, and mean-faced to lighter (literally!) and almost childlike, quiet with wide-eyed curiosity.

I asked Angel whether he wanted to release the cord that bound his minion to him, so the minion could, of its own free will, choose whom to serve. The idea that he could release his minion was very new, and he had to think over that possibility. We inquired what new job Angel would like to have working for the Light and listed a number of possibilities. Angel did not feel ready to take on any of them. We asked if he wanted to have a time of job training to prepare him for his new role as a Lightworker, and that solution was very agreeable to him. He went off to Lightworker School, surrounded by his new comrades.

We multiplied the benefits, and Fatima muscle tested that over six thousand other Fallen Angels accepted job promotions and came to work for the Light!

Lifetime on Mars

Next we muscle tested when this dark energy had attached to Fatima. We found that the Fallen Angel had been with her ever since a lifetime on the planet Mars two thousand years before the flood. Earth was in the year 13,000 BC when this lifetime happened on Mars. The trauma of that incarnation was being martyred together with her mother when she was an eight-year-old female, though either Fatima was already an "old soul" at that time or, in that realm, eight years old was much more mature than on Earth. They were burned to death over a struggle/conflict relating to freedom, and Fatima's spirit left that physical body quickly, so as not to experience the full trauma of that fiery death. The dark force had targeted her when she was feeling upset and vulnerable and had been tracking future incarnations of her soul. Whenever she had a

61

lifetime in which she rose too high in her spiritual development, the Fallen Angel would throw her into depression to try
to stop her.

One of the other Soul Detectives present saw that 15,000
years ago, Mars had been green and lush, very different from
its present condition. Alima had never taken an intuitive trip
to Mars before and was excited to take a look at another planet! She saw a lone bulldozer-type machine crawling along the
dim, dusty, and rather barren surface, although she thought
this vision was probably at a different time period. We desen-
sitized the trauma of that lifetime and healed and sealed the
wound where the dark force had attached.

After giving thanks and closing our octahedron of light, Alima saw Jesus go around and place his hands on the head of
everyone present in our session, giving us a blessing. We were
all absolutely glowing!

Results

Fatima came out of her depression after this session and went
back to working on her book. Although she still had some
mood fluctuations with the seasons over the coming years, she
was able to get off all of her medication and did not fall into
the despair that had plagued her before. She was grateful for
the healing that came to her soul from this group intervention!

h. *One or more Impostor Spirits. In cases of severe mental distur-
    bance, clients may hear a disembodied voice, either coming from
    inside their head or from outside just like a regular voice, claim-
    ing to be the spirit of a deceased person known to the client or a
    living person. With an Impostor Spirit, however, this voice is not
    really the person it claims to be. The voice is just masquerading
    as someone else to cause trouble. Just like a virus that mutates to
    avoid detection, these spirits can hide by changing their labels*

after the first identification. They may also jump to other family members or close contacts to escape detection when other detrimental forces are converting to the Light. Clients with major mental illness such as schizophrenia may or may not have Impostor Spirits. The bottom line of the Impostor Spirit is likely to be the idea that the client should die so the client can be in spirit form with the deceased person the Impostor Spirit claims to be. If suicidal ideation, strong thoughts of death, or major mental illness are present in the situation, the case belongs in the hands of a licensed mental health practitioner trained to deal with these risks.

5. *GETTING PERMISSION FOR EACH ITEM OF THE INVENTORY*

   a. *Muscle test whether or not you have permission to work with each item in the inventory of detrimental energy. If you get permission, you can proceed with the confidence that you have the skills necessary to deal with that item.*

   b. *If you do not get permission to proceed with one or more items on the inventory, turn that item or items over to Archangel Michael, the angel of protection, asking him to do whatever is necessary to resolve the problem and free the client from this detrimental energy.*

   c. *Impostor Spirit Advisory: When we test for permission to work with an Impostor Spirit, we are not asking the Impostor Spirits directly if we can change them from "bad guys" into "good guys." You can imagine what their direct response would be! Rather, we are asking Source energy if it is in the highest good of the Impostor Spirits, the client's highest good, and everyone's highest good to take the next step of converting the torsion spin on their energy from detrimental into beneficial. If you get permission to work with an Impostor Spirit, first run the Torsion Spin Conversion Protocol and then proceed with Step 5 of this Detrimental Energy Protocol.*

In the following case, a client was being affected by a Dark Force Entity attached to her husband, compounded by fragments of her soul stuck in two past lives which left her unable to move forward in her life. We got permission to work with the Dark Force Entity that was weighing down her husband and affecting the whole family.

Ostracized

As Lori started standing up for herself, her husband's drinking got worse. She loved and cared for him but could not tolerate his drinking and emotional withdrawal. She wanted to resolve the relationship one way or another but felt stuck, unable to resolve the situation.

Her husband had been abused in Catholic school, with the nuns locking him in a closet because he had a lisp and putting him in the preschool, saying, "If you're going to talk like a baby, you have to be with the babies." Religion was used abusively in his family and in the Catholic school and was the entry point for infection by a dark force.

We muscle tested that Lori had three patterns interfering with relationship harmony with her husband: a spiritual issue of a Dark Force Entity attached to her husband plus two past life traumas affecting Lori.

Spiritual Issue: A Dark Force

The purpose of the dark force attached to Lori's husband was to weigh him down with anger about the ways he was abused and to make him bury his head in the sand, put him down, and hold him back. A psychic told him that his animal totem was an eagle, but his four children said he was an ostrich! The force working for the darkness was hiding, like a shadow, and did not want to be discovered. It was surprised it had been able to stay with him so long and was waiting to be kicked out.

In its center was a hurting child who did not like its job. The heart of this child had light in it that began to expand when we focused on it. The Dark Force Entity willingly quit its old job and accepted a new job working for Archangel Michael and his band of New Lightworkers. Then we visualized pouring healing energy into her husband's heart to give him all the love he had needed as a child and never got. It poured in for a long time before it felt complete.

Lori's Past Life Trauma

Lori's soul incarnated into a tribe in western South America in 561 BC, and this incarnation wanted to be called Christopher. The happiest time was feeling lightness, sunshine, and a golden color. A marriage was arranged for Christopher to a woman who wanted to be called Mary, now reincarnated as Lori's husband. Christopher's feelings were neutral at the time Mary was presented to him. He thought, "Oh, there is the wife." A tragic scene ensued, however. The tribe practiced ritual human sacrifice and wanted to sacrifice Mary to their gods. Christopher could not accept this practice of human sacrifice and objected. Both he and Mary were ostracized from the tribe because they were not following tribal custom. On their own, Christopher could not find enough food, and Mary starved to death. With his wife gone, Christopher felt totally abandoned. He knew the tribe could come after him, so he took his own life by poisoning himself to prevent what they would have done to him.

We tried to treat Christopher for his rage and trauma, but he did not want to let go of his anger at the ultimate betrayal by the tribe. We pointed out that he had been holding this anger for over 2,500 years, and it was not hurting the tribe—he was the one who was suffering by remaining earthbound. We repeated his treatment, asking him to forgive himself for standing up for his belief that human sacrifice was wrong, even though he suffered the drastic consequences of his action. Then he felt better. Mary had also remained earthbound. We called her spirit into the octahedron of light, and Christopher giggled when he felt her presence with him. Condor came to fly them home in a joyful crossing!

Soul Lesson

"Stay true to your own spirit."

Application to Lori: In the recent past, she had been carrying the fear that standing up for her beliefs could cost her not only her life, but the life of her partner, too. She walked the labyrinth at a church and felt power in the vortex at the center. She looked up and saw Jesus hanging on the cross, dripping blood. She thought, "You wind up in prison either way, but hiding is a worse prison." We treated her fear in her current life about truly standing up for herself, and then she was able to release the fear that if she made a decision, it would kill both her and her partner.

One More Past Life

In the incarnation just previous to this one, Lori had been a soldier in Vietnam. He was running from the enemy, in panic. He got separated from his group and was terrified. He was killed but did not cross to the Light because he was so locked into his fear that he just kept running. As a child, Lori had vivid nightmares and drew pictures about this soldier's experience. His presence would come and go. We treated his trauma and explained the situation to him. The transition to receive the help of the angels that were all around him was difficult at first, but then he was able to stop running and move into the Light.

Soul Lesson

"Let go, let go, let go!"

We multiplied the benefits for all of this work, and Lori was able to come to peace about letting go of her dysfunctional marriage.

6. *INTERVIEWING FOR PURPOSE: If you have permission to proceed, ask the detrimental energy what its purpose is in the client's life. (Frequent responses are to destroy the person, cause as much pain as possible, to make the person miserable, split the family, etc.) Here you are going into the heart of the negative pattern that has been controlling the client's life. When you understand the goal of the dark force, you gain insight into its point of view of the situation. Especially in cases where the dark force has been quite successful at doing a lot of damage, you might want to flatter this energy by letting it know it has been doing a good job of its stated purpose. The dark forces seem to have very large egos and revel in a sense of their own power. This flattery may help to build rapport. Later, when you invite the dark force to get a new job working for the Light, you can mention again that it is a good worker, and the Light needs more good workers.*

One client was working with a Dark Force Entity whose job was to frighten and scare her. While we were working with him, she spotted a big fat spider about two inches long including the legs crawling along the wall over to the bookcase. I, too, saw it, and it was ugly and menacing. It crawled behind a bookcase. We went on with the session, and the dark force attached to the client found its light and converted to becoming a Lightworker. After the session, I went to look for the spider to escort it outside, but it was nowhere in the bookcase.

Double Agent

A Soul Detective student noticed increased attack from dark energies and felt a serpentine dark energy with octopus-like tentacles reaching all through her body. Rather than going through the whole protocol, she just asked Archangel Michael for assistance and offered the Darkness a promotion to get a better job. He jovially accepted and began his transformation. Even his little minion joined in! The minion was impossible to transform, however, so Michael just eradicated the mini dark energy. This action raised a red flag for the student, so she started at the beginning of the dark energy protocol and watched closely. Here is her first-person account.

Façade

When I asked the Dark Angel what his job had been and why he was bothering me, I could see his façade start to drip away, melting like it was above a flame. When I looked at him from behind, I could see dark spots up the middle of his back. Suddenly, he could not hold the pretense anymore and grew to ten times his original presenting size, spouted a few angelic profanities, claimed he never changed, and threatened me. He told me that I was about to start work that was intensely dangerous to his kind, and it was his intent and mission to stop me from this new beginning. In the background, I saw an army of darkness coalescing and moving toward me.

Of course, Michael knew the scoop from the start. And in retrospect, he acted differently to this "new Light convert" than I had ever seen him do before. Michael was present, strong, and angelic but had firmness about him, as if he were ready for battle. When the dark army appeared, even before I finished asking for help, Michael's Light Troops had surrounded me, spreading so much Light that the Darkness was completely overtaken.

Slight Sidetrack

After the ordeal, Michael explained that the coming significant growth period for humanity might have some disruption
and chaos. More and more, darkness may try to pretend it is
Light. If the dark side can distract Lightworkers even just a
little from their paths, they're hoping for a critical mass to be
reached where everything is just slightly sidetracked, making
their ultimate dark missions easier to achieve. He told me to
be vigilant of this possibility and asked me to share it with
others. I can feel that the dark forces are still out there, but I
also feel an intensity of Light around me, stronger than I have
ever felt before.

7. *EMPLOYER: Ask this force, "Who do you work for, the darkness or
   the Light?" Some will say the darkness or may sneer, wondering how
   dumb you could be to ask such a stupid question, given the job they
   just disclosed. Others may never have thought about who they are
   working for. If they say they are working for themselves, don't believe
   it! Some will mistakenly believe they are working for the Light. If they
   turn a cold shoulder and do not answer, you can say, "With a job like
   _____(mention their job), we are assuming you are working
   for the darkness. Is that correct?" At this point, they usually admit
   they are working for the dark side.*

Protective Angel

Peter, a mechanic in his fifties, was volatile with his wife and
other family members. He would fly into rages, and the whole
family tiptoed around him, afraid of another outbreak and
cowering before his fury. Peter had gone through open heart
surgery, but the physical intervention to remove the blockages
in the arteries to his heart did not open up his emotional heart.
His wife loved him and did not want to leave him, but she had
difficulty tolerating his outbursts and watching his behavior

69

and attitudes threaten his life by putting him at high risk for a fatal heart attack.

One Dark Force Angel

The dark force angel launching these attacks communicated that it had stepped in to protect Peter when he had been severely physically abused as a child. Whenever Peter felt threatened, the angel launched an all-out defense of filling Peter with rage to destroy the enemy, even though the offending person was a family member. The angel insisted he was working for the Light, to protect Peter.

We had to work with the dark force angel quite a while to help him realize that this defense action had been necessary when he was a small child, but that he was a grown man now, and nobody was going to beat him up again. Then the angel converted and got a job that was really working for the Light.

Rage Is Better Than Fear

Each emotion has a calibration of life energy, which David Hawkins has delineated in his Map of Consciousness.[17] This scale maps the vibrational level of each emotion on a logarithmic scale of zero to 1,000, with Shame at the very bottom calibrating at only 20 and Enlightenment at the top calibrating from 700 to 1,000.

When children are abused, they distort their reality to believe that the abuse was their fault. Living in a world where one's caretakers are evil would be so frightening that, in an attempt to feel more secure, the children create the illusion that their caretakers are good, and that they are the ones who are guilty. In other words, they put themselves down into the lowest two categories, Guilt at 30 and Shame at 20. From this place on the scale, Anger at 150 has a lot more energy to it. Dark forces exploit the vulnerability of these children. They

---

17 Hawkins, *Power Vs. Force*, 52-53.

enter through the emotional wound as protectors against feelings of helplessness with the messages of anger and rage, saying, "Fight back! Get even!" *These dark forces often think they are helping the children by raising their vibration.* They may claim that they are working for the Light. The problem is that anger is still an emotion that pulls a person down. When these children reach adulthood, they may stay stuck in the chronic response of rage toward the injustices of their daily lives.

Dark Force Entities who think they are working for the Light are using the only tools they know: hatred, antagonism, and aggression. When working with a dark entity that is under the illusion that it is helping the person, first of all, support its underlying desire to help. Then bring awareness to the effect its influence is having on the adult, and then show it *an even better way to help.* When these angels get new jobs working for Archangel Michael, they are thrilled to finally be in alignment with the true desire of their hearts to serve!

Courage at 200 is the dividing line between the emotions that are "uppers"—Neutrality at 250, Willingness at 310, Acceptance at 350, Reason at 400, Love at 500, Joy at 540, and Peace at 600—and the emotions that pull us down.[18] People need courage to face the emotions beneath the rage that covers up the fear, trauma, despair, and humiliation of their abuse.

The love that the Divine realm has for each of us, no matter what has happened to us, is a powerful force to lift our spirits. Love says, "Come hither," while fear says, "Go away!" In the Dark Energy Protocol, we surround ourselves in the Light of the Divine and the love of the angelic realm to find and desensitize emotional wounds and to reveal the distortions people have believed about themselves and to help them see the truth of their innocence.

The Healer Trap

Jane, a psychotherapist in her mid-fifties, loved her job and had deep insight into the way the mind works, yet she had struggled with multiple health problems for half of her life. She had nutrient absorption issues and felt depleted.

---

18 Ibid.

Her entry into this world had been traumatic, as her low birth weight put her into an incubator for the first month of her life. When she finally got to go home, she suffered from her mother's undiagnosed depression and paranoia. Her mother often attacked Jane with vindictive emotional tirades that lasted hours, blowing insignificant issues out of proportion. Both of her parents, who died in their late sixties, were atheists.

In her twenties, Jane had an awakening in which she realized that she would die some day, and she tried out various forms of religion to help form a plan for the hereafter! Zen Buddhism resonated more than some other religions, but she had difficulty with meditation, the cornerstone of this spiritual practice. Whenever she began to sit quietly, disturbing emotions distressed her system so much that she could not continue.

We found two interference patterns with her goals of improving her physical and emotional health:

1. A Trance State, defined as "Unconscious tendencies to slip into old ways of feeling and behaving, usually based on childhood reactions to life, that prevent a person from being present and able to effectively deal with life." 2. A Past Life Trauma.

Interference Pattern #1: Trance State and Dark Energy

A Fallen Angel and its three minions held the trance state in place, constantly pulling Jane back into the helplessness of her early childhood.

Dark Energy Protocol

Job: The Fallen Angel appeared to Jane like a shadowy energy crowding around her, wanting to be part of the action of her life. This Fallen Angel wanted sexual energy, which it mixed up with love. Asking the Fallen Angel what his job was with her confused him. He was so enmeshed with her energy that he responded, "I am you." He fed off her energy, like someone eating a piece of fruit. Since he thought of her as food, he was confused by his food asking, "What are you doing eating me?"

Employer: When we asked the Fallen Angel whether he was working for the darkness or the Light, he let out a nasty laugh. "Definitely not the Light," he responded. But he denied that he was working for anyone else and asserted that this question was none of our business. We answered that since he was feeding off Jane's life energy, it definitely was her business!

Cognitive Distortions: When we asked what the Fallen Angel had been told about the Light, he became confused and frightened. He felt the light would burn him, but he was even more afraid that he would get punished by the dark force behind him. We did a heart massage and assured him that we were working for his highest good, and that we would be sure that the energetic cord connecting him to his dark employer would be severed so he would not get punished.

Center: At his center, he saw a frightened, helpless infant being terribly punished. Jane related this image to how she must have felt as a newborn, being locked up in an incubator, poked and prodded, and cut off from the human contact every baby needs. We paused to do a tapping treatment to help the Fallen Angel get through this fear.

Then we told him he had the right to know what was in his own center when he was created. However, he felt so helpless, like an infant, that *he asked for an Angel of Light to come and help him*! I was so moved by his request for help that I wept

73

as I told him, "Thank you for asking! The angels have always been there ready to help, but you needed to ask!" This request, made of his own free will, marked the change in attitude necessary for him to transform from a Fallen Angel into an angel working for the Light. He felt more connected and supported once an Angel of Light was present, but he was still confused. He was worried about the physical health of the heart of the baby he felt in his center. We called in the energy of Divine Mother to heal this baby's heart.

Third Eye Linking

We again asked the angel to see what was in his own center. Jane was unable to focus on his experience. As if her focus were locked in with a wrench, she was unable to look anywhere other than her own third eye. We saw that the Fallen Angel had been linked into her energy field through her brow chakra, the third eye. The angel was also linked to his dark employer through his third eye.

We tried to skip the step of finding his own light since he was having so much difficulty with this part of the protocol. Instead, we went to the next step of his asking Archangel Michael to free him from these energetic cords. He asked Michael to set him free from the delusions of dark side, but then the angel became anxious. He asked, "Where will I get energy?"

Once again, we asked him to find out what was in his center. He knew it should be the nice warm feeling of Light, but what he and Jane experienced was an empty place, more like a desert than a garden. Jane recognized that the Fallen Angel had led her straight to her core fear of her inner desert. The goal of Eastern religion is to embrace the void, but her fear and anxiety skyrocketed whenever she got close to this inner barren place.

I had her inquire of her spiritual mentor how to handle this situation. He responded that she needed to trust this place, even though she did not want to. She needed to be okay with this place, even though it did not match her internal image of what the Light would be like. She reflected that Jesus had to go into the desert to face the trials of temptation and illusion.

We customized a meridian treatment to handle this fear. First, we cleared the shame blocking her path by tapping under the lips and having her say vigorously, "I demand to be set free from what is not true! I demand to release the trance state of the shame my mother heaped on me in my early childhood!" Then we tapped a sequence for trauma to clear her feelings as a little baby in the incubator. She reflected that her mother trained her, at every step, not to go into the bliss and peacefulness of the void. Jane then asserted that she had picked her mother because she had carried this fear of the void into this life from a previous incarnation. This realization took us to the second interference pattern, a past life trauma.

We turned the Fallen Angel over to Archangel Michael and his band of New Lightworkers to find his inner light—a new and better place for him to get energy—and to get a new job working for the Light.

Interference Pattern #2: Past Life Trauma

We muscle tested that Jane's soul had incarnated as a female in this past life, which happened in another galaxy. When we asked what year it was on Earth when the lifetime happened, the response was, "This lifetime happened before years started being counted on the Earth." We realized this soul wound was extremely ancient!

This woman wanted us to call her Birdie. She was especially happy when she was helping others with medicines and herbs she had gathered. Jane also felt some egotism in Birdie's attitude; helping made her feel special and important. One person she was treating did not respond to the medicine she gave, and the patient died. Birdie felt disgraced and traumatized by this event. "I made a mistake," she told herself. She felt she was no longer special. Jane realized this experience gave Birdie a taste of the void, the opportunity to be in the desert instead of the inflation of being a helper.

Birdie's spiritual guidance team showed her that the patient had some kind of program running that blocked the ability of the medicine she had given from working. In energy psychology, we call these limiting beliefs "reversals." Birdie chided herself for being so puffed up with feeling special that she did not attune to the programs inside the patient that had blocked the healing process. She deeply carried the negative life belief "*I am not good enough.*" This blockage pattern was still lodged in Jane's throat. We did an energy healing treatment to release this negative belief and installed two positive beliefs: "*I did my best, and I keep on learning,*" and also a revolutionary new idea Jane thought up of "*The Universe wants me the way I am!*"

Birdie's spirit had not been able to move fully into the Light because she had been weighed down by her shame. As these healing programs took effect and her spirit healed, Birdie felt loved. We called the energies of Divine Mother and Divine Father to take her to the Light, but Birdie first wanted to find the spirit of her patient who had died and take that person with her! The angels brought in the earthbound spirit of that patient, and Birdie reflected, "I couldn't help you then, but finally I can help you now!" Both of them joyfully went into the Light together.

We multiplied the benefits, inviting soul fragments of any other healers who had lost a patient and stayed earthbound to couple to this healing and to invite the patients they had lost to come cross into the Light with them.

Soul Lesson

Birdie's soul lesson was all about surrendering and letting go, the opposite of what the ego wants to do! She reflected, "If I let go, I can finally open the door. I can just jump and embrace the void. I need to trust and accept everything is as it is supposed to be. We are supposed to make mistakes so we can learn, and keep letting go and entering the desert. When we completely embrace our ignorance—not knowing—then with this humility, we can let go of all of the wrong teachings we have absorbed and go back to what meditation teachers call 'the beginner's mind.' Healers need to know that we do not always know all of what is going on with our clients, and we are going to lose some of them. That is just how it is supposed to be." She further reflected that she needs to be in this dualistic world where we label things good or bad, and then the next step is going into the void where all this dualism disappears!

We next checked back in with the Fallen Angel who had gotten connected to his own light—a source of energy that never dries up—and had become a New Lightworker! We asked him to call his three minions into the Light with him. Jane felt something shift in her forehead as they left her energy field and also moved into the Light.

Universal Healing Frequencies

To support Jane's physical healing process, we added healing frequencies for clearing posttraumatic stress disorder, spiritual cleansing, and resetting the genetic templates. With her

Fallen Angel having a new job and healing her core emotional wound, the path was paved for her physical body to recover!

8. *COGNITIVE DISTORTIONS (CDs): Ask the dark force what it was told about the Light. (The Light is bad, the light would annihilate them, you can't trust the Light, it will burn them up, etc.)*

> *Love.*
> *Where to find truth?*
> *Well, it has to be sought within one's own self,*
> *within one's own self*
> *within one's own self*
> *within one's own self.*
> *It is definitely there.*
> *One who seeks it elsewhere loses it.*
> *—Osho[19]*

Crucifixion Trauma

Clarissa would get sensations several times a year of the smell of the face of Jesus after the Crucifixion—blood, sweat, and torture. Then these images started coming more frequently, and she sensed a dark force jumbled into the mix. In a previous session with another healer, she had relived a memory of a woman named Mary at the foot of the cross screaming, "Nail me up there too, with my beloved!" A soldier harshly shoved Mary, jabbing her hip with his spear. Jesus witnessed this act and shouted "No!" in his mind, not happy that she got hurt. He sent energy directly into her heart with the message, "Live in me." Mary was so angry at the unjust, cruel slaying of that wonderful man that she looked into the crowd and vowed to hate all men for all time.

---

19 Osho, *A Cup of Tea*, 64.

After his death, Mary helped to clean the body of Jesus and to prepare it for burial. Mary smelled his hair, and every time it still smelled like the blood, sweat, and torture of that day, she washed it again. Mary found comfort in the scent of the oil they rubbed all over his body. After finishing with the burial preparations, Mary went back to the scene of the cross. From that hill, she cursed all the perpetrators of the Crucifixion and all of their descendants. Others tried to comfort her, but she refused to release her rage. She remembered that Jesus had told her not to come to the Crucifixion. She was so sorry she did not listen to him, though he knew she wouldn't!

The Beast

Clarissa recognized a man in a class at a local healing center as the reincarnation of the soldier who had jabbed Mary's hip. She felt that dark forces had been at the Crucifixion and entered Mary with the purpose of stopping her light. The Dark Force Entities believed the light would destroy them. When we began the Detrimental Energy Protocol, the dark forces were very angry, snarling and growling. Clarissa saw a shape inside that started bobbing its head back and forth, like an animal in agitation. It was extremely resistant to our request for it to look within. The animal retorted, "I would rather chew off my limbs than listen to what Barbara wants me to do. She is a liar!" Clarissa reported it was the beast itself and that it had red eyes and a thick neck.

I mentioned that in the story of beauty and the beast, the feminine has to kiss the beast for it to find its own heart. We called in the love of Jesus for all of creation to the heart of the beast. As the angels encircled the beast, it got frightened. Clarissa felt huge compassion because the beast was like an animal in a tiny little cage with no place to go. It collapsed, submissive and weary, and Clarissa put her arm around its neck in compassion. She requested the angels to back up a little. Then Jesus approached the beast, which was lying on its side, putting both of his hands over the beast about eighteen inches apart and saying, "Hello, my old friend."

As the beast looked within and found its light, it began to melt. The beast wanted to stay away because it felt totally unworthy of God's love, but Jesus embraced and comforted the beast. As Beings of Light came to help, the beast wept and reported that nobody had *ever* cared for it before. We wept with compassion for this poor creature who had never known love. As Archangel Michael prepared to take the beast to the spiritual recovery center, the beast wanted the spiritual presence of Clarissa's past life as Mary to go with it. With great compassion, Clarissa gladly consented and saw blue tinged Light coming from a point in front of the beast where Jesus and Mary were walking with it toward the Light. She could see the shape of the beast's back legs, haunches, and hoofs.

Multiplying the Benefits

Mary rescinded the curse she had put out and released her hatred. We asked to multiply these healing benefits for all others who had been traumatized at the Crucifixion. When we multiplied the benefits for the conversion of the beast, it invited all of its servants to come. Clarissa reported that the response was like a huge poker party!

9.   *GOING TO CENTER: You can communicate to the dark force, "We have reason to believe that your employer has withheld some very important information from you that would enable you to get a more powerful job. Are you interested in knowing more?"*

Then you can add, "The key to getting your job promotion is knowing what is in your core energy, right in your center. It

*will be what was there when you were created, and it might
be a surprise." Ask the dark force to look at its center and
see what is in its core energy. If they say anything else other
than light, tell them to keep going past that, deeper, to see
what is underneath it. What was its original essence when it
was created?*

A spark of light or a golden nugget or light in some form is always in the center. If they say darkness is at the center, ask to go past the darkness into the very core essence of their being. If they say they have a black hole in their center, ask them to go into that black hole and see where it takes them. If they see some kind of flame inside, have them focus on the light coming out of the flame.

Note: If the dark energy gets frightened by finding light inside itself, pause and do a heart chakra clockwise spin together with the dark energy, saying, "Everything is going to be okay. It's all going to be all right. We are working to get me a job promotion." Then you can both tap the Thought Field Therapy algorithm for fear: under the eyes, under the arms, and under the collarbone. Once the entity has calmed down, proceed.

Note: Dark Force Entities may get very upset when they have been discovered because "this exposure is considered a failure by Satan" and they know they will be punished.[20]

We can see how Satan's manipulating through fear feeds the atrocities of war, when people seem to become possessed by dark forces. The genocide in Rwanda in 1994 is an example, with its government-sponsored plan to kill all Tutsi and Tutsi sympathizers in the whole country. A million people died in one hundred days.[21] The survivors of this genocide are highly traumatized in a country that does not have the mental health infrastructure to deal with the massive amounts of PTSD created for those who survived. Teams of human-

---

20 Modi, *Remarkable Healings*, 302.

21 Hatzfeld, *Machete Season*.

itarian workers using Thought Field Therapy (TFT) have published several studies on the efficacy of TFT with this population.[22]

The Dark Force Entities also have PTSD, and meridian tapping seems to help them calm down so they can find their inner light. Sometimes the healing image in the center is not light, but instead a beating heart or the emotion of love. In the following case, what was at the center of the Dark Force Entity was a cup of the water of life, a healing image that worked to help the entity transform.

Catastrophe in Atlantis

Regina wanted help with both her physical eyesight and getting a clear connection with Spirit. After setting sacred space, we found three interference patterns running to block her goal of being able to see more clearly, inside and out.

Interference Pattern #1: A Dark Force Entity

We muscle tested that the best pattern to clear first was a Dark Force Entity that had been with Regina from the time of Atlantis. Its purpose was to pull her down through self-doubt, and it believed, "The Light is guarded and inaccessible to me." Additional messages were, "I don't belong there" and "I can't trust it."

Center

At the center of the Dark Force was a crying infant, male. The Dark Force was constantly in the pain of the infancy state, having crying as its only hope for release. We went deeper, and in its very center was a cup of healing water. We let the

---

22   S. Connolly and C. Sakai, "Brief trauma intervention with Rwandan genocide-survivors using Thought Field Therapy," *International Journal of Emergency Mental Health* 13:3, 161-172.

infant drink this healing water, and he began to relax and to feel his own movements.

New Job

The Dark Force definitely wanted a better job. Regina said, "Its only way to fulfill its true purpose is to work for the Light." It wanted to be a torchbearer, a light to be carried everywhere and anywhere. Regina felt she had been working toward that goal her whole life. We multiplied the benefits by asking this torchbearer to hold its light high and call out to other dark forces with similar jobs. We muscle tested that over 700,000 other Dark Force Entities raised their consciousness into the new dimension by coupling to Regina's intervention. We then worked on Regina's crown and brow chakras to repair the physical damage done by the Dark Force Entity.

Interference Pattern #2 and #3: Past Life Trauma

The Dark Force Entity had entered during a past lifetime as a woman named Marguerite who incarnated in the time of Atlantis as a Hebrew. Her happiest moment was having her own child, a little girl named Ophelia. Marguerite felt, "Life is the experience of the sun shining on my circumstances day and night!"

When Marguerite was thirty-two years old, a meteor was heading toward Atlantis. Marguerite relived the horror of oblivion, knowing the meteor was coming, and knowing that all of the goodness and joy of her life would be cut off and replaced by only pain and misery. The worst part of the trauma was not what it would do to her but knowing how her child was going to be affected.

We treated Marguerite with meridian tapping to release the depression and trauma that resulted from this event. As she

83

released these feelings, Regina realized that the catastrophe in Atlantis has colored all the talk of global warming and its effect on our current civilization. She set her intention to release from her present situation all the fears of annihilation she had been carrying from that lifetime. Then Regina breathed a sigh of relief!

Melchizedek's History of Atlantis

Author Drunvalo Melchizedek says a spiritual teacher named Thoth communicated telepathic knowledge to him. He shares what he learned in his books *The Ancient Secret of the Flower of Life, Volumes I and II,* which weave together science, sacred geometry, occult knowledge, and the history of human civilization, including Atlantis and Lemuria. Melchizedek developed a special way to spin the sacred geometrical fields around the body, called the MerKaBa meditation, which is taught in workshops internationally. I had the pleasure of attending one of these workshops in Hawaii in the 1990s. Some of the things Melchizedek said back then sounded so outlandish I was sure he was mistaken. For example, he said that long-distance phone calls would be free. Back then I could not imagine a world like that!

Melchizedek says the continent of Atlantis had ten vortexes, with a city built at each one. The Lemurians migrating there filled only eight of them, which left two vortexes empty. "These two vortexes were pulling life toward them, and in life you just can't have an empty place."[23] Melchizedek says that the Hebrews stepped into one vortex and the race that stepped into the tenth vortex was from Mars. He asserts:

---

23 Melchizedek, *The Ancient Secret of the Flower of Life*, 97.

> ...this same race is still causing major prob-
> lems. The secret government and the trillion-
> aires of the world are of Mars extraction or
> have mostly Martian genes and little or no
> emotional/feeling body.[24]

Cutting the love bonds between beings on Mars disconnected their emotional bodies, and the Martians became predominantly male energy, with almost no female qualities in them. According to Thoth, Mars looked much like Earth a little less than a million years ago. It was beautiful. It had oceans and water and trees and was just fantastic.[25] But without compassion, the Martians were in constant war with each other. Mars became a battleground that just kept going on and on, until finally it became clear that Mars was not going to survive. Eventually they blew their atmosphere away and destroyed the surface of their planet.[26]

Melchizedek says that around 13,000 to 16,000 years ago, a comet was headed toward Atlantis from deep outer space, and the Atlanteans were divided on how to approach the problem. The left-brained Martians wanted to blast it out of the sky with their laser technology. The other nine groups on the continent felt that this meteor was God's will, and nothing should be done to intervene. Reluctantly, the Martians conceded to the will of the majority. The comet hit in the area where the Martians were living, killing a huge portion of their population. From that time on, the Martians decided they were no longer going to pay attention to what others wanted. They told the others, "You can do whatever you want, but we're going to

---

24   Ibid., 98.
25   Ibid., 98-99.
26   Ibid., 99.

lead our own lives and try to control our own fate. And we're not going to listen to you ever again."[27]

The Martians set about to build a device that would give them the power to take complete control of Atlantis. They built a synthetic MerKaBa machine with counter-rotating star tetrahedrons inside of a pyramid and activated the power to the machine. Unfortunately, they did not remember exactly how to set the proper rotations on the star tetrahedrons, and when they activated this device, it ripped a gigantic hole in the time-space continuum. It still sits at the bottom of the ocean floor with its star tetrahedrons rotating and is known today as the Bermuda Triangle. Ships and planes that get into this area are sucked into its black hole and are transported into other dimensions of time and space.

Ripping Membranes

Worse yet, this ripping of the membranes between dimensions flooded Atlantis with lower dimensional spirits who were terrified of being on the earth plane, which vibrated way too fast for them. Multitudes of these dark forces entered the bodies of everyone in Atlantis, and the people had no way to stop this invasion—one explanation for why we have so much darkness and dark force activity on this planet. Fear and terror replaced all the goodness and joy in the lives of Marguerite, Ophelia, and everyone else on the continent.

Ophelia crossed into the Light when she died, but the trauma of seeing her daughter tortured by these dark forces kept Marguerite earthbound. Ophelia came into our octahedron of light and called to her mother, "You have wandered and suffered

---

27   Ibid., 102.

long enough. You need to rest in the Light now." Angels took them home, with Ophelia holding her mother's hand.

Soul Lesson

The Council of Elders knew about the upcoming catastrophe, and it was in Divine Order. However, Marguerite felt that she did not know before she incarnated that it would happen, or she would not have chosen to go through that suffering. The purpose for Marguerite's soul was to be a fellow soldier/warrior for the recovery of peace and joy and the restoration of the Light on the planet.

Multiplying the Benefits

We invited any others still earthbound from Atlantis, any other parents who had stayed earthbound because of the pain they had over what happened to their children, and any others weighed down by dark spirits to couple with the healing in our octahedron and cross into the Light. We tested that the third interference pattern had been another past life trauma, and that one also cleared with this invitation.

10. *FOCUSING ON THE LIGHT: Ask the dark force to focus on the spark of light within and see what happens. (It will expand.)*

Vietnam Vet

This case shows how Soul Detective procedures found a nested set of issues all related to each other and, step by step, unraveled the mystery until the presenting issues were resolved.

Negative Rays

Karen, a talented psychotherapist, had been physically ill more often than usual in the past few years. Her grandson came to visit and became so ill during the night that he hallucinated a dog was trying to eat him and that people were coming to get him. Karen suspected something unusual was unfolding in this situation, and we found negative rays aimed at both Karen and her highly intuitive grandson.

Karen's negative ray was coming from a man named Victor, the emotionally and physically violent and terrifying husband of one of her clients. Victor, a Vietnam veteran with posttraumatic stress disorder, was not happy about his wife seeing Karen for psychotherapy. Victor was carrying one earthbound spirit and four Dark Angels. We muscle tested that we had spiritual permission to work with these Dark Angels, so we set up an octahedron of Light with archangels on each side.

Four Dark Force Angels

The lead Dark Angel reported his mission was to wipe out every smidgeon of Light that exists. He was trying to create hell on Earth and felt thrilled with the carnage in Vietnam. His employer was coal black—pure darkness. This angel believed that Light is chaotic and ruined his plans. He saw Light as his enemy and believed he would be incinerated if he got too close to it. He was convinced that the Light was "unbelievably unsafe!" He was so afraid of Light that we had to tap the sequence of energy points for fear (under the eyes, under the arms, under the collarbone) before he was even willing to take the risk of looking inside of himself.

When he finally found a spark of Light at his center, he screamed in terror! We did more calming work and invited in the New Lightworkers to assist their fallen brother who was now waking up to the true nature of Light. They tenderly supported him as he realized that light had been inside his core all along. Multiple negative cords enslaved this angel to his dark employer. We let him know that because of the law of free will, he himself needed to ask to have his cords cut, or they would grow right back. Archangel Michael responded instantly as the dark entity asked to be freed from his former employer. All of the detrimental cords melted away.

Multiplying the Benefits

Then this angel invited all the dark force angels under him to follow his lead. They looked within and also converted into Lightworkers. The whole bunch got very excited about their new roles. They invited all of the dark force angels involved in the Vietnam War and all Dark Angels involved in any other wars to couple to their own conversions and to join the brotherhood of New Lightworkers! Many came.

Dark Force Entry

During the war, American soldiers had been pushed to the edge of insanity. Often they could not distinguish between civilians and the enemy, as the Viet Cong did not wear uniforms, and sometimes they wound up killing civilians. The dark forces had entered Victor during this mayhem.

Next we addressed the earthbound spirit attached to Victor. Muscle testing indicated the presence of an eight-year-old boy who wanted us to call him Chen. He was a Vietnamese civilian Victor had killed during the war. After clearing Chen of his rage and the reversal pattern blocking his heart, he was ready to reunite with his family members and cross into the Light. As we multiplied the benefits, Karen saw many Vietnamese family groups uniting and crossing together into the next world.

Split Personality

Victor had recently gone through another trauma, which is considered the most traumatic event possible for humans—

the death of a child. We invited the earthbound spirit of Victor's deceased son to couple to this healing and cross into the Light. We found that his son's personality had fractured into three parts. One part had crossed at his death, but the other two parts had stayed earthbound. One of these earthbound parts carried his shame and another carried his fear. We cleared both of these parts with energy tapping, and then with the shattered parts of his son's personality reconnected, the young man was able to fully cross into the Light.

Follow-up

The next time Victor's wife came for a session, before Karen told her about the Soul Detective work we had done together, the wife reported that Victor had mellowed a bit. She noticed he was not as reactive when things did not go his way. She had also made some adjustments to change her household habits, which had made him explode prior to our work. After Karen told her about the release work we did on Victor's behalf, she felt that the positive shift in his attitude made more sense and was very grateful. After a month, Victor's wife reported that he was smiling again and teasing her, and she now found it manageable to live with him.

Victor's Cord to Karen

Ordinarily, Karen would not have worked on a family member of her client on her own time, but since the negative ray from Victor had been having such a negative impact on Karen's physical well-being, she felt she had the right to do what she could to help Victor heal so that she could reclaim her own strength. Karen noticed an increase in her sense of completeness and well-being as the negative ray that Victor had been sending her was terminated. She even noticed that her visual acuity increased.

Karen felt that her grandson, who was highly intuitive, had registered the psychic impression of the negative ray aimed at him as the dog he dreamed wanted to eat him. We did a protocol to convert the detrimental energy in that negative ray into beneficial energy, and her grandson moved out of fear and back into physical health.

Karen told me, "You have such a gift! What you do for everyone you touch is a blessing in the world. No other person on Earth has your blend of history and skill, and that combination plus your desire to help others makes you unique among healers. You are very giving with your knowledge, time, love, and talents." When Karen tried to tell me I am one-of-a-kind, I pointed out that others in my Soul Detective trainings are also doing this amazing work and that the real power of transformation comes from our connection to our angelic helpers! Thank you, Lightworker Angels!

11. *POINTING OUT THE DECEPTION: Go through whatever cognitive distortions the dark force had held about the light, pointing out the truth. For example, if it was told the Light would kill/annihilate it, inquire whether it is dead. (No, it is still present.) If it was told the Light would burn it up, ask point-blank, "Did it burn you up?" (Of course not.) Ask how the Light feels. Usually, they say it feels warm, safe, and peaceful. Then contrast their direct experience with what they were told about the light and note, "Your employer lied to you."*

With one set of extraterrestrials (ETs), the dark employer had put pronged covers over their hearts, to block them from knowing about their own light. The prong was black with a hint of green, and the green started pulsing as they searched for the truth about what was at their centers.

Angels of Darkness

A client asked to do some surrogate healing for the granddaughter of a friend. The granddaughter had two little girls who were extremely active and difficult to discipline. Muscle testing indicated that we had spiritual permission to do this work and that the granddaughter had two dark energies attached. We asked to speak with the more powerful angel first, and this angel asked us to call him Simon. He had been attached to the granddaughter for fifteen years. He worked for the darkness, and his job was destruction and dissolution. His employer had told him that the Light was destructive, and he believed that the Light would totally destroy him and the angel under him, and they would both be gone.

When we asked Simon to look inside to see what was in his own core energy, he found Light. He reported this light felt "kind of good," but then he worried that he could not trust us. We asked him to check with the Light itself that was within him to find its true nature, rather than taking our word for what it was. Simon realized he had been lied to about the Light, because his direct experience demonstrated that it was beneficial, not destructive. The light had not destroyed him, and Simon felt angry about the deception his boss had used to get him to try to destroy the granddaughter's life.

We offered him the chance to quit his job of working for the darkness and go with Archangel Michael to join the band of other dark force angels who had found the light within and converted into Lightworkers. We assured him that the Creator of All is a God of only love, and that all heaven rejoices when one fallen angel converts back to the Brotherhood of Light.

Job Interviews

First, Simon wanted to interview some of the former dark force angels who had changed jobs. He inquired of them, "Why did you change?"

They responded, "Nobody made us do anything."

He asked, "What if I don't like it there?"

They assured him he could go back to his old job if he wanted to and told him they felt a lot better in their new jobs. Simon decided to try going with Archangel Michael.

"Angel"

The second of the two dark energies had been attached to the granddaughter for only three years. His job was to drive the granddaughter crazy and to keep everything and everybody away from the Light. He also worked for the darkness.

We inquired what he had been told about the Light. He responded, "Not much of anything, except that the Light is not good for us, not healthy, and we are not supposed to be around the Light."

When we asked what name to call him, he smirked and said we could call him "Angel." He boasted, "I'm an Angel of darkness and proud of it!"

Core Energy

We asked him to look deep within. He wanted to know why, and we told him it was so he could see for himself what was in his core energy. He retorted, "I don't want to." This Dark Angel was less developed than Simon and had depended on Simon for guidance. With Simon gone, he was unsure of himself, so he obstinately dug in his heels.

We countered that nobody was forcing him to do anything but that we just wondered if he had the courage to see what was really in the center of his own being.

Angel interjected, "I've been around for a long time. Why should I do what you ask?" We confided that we believed he had been lied to about the true nature of the Light and had been deceived about what was really in the center of his being. He queried, "Why should I believe you?"

We told him, "Don't believe us—look for yourself!"

He drawled, "You're tricky!" He paused, then exclaimed, "There is Light!"

Multiplying the Benefits

Angel decided to join Simon in switching sides, and we invited any other angels with jobs working for the darkness to couple to this opportunity and to get a job promotion working for the Light.

I noted that Angel was a hard worker. He had done a very good job when he was driving his host crazy and trying to keep everything and everybody away from the Light. Now that Angel had gotten promoted to working for the Light, we asked if he would like to do some repair work for the family he had formerly been tormenting. Angel responded with pride that yes, he was a good worker and that he would apply his hard work to his new job as a Lightworker. Both Simon and Angel readily accepted this new job assignment, and my client saw them filled with Light and playing with the two little girls.

12. *WORKING FOR A LIAR: Ask, "How do you feel about working for a liar?" (They get mad. Let them have a little hissy fit.)*

Vow of Suffering

Gabriel, an extremely gifted energy worker, wanted to break through the pattern of stagnation in his profession. One of the interference patterns we found was a vow of suffering from a lifetime many centuries ago, in which he was named Herman.

Born in 1573 AD, Herman consecrated his life to God and became a monk in the Catholic Church. He took vows of poverty, obedience, celibacy, and suffering—a vow he took very seriously. He then went on a mission to South America to serve in the early years when the conquistadores were penetrating the area that is now part of Argentina. The happiest moment in his life was teaching children in a setting like a monastery.

Just before the trauma that was still locking him into suffering, civil unrest broke out among the people, and he felt overwhelmed. We cleared limiting beliefs and then tapped points for Herman to clear his fear and anxiety.

A Bitter Death

Herman developed an extremely painful chronic disease. He felt alone, lonely, and uncared for. He developed bitterness toward the teachings of the church and resented the suffering of his disease. At age forty-seven, he died, with part of his soul energy going into the Light, but part of it staying earthbound, locked into the suffering of his hatred and bitterness.

One Fallen Angel and Its Minion

We muscle tested that a Fallen Angel and its minion (servant) were attached to Herman's earthbound spirit with the job of continuing to torture him and to keep him from being happy. *With his vow of suffering, Herman had asked for this torture.* By choosing suffering, he had removed himself from love, and this Fallen Angel was attracted to him and able to enter through his physical and emotional pain.

Employer

The Fallen Angel first claimed he was working for the Light, as Herman had wanted to suffer for spiritual advancement.

The Fallen Angel claimed he was just helping Herman achieve his goal. But Gabriel's head kept shaking a "no" for this angel coming from the Light. We did not believe that making someone suffer was anything the Light would ever sponsor! The Fallen Angel was afraid to tell us for whom who he really worked. After we did some calming work with the angel, assuring him everything would be all right, he simply called his boss "My Lord."

His dark employer told him to refuse the Light because it was bad and would burn him.

Working for a Liar!

When the angel looked into his own center, he was surprised to find a bright warm light. It brought tears to his eyes and felt good. He realized His Lord had deceived him. He felt angry about working for a liar! We offered him the chance to quit his old job and come work for Archangel Michael—a job promotion he was grateful to accept!

Cords

The Fallen Angel asked Archangel Michael to release the energetic cord His Lord had wrapped around his throat, to set him free to join Archangel Michael's band of New Lightworkers. The Fallen Angel's minion had been attached to Gabriel's hands, making him do detrimental things. The minion also converted to the Light. To multiply the benefits, we invited any other Fallen Angels with the job of torturing people to come into our octahedron of Light, couple to the process, and also get job promotions!

Next we called in a healing frequency to cleanse Herman of the damage done by the dark forces. Tears came as this deep soul wound healed. Then Herman called back the soul fragment that had been locked into the suffering of this death so long ago in Argentina, and that part of his soul energy went into the Light.

Soul Lesson

The lesson for the soul that Gabriel and Herman shared was spiritual discernment, to distinguish between true power and false power. Suffering is a false power. True power is serving God with love. False power would deny his humanity, but true power loves his humanity.

The application to Gabriel's current life was "to remove from my heart the hatred of the cruel things that men do." When we asked to release this hatred of man from his heart, we ran into the interference pattern of an ancestral belief that had come through an imprint from his mother that "men are bad." Gabriel experienced an inner conflict: he had to be loyal either to his mother or to his manhood, but he could not do both at once. We did a Matrix Energetics Two-Point technique[28] to collapse this negative belief. Next we rescinded the vow of poverty and replaced it with the joy of abundance as a path to God. At the end, Gabriel felt a wave of joy and prosperity flood his soul.

13. *A CHANCE TO QUIT: Ask the Dark Force Entity, "How would you like to quit this job and get a better job working for the Light? Ask Archangel Michael to offer the Dark Force Entity a job promotion working for the Light. If the Dark Force Angel hesitates, you can explain that Archangel Michael has a band of brand new Lightworkers that used to have jobs like yours and chose to get a job promotion and go work for the Light. Invite the Dark Force Angel to interview*

---

28   Bartlett, *Matrix Energetics*, 91.

them to see how they like their jobs. Then invite it again to get the job promotion.

This energy still has free will and can refuse or ask to take the new job on a trial basis to see how they like it. If the dark energy stalls on this decision, you can point out the strength of the Light with an example of two rooms with a wall between them, one dark and one with a light on. Take out the wall between them and what happens? Does the darkness overcome the light? Of course not—the light shines into the darkness because it is more powerful. Give them a chance to get on the powerful winning team!

If the dark force expresses fear of getting into trouble with its employer, you can do a heart massage and perhaps even tap the phobia algorithm (under eye, under arm, collarbone), assuring the dark force that we have its highest good in mind and that everything is going to be okay. Once the dark force makes a decision to quit its old job and work for the light, proceed. If you are working with a dark force angel, you might want at this point to announce that you will now be calling it an angel rather than a Dark Angel.

Soul Destruction

Sarabella never got to meet her stepson Chuck because his life was tortured by addictions, and he took his life fifteen years before she married his father. The night before our session, she heard Chuck's voice saying, "I keep digging in." We did a Soul Detective session to help this young man. Highly intuitive, Sarabella saw darkness around Chuck. He did not know that his spirit was out of his body and thought the date was two decades earlier, the time of his suicide.

Dark Force Entity

Chuck had one Dark Force Entity around him whose purpose was to destroy his soul. This entity had egged him into suicide. The dark force believed that the Light was controlling and bad. When he found the spark of light within his center, which grew, he promptly quit his job! Sarabella noticed

Chuck brighten up when the Dark Force Entity turned to the Light. We multiplied the benefits, and about eight hundred to nine hundred other dark entities also quit their jobs.

Joe

Chuck was so also carrying the earthbound spirit of a man named Joe who had died at age twenty-three of an overdose of drugs. We helped Joe release his shame and fear, and his mother came to take him into the Light. Chuck asked, "Why can't I go too?" Sarabella had sensed that Chuck's mother, her husband's first wife, had stayed earthbound searching for her son, whose death had preceded hers by a decade. We called the spirit of Chuck's mother into the pyramid, and then together they crossed into the Light.

14. *CHECKING FOR ENERGETIC CORDS: Assume that the former employer of the dark force has been controlling it with one or more energetic cords that distort its perception of reality and control its actions by filling it with fear of getting punished if it does not carry out the will of its dark master and its orders.*

Ask the formerly dark force to check for any and all energetic cords of deception and/or mind control leading back to its employer. Let this entity know that God gives every being free will, and its enslavement has violated the law of free will. Archangel Michael could free it from these cords, but they would just grow back if the entity does not use its own free will to ask Archangel Michael to free it from these cords. Often this cord will be at the solar plexus, but it could also be at the tail, the heart, the head, or other places. Sometimes the dark force will have more than one cord of control. If these cords are not severed or removed, the dark force employer can yank on the cord to reactivate the problem for the client.

It's All Lies!

Rachel (the client in "Cockroaches on You!") wanted another session to work on the resistance she had felt when returning to her spiritual group. When she first joined the group, she had a nightmare of a large man pulling a gun on her and coming toward her. She tried to scream but had trouble connecting with her voice. We went back into the dream, flanked by guardian angels, and asked the man in the dream, "What do you want?" When Rachel looked him in the eye, he metamorphosed into a bat with fangs. We muscle tested that this bat was a Dark Force Entity whose purpose was to block Rachel's spiritual progress.

When we asked whether it worked for the darkness or the light, it gesticulated wildly to try to scare us off. After this tactic did not work, the entity, who wanted us to call it Metatrón, admitted it worked for the darkness, threatening, "Yes, and I'll get you!" (Note that this entity wanted a name spelled like the Archangel Metatron but with the accent on the last syllable rather than the first one.) Metatrón believed, "The Light is red and will burn you. If I got really into the light, I would get all burned up and shrivel to dust." When we asked Metatrón to look inside into his center, he protested, "All lies—it is all a lie."

Dr. Stone: "Don't believe me—look for yourself."

Metatrón: "Oh no, no! It's white—getting big. Aaaarugh!"

Dr. Stone: "Do you realize your employer lied to you?"

Metatrón: "No, it couldn't happen."

Dr. Stone: "Well, your employer said the light was red, and you can see that it is white."

Metatrón: "The white is getting bigger. Only my head, hands, feet, and wings are still black. Maybe it's ice."

Dr. Stone: "Check it out."

Metatrón: "It's soft. I can't go home like this!"

Dr. Stone: "Would you like a job promotion?"

Metatrón: "I'd rather die. It's all lies, everything is lies."

Dr. Stone: "Don't take my word for it; check things out for yourself. We call in Archangel Michael and his band of New Lightworkers to talk with Metatrón so he can see the situation for himself."

Metatrón: "They look like me, but they will tear me to shreds. I still want to go home. It's all lies."

Dr. Stone: "Go into your heart and ask where is your true home."

Metatrón: "In the Light."

Dr. Stone: "We call a big welcome home party for Metatrón."

An Energetic Cord

Rachel saw Metatrón walking away with the New Lightworkers, but the tip of his tail got longer because it was still attached to home. We explained to him that keeping an energetic cord to his past job was like trying to fly an airplane with a rope around its tail anchoring it to the ground. The plane would never be able to fly. Then Rachel saw that Metatrón's tail had been pinned down, like a push pin. He took the pin out and gathered his tail. He shed a tear and dropped it on the spot where his tail had been pinned.

In addition, allow more room for creativity by having the entity ask Archangel Michael "to do whatever is necessary" to free it from this control. Sometimes the entity may unplug the cord itself. Archangel Michael may sever the cord or touch the cord with his sword, filling it with light that dissolves the cord or sending a bolt of Light back to the employer. Once the process feels complete, muscle test whether or not this force is now free from *all* detrimental energetic cords to its old employer.

These cords of control could also be seen as reactivation cords or reactivation programs the client has that make the problem recur. If the reactivation cords are not removed, no matter what the client does in therapy to remove the dark force, the problem will always come back. Clients get very discouraged when they work so hard to recover but always fall back into the same black hole.

Invitation to the Employer

In another session, when a client inquired whether the Dark Force Entity wanted to ask Archangel Michael to cut the reactivation cord to its employer, it refused. Instead, it wanted its employer to come get a job promotion, too! The employer accepted the invitation to work for the Light. He communicated that he was a Fallen Angel who knew he was doing something wrong. With sorrow, this dark force told us he thought the angels of Light had forgotten him. He had been working to increase the seductive pull of the darkness in a spiritual growth community. After converting, he wanted to work to help the people in that community find their own Light and release the pull of addictions. The angel called in all its minions to help it in this new mission!

No Cords?

Occasionally, an entity will say it has no energetic cords to the former employer. In this case, check for proper polarity in both the client and the energy practitioner, and then muscle test to be sure that this situation is true.

15. *INVENTORY OF THE DAMAGE: The first task of this new Lightworker will be something like the Catholic practice of confession. Ask it to give a list of all the specific ways it has been affecting the client's life. This step raises awareness for the clients of the extent of*

the emotional infection they have been suffering. After the inventory is complete, go through each item on the list, asking to heal and reverse the damage. You can also install positive affirmations to replace negative patterns.

Things That Go Bump in the Night

Darlene felt frightened by hearing things moving in her room at night. Others also heard the activity and got scared. Her therapist referred her to me for a Soul Detective consultation. We muscle tested that the nighttime activity was caused by a dark energy whose purpose was to create misery in her life and to flat-out destroy her. This employee of the dark side believed, "The Light is blinding, not friendly."

In his center, he saw a swirling blackness with a tiny spark of light. He was so afraid of this light that we did a meridian tapping sequence for fear with him. Then he was able to focus and find his inner light. It felt warm. Transforming very quickly, with a broad smile, he asked for a new job! As he was freed from cords to the darkness, Darlene saw that he had wings and looked like a ball of Light doing flips in the air. We invited other dark force angels with similar jobs to also get job promotions.

Inventory

In his first job as a New Lightworker, we asked him to give Darlene an inventory of the destructive things he had done to her. He gave Darlene the following list of his interference in her life:

1. Talking to her ego.
2. Making her dissatisfied with her job.
3. Destroying both of her marriages.

4. Making her feel like less than what she is.

5. Taunting her to keep her scared.

Origin

He had attached in one of Darlene's past lives where she had been beaten as a child. As we cleared that trauma and installed healing frequencies in her system, Darlene felt much better. With tingling and tears of gratitude, she thanked her therapist and me for our parts in liberating her from this dark force so that she could reach her highest potential.

Follow-up

A couple of years later, Darlene noted how far she had come and how much this session and her ongoing work with EFT had released her fears. She reported, "I no longer hear things bumping in the night. I believe that part of it is that I'm no longer afraid of the invisible force that I cannot see, because I know that it's all for my higher good—whether it's something I need to heal and clear or it's a spirit guide letting me know I'm not alone." She was able to mobilize herself and enroll in a training program for the profession that was her heart's desire.

16. *NEW JOB ASSIGNMENT (optional): You can ask what this entity would like to do in its new job or simply send it to the Lightworker Orientation Training to learn how to be a Lightworker and then look at the job openings.*

Confusion

Franchesca loved her husband very much. He was a loving father to their children and very responsible financially, always taking care of the bills. But he was not responsible to his marriage vows. He had a hole inside of him that he kept trying to fill with having another woman in his life. He isolated himself from Franchesca emotionally and only opened up during sexual contact. His pattern of closing up again after making love was extremely painful to Franchesca, but she felt powerless to change the situation. Both of them had traumatic histories. Her husband had been abused, mistreated, and abandoned by his family. Franchesca's biological mother tried to abort her, but her will to live was so strong that she survived. Her adoptive parents were emotionally and physically abusive.

Dark Force Entity

After setting sacred space, we found a Dark Force Entity who wanted to be called a minion. His purpose was to destroy both Franchesca and her husband. When I noted that the minion had been doing a very good job, it strutted with pride in its accomplishment and effectiveness, bragging, "I'm a good worker—the best." The minion said it worked for "the only King there is, the King of darkness. He is strong." The minion told us that others sent to destroy this couple had been taken out of the marriage, but he was determined to stay. He claimed he lived in the center of their bed and kept telling her husband that Franchesca was making a fool of him by being with other men. Her husband listened to the minion, but Franchesca did not pay as much attention to him. His goal was for them to separate.

Cognitive Distortions

The minion believed that the children of this marriage were dangerous because they had too much light. He complained, "These people are too strong." He believed the light would blind him and make him bad. His goal was to put out the light. He was trying to stop the husband's creativity. Franchesca had a healing room so full of light that this minion could not enter it. The minion said, "The angels in that room are stupid. They think the Light will win. This office where we are working

105

(Kristin's) makes me mad because it has too much light. This lady here (Dr. Stone) converts everyone, but she's not going to convert me! If I get too close to the light, I will be in trouble with my employer. I would go to jail forever, in a place with no windows."

(Note the humor in the minion who was so opposed to the light being afraid of going to a place with no windows!)

Center

The minion became very upset when it looked into its center. It exclaimed, "Oh, this light is infecting me, making me weak. It's growing, spreading from my chest out. Oh no, beautiful clothes are growing on me, purple and green. Oh God—wait a minute, God doesn't exist. What am I saying! My claws— I'm losing my claws. How will I scratch? The light is getting bigger and stronger. Barbara, you're not a good doctor. You said you were here to help me, and I'm getting more and more infected with this Light virus. Do something! I can't go back looking like this—paint me black! How am I going to walk with my gals looking like this? Oh no, now wings are growing on me."

Ambivalence

As the minion became aware of its own light, it saw a beautiful little girl in its center. It continued, "I want to work with Archangel Raphael, to heal everyone. Wait a minute, what am I saying? I want to destroy everyone. You don't understand me—Light is a virus, and it's infecting me, spreading almost everywhere in my body. Take it away! You are doing this to me."

I replied to the minion, "I have no power over you. I'm not doing anything to you. You just found your own light within yourself."

The minion responded, "That's right, you have no power over me." When we offered this minion the chance to quit its old job and get a new job working for Archangel Michael, the angel's brilliance made the minion nervous. He said, "Ask Michael to stand back a little. But wow, he has a really nice sword."

New Job

We invited the minion to talk with some of the other New Lightworkers to find out how they liked their jobs. The minion reported that their job satisfaction was high. When we talked about a possible list of new occupations, the minion wanted the job of guarding the earth by stopping earthquakes. It reported, "I see how the earthquake in Chile happened last week. I know what they do, and I want to stop them. No wait, I want to make more of them and destroy the earth. Oh help, I'm confused! The Light is everywhere in me now."

I inquired, "How do you feel?"

The minion replied, "Strong, actually stronger than I felt before. I do want to work for Archangel Michael and the Light. The earth is sick, and I will take out the origins of the earthquakes." The minion found the cord of control to its master that had made it a slave of the dark forces. When Archangel Michael cut that cord, Franchesca's body moved around in her chair, shaking her shoulders as if shaking off a body suit that was too small. Then the minion was free from its confusion and fully wanted to work for the Light. It declared, "I want to work for Archangel Raphael, the angel who heals people."

Following up one year later, Franchesca glowed as she reported that her marriage was improving.

17. *ADDITIONAL INVENTORY ITEMS: Invite any other Dark Force Entities and/or minions involved to also get job promotions. They may all transform, following the leadership of the most powerful one, or they may have individual fears that need to be addressed. Address whatever may come up with each item on the original Detrimental Energy Inventory in step 4 of this protocol to be sure the client is free from its influence and the issue is resolved.*

Beelzebub

Adrienne had chest pains during the time her partner was talking about how North Korea was threatening to send an atomic bomb to Hawaii. We traced these pains to two inventory items:

1. A Dark Force Entity influencing her mother.
2. A negative life belief of "Nobody cares for me" that was carried by a soul fragment of her older sister. This fragment had separated when their mother beat the sister.

Dark Force Protocol

Adrienne realized that her mother had been under the influence of a dark spirit named Beelzebub when she was beating her children. The purpose of the dark force was pure destruction. When the mother felt weak, Beelzebub stepped in to give her power and strength. He was able to enter through the mother's wound of her unresolved childhood abuse. When we asked Beelzebub who his employer was, he jeered, "Who do you think I work for?"

He believed, "The Light is for sissies. It has no real power." When Beelzebub went within, he saw a portal of Light taking him into another dimension, one of true peace, and it was extremely powerful and calming. He hated working for liars and accepted the offer of a job promotion. We told him we had a big job for him and the others we invited to multiply the benefits. The new job was to work with the leaders of North Korea who were under the same delusion that Adrienne's mother had been about the ability to destroy others granting someone power.

Additional Inventory Item

The three-year-old part of Adrienne's sister healed with tapping a sequence for sadness and went back to her sister's soul energy. She had attached through the wound in Adrienne's heart of feeling like nobody really cared. We did a counter-clockwise chakra spin to pull this illusion out from Adrienne's heart chakra and then did a clockwise spin to install the truth, "My creator loves and cares for me."

18. *MULTIPLYING THE BENEFITS: Invite any other dark spirits and minions with similar old jobs to come into the octahedron of light, look within, find their own light, quit their old jobs, release their cords to their former employers, and go with Archangel Michael and his band of New Lightworkers. You may want to muscle test how many took this offer!*

Jasmine and the Galactic War

Jasmine, a highly intelligent and gifted energy practitioner, had difficulty owning her own capabilities. Every time she excelled, a pattern would come in to destroy her self-confidence. Using muscle testing, we uncovered two interference patterns blocking her goal of self-realization.

Interference pattern #1: Past life Trauma in the Pleiades

The first interference pattern was fear of failing God, a traumatic pattern imprinted in a lifetime as a young woman named Rae. Jasmine felt surprised when we muscle tested that this

lifetime happened on a planet in the constellation of the Pleiades, also known as the Seven Sisters, about 300,000 BC.

Rae had a body made of light and wore colors. She floated in
the air, and her whole life felt like a ballet, graceful, happy,
and blessed. Then everything got dark and heavy on the whole
planet. A Galactic War broke out, and their planet was invaded
by 553,000 dark force entities. Rae's body was mashed, com-
pressed, and crumpled up like a waffle so she could not move.
Rae was stuck.

World Control

The Dark Force Entity leading this invasion had the mission
of destroying their planet to stop the beings there from their
Light energy infiltrating the rest of the Universe. His dark
boss wanted control of the world, much like the energy of
ancient Rome and Hitler. This entity believed the Light would
destroy everything.

Center

When we asked the entity to look into his center, he found a
ball of Light, just like the sparks and beams the Pleiadeans
emitted. He wondered why he was not dead, as he was taught
that Light was destructive. Then he saw a container around his
own Light which had been squelching his Light and sending
cords of energy to control his mind. The Dark Force Entity
asked Archangel Michael to release him from this mind control, and then he was able to see the truth. When we offered
him the chance to quit his old job and go to work for Archangel Michael, he gladly accepted. His first new job assignment
was to order the rest of his 553,000 troops to look inside themselves to find their own Light. He invited them to convert,
letting them know, "That Light is who you are!"

The next job was to decompress Rae. First, one of the entities who had converted to a New Lightworker turned a knob on the whole planet, and a cloth-like web was rolled back. The beings there became more animated. Then he did an extraction on Rae so her body could expand to its full measure of Light. Rae was dancing, and Light filled the entire planet.

Jasmine saw the dark forces changing into Light bodies, which were more solid than etheric bodies. We multiplied the benefits by inviting other Dark Forces throughout the Universe to couple to this job upgrade opportunity, and Jasmine muscle tested that 642,000 others also converted!

Soul Lesson

The lesson for the soul that Jasmine and Rae shared was to maintain her presence and her Light. She saw that the dark energies misuse power because they use force. The power of the Light is innate and cannot be destroyed.

Interference Pattern #2: Another Dark Force

At this point in the session, Jasmine started to zone out, becoming very sleepy. Then the face of a man who had swindled her in her current life as Jasmine appeared on the screen of her consciousness, as if the dark forces assigned to her in this lifetime were still trying to stop her from coming into her full potential.

We tapped meridian points to clear blockages and reduce her fear. Then we ran a protocol to convert any detrimental energy coming her way into beneficial energy and set it to run through all of her lifetimes.

The Test

With this expansion of the Light in her soul, Jasmine thought of a difficult family gathering coming up. Her siblings had cheated her out of her share of her inheritance, and the bitterness of being left out kept surfacing every time she saw them. Jasmine set her intention to shine her light even in their presence. She quoted a line from *A Course in Miracles*: "I am the Light of the world. Light is my only function."

Jasmine decided to take Rae along to the family gathering to help her hold her Light! At the end of this session, Jasmine felt an expansion of her spiritual light and the ability to hold responsibility for her own capabilities. She was very pleased at how much more smoothly the family gathering went with the spiritual healing that came to her from this work.

19. *GIVING THANKS*

Tenacious

Aimee came into this world the year after Pearl Harbor was bombed, into surroundings that were caught in the darkness of ritual abuse. Even through the devastation of her childhood suffering and the marks it left on her physical system, her heart remained so full of love that all those who knew her quickly came to adore her. Aimee had suffered seven miscarriages and had recently been in the hospital for a problem with her left leg swelling to the point that she had great difficulty walking; she also had severe problems with her eyes. Three days before she was scheduled to have surgery on her leg, she came to an Integrated Energy Therapy class I was teaching. After her surgery, Aimee reported that she felt the emotional healing she did during our practice sessions helped her get through the operation.

In our class, we set the intention to heal our ancestors. Over the lunch break, Aimee turned to hold the door open for a classmate, tripped, and fell down. An ambulance came to take her away. The hospital X-ray showed a bone fracture, but the doctors did not want to operate. Instead, they prescribed physical therapy for her.

FIRST SESSION

She had been outside only once in the three weeks after the fall and called for a session, feeling "mean, ornery, and shut in!"

The root cause of the accident tested as two earthbound spirit attachments. One traced back to her paternal great-grandfather in the male lineage. However, the earthbound spirit was a female who had died at age forty-three of an illness. She had been an earthbound spirit her great-grandfather carried and passed down to her grandfather, father, and then to Aimee. The spirit came in screaming, "Ritual Abuse!!!"

First Earthbound Spirit: Sibyl

She wanted us to call her Sibyl. When asked what year she thought it was, two answers came: 1925 and 1932. Sibyl had multiple parts with different time realities. We called all of Sibyl's parts to play a "Simon Says" game of tapping. They cooperated. Later, when I forgot to add "Simon Says," Aimee kept correcting me, because the child parts wouldn't do it otherwise! We cleared her limiting belief around feeling she deserved to suffer, and then did a meridian tapping sequence to desensitize her trauma.

Sibyl's heart felt better, but then she felt disturbance in her solar plexus. We cleared more limiting beliefs and then addressed her sexual abuse and sadness. Sibyl wept violently as she mourned for the six babies the cult she had been involved with had killed. She felt totally alone and bereft. We muscle tested that five of these babies had remained earthbound, searching for their mother. Only one was already in the Light. We called to the guardian angels of these five babies to bring them to Sibyl, and one by one, they came. One was afraid to come, so we tapped for the fear. Sometimes trapped souls actually fear the Light. Then that one came also. We called for all the siblings to join their mother, and the one in the Light came running to be with the family group! That one guided Sibyl and the other five into the Light. Aimee then still felt tired but less weighed down.

Second Earthbound Spirit: Hope

The second earthbound spirit tested as a female who died at age fifty-three from suicide. Hope had been a nun who was sexually abused by a priest. She was in absolute agony. She had dissociated from the abuse and also dissociated from the pregnancy that resulted. She confessed to us that when her baby was born to her, he was alive, but she killed him by burying him. Aimee felt strongly that Hope was a past life of one of her good friends named Penelope. This time Penelope got pregnant and wanted her baby boy, but he died at birth.

In this life, Penelope told Aimee that she felt that if God was not present in her life, she did not want to be here on the planet. When she said these words, Aimee flew off the handle and yelled at Penelope, telling her not to kill herself. Aimee was enraged at Penelope's attitude. We realized that this strong attitude could have come from the spirit attachment of Hope, who did not want her soul's current incarnation of Penelope to make the same mistake of suicide again.

Hope's suicide had been her way to punish herself for killing her baby. She reported, "I paid a life for a life." She wept, asking if God could ever forgive such a thing. We reminded her that God is always ready to forgive and asked her to beg forgiveness of her baby. His soul communicated to her, "There is nothing to forgive."

Hope did not feel that she was worthy of standing before God. As Aimee went through this memory, she gagged, choked, and coughed incessantly. We realized that Hope had ended her life by hanging herself. Our class had been held at a convent, which triggered this past life memory.

We reminded Hope of her belief that at death she would have to suffer in purgatory to pay for the sins she had committed. We told her the date was 2008 and asked if she had been suffering. She responded, "Yes!" We inquired if she felt she had suffered enough to pay the price? Yes, she agreed she had suffered enough. At last, Hope was able to forgive herself and let God wash her off so she could stand before him white again— cleansed from the shame of the sexual abuse, resulting birth, and infanticide.

How did Hope attach to Aimee? I asked Aimee if she had ever felt like the abuse heaped upon her was too much and that she had wanted to get out of this life. Yes, she knew those feelings! And she felt that in a past life, she had made the choice to do the same thing, to end her own life.

Aimee made a vow to her soul: "I, Aimee Joy, of my own free will, do hereby renounce the decision I made to take my life in the past and commit to never again making that choice. I commit to facing my feelings as they come, no matter what happens, and taking some time out of my body if the pain is too great, then returning to the body."

She said it three times, so it would be binding, to body, mind, and spirit. I said that the law of karma states that actions must

115

be balanced, and the theory is that most people who have been victims of abuse in this lifetime abused others in the past and volunteer to go through the pain of the abuse in this lifetime to balance that karma and learn never to perpetrate again.

I added that there was another theory, a second possibility, that some advanced souls from other realms see the suffering on Earth and volunteer to incarnate in this plane to help bring the suffering to Light and to heal it, setting a template for others to heal also. I asked which one felt true for her, and she said the second, as other healers had already seen this pattern in her. This answer felt true to me also. I told Aimee, "I respect you and honor you and bow to you." She accepted the first two statements but not the last one. I clarified bowing as in the Namaste greeting in the East, "The God within me bows to the God within you." That she could accept!

We completed the work by checking to see if all the places where Aimee had similar pain to that of Sibyl and Hope had been cleansed and repaired, and we felt they had.

SECOND SESSION

A month later, Aimee scheduled another appointment. She was doing well, but another baby was present on the fringe of her awareness. She felt this baby was like a "stopper in a bottle," and a flood of clearing would come out with this work.

After centering, we called pyramids of Light around us. I mentioned that I had recently become aware that establishing a pyramid of light on the earth creates a mirror pyramid under the earth, and Aimee exclaimed that she had seen the same thing, years before, with a mirror pyramid pointing down into the earth. In Sacred Geometry, this shape is called an octahedron. We called the Archangels Raphael, Gabriel, Ariel, and Uriel to anchor the sides of the pyramid, Michael to stand at the apex, and Zadkiel to stand at the point under the earth. Into this pyramid, we called the spiritual helpers for Aimee and me, for the baby, her parents, and anyone else involved in this issue.

This baby, Elizabeth, lived for only an hour and a half, and her spirit was earthbound. Her mother, also earthbound, wanted to be called "Tenacious" and had been taken captive at age fourteen. She came over to the United States from England on a ship and was sold as an indentured servant to pay for her ship's passage. Her owners raped her, and then forced the abortion of her babies. Her last baby was Elizabeth. They killed this baby when she was only seven and a half months through the gestation period, in a ritual sacrifice in the year 1876. First, we treated baby Elizabeth for the shame, heartache, and fear she had absorbed from her mother's terror while she was going through this nightmare. Next, we connected with Tenacious, who had been used as a "brood mare" and had lost four other babies before Elizabeth to ritual sacrifice, as well as her three children, ages ten, eight, and six.

We tried to have Tenacious do a heart massage, accepting all of her feelings about all the horror she had been through, but she was angry and did not want to accept anything. Feelings gushed forth, so we switched to scream therapy and invited her to scream out her feelings, all the things she wanted to say to her abusers. Tenacious yelled, "You're evil! You're wrong! Nothing about this is right. This is wrong. I know that I'm right and you're wrong." Every time they did a ritual sacrifice, they demanded that Tenacious say that she was wrong and they were right. When she refused to lie and say they were right, they killed her child as "punishment" for not complying. In this way, they twisted the truth to produce false guilt in her soul and to make her think that her actions had killed her child.

117

Reversed

I told Tenacious that everything the abusers did was backward. What they said was just the reverse of the truth. I added that they would have killed her babies even if she had said that they were right and she was wrong. I gave an example of how they distorted the truth to try to make a victim feel guilt, shame, and self-hatred. To break a child's heart, they would put a knife in the child's hand, place an adult's hand over the child's, and then use the knife to kill a beloved pet, saying that the child had killed it. This example triggered Aimee's memory of the cult killing her puppy in exactly this way. The sound of her puppy screaming as they plunged in the knife still haunted her. Although none of her own children had been sacrificed in a cult ritual, she felt that her abusers had changed her DNA and had programmed her body so that she could not carry a baby full term.

Trying to find a way to connect with Tenacious, I told her that we were in the year 2008. She replied that there was no such year. She could not even imagine it! She was in what she called the "fog world," searching for her babies. We let her know we understood that her spirit could not leave without her children, and that we would help her find them. We asked her to hold a hand over her heart and say, "Even though they told me I was wrong, it's not true! Even though they told me I killed my babies, it is not true!" She was willing to make these statements, and ended with the exclamation, "They did not break me!" She realized that they had been trying to make her lie and say wrong was right, but that she had the tenacity to hold to the truth!

Choosing the Darkness

I explained that having chosen the darkness, the cult members had cut themselves off from the flow of life energy that

118

constantly streams from the Creator to all beings. Since they had no way to regenerate their life force from the inside, they had to "recharge" by stealing the life energy of the sacrificial victim. This solution to their energy depletion had to be repeated, however, because the energy they stole lasted only a short time.

Rather than doing any more tapping, at this point we employed a technique from the teenage healer Adam of standing under a waterfall to cleanse the energy system. We invited Tenacious to stand under the waterfall and let it wash off all the lies, the sorrow, and the contamination from contact with this evil. Soon she felt clean, and then we invited her children to go under the waterfall to cleanse away all the darkness around them. We invited Tenacious to hold them in her arms, but her arms were not big enough to go around them all. Instead, we had them hold hands, and soon she had a circle of eight, her with all of her children. Only one of her children, her ten-year-old son, had crossed to the Light when he died. He came to this cleansing, got under the waterfall, too, and then led his family back through the doorway into the Light. Aimee commented that they had to open that door big and wide to get this party of eight through it!

Multiplying the Benefits

Next we multiplied the benefits by inviting all other children killed in ritual sacrifice and all other bereft parents of those children to stand under the waterfall, wash away the entire trauma, and find each other again. Aimee saw so many spirits answering this call that we asked for a thousand waterfalls. She reported that the Angels were rejoicing and singing at the healing taking place.

The soul lesson for Tenacious was, "I was right. God is real. Evil is wrong. My family is still alive and with me." Aimee responded that a couple of weeks ago she had felt that her light was being crushed by the darkness. I asked her, "What happens if we have two rooms, one with a light on and the other one in darkness and we take out the wall between them? Does the darkness crush the light?"

She laughed and responded, "No, the light shines into the darkness."

To consciously shine the light of truth into the darkness, we next sent out a cosmic invitation for any souls who had been trapped in the darkness of cult abuse, including those who had been abused as children and joined the perpetrators, who now wanted to get off the losing team (the darkness) and switch over onto the winning team (the Light) by making the choice to choose good instead of evil. We asked them to look within, find their light, let it grow, and then invited them to go under the waterfall to wash off all of the lies they had been told, to wash off anything that was not true, and to cleanse their souls. Aimee saw very long lines at the waterfall, even longer than the ones for the victims.

I asked Aimee if Tenacious was someone she had contact with in a past life. To her surprise, Aimee realized that she was one of the teachers that Tenacious had studied with before she left England, and she helped shape her faith. Currently in this life, Aimee had been feeling useless, not being needed by anyone. Knowing that she had helped Tenacious learn to hold on to the truth in spite of everything was very healing to her heart. As everyone was being washed clean, she saw a beacon of light radiating down into and onto the earth, then radiating across the face of the earth, with lights coming on all over the place.

Tenacious communicated to Aimee, "Thank you for your love and guidance."

Next I asked for a message from Spirit: what does God want for Aimee right now? Aimee narrated the following message from Spirit to her soul:

Love is the greatest power of the Universe. Earth has to come into alignment with the Universe. Remember that love is greater than the darkness. Don't be fooled by the façade. God's love is the greatest power in the Universe. I am to continue to teach this truth.

I asked Aimee to open up all of her chakras to take in a big drink of the love that God has for her. At this point, Aimee asked me to write up this session. She noted that in a session with another therapist, seeing a misshapen Star of David against a black background had triggered a memory. We put that one under the waterfall, too! Many times the cult will deform sacred objects and say things exactly the opposite of what they truly mean.

We talked about how the upward shift in evolution associated with the end of a 26,000-year cycle that completes in 2012 starts a new cycle with the possibility of moving into a higher plane of love. Instead of splitting and sending good people to heaven and bad people to hell, the new goal was to help the people who had made choices of darkness see the power of the Light, because we are all connected in a web of unity, and to transcend to a higher level. Either we all shift upward, or the planet may need to wait another 26,000 years before being able to make this leap in consciousness to letting love rule. Rather than polishing the brass on our shining fence posts, we need to clean out the sewers! Aimee had only recently realized how much Hitler had been involved with the dark forces. We invited his soul, too, to make a different choice, as his former choice did not lead to a happy ending in his lifetime as Hitler.

Teaching Love

Aimee could see that her soul had been involved with the evolution of this planet for a long time. She came to teach love, show love, and know love. Sometimes she was a sacrificial victim, and sometimes she was a teacher. Like Tenacious, she has also stayed true to the power of love.

We were ready to end the session, but since the waterfall still had long lines, we asked Spirit to manifest a personal waterfall for each person in the line. Aimee burst out laughing, reporting that the waterfall was so very, very big now! She broke into giggles, saying the angels were singing, dancing, and clapping, and the souls who had converted to the Light were having a huge, joyous, party!

20. *TRACING THE ORIGIN: Investigate how this dark energy was able to attach to the client. Did it come from an ancestor? If so, who and how many generations back? If it came in this lifetime, when? Did the host ever see such gruesome destruction of human life that they felt like God had forsaken them/God did not exist/they were traumatized and powerless to defend themselves? Heal this wound also.*

Seven Generations Back

In one session, we traced entry of the dark force back seven generations through the male lineage. Invaders had come and killed everyone in the family. As the ancestor was dying and seeing all of his family slaughtered, he decided that God could not exist in a world this awful. The dark force entered in at that point. We also realized, however, that this man seven generations back could not have been an ancestor if none of his children survived. When we took a deeper look, we saw that one son and one daughter had survived and reproduced, but that the dark force of rage had been handed down through the generations, poisoning the actions from father to son.

Was the person abused as a child and left feeling helpless and vulnerable? Sometimes dark spirits step in as "protection" for the child to fill the void and make the child feel powerful by getting angry about the abuse. The dark forces think that anger and rage are powerful.

The Fighter

A loving and concerned mother asked to do Soul Detective work to help her young son Dakota, who was quite ill. We muscle tested that, two lifetimes ago, his soul had an incarnation during World War I as a child named Aaron. At the tender age of four years old, Aaron witnessed his parents and others being slaughtered before he was also killed. The dark energies behind this carnage attached to Aaron's spirit and kept him earthbound. They had followed his soul energy into this lifetime as Dakota with the purpose of killing him. The dark forces were frustrated by not being able to accomplish their goal because Dakota fought them. He had often said, "I love to fight, Mom." Suddenly, she understood why.

As we treated Aaron's past life trauma, the top of the pyramid of light we had set around ourselves beamed radiant Light to him. It was so beautiful! Aaron's trauma cleared, and we called his parents, who were already in the Light, to come get him and take him home. Then we worked to help the Dark Force Entities find their inner light and get job promotions.

In this lifetime, we felt that Dakota's soul chose to incarnate to his mother because she would bring him the possibility of knowing about the Light. After the session, Dakota rapidly recovered from his illness.

21. *REPAIRING THE ENERGY FIELD: Do whatever trauma healing work is necessary to resolve the original emotional wound. Then ask the angels to wash away all damage done in the energy bodies by the presence of the dark force. A healing visualization I like to use is standing under a cleansing tropical waterfall that washes away the entire trauma. If the problem has been generational, ask all of the ancestors affected to come stand under the healing and cleansing waterfall.*

Dad's Last Days

Patience had done forgiveness work with her father over and over for the emotional abuse he had heaped on her and her mother. Her father, Roscoe, had always been mean to her. Diagnosed as a paranoid schizophrenic, he had burned his house down five years earlier and had tried to commit suicide. Patience tried to help him, but he kicked her out. A psychic predicted that he would not live to eighty-three, and two weeks before his eighty-third birthday, he had to be hospitalized. During those two weeks when death seemed imminent, he let Patience pray with him, and after that prayer work, he turned into a sweetheart! He was warm and welcoming to Patience and her two sisters, and they laughed and cried together. They had always wanted the healing balm of having this love relationship with their father. Joy filled their hearts!

But then Roscoe turned mean again. He went into a nursing home and was fine with the staff, but he acted out when Patience and her sisters came to visit. They always went in twos, not wanting to stand in the "firing line" alone. Her father would not make eye contact with her and complained, "I can't think. I don't know what the words you are saying mean." Although Roscoe said he wanted to die, he was also terrified of death and asked for every resuscitation method possible. He saw his good friend who had died and also saw people coming up out of the floor. Patience told him, "Dad, if your friend comes again, just go with him!"

As Roscoe kept scraping by each medical emergency, even though he had internal bleeding and was bedridden, Patience found, to her horror, that she was angry at the recurrence of his emotional abuse. His eyes would get glassy and then a virulent attack would erupt. He would yell at Patience, "Get away from me! You are worthless!" His outbursts hurt her heart more than words could tell. While she did not want to come down to his level, she found anger welling up in her heart. We had a session on Roscoe's eighty-third birthday.

Jeffrey

Muscle testing indicated that Roscoe's personality was split into two parts. One part had converted to the Light when Patience prayed with him for forgiveness, but another part of him held all the enmity of the abuse he had received at his own father's hands and had a Dark Force Entity attached to it. This entity, who called himself Jeffrey, would come out whenever the people came around who loved Roscoe the most. Jeffrey tried to destroy all of Roscoe's love relationships.

Jeffrey admitted he worked for the darkness and felt it made him important and powerful. We muscle tested that the evil spirit had attached around thirty years earlier, when Roscoe was about fifty-two years old. Jeffrey had been told that if he got close to the Light, he would die. We asked him to look into the core of his very being to see what was there. To his amazement, he first saw purple and red, the far ends of the light spectrum (infrared and ultraviolet), and then he saw a brilliant yellow neon light in an eye and a cheek. This light within him was so amazing and so strong! We asked if the Light had hurt him and had killed him.

Working for a Liar

When Jeffrey realized that the light had definitely not hurt him, we pointed out that he had been lied to about the true nature of the Light. We inquired how he felt about working for a liar. Jeffrey got extremely angry. He decided to convert to becoming a Lightworker so he could be on the winning team in the struggle between darkness and Light. As we multiplied the benefits of his conversion, over 1,500 other dark energies looked within, found their own connection to the Light, and went with him.

Next we worked with the wounded part of Roscoe. Initially this part of Roscoe communicated the thoughts, "Women are no good! They cause me pain. My wife, my sisters, and my daughters are all lesbians!" Then we connected with an eight-year-old part of Roscoe who was so frightened that he felt he had to hide. We helped clear his heartache and shame over his own abuse. Then he apologized to his late wife for his abusive behavior toward her and softly added, "You're not a lesbian. I love you so much!"

This split-off part of Roscoe's personality rejoined his essence so that when his time came to cross into the Light, he could take *all* of himself with him. Otherwise, the split-off part of his personality would have stayed earthbound, and the tormented feelings he had carried would land on someone else in the family system—the most sensitive person.

Next we worked with Patience to remove her emotional scars from years of her father's abuse. Knowing that Jeffrey targeted her and her sisters precisely because they loved Roscoe so much helped her understand that she had not done anything wrong, that the darkness always attacks the strongest love relationships, because love is the only truly important quality in the whole universe!

E-mail from Patience the Following Day

Within fifteen minutes of getting home from our session, Patience got a call from the nursing home that Roscoe had started bleeding internally and blood was emptying into his catheter bag. They wanted to send him to the emergency room, but Roscoe refused and said he wanted to be left alone to die. This attitude was different from his former stance of wanting every resuscitation method possible. Patience felt he was now flowing with the process of leaving this world instead of resisting it. Roscoe did not ask for Patience to come into his room, so she slept in the lounge by his room all that night. When she told her sister about our session, her sister realized that Jeffrey had attached to Roscoe right when Roscoe's father had died. Patience and her sister described Roscoe's father as "the meanest man on Earth." His wife had died at age twenty-eight, right after Roscoe's birth, and their grandfather blamed Roscoe for this loss. When Patience next visited her father, he looked at her, smiled, and laughed. She recounted:

Then he said, "Well, you're the last person I expected to see here. You look beautiful; you even dressed up to come and see me." He was so talkative and unbelievably kind. Two more times before he went to sleep, he said, "Tell me again why you came." I told him because I wanted to come and because I love him. He said softly that he needed to take a nap and drifted off. He woke up five minutes later and said, "You better go before it gets dark."

I gave him a kiss good-night and said, "I love you, Dad." For the first time since Jeffrey had infected him decades ago, he

127

said, "I love you, too, Patience." I will always praise God for this night. Your work for the light is beyond words.

Her following visit with her father was again precious and filled with love. Roscoe kept telling her how much he appreciated visits from his children. She said, "He laughed, and just sat and talked in such a soft voice, one that I have never heard before." He was in pain from multiple blood clots and started craving hard salami and bologna, onions and pickles. When she promised to bring those foods on her next visit, he laughed and said, "You are not going to believe this, but you smell like hard salami and you have hard salami hanging from your face." She brought the food he was craving on her next visit after she got off work, put in his false teeth, and they had a picnic at 10:00 p.m.! He cried and wept that no one had ever done something so sweet for him. As she kissed him good-night, he said, "I'm really going to miss you, kid. Drive careful; I love you more than you'll know."

The whole family was so blessed to have this special time with the man they never knew because of Jeffrey's interference. Patience reflected that Jeffrey was also blessed to have a new job. Formerly, Patience had seen Jeffrey in her mind's eye with a hard hat and dirty clothes scrubbing sewers. But her inner vision changed and she reported:

Now I see Jeffrey in a suit and tie with well-polished shoes. He carries a briefcase that has all the tools necessary to become a child of God. He carefully opens his briefcase to expose love, forgiveness, kindness, and, most important, the light to show the way, never to be lost again!

Patience reflected that she had come to me to heal her own heart, and the work wound up healing the whole family! She e-mailed me this blessing:

"May you skip on fairy dust today, and have a LIGHThearted song in your heart forever. You are truly a blessed one!"

The Last Days

After a couple of months of living with an open heart, expressing his love for Patience and connecting with God, Roscoe's dementia and Alzheimer's disease progressed and affected his cognitive processes. He deteriorated mentally, emotionally, and physically. He hit the nursing staff, her brother, and Patience. He would swing her purse at her, trying to clobber her, and blasting her with verbal abuse. He was paranoid and accused Patience of trying to kill him. Once he held his nose and his mouth shut, glaring at Patience. When she inquired why he made this strange gesture, he accused her of doing the same thing to him so he could not breathe.

Mental Illness Distortions

I acknowledged how difficult the distortions of mental illness are for other family members. In the last five days of his life, Roscoe was totally unable to move or communicate in any way. He could not even blink his eyes. The nurses instructed the family to use a wet cotton swab on his mouth and to put cream on his lips because his whole mouth was so dry. On the very last day of his life, when Patience tried to swab his mouth, he clamped his mouth closed tight and shot darts at her with his eyes, as if he were screaming at her. The family did not believe her when she told them what he did, insisting that Roscoe was incapable of any action, including closing his mouth. They must have thought she had gone "over the edge," but that look sent chills down her spine. From then on, Patience sat in the corner of the room as a prayer warrior but did not go close to her father's bedside. She left the hospital at 11 p.m. that night, and he died three hours later, on her sister's watch.

I explained to Patience that because Roscoe had the delusion that she was trying to kill him, he probably thought she was trying to put poison in his mouth and protested the only way he could. Also, because of the mental confusion of his dementia, he could have twisted past events. Months before, he had wanted to die and asked Patience to pray with him that God would take him soon. She'd honored this request, and together they'd asked God to release Roscoe from his physical body and take him Home to Jesus. None of the other siblings prayed with him in this way. Later, he could have misconstrued this action as her trying to kill him.

Dream

Patience came for another session after Roscoe died. The previous night, she'd had this dream:

Young students are at a nursing home. They want people to think they are nurses so they dress all in white to hide their colorful uniforms. Then they leave. I go into the bathroom. When I come out, someone says, "We saw your car out in the parking lot. You don't have to hide."

I ask, "Is he mad? Does Dad know I'm hiding?" They are not sure, but they say Dad is out with everyone else in the parking lot, eating hot dogs. He knows my car is here, but he's having a good time, so it's okay. Then I wake up.

The dream reflected three themes that resonated to the situation:

1. Patience was trying so hard to be loving and forgiving, but her heart was ripped apart by her father's

abuse. Like the students who were trying to be more advanced than they actually were, she was trying to hold the energy of forgiveness, but her heart was broken. 2. She had been avoiding her father on that last day, not trusting his actions. In the dream, she was hiding in the bathroom. 3. Roscoe himself was all right, an encouraging sign that he had crossed into the Light when he died.

Distraught by the outright lies her father had believed and his physical and verbal abuse at the end, Patience felt anger with him and with every other man in her life. Roscoe had hated her husband because of his religion and because he was from an ethnic group Roscoe disliked. Her husband didn't go to the nursing home to make his peace with Roscoe those last few months when Roscoe was in his right mind, and he did not attend Roscoe's funeral. Patience's only brother had molested her daughter. Underneath all her anger toward men was raw, seething pain.

We did a counterclockwise chakra spin to release the pain in her broken heart. After hauling out tons of agony and emotional damage, we did a clockwise spin around the heart and called on Mother Mary to fill her heart with love. We asked Mother Mary to reset the grid work for her heart chakra. Then Patience was able to realize she had a good relationship with at least one man in her life—her only son.

Totally in the Light?

Next we muscle tested to see if all of Roscoe's spirit had crossed to the Light. Testing indicated that 93 percent crossed (and was eating hot dogs) but that a soul fragment of 7 percent was still earthbound. I had been thinking that if 100 percent of him had crossed, he would either make a more nutritious food choice or wouldn't need to eat at all! Patience did not want to deal with this part, as she was still afraid of her father's irrational outbursts and the physical violence of his last days, so I did a surrogate treatment for this part of Roscoe. We released his fear of being unloved, and this fragment from his severe childhood abuse was pulled into heaven to join with the other 93 percent of his soul energy. Then I saw that Roscoe had had great courage to incarnate into the situation he chose, given the long history of wounding in the family. I felt him declaring as he incarnated, "One of my children will heal this wound!"

We extended an invitation to all other ancestors and all others in the universe who had suffered in a similar way. Patience began pulling in all around her, as if pulling in lifeboat ropes for those who had also been fragmented and trapped in their fears to come into our pyramid of light and claim healing and wholeness. We set up a stairway of Light for them to cross. After the session, we moved this stairway out into the woods in my yard for any "stragglers."

Patience experienced much healing in her heart from this session. Then she was able to remember the good times with her father. She related how he had wanted to pray together—such a great spiritual blessing for them both. He would raise his hands and pray out loud as she rolled his wheelchair up and down the aisles at the nursing home. This time together was so precious and beautiful! One day she came in and asked, "How are you, Dad?"

He responded, "I'm having a great day." That was the first time in her life she ever heard him say something that positive, and her soul rejoiced.

Later, Patience brought in one of her sisters for a Soul Detective session, and we did healing work for the whole lineage.

Then Roscoe came to get his father and grandfather and take them into the Light.

Pennies from Heaven

After her father's death, Patience asked to find pennies as a sign of her father's spiritual connection to her from the other side. Pennies began to show up regularly. She would be walking around the track and find a new penny where she had just been a lap earlier. Then she began to find nickels, dimes, and quarters. Roscoe apparently really wanted her to know they were connected!

Soul Lesson

Patience reflected, "Hearts carry so much damage!" She felt that the lesson of this whole experience was to teach others the love of God, forgiveness, and the peace that comes from God's guidance. She wanted everyone to know about the miracle that happened to Roscoe after we helped Jeffrey, the Dark Force Entity, get a job promotion and start working for the Light.

I sent Patience the write-up of this story and asked for her additions and corrections. She responded:

My, my, my, you have captured this mystery/miracle so eloquently. Things that seemed so ugly and discolored have been all washed, and pressed. All the wrinkles are removed and all that remains is a smooth crisp soft cotton robe, one that Roscoe will wear with pride, a robe that he will be so excited to show me when we meet again. I am so thankful you are our Laundry Lady. You took my dirty laundry and mended the rips and holes. You washed my laundry in a delicate heavenly soap supplied only by God. Then in the rinse cycle you made sure all the soil was gone. You added your heavenly fabric softener of God's love before you hung it out to dry on that sunny, breezy day. When my wash was dry, you pressed it with love, understanding, and kindness and then added the crispness of Jesus. Roscoe is so proud that you are writing his story. He is so happy to be on the other side and free to think as Jesus does. But I know he wants his story repeated so others who may be suffering like he was can get complete forgiveness and unconditional love, and be clothed in his new heavenly clean and pressed garment.

You are just too awesome for me to find words to describe how free I feel. I am Patience, and I have never ever been so free! I love you, dear friend. You have such a special gift; I thank God you have come into my path of life. Peace to you.

22. *CHECKING FOR OTHER WOUNDS: Find out whether the client has other open emotional wounds making the person vulnerable to invasion by Dark Force Entities. Sometimes the dark side has more Dark Force Entities lined up to take the place of the ones that just converted. If you find this situation, ask Archangel Michael to do whatever is necessary to help all the other dark entities lined up to find their own light and come back to the Brotherhood of Light. One technique you might use is to ask Archangel Michael to zap each dark entity with a beam of love and light from his sword, to ignite the spark of Light within each one and flood them with their own Light.*

Dragon

No matter what Draco did, it turned out wrong. Highly intelligent and articulate, he worked very hard in therapy to break out of his negative patterns, but everything he did seemed to disappear down a black hole. He worked through multiple issues with seeming success at the time, but the pervasive negativity always returned. Draco felt completely invisible and stymied by his lack of success even though he was exerting tremendous effort to improve his life. Angry and frustrated, he felt as if he were cursed and living in a goldfish bowl, unable to escape the suffering of his life.

The Curse

Muscle testing confirmed his suspicion that he had a curse on him. Draco's father had engaged in an extramarital affair. When he broke it off, the rejected woman sought revenge and placed the curse on him and his offspring, "Go to hell, you and all of your family!" The woman invoked demons to carry out this curse. Draco commented, "I do feel like I'm in hell!"

Dragon

The lead Dark Force Angel enforcing this curse was named Dragon. His purpose was to disrupt everything. The only emotions he could resonate with were anger and hate. He had no personal freedom, because he was corded to his employer, forced as a slave to do the will of his boss. He believed that Light was not available to him and focused on death energy.

We asked Dragon to look within himself. He was surprised to find a fine white line on the horizon. He floated above this space, batting his wings. Then the color shifted to silver, and Dragon found his own light! He wanted a better job and accepted the offer of Archangel Michael to come work for the light. All four of the other dark energies followed suit, found their own light, and switched sides.

Subtle Shifts

After this intervention, Draco felt hopeful. He felt he was at a cusp in his personal life and that a definite shift had happened. He reflected, "The whole curse thing baffles me and at the same time seems to explain a lot. I have put forth effort, like Sisyphus, and just never thought to question why so much effort would result in so much nothingness and pain. Thank you for being willing to try to help me find life again, as I am looking hard for it."

After this session, his regular therapist had a stringent talk with him and gave him a "one-two punch" challenge to force him out of his negative perception of himself and to like himself. She gave him an assignment of making a daily gratitude list. His lists reflected how much his life had changed from the days when he was so immersed in negativity that he could not even leave his home.

After a couple of weeks, Draco reported, "I admit that I tend to be somewhat of a skeptic, but I have to be honest and say that something seems to have shifted. What I started to notice right away was a sense of small things falling into place more easily, and I could also be grateful in the moment for them. As these things happen, I notice myself feeling grateful more readily. Not every day, or every moment is as smooth as possible, but I am able to risk being available and less defended. It's a little odd to me since my situation, truthfully, has not changed with regard to the logistics of my life. My finances are still in disarray, I don't have a regular job, and I still have health and lifestyle issues that I'm dealing with. What I am noticing, though, is that I'm not feeling as overwhelmed by these challenges as I was. Rather, I'm doing my best to address them and acknowledging the efforts that I'm making in a positive way, without self-recrimination or doubt. Now, that may seem like a small thing, but there are a lot of these small things that seem to be adding up so I'm more in sync with life, rather than rubbing up against the fabric of the universe in such a way that I always feel like something is wrong."

23. *GIVING THANKS AGAIN AND CLOSING THE OCTAHEDRON: The energy of gratitude has a very high vibration and is an excellent way to close a session. If you called in transpersonal help, give thanks for this Divine assistance. Thank all the Dark Force Entities who became New Lightworkers, thank the client for having the courage to do this deep emotional healing, and thank everyone else who multiplied the benefits to help lighten the load of trauma on this planet.*

BE SURE TO CLOSE DOWN THE PYRAMID!

Stragglers

When I went to visit my sister in a distant city, she let me see some clients in her home. One client did some wonderful release work to help her earthbound grandfather get into the Light. We multiplied the benefits and invited any others with similar issues to cross into the Light, too.

The next morning, I asked my sister, "How did you sleep last night?" She told me she couldn't sleep and went out on the couch. While she was lying on the couch, she felt frightened by an invasive energy hovering right over her, staring at her. Then she heard a crash in the kitchen and sensed two people there—people without their physical bodies.

Suddenly, I realized that I had neglected to close down the pyramid of light I had set up the day before. We muscle tested that the entities my sister had sensed were earthbound spirits who had been drawn to the light of the pyramid. By the morning, they had all found their way home to heaven, but I felt embarrassed that my forgetfulness had caused my sister to have such a frightening night.

We closed down that pyramid!

137

E-mail from a Soul Detective Student:

One of the reasons I felt so "whacked" yesterday was that I forgot to close the pyramids after working with a client. I even went to sleep last night with them open. I had horrible dreams and woke up feeling awful. I started to balance myself and sprayed my house with a clearing essence. I could feel the dark energies. Then bingo! I remembered I had forgotten to close down the pyramids. At first I got scared—just wanted to chase the dark forces away. Then I stopped. I remembered who I am and my Soul Detective Training and connected with the dark energies and asked for *a very large team of angels* to come down and escort them all to the light. Gosh, everything shifted instantly and I was myself again! Only better, because I used what I am good at and with full confidence in myself and what I was doing. Barbara, as you can imagine, there were a lot of dark energies in that pyramid! It's funny now!

24. *FINAL GROUNDING: Be sure the client is grounded again after this work, especially if they are going to drive home from the appointment. Reconnect clients to awareness of the physical body and connection with the earth under their feet. The Hara Alignment is one way to ground a person's energy.*

Hara Alignment

- Standing, bring your awareness to the tan tien, an energy ball in your belly a couple of inches below the navel. This is the point from which all martial arts forms draw their power. This belly center can also be called the hara.

- From the tan tien, send a line of energy down your pelvis, down through your legs, through the balls of the feet, deep down into our beautiful Mother Earth, imagining you are a tree growing deep, strong roots. Then let these roots draw up nourishment from the earth into the tree trunk, into your tan tien.

- Next, become aware of the energy around your heart. Feel your physical heart beating. Call to mind a list of things you are grateful for, bathing your heart in the elixir of gratitude. Then from your heart, send up a line of energy through your throat chakra, third eye, and out the crown chakra, up to the sky. If you have a relationship with spiritual helpers, you can send it up to the heart of your guardian angel, the heart of Divine Mother, Divine Father, or any other spiritual figure that holds meaning for you. Then breathe in energy from the sky through this energetic cord back into your heart. If you have spiritual helpers, feel how grateful they are to you that you are doing this powerful healing work.

• Next, bring the energy of the belly up to the heart, so that you are simultaneously breathing in energy up from the earth and down from the sky, meeting at the heart. On the in-breath, draw energy in from above and below, and on the out-breath, send your love and caring out through your heart to the world around you.

SECTION TWO:

I Want
This Nightmare to End

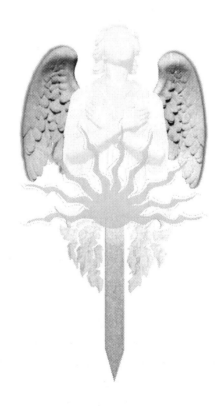

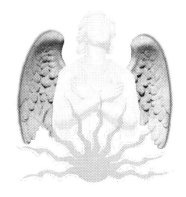

CHAPTER 3

Dissociation and Satanic Ritual Abuse

When Paula first walked through my office door for psychotherapy, the chaos and turmoil behind the walls in her memory were carefully guarded secrets concealed within the quiet, mild-mannered widow I saw before me. In our second session, Paula reported that she had been ritually abused. She denied any elements of satanic worship in what happened, saying that her abusers just did the same things to her in the same order every time—ritualized abuse. The full impact of her abuse unfolded gradually, as she felt safe enough to let the walls in her memory start to come down. It is extremely hard to believe that anyone could live through the severity of the physical torture she reports was inflicted upon her. The mere fact that Paula survived, living to tell what happened, is a miracle in itself. This section includes pencil drawings Paula brought to her sessions to tell her story through art, as a picture is worth a thousand words.

Pencil Drawing by Paula

Defining Ritual Abuse

Ritual abuse is a brutal form of abuse of children, adolescents, and adults, consisting of physical, sexual, and psychological abuse, and involving the use of rituals. Ritual does not necessarily mean satanic. However, most survivors state that they were ritually abused as part of satanic worship.[1]

According to this report from the Los Angeles County Commission for Women, the purpose of the abuse is indoctrination into satanic beliefs and practices. Usually, ritual abuse involves repeated abuse over an extended period of time rather than a single episode. Sometimes torture and killing are involved in the rituals. Sadistic, humiliating sexual abuse is used in this system to gain dominance over the victim.

> The psychological abuse is devastating and involves the use of ritual/indoctrination, which includes mind control techniques and mind altering drugs, and ritual/intimidation which conveys to the victim a profound terror of the cult members and of the evil spirits they believe cult members can command.[2]

---

1 Los Angeles County Commission for Women, "Report of the Ritual Abuse Task Force," 1989.
2 Ibid.

The heightened state of terror created during the abuse persists afterward. Combined with the effects of dissociation, disclosure becomes extremely difficult.

Advisory

This extended case history is not for the fainthearted, because just hearing about the horrific abuse Paula reported may produce vicarious traumatization in the reader. We know that the physical body reacts to the mental pictures it sees, as in the heart pounding while watching a scary movie. This section contains explicit details of satanic ritual abuse, including sadistic physical, emotional, and sexual abuse. Please skip this section of the book if you do not feel prepared to face the vicarious traumatization that may come from reading about these practices.

Emotional Freedom Techniques Free Manual

If you are not already familiar with an energy therapy self-care method to release your own trauma, a self-help method called Emotional Freedom Techniques has a download of a free manual at www.eftuniverse.com. It shows the reader where and how to tap on acupressure points to release disturbing emotions.

When I first met Paula, I had never heard of these rapid, highly effective trauma release methods. The vicarious traumatization I experienced as her therapist drove me to learn a broad range of energy therapies to deal with my own trauma as well as to help my clients.

Belief Systems

Reading this section may challenge one's belief systems. Most of us do not want to believe the abuse Paula reported is true. We feel safer behind the walls of denial. Yet this denial gives evil the freedom to continue its dark practices. According to Paula, the cult tries to hide behind an invisibility cloak fed by collective denial of their existence. They purposely cultivate dissociation in the people they abuse so the survivors themselves do not remember what happened. Masters at using energy work for darkness, they also program their subjects to self-destruct if their memories come to their awareness. Thus the

143

risk of suicide heightens tremendously when people recover their memories of satanic ritual abuse.

Another tactic abusers use is trying to discredit people who disclose their memories. The False Memory Syndrome Foundation (FMSF) was created by the parents of a woman who accused them of sexually abusing her as a child. This foundation sparked a huge controversy in the mental health field between the therapists who hear the stories and see the signs of trauma in their clients and the vehement denial from those accused of being perpetrators. This conflict goes back to the founders of psychotherapy. Sigmund Freud initially attributed hysteria in his female patients to forgotten childhood traumas of being sexually abused by their fathers.

> However, Freud soon experienced a reversal of opinion. He had been wrong. These childhood sexual assaults he now decided were not real experiences but fantasies produced by sexual feelings toward the parent, which violated the incest taboo and therefore had to be repressed.[3]

Could some children make up stories of sexual abuse? Sigmund Freud decided they did, because he could not believe the material disclosed to him, which involved naming a colleague of his as a perpetrator. Could some memories of abuse come from past life connections between people? It's possible, especially with a client whose boundaries are permeable to other realities. I always treat the trauma the client presents because it is emotionally real in the present moment even if it physically happened in another incarnation. I never pursue punishment of the perpetrators, but rather work to help the shattered parts of the client heal and come back into relationship with the core personality. Because satanic ritual abuse is often intergenerational, with the parents first being abused themselves, then under pressure joining the satanic cult and abusing their own children, the ancestral wounds also need to be healed.

---

3   Bliss and Bliss, *Prism*, 105-106.

Veracity

Is everything in this story true? I do not know, and I do not judge. We know that truth is always filtered through one's perceptual lenses, because five eyewitnesses of an accident will give five different versions of what happened. At one point in her treatment, Paula's psychiatrists diagnosed her as having factitious disorder, which would mean that she feigned her illnesses and deliberately produced or exaggerated her symptoms to get attention from her caregivers—especially me. While we strongly disagreed on her diagnosis, the psychiatrists and I agreed on the main aspects of her treatment plan, which were:

1. Continue working together in therapy, as we had developed a strong therapeutic bond.
2. Focus on getting Paula grounded and functional.

Frankly, I wish those psychiatrists were right. I would much prefer to think that I was fooled and that the atrocities Paula reported never happened. I wish that nobody worshipped Satan and everyone knew the power and joy of the Light. Throughout our work together, I kept my eyes and ears open, looking for inconsistencies in Paula's story and questioning its veracity because many of the things she told me were extremely hard to believe.

Paula kept saying all through treatment, *"I want this nightmare to end."* By reading this book and passing it along to others, I pray that we can collectively wake up from the nightmare of the darkness, negativity, and fear that manifests in these dark practices. Carl Jung talked about the pooled field of all the memories of human experience, which he called "the collective unconscious." I pray we can spot the lies in this piece of the collective unconscious and see the distortions we have believed about who we are and what God wants from us. When we see the real truth, we can heal the damage and get in touch with the golden light in the center of each of our hearts. I pray that therapists will listen with an open mind to this account and learn to recognize the signs of dissociation, whether from ritualized abuse or the more severe cases of satanic ritual abuse. I pray that healers will use whatever tools resonate for them—traditional methods using hypnosis, spiritual interventions, and energy therapies, including the Soul Detective protocols in this book—to stop the pain of this nightmare for those caught in its web, either as victims or as perpetrators.

Janet Thomas, an author who has spoken out about her severe childhood sexual abuse, writes:

> It was only after I'd faced the abuse done to me that I could face the creation of the nice, thoughtful "me" that everybody in my life took as true. It's complicated. Whenever I try to describe and explain the map of my mind and the inchoate geography of my body, I am stymied by the reality of it all. It is as unbelievable as nature. And as true.[4]

Multiple Personality Disorder (MPD)

My understanding of multiple personality disorder (though I didn't yet know the term) began when I was eighteen years old. A college classmate told me her mother had two personalities. One was nice to her, and the other would viciously beat her up, chase her with a knife, and threaten to kill her. I wondered how a person could have a split like that and realized how insecure this friend would feel around her mother, never knowing which personality would be out.

Introductory Lecture

In 1990 I was in a doctoral program for clinical psychology, and one lecture by psychiatrist Marcus S. Barker stood out from all the rest as being difficult to comprehend. Dr. Barker told us about a rare condition called "multiple personality disorder," a psychiatric term later changed to dissociative identity disorder (DID), although the International Classification of Diseases and Related Health Problems continues to call it multiple personality disorder. I could not comprehend how a single mind could have several personalities, with separate memories, conflicting food preferences, different allergies, distinct medical conditions, separate languages, and sometimes even different

---

4 *Day Breaks Over Dharamsala*, p.322.

scars. Wasn't a scar a record of something that happened to the body? All the personalities shared the same body, so how could a scar disappear when a different personality appeared? How could one physical body have different medical problems, depending on which personality was out? My model for how the physical body worked did not allow for this much plasticity to come from a change in psychological state. Dr. Barker instructed us to get supervision help when we found our first case of dissociation.

The Strangler

After the lecture, I spotted a woman in my caseload with signs of being a multiple. She felt frightened by threatening notes she had been finding from a guy who called himself "The Strangler." I asked her to bring the notes to therapy, and I photocopied them. Then one day this woman left me a note saying she had to change her appointment, and I noticed the notepaper and the handwriting were quite similar to the notes from the Strangler.

I presented to her the possibility that she might have different personalities inside her, and that the Strangler might be right inside her own body. She thought the idea was totally ridiculous! Even though she was resistant to the concept, she agreed to let me assess her for dissociation. I felt pretty silly as I used a technique I had learned from Dr. Barker. First I talked her into a state of relaxation by having her focus her awareness on her breathing. I had her relax each part of her body, from her toes up to her head. Then I counted from one to five with the suggestion that she would be totally relaxed by the time I got to the number five. Then I asked to speak with the Strangler. To my disappointment, he did not come forth, nor did any other dissociated part come forward. My client probably thought I had gone totally crazy. Perhaps she was not multiple, or perhaps she did have dissociation but was not yet ready to face the trauma that would be uncovered if she went behind that wall in her memory.

Witnessing Switching

Since I am bilingual, I translated for my Spanish-speaking clients during their appointments with their psychiatrist. Once, a colleague was unavailable and asked me to translate for one of her clients. The timid, hunched-over young man wearing glasses did not speak any English, so I translated his Spanish for the psychiatrist. Halfway through the fifteen-minute appointment, he switched personalities, took off his glasses, sat up straight, laughed, and told the psychiatrist in English, "I don't need any of that medicine!"

I was amazed to see a totally different energetic imprint in his personality, as if he were two people living in one body. The part of him that came out at the end of this session liked to party, did not want to take his antidepressant medication, and frequently got the other part of him into trouble. At last I had witnessed the phenomenon of "switching," seeing a different personality take over the physical body. The sudden difference in demeanor, eyesight, and language astonished me.

Dr. Eugene Bliss

Several months before I met Paula, my daughter called me to say she was reading a great book titled *Prism: Andrea's World*, by Jonathan Bliss and Eugene Bliss, MD, about a woman who had developed multiple personality disorder from an abusive childhood. She said she would loan me the book when she was finished, knowing I would be interested because I was studying psychology. I wanted to find out from reading this book what a flesh-and-blood case looked like. I also wanted to learn the innovative treatment techniques developed by Andrea's psychiatrist, Dr. Eugene Bliss. Just in case I ever got someone in my own caseload with multiple personalities, I wanted to be prepared! Now I am laughing at how naïve I was about the complexities of multiplicity.

Initiated by Cancer

My doctoral dissertation on the emotional factors influencing cancer survival was published in popular form under the title *Cancer as Initiation: Surviving the Fire*. It includes the autobiography of my diagnosis of breast cancer in 1991, the integrative treatment approach I used, and the role of Divine intervention in finding the tumor and healing my soul. In gratitude for the gift given to me of having more time on this planet, I surrendered my will to Divine will. From deep in my heart, I prayed to Spirit, "Please use this additional time you have given me to do whatever would serve you best and to work for the good of all of humanity. May God's will be done in my life." God took this prayer seriously and sent me Paula. She was the catalyst that began my search for tools to turn darkness into light and fear into gold.

CHAPTER 4

Paula's Background

Overview

*P*aula's acupuncturist referred her to my practice, saying that a recent car accident had aggravated some long-standing problems that needed more than the thirty acupuncture sessions allowed by her health insurance. Her acupuncturist told me, "It's not just the accident, it's everything! You'll see."

The drama of Paula's story is narrated as it unfolded, but with names and other identifying details changed to protect the identities of the people involved. The beginning stage of therapy is elaborated in detail, including the progression of the unfolding of memories in the first ten sessions. Nine chapters are devoted to the stories of individual parts. The final section includes a synopsis of the last six sessions we did together.

Initial Consultation and History

Paula presented as a soft-spoken, emotionally withdrawn, and reserved but cooperative fair-skinned Caucasian female in her early thirties. She lived with her daughter, who was in grade school. Her gait was unusual, as her arms did not swing as she walked; she moved stiffly and cautiously. She exhibited a startle response to any loud noise in the environment and had been having psychological difficulties for over a decade. Paula's face was scarred, as if she had suffered from severe acne. She was dressed neatly in a black-and-white polka-dot blouse and black skirt, with straight hair pulled back away from her face into a ponytail.

Both of her parents were alcoholics. She had a younger sister who was crippled, and Paula cared for her and tried to protect her sister from the abuse of their parents. From her mother's side, Paula had two much older half brothers who were deceased and one half brother close to her age who was still living. Paula felt that both her older brother and younger sister got everything they wanted, but she got nothing. She reported severe abuse from her father and others from the ages of four through fifteen. The three-story house her family had lived in burned down when she was fifteen, and after the fire, the abuse tapered off. In her early twenties, she was raped by a stranger who abducted her while she was walking from her car to her house.

Paula's mother never participated in any of her physical abuse. On the contrary, her mother had tried to stick up for Paula on several occasions. When she intervened, however, Paula's father beat her mother badly and then beat Paula twice as hard. Usually, her mother observed the abuse without trying to stop it, numbing her feelings with alcohol. Her mother wanted Paula to stay quiet about the sexual abuse. Paula decided otherwise and told her mother, "What was good for you may not be good for me."

Her relatives used to come to visit her parents, and Paula would babysit for about ten kids who were younger than her while the adults played cards and drank. Then the adults would start to abuse her. She could not leave because she felt she had to stay present to protect her younger sister and the other children. The adults also used drugs and forced her to take drugs when they abused her, and she became addicted. She was currently clean and sober having done a 12-step recovery program.

Her parents often kept her home from school, using the excuse that she had to care for her sister; however, she believed that the real reason they kept her out of school was to isolate her and to abuse her further. Her grades were low and her absences high, but the teachers pushed her through anyway, and she graduated from high school.

Her mother had been married four times to abusive alcoholic men, but her mother never married Paula's father. Paula would see her mother shift into looking like a frightened, helpless child when her father was beating her up. Also, her mother would have episodes of heaping verbal abuse on Paula, though she never abused her physically. After years of physical, emotional, and sexual abuse from her father, her mother finally tried to throw him out. The police would come several times a night to deport him to his mother's house, but her father would always return. Sometimes he stole all the food in their house.

Medical Problems and Medication

Paula had a blood abnormality in which her blood clotted too rapidly. She was taking medication to thin her blood to avoid a blood clot that could travel to her brain and kill her. She reported her physicians had installed a filter in her groin to reduce the risk of a clot going to the brain. At the time of the intake, she was bleeding from her vagina more than when she had given birth to her daughter. Once she had bled continuously for nine months straight. The doctors could not figure out the cause of this bleeding. They noted that her body was constantly in the first stage of her menstrual cycle. She wanted a total hysterectomy, but the physicians refused to take the risk because of her clotting disorder. She also had asthma treated by an inhaler and oral medication.

She was on major tranquilizers to try to stop the auditory hallucinations that cried out obscenities and clamored for blood. She was on minor tranquilizers for her anxiety disorder and startle reflex. She was also on sedatives for insomnia, but medication never seemed to work very well for Paula. It helped take a little bit of the edge off the problem but never fully resolved the issues.

First Breakdown

Paula's first breakdown came while her daughter was learning to crawl. One night Paula dissociated and came to with her hand holding a butcher knife at her own throat. She threw the knife on the counter and called the doctor for help. She went into psychiatric hospitalization for the next three months.

Paula reported having been through twenty-seven psychiatric hospitalizations. In the previous ten years of psychotherapy, she had been diagnosed with major depression because of multiple suicide attempts and also with borderline personality disorder because of frequent self-mutilation. The inside of her arms had many scars where she had cut her wrists. She was also diagnosed with posttraumatic stress disorder because of her trauma history.

Multiple Losses

Paula reported multiple losses in addition to ritualized abuse. On their first birthday, her twin brother, Paul, died of sudden infant death syndrome (SIDS). She reported that the family blamed her for his death and wished she had died instead of her brother. After she saw Paul's birth and death record, his death certificate was burned. Something was hush about that issue, as other family members refused to talk openly about how he died.

When she was nineteen, her boyfriend witnessed Paula being beaten by her father at home. Four months later, he asked her to marry him to get her out of that abusive situation. They eloped together. Soon after their wedding, she became pregnant. This beloved husband was tragically killed in a car accident a few months before the birth of their daughter, Megan. He never got to see his baby girl. She never remarried, but she had one miscarriage from a boyfriend after her daughter's birth.

A natural caretaker, Paula compassionately ministered to others in need no matter how bad she felt herself. She complained that others did not reciprocate with helping her when she was in need. She had been the primary caretaker for her mother through a long physical illness. They lived together in an apartment, and with both of their social security disability checks, she had just been able to make ends meet. Her mother died eight months before we began therapy, followed by her father's death several months later. Paula was still in mourning for her mother. Poetry is a creative art form that helped her to manage her feelings. She wrote the following poem, expressing her grief about her mother's death.

Mourning Still

I was doing okay until I read the date on the wall.
Then, I started to crumble and fall.

For it is one month to the day
At rest, I put her body to lay.

I opened her door:
I was in shock no more.

Reality is finally setting in,
And the impulses are trying to win.

Many feelings I cannot shut out,
And feeling full of doubt.

For, I am feeling weak.
And deep inside, I weep.

Feeling angry and alone.
And finding no one home.

Alone, feeling bitter and cold.
Wishing I had someone to hold.

Mourning still,
And trying to find my will.

Both grandfathers had been killed in wars. Her paternal grandmother immigrated to the United States from Germany with her three sons and her sister, Aunt Martha. Grandmother was a strict Catholic and had difficulty accepting Paula because she was born "out of wedlock." Paula's maternal grandparents were Hispanic, and her maternal great-grandmother was Navajo. Highly intelligent, Paula had learned German, Spanish, and the native language of her tribe as well as English, her native tongue.

Paula's Artistic Talent

Another coping skill that Paula had developed was using art as therapy. When she could not verbalize her feelings, she could draw them.

> *Art washes away from the soul the dust of everyday life.*
> —Pablo Picasso

Nude Sketch

Paula had always shown artistic talent. In school, if a poster needed to be made, the teachers always asked Paula to do it. During her twenties, she took art classes to refine her talent. The following drawings are some of her sketches from those classes. Her finely detailed partly nude studies of human figures show a high degree of artistic skill that makes the models seem to come to life.

Three Nude Bathers

Paula's Sandtray

In our first psychotherapy session together, I asked Paula to do a sandtray,[1] a diagnostic tool I had learned when I studied at the Jung Institute in Switzerland. Paula did not touch any of the myriad objects available and instead drew pictures in the sand with her finger. Paula's sketching in the sand included a broken heart, a mountain with "everything piled up," a cross-section of the brain with flashbacks coming out in confusion, and a mask of a woman's face with the right side smiling and cheerful and the left side tearful and in pain. Paula reflected that she was like the woman's face. The face she presented to the world was cheerful, but inside she was crying.

Flashbacks

Paula's primary complaint was having recurrent flashbacks of sexual and physical abuse. She was hallucinating voices that clamored, "We want blood!" Five days after our intake session, Paula called me, asking for psychiatric hospitalization to prevent her from hurting herself. She stated, "Every road I take is a dead end, ready to go over a cliff," and she added that sometimes she felt like other people were inside of her. This last statement is one of the diagnostic indicators of multiple personality disorder that Dr. Barker defined.

The Dissociative Experiences Scale (DES)[2] is a simple inventory of twenty-eight questions about experiences in daily life developed to screen for dissociation. Available online at no charge and needing only ten minutes to take and five minutes to score, the scale has good validity and reliability. The average score of a DID client on this scale is in the 40s. Paula's score was well over 40.

---

1   Sandplay, a form of art therapy developed in Switzerland by Dora Kalff, allows the creative forces within a client to express themselves. It aids bringing up unconscious parts of the mind. The client can choose from an array of miniature figures of plants, animals, buildings, vehicles, people, and nature objects to form a three-dimensional picture in a 23-by-28-inch tray of sand four inches deep. A photograph is taken of the completed sandtray.
2   The DES was developed by Eve Bernstein Carlson, PhD, and Frank W. Putnam, MD, and is available online at http://counsellingresource.com/lib/quizzes/misc-tests/des/

Refusal

To Paula's chagrin, the hospital refused to admit her, claiming that on her last admission, she had given someone a razor blade. Paula was quite hurt by this accusation, since she placed a high value on never ever harming anyone else. Rather than hospitalization, Paula was given a new psychiatrist and medication changes.

CHAPTER 5

Diagnosis of Dissociative Identity Disorder

*S*ince Paula had mentioned feeling as if other people were inside her, I inquired whether she would like to do a progressive relaxation technique I had learned to get to a deeper level of her own truth and assess for dissociative identity disorder (DID). She agreed. When she was relaxed and breathing deeply, I asked whether any other parts of Paula would like to speak. "Marge," ten years old, came out. She did not know Paula and was very confused. She reported others were inside with her, locked up, screaming for help. Marge cut herself because she "wanted to cut free." Marge did not want love. She felt afraid of love because family and friends had hurt her, saying they had done it because they loved her.

Dissociative Identity Disorder

When Marge left, Paula's whole body jerked, and she got a terrible migraine headache. Paula did not remember Marge speaking and had trouble accepting the possibility that part of her personality might have dissociated from her awareness. Even when we reviewed the content of what Marge had told us during the session, Paula remained skeptical. Since I had seen both parts of Paula, she had met the criteria for DID:

- The presence of two or more distinct identities or personality states (each with its own relatively enduring pattern of perceiving, relating to, and thinking about the environment and self).
- At least two of these identities or personality states recurrently take control of the person's behavior.
- Inability to recall important personal information that is too extensive to be explained by ordinary forgetfulness.
- The disturbance is not due to the direct physiological effects of a substance (e.g., blackouts or chaotic behavior during alcohol intoxication) or a general medical condition (e.g., complex partial seizures). Note: in children, the symptoms are not attributable to imaginary playmates or other fantasy play.[1]

Over the next two weeks, Paula experienced increased flashbacks and difficulty accomplishing routine tasks. She was hospitalized for five days to stabilize an allergic reaction to one of her new medications. She reported that her psychiatrist thought she had a biological chemistry disorder that made the natural changing of body rhythms with the seasons not shift right for her. She also reported getting blood clots, with abnormal PTT (partial thromboplastin time) tests, which measure how fast the blood clots, and abnormal PT (prothrombin time) tests, which measure other clotting factors. She was unable to sleep, even though she was on major and minor tranquilizers, an antidepressant, and a strong sedative. Medications never seemed to work well for Paula.

Ashamed of all that had happened to her, Paula found talking with me over the phone easier than speaking to me in person. After our second appointment, she called to tell me what was going on with her. At that time, I did not realize

---

1 http://psychcentral.com/disorders/sx18.htm

Flashbacks and Personality Fragments

that I needed to model good boundaries and not do psychotherapy over the telephone.

Why Me?

In our phone call, Paula reported she had blanked out for a while the previous night. When she snapped back in, she found herself holding a razor blade in her hand, and she had carved the words "Why me" upside down and backward on the inside of her left knee.

She cleaned the wound with hydrogen peroxide and bandaged it. She

∃ W ⅄ H W

said flashbacks of the following memory from her teenage years were disturbing her.

A Robbery

She reported flashing to the scene of a double murder she had witnessed in a male friend's apartment, which was above a local store. She had not known that drugs were in the house, but while she and other friends were drinking and playing cards, the apartment owner answered a knock on the door and then came back to the card game. Another knock came. Two men wearing ski masks entered the front door, and a third man entered through the back door. One intruder hit the apartment owner on the head with the butt of a revolver, knocking him out. Another intruder held Paula hostage at the kitchen table with a cocked gun to her head. The other two robbers put everyone else in the bathroom, robbed them, and then stole the drugs. On their way out of the building, the robbers shot two other men. After this event, Paula had never been able to go back into that store, but she had never understood why until

159

she recalled this flashback. She feared reporting this information to the police, even anonymously. She thought that the others, too, had kept silent. She had wondered why she got such a funny feeling every time she went near that corner store and apartment.

I consulted with Paula's psychiatrist on the issue of this flashback. He advised against trying to report this information to the police since it was nearly two decades old and lacking in specific details. He agreed to the idea of tape recording future sessions since Paula was resisting the diagnosis of dissociative identity disorder and did not remember what she had said to me when Marge came out.

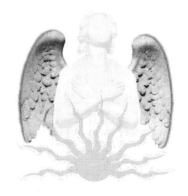

CHAPTER 6

Sessions Three to Eight

I n her third session, Paula reported increasing difficulty coping with everyday tasks. She felt as if her creative side was blocked and refused to do another sandtray or any other form of art therapy. We looked at her attitudes around playing, noticing how her daughter plays

Session Four: Seven Stitches

The night before our fourth session, Paula cut her forearm and needed seven stitches. She did not remember cutting herself and felt no pain from the wound, even when the doctor stitched it up. I was very surprised that the wound did not hurt. I could not figure out how she could not feel the stitches I saw with my own eyes.

With her permission, we tape recorded the following session so she could listen to any other parts of herself that came out. To make the atmosphere safer, I suggested that she would find out only as much as she could handle right

Crystal Glass

Mind of the Crystal Glass,
Seeing nothing but my past.

Crystal Glass that is so clear:

I see all that fear.
Scared to let anyone near.
Only I can see
What they have done to me.

Crystal Glass of mine,
Why are you bringing me back to
that living hell,
When I have been doing so well?
What is it you want me to know
About years ago?

Where are my tears,
Of my childhood years?
Mind of the Crystal Glass.
Seeing nothing but my past.
How much longer will it last?

Paula

then—only what she needed to know at present for her healing. We did our guided relaxation exercise, and then had the following dialogue:

Dr. Stone: "Who cut Paula?"

Paula: "Karen, age eight."

Dr. Stone: "Has she ever cut before?"

Paula: "Lots of times."

Dr. Stone: "Why did she cut?"

Paula: "Hurts so much, beaten so bad, one more cut will not matter. Cutting is the only way I can cope."

Dr. Stone: "Beaten by whom?"

Paula: "Dad and his friends."

Dr. Stone: "Why did you separate from Paula?"

Paula: "Beaten up so much, didn't want to feel it anymore. Am locked up in the wall, all alone."

Dr. Stone: "Anyone else there?"

Paula: "Marge, age ten. Others there, locked up. Screaming for help. Can't see their faces."

I inquired what the relationship was between Karen and Marge, and Paula replied that they helped and protected each other. In retrospect, my next question to Paula seems pretty silly. I asked, "Who is stronger, Karen or Marge?" I was trying to figure out how dissociative identity disorder worked in her specific case.

After a pause sufficient to reflect on the absurdity of my question, Paula replied, "We don't compete with each other." Further questioning revealed that Paula could not paint because kids in her inner world were not allowed to play, ever!

Karen had no sense of anyone being present to help her and felt scared and confused. I told Karen that Paula wanted to send her help, but Karen did not believe that. I told Karen that she was safe because her dad was dead and could not hurt her anymore. Karen did not believe that either and told me, "He'll find me."

My head was spinning at finding a part of Paula that did not know about her father's death. This part was still operating under the reality that she was eight years old, and that her father was going to find her and beat her again. I informed Karen that her dad got sick and died. I told her that he and his friends could not hurt her anymore, fully believing that I was speaking the truth. At the time, I did not know that in her belief system, a malicious earthbound spirit could continue to abuse her just as the person had done while living. I told Karen that the rules had changed and kids could play now. I encouraged her to learn how to play to help stop the pain. The next time she felt like cutting, I suggested she paint instead. She agreed to try to remember to paint instead of cut.

Decision

At this point, I felt like I was in way over my head. In my bones, I felt the abject terror in this child part of Paula and with shock realized how different Karen's worldview was from mine or Paula's. Was I doing the right thing? Would she be dead before our next appointment? I had a big clinical decision to make. I knew that people had to be extremely severely abused by or before the age of five for the personality to split and wall off part of itself from awareness. I also knew that when a trauma arose that had an emotional charge that

On the Line

My life is on the line.
No fight in me at this time.
The flashbacks have a tight hold,
and I feel very bitter and cold.

I shake with every flashback that
flashes in my head.

And I am wishing I was dead.
Many images are attacking me.
And I want to be free.
Full of anger and hate.
Ending it, I am starting to debate.
Many thoughts of cutting.
A blade would be so inviting.
Many tears, I need to cry,
For I hurt so much inside.
My moods change very fast.
Especially after seeing a little girl
getting slapped.
I wanted to help that little girl.
But my mind went into another
world.
Back into my childhood years
And feeling insecure and full of fear.

Paula

was too great to handle, a person had to either wall it off or go crazy. Building the wall around the memory was the healthier option, but it required a great deal of intelligence and energy to keep the wall in place. Dr. Barker also told us that once a child learns how to make this wall, other traumatic experiences will split off, with a wall of their own.

The DID population is among the most severely traumatized of the people who come for mental health treatment. I was a relatively new therapist, with just over five years of paid clinical experience, and I did not have the specialized training this diagnosis requires. It was definitely outside my scope of practice. My choice was either to refer Paula to a practitioner experienced in working with dissociation or to get the training I needed to be able to continue working with her. In my heart, I wanted to continue seeing her, but I also wanted to do what was best for Paula. I felt totally inadequate to deal with the level of trauma that made Paula self-mutilate and attempt suicide. At that point, I had never heard of energy therapy and only had talk therapy skills and limited training in relaxation methods. I had very little experience working with earthbound spirits and felt frightened by the dark energy around her case material.

Attempted Referral

I tried to refer Paula's case to an expert and made phone calls to other therapists in the area specializing in working with dissociation. Nobody anywhere was taking any new clients with a diagnosis of DID. But I did find a compassionate therapist who was willing to do supervision with me and help me understand how to handle the case. I also found a local chapter of the International Society for the Study of Trauma and Dissociation (www.isstd.org), which had monthly support group meetings I could attend to learn more. They highly recommended the recent book by Judith Herman, *Trauma and Recovery: The Aftermath of Violence—from Domestic Abuse to Political Terror.*

I had been seeing Paula for free because her health insurance did not cover my private practice. I did not mind doing this pro bono work, but my supervisor (whom I paid) told me that this setup was not good for Paula since it made her indebted to me. With the help and support of Paula's psychiatrist, we arranged for me to see Paula in a clinic where our sessions would be covered by her health insurance.

Paula's psychiatrist cautioned me to take care of myself. He told me, "She's a survivor. I'm not worried about her. But I've seen too many therapists working with cases like these get scared and burned out when objects start flying around the room and other supernatural things happen." He asked me to make a two-year commitment to staying with her case to keep continuity of care. Paula and I had established a strong therapeutic bond, so I decided to commit to her case, get more supervision and advanced training in dealing with dissociation, and bring in consultants with expertise as needed. That two-year commitment turned into working with her regularly for twelve and a half years plus some crisis work several years later. I also began studying Frank Putnam's textbook, *Diagnosis and Treatment of Multiple Personality Disorder.*

Paula's Strengths

In the two decades that I worked with Paula, I never found any noteworthy inconsistencies in the information she gave me. She often told me stories and details about her life that were very hard for me to believe at the time, in my naiveté. I thought that surely she had exaggerated parts of the stories or that they had come from an overactive imagination. But over the years we worked together, time after time, the stories stayed the same. Some of them were backed up by events that unfolded, and others I had no way to verify. Several times, Paula was so physically ill that she thought she was dying. Once she even made out her will and planned her funeral. Yet somehow, each time she found a way to pull through. A critic might say that she exaggerated her symptoms, but I believe she truly thought she was dying. I could see and feel her grief at leaving her child.

Eventually, I came to trust that Paula's word was reliable and that she always told the truth, from the point of view of whatever part of her was "out" at the time. Being truthful was part of her deep spirituality, which sustained her. She was dedicated to the spiritual goal of forgiving everyone involved for all that had happened.

Another endearing quality that Paula had was a well-developed sense of humor. She could find something to laugh and joke about even in the most difficult circumstances. One of her standing jokes was that when someone asked her how she was, to avoid lying, she would say, "FINE." To Paula, those initials stood for "*F*rustrated, *I*nsecure, *N*eurotic, and *E*motional!" Another standing joke was that when I asked her what she needed in the moment, she would ask me to bring in a sledgehammer to clobber her to put her out of her misery. I always refused, and then we laughed!

Paula's empathy for others was outstanding. She could feel what other people were going through and always knew the right thing to say. She never tried to make me feel guilty when I would go on a long vacation. Even though I knew my absence would be difficult for her, she would tell me, "You need some time off. Enjoy yourself. I'll be okay."

Session Five: Why so long?

In our fifth session, Paula speculated on why finding the other personalities inside of her had taken so long. She was now in her thirties and just figuring out what had happened in her childhood. She was wary of the situation but wanted to know more to understand the tangle of her own confused and conflicting feelings.

She also gave the additional history that after being raped in her early twenties by a stranger, she had lost the use of her right leg for five years. Severely beaten in this rape, her joints and ligaments had been damaged. At present, she still had physical pain, but she could walk. She reported that the emotional scars from this rape by the stranger were worse than the physical ones. Paula started writing a journal to express and sort out her feelings after this trauma. The following is her first journal entry:

A Cry Out Loud

The tears I cry are real. The rage I am feeling is very strong and very painful.

I no longer feel much like a survivor. Being victimized once again has brought back many painful feelings for me. It has also given me a very poor self-image.

This time the feelings are stronger than ever before. I am feeling very much alone, helpless and overwhelmed.

I keep asking myself, "Why me? What am I doing wrong? Will it ever end for me?"

Feeling frustrated and very empty as I cry, the tears fall heavy at this time.

Please hear what I am not saying. The words just will not come out. Feeling locked behind a wall that I cannot knock down.

I scream, but nothing will come out. I panic at the thought of my weakness and the many fears I have of being exposed. I don't want everyone to know. Afraid of not being accepted by my friends, family, and those I do not know.

Feeling screwed up and not much like a person, wondering if I will ever be the same again.

Before this happened to me, I started

to feel like someone, but now I feel like a nobody. Feeling like I am, reliving my past, and finding it very difficult to cope with it all.

What is wrong with me? Will I ever feel like a real person again?

Rage

Paula had to work on the feelings from the rape for a long time. After five years, a shift came when she was in a "speak out," talking in front of a group in public about what had happened. She shared with the speak-out group a piece she wrote during her recovery:

169

Rage to Recovery

I am a rape victim trying to recover.
I am isolated in a wall of anger, the rage.
Old behaviors return.
Strong feelings of hurting myself versus the quest to end it all.

I cry but no tears fall.
All the bitterness and bad feelings return, tied into one big ball.
The anger turned inwards is the rage that I can recall.

Oh rage, Oh rage, please go away!

I am the victim of it all.
My mind sometimes races, which makes it a struggle to cope and survive with it all.
But I am a survivor and a fighter!

So if you should hear my cry, please be patient with me.
I am just trying to knock down that isolated wall of anger,
the rage I chose to call.

Paula

She was tired of feeling so rotten inside and wanted to get better. Her memory was fragmented, with bits and pieces, some things vivid and others missing. She formed these questions to ask her other personalities:

1. Why have you waited so long to come out?
2. Who else is back there? I really want to know!
3. Why did you separate from Paula?
4. What does Paula need to do for them to trust her?

After going down our relaxation elevator again, we called out Karen. She reported she had separated from Paula to distance from the pain. Karen stated, "All the adults beat me, used me like a toy." Karen was not sure who Paula was, but when I inquired what Paula could do to get her trust, Karen responded, "Don't let me get hurt anymore." She said she wanted the pain to stop and began trembling, with visible emotions of pain coming up, as if she wanted to cry. I told Karen crying was okay and gave her a tissue, but she objected strenuously, "Not okay to cry!" The adults had cut her for crying. When I insisted that the rules had changed and she could show her feelings now, Karen said she had to go.

Marge then came out and reported she had separated from Paula because she did not know how to deal with what had happened. Marge told us, "Nobody cared when I asked for help." She said she was able to come out now because Paula had talked with her. Marge told us, referring to Paula, "She's the adult, and I'm the child stuck inside her." She had some trust in Paula. I asked what she needed, and she responded, "Can't leave the others. Have to take care of them."

Dr. Stone: "Who are you taking care of?"

Marge: "Others more confused than I am."

Dr. Stone: "Who else is there?"

Marge: "Tami, fourteen, she doesn't talk to anybody."

Dr. Stone: "Why doesn't Tami talk?"

Marge: "The pain. They beat her up. The baby. She was pregnant and the baby was stillborn because of the beatings."

Dr. Stone: "Who else?"

Marge: "Katie, age nine. Got burned."

Dr. Stone: "Who burned Katie?"

Marge: "Dad."

Dr. Stone: "Dad died. You are all safe from Dad now. Do you believe me?"

Marge: "Want to."

Dr. Stone: "Anybody else?"

Marge: "Carol, seventeen, very angry. She locks herself up and doesn't talk to anybody either."

Dr. Stone: "Why is Carol so angry?"

Marge: "Friend got shot, died."

Dr. Stone: "What was the friend's name?"

Marge: "Jerry."

Dr. Stone: "Did she see him get shot?"

Marge: "She was upstairs. Because he wouldn't get his uncle the beer, his uncle shot him."

Dr. Stone: "How many are there all together?"

Marge: "Five of us. That's who I'm taking care of, just five of us."

Dr. Stone: "What can Paula do to take care of you and the others?"

Marge: "Not sure."

Dr. Stone: "My name is Barbara. Thank you for talking with me. Anything else?"

Marge: "Hard to cope."

I again encouraged Marge to cope by painting instead of cutting. Since Marge did not know how to play or paint, she agreed to let Paula teach her how. Marge then left, saying, "Gotta go, kids are crying."

As Paula came out of this memory, she asked, "What's this tissue doing in my hand?" She did not remember anything she had said to me. After giving her a synopsis of what her parts had told me, Paula said she remembered Jerry's death because she remembered going to the funeral. She did not remember him getting shot, but she knew booze was involved. Paula remembered a miscarriage at age sixteen from being beaten, but she did not remember losing a baby at age fourteen. Later in therapy we got to detailed accounts of both miscarriages, but Paula was not yet ready to face these feelings at this time. After this session, Paula brought in the following poem:

Hurting in the Soul

So much I hurt in my soul.
I once again no longer feel whole.

My mind goes back in the past. Not sure how much longer I can last.

I feel so much like a failure,
For the impulses once again have won.
And all I want to do is run.

Not feeling safe with my thoughts,
For in the self-destruction, I feel I am caught.

Not able to sleep.
And deep inside I weep.
Not able to let go.
And feeling so bitter and cold.

Feeling too scared to let others in.
This fight, I feel I will never win.
For I feel my broken heart,
And I am not able to make a new start.

The night after Marge introduced Karen, Katie, Carol, and Tami, I had the following dream, which laid out the course of treatment and showed the beneficial results it could have in Paula's life five to ten years down the road.

Barbara's Dream: Transforming Fear

I am with Paula and do healing work with her. We go through each of the split-off personalities, healing each one. We do the ones who got beaten and the one who got burned, stating the offense, expressing the feelings, releasing the feelings, and forgiving everyone by seeing that each perpetrator was also a victim. The one who lost the baby is still carrying around the dead baby—we need to bury that baby. I ask her for help in how to bury the baby. Paula cuts off the feet and wants to bury them first. We finish healing work with four of the personalities but do not yet get to the last one, the angry one.

Paula leaves, carrying a huge pole, about half the size of a telephone pole. I help her navigate crossing the street. Then I want to go back into her house to turn off the light and lock the door, but it is dark, and fear enters. Would someone attack me in the hallway? Something inside of me wants to leave, but my sense of responsibility to the client wins, and I return to the house to lock up. As I step over the threshold of the doorway into the house, instantly time changes from night to bright day, and the house changes from Paula's apartment to a different apartment, with much light in it, white walls, and comfortable white chairs with flower prints on them. I try to find the door to leave but at first can't locate it.

I hear someone coming and panic a little. I find the door and step out. A nice-looking older woman comes out, and I apologize to her for intruding in her house. As she recognizes me and talks with me, I realize that I have landed in a time five to ten years later than before I stepped through the door. I walk down the street and notice things that are different.

The dream points out several facets of healing from dissociation. It guided me in forming a belief system about how healing could work for Paula. Following are some principles of therapy that emerged from the dream:

1. Healing comes to the personalities one by one.
2. The offense needs to be brought to consciousness and stated. Then the emotions locked in the memories need to come to awareness before they can be released.
3. Forgiveness is an essential and powerful part of the healing process.
4. Seeing the perpetrators as victims helps to understand how this kind of abuse can be handed down through the generations. According to Paula, people were forced to join the cult under the threat of death if they refused.

In the dream, we do not get to the angry part. Perhaps neither of us was ready at this point to face the full blast of the anger still burning within Paula from the unspeakable acts that were buried in her memory. The dream shows her leaving therapy not with a chip on her shoulder but carrying half a telephone pole. Imagine how difficult getting close becomes when someone is holding a pole that big! Even though she did a great deal of healing work, she leaves therapy marked by the experience of her abuse and still carrying a heavy weight. The therapist helps her navigate this load.

The next emotion that came up is a very difficult one: *fear*. In the dream, it arises not in the client, but in the therapist. I saw that Paula walked in fear every day of her life, but I did not realize how remembering her past would increase the threat she felt to her personal safety. I did not know at that time that satanic ritual abuse survivors are programmed to self-destruct if they recover their memories of cult activity. The dream was preparing me for the fear I, too, would face in the process of working with Paula and writing her story, but the dream was also letting me know that, as I faced this fear and stepped over its threshold, the situation would change into light.

In the dream, as I go back to Paula's house to turn off the light (to prevent wasting energy she will have to pay for) and lock her door (to secure her psychological space from attack by others), I sense danger and fear for my own safety. This fear gradually came to consciousness as the horror of the nightmare of Paula's past unfolded in the course of our therapeutic work together, and we both experienced harassment and psychic attack from the cult. In the dream, I waver in ambivalence between escaping from the situation so I can be safe and going back into danger to help Paula. My sense of responsibility to her as my client helps me overcome my fear, and I return to lock up her house.

Transforming Fear

As love wins out over fear, I step over a threshold, and night literally turns into day. The home of my client is now very different, beautifully furnished and filled with light. In the dream, I do not immediately realize what has happened, and my first reaction to the change is fear that I am intruding. I could not find the door at first, could not get out of doing the psychological work we were called to do.

The ending of the dream flashes forward five to ten years and shows the improvement that Paula's healing work would make in her psychological situation in the future, drawing more light and beauty into her life. When I had the dream, I did not understand its meaning. I was feeling bewildered and confused by the discovery of five additional people inside Paula and felt muddled by the concept that ten-year-old Marge was taking care of eight-year-old Karen, nine-year-old Katie, fourteen-year-old Tami, and seventeen-year-old Carol, each of whom had a horror story of her own. I only came to understand this dream later, two years into Paula's therapy, when she felt totally overwhelmed by her memories, and I, as her therapist, felt almost totally overwhelmed by fear and feelings of helplessness. I had been studying dreams for the previous fifteen years and living by the Divine guidance they brought into my life. This dream had been sitting in my computer for two years like a letter unopened. I went back to the dream at a time when I was struggling with fear that Paula might commit suicide, and it brought me hope for a positive resolution in our work together.

Session Six

In our next therapy session, Paula reported that flashbacks continued to pour into her awareness, primarily of her father and others abusing her. She reported a lot of "disconnecting," the word she used for dissociation, but she had started to do artwork again. As Karen had disclosed, she was not allowed to cry or express her feelings. She got cut if she cried. Art was a lifeline for Paula. It was a way that she could express her feelings about what happened without getting into trouble with the adults. The different parts of Paula used many different techniques to make their feelings visible.

Artwork Styles

The artwork she brought to our sessions was very different in character depending on which part was doing the drawing. I knew the sketches were hers, because sometimes she did them during the therapy hour. I was amazed how deftly her hand-eye coordination produced the drawing. Sometimes her sketches showed a special technique of drawing, then going back with an eraser to remove some of the pencil. Other drawings showed an abstract portrayal with almost no recognizable facial features. The dynamic jagged movements in the pencil lines convey the chaos of feeling torn apart and the severe fragmentation that comes with dissociation. In other sketches, many tiny faces appeared, personality fragments struggling to emerge, tell their stories, and stop their pain.

Personality Fragments

177

Some parts loved to draw cartoon characters, and others animals: a tiger on the left and a crow on the right. Note the sadness the tiger's eyes convey.

Tiger and Crow

Between this session and the following one, Paula—or rather, one of Paula's parts—cut herself on the forearm three times. Paula did not remember cutting herself and felt no pain from the wound.

Session Seven: Cutting Hand

I felt perplexed and helpless as Paula continued to self-mutilate. I did not know how to prevent her from harming herself. Paula brought in the following poem, which helped me understand why she cut and the emotional release that came to the part who had done the slicing of her arm.

Cutting Hand

It's the release I use to go on,
So I can be strong.

This release gave me so much relief.
The fog is starting to clear,
And I am shedding my tears.

Identifying my feelings,
Feeling strong enough to deal
With the cards I have been dealt
And letting others know how I felt.

I will not let them pull me down
once more!
I will find my cure,
My anger turned into rage.
My feelings were locked in a cage.

With the edge, I cut into the skin.
Relief I felt once again
No one understands truly that cut-
ting hand.

Needed to release,
For I was not feeling at peace.
The edge was smooth.

Paula

Although I hated seeing one more scar on Paula's arm, I also remembered that from times of antiquity up to the late nineteenth century, bloodletting was a common medical practice. In ancient Greece, physicians believed that bloodletting balanced the body's "humours"—blood, phlegm, black bile, and yellow bile. The shock bloodletting produces in the body actually has an indirect medical benefit of arousing the body's defense system, but overall, the practice is generally harmful to a patient's health.

CHAPTER 7

Tami's Memories

Session Eight: Joseph's Abortion

D uring the next therapy session, Paula used our elevator relaxation technique to connect with the internal part that
had cut. Marge told us that Karen and Katie had cut Pau-
la's arm. Katie had tried to hurt Paula lots of times before. Marge reported,
"One time she took a whole bottle of pills. Katie wants to kill herself." Katie
would not talk and she was angry because she felt that nobody cared. I asked
Marge just to hold Katie and explained to the system that since Katie was sharing the same body with Paula and Marge, if she killed herself, all of the others
who shared the body would die, too.

Marge then said she was worried about Tami, so I asked Tami to come and
talk. I could see Paula cradling her stomach as she was connecting with Tami,
who was fourteen years old, so I gently inquired, "Tami, are you holding your
baby in your arms?"

Tami began to cry. She was not ready to let go of her baby yet. We worked on giving her baby a name to honor his importance in her life. Tami chose to name this little boy Joseph. I asked if she were ready to let go of him to bury him, but she objected, "No! Can't! I don't want to lose him." She could not bring herself to let go, so I asked what she wanted to say to Joseph. She wept, "I'm sorry." Tears flowed from her eyes as she told the story. She had tried to protect Joseph, but her uncle and cousin beat her to abort the child. She asserted, "NOT FAIR! He never had a chance."

Beaten

Tami blamed herself for Joseph's death because she could not get out of the house when she realized the perpetrators intended to beat her. She had tried to escape but could not. I tried to comfort her by reflecting that she had done the best she could. When I asked whether she could forgive herself for not being able to get out of the house, she just sobbed. I reflected to her that she never had a chance either. Noticing her fists were clenched, I inquired who she wanted to hit. Tami responded, "I hate them!" Tami wanted to beat the uncle and cousin who had beaten Joseph to death.

Next I asked another extremely naïve question: "Tami, who was Joseph's father?" Paula had been raped by so many men that she could not distinguish which perpetrator had fathered the baby. I inquired what she needed to stop her pain—did she want them to be beaten, or did she want to let them go? Tami replied that she had to go. I let her know I would pray for Joseph. Tami cried for a while, and then Paula switched to Marge.

I asked Marge to hold Tami's hand and thanked her for the big job she was doing holding Karen and Tami. Marge was also trying to paint. Marge reported she had trouble sleeping, so I suggested that to help her relax, she could watch her breath going in and out of her body. Marge reported she was "trying to hang on," and I added that we were trying to give her more to hang onto! Paula came out of this conversation with partial memory of what had happened, remembering the feeling of how mad she was at the men who beat her and caused her baby to abort. Later as she had integrated more of her memories, she remembered that the beating started without being tied, and then they tied her up, blindfolded her, and aborted the fetus. She also noted that she had split twice: once because of the pain, and then Tami split again and some other part came to do the healing of her physical body. She did not know who this other part was, but she felt that she had often done a double split.

Quitting Her Job

Between this session and the next one, a part of Paula called up the place where Paula worked part time and quit her job. Because Paula had no memory of this action, she felt terribly embarrassed when her employer called her back and told her they were not letting her quit! In our next appointment, we called out the one who had quit the job. It was Tami who did not like that job. After all, how many fourteen-year-olds like to work? Tami's body hurt all over from the memory of her abortion, and she just wanted to quit and go be with Joseph.

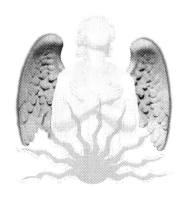

CHAPTER 8

Jesse's Memories

etween sessions, Paula continued to dissociate. A walled-off part of Paula that she did not know would jump into the driver's seat of her mind, unbeknownst to Paula, and do things outside of Paula's awareness. Paula experienced these episodes as "losing time," when she would disconnect from awareness of what she was doing and sometime later would find herself in a different place with no memory of how she got there. During one of these dissociative episodes since our last session, she cut herself again, this time on the left wrist. Another time, she dissociated and then "reconnected" to find herself at the graveyard, kicking her dad's grave. I sensed the chaos rising and felt very concerned about Paula's continued self-mutilation. I dug out the notes from my doctoral course on multiple personality disorder and pored over them, searching for some foothold into healing. My notes said that until the core personality was integrated with the personality who was out most of the time, chaos would reign. I certainly felt the chaos!

I did not know how to do an integration of different parts since Paula was the first client in my caseload with a dissociative disorder who was ready to work on the issue. Between sessions with Paula, I was furiously reading about dissociation to figure out how to facilitate integration between parts.

Session Nine: Jesse

Since the core personality plays such a critical role in the healing process, I talked with Paula about finding her core, the part of her that was present when she was born.

> There is one, and only one, core. She is the original person born with the body. She can't die or cease to exist unless the body dies. And she can't abdicate her position to another part....The core owns the dissociative system, the entire inner world.[1]

Paula agreed to ask for her core. We went inside again to talk with Marge, who reported she was having trouble controlling the parts. I asked Marge who was there first, when Paula was born. Marge did not know the name but said the core part was sixteen years old and kept "comin' and goin'."

We called out this part and asked to speak with her, inquiring, "What is your name?"

Paula's posture shifted to a hunched position reflecting extreme sorrow. In a deep, low voice, her core personality spoke her name: "Jesse." She began to weep quietly. I inquired how old she was and she said she was sixteen. I introduced myself and asked to get to know her. I inquired what she was crying about right now, and she responded, "I don't know who I am anymore."

Jesse felt hopeless and coped by getting high. She wanted to become numb. She did not know who Paula was and did not know the names of any of the others. I introduced the idea to Jesse that she was sharing the same body with Paula and others. I talked about trying to understand what was happening

---

1 Karjala, *Understanding Trauma and Dissociation*, 26.

184

and putting the pieces back together. I talked with Jesse about reconnecting with Paula when she was ready. I asked Jesse, "How do you feel right now?"

She replied, "Tryin' to kill me." She experienced the self-mutilation and suicide attempts of the other parts as attempts on her life—an accurate assessment! I talked with Jesse about wanting her to be safe and let her know that we were trying to get the others to stop their attempts to kill her. I spoke with her about her importance as the one who was there first. I asked whether she was ready to get together with Paula, the adult part who wanted to get to know her better. She did not know whether she would be able to reconnect. I assured her there was no hurry, and we would wait until she was ready and would check again at our next session. I could see by the pained expression on her face that she hurt a lot. Jesse told me that she did not want to live because "the pain just won't stop."

I asked, "Who is hurting you, Jesse?"

Hit with a Fist and Cut with a Beer Bottle

185

She replied, "Emily." I asked to speak with Emily but got no answer. I inquired how old Emily was, and Jesse replied, "She's not here now."

Confused, I asked, "But how old is she? Is she gone? Is she going to come back?" I thought at first that Jesse was being hurt by another part of herself. It took me awhile to figure out that Jesse was frozen in the past at age sixteen and was still feeling the hurt one of her perpetrators had caused her. Finally, Jesse told me that Emily was her aunt, who was still living. I asked how Aunt Emily had hurt her.

Jesse's face formed expressions of extreme pain as she replied, "Broken glass on me all the time. Stuck things in me." Jesse revealed that Emily had constantly stuck things into her, including sticking a broken beer bottle into her vagina.

When I heard that Aunt Emily had raped Jesse with a broken beer bottle, I felt enraged at this abuse and was overcome with vicarious traumatization from simply hearing the story. Later I learned that Paula's perpetrators purposely hurt Paula internally, where it would not show to the outside world, to avoid having the abuse discovered. Jesse was making a fist, showing her anger toward Emily. She was still feeling the pain from that abuse.

Aunt Emily was still in Paula's life. While she was not really a blood relative, her family had pretended that her major perpetrators were relatives and called them aunts, uncles, and cousins. The last time Jesse had seen Emily was the previous year, after her father's funeral. Jesse spoke fluent German and came out at

Anger toward Aunt Emily

the funeral to talk with her German-speaking relatives. When she saw Emily, she ran.

Jesse knew that her dad was dead because she had been out at the funeral. The parts that were not out at the funeral did not know he had died. Jesse felt both angry with her father and also glad that he was dead so he could not abuse her anymore. She said she just did not want to feel anymore. I thanked Jesse for talking with me, and she promised not to hurt herself until we talked again in our next session.

Marge came out, and I explained the situation with Jesse to her. I asked if anyone else needed to talk with me. Marge cried and said that taking care of them was too hard for her, lamenting, "They're just all out of control, angry. I don't know what to do anymore." She wanted the internal pressure to stop.

Marge Caring for Other Parts

Next we called on the angriest one of all, the one who had just cut Paula several days ago. Karen came out, age eight, and admitted she was the one who had been kicking Dad's grave. She wanted him to pay for all the pain he had caused her. Karen felt overwhelmed with her anger and did not know what to do with it. I asked her to yell out what she wanted to say to her dad, but she refused: "Can't. I'm scared!" I asked whether she knew Paula, and she said she had heard the name. I explained to her that she shared a body with others, and when she hurt herself, she hurt the others, too. That concept was new to her. I asked her to promise not to hurt herself until we talked again at our next session, and she said she would try.

Session Ten: Values

In this session, Paula expressed concern about reconnecting with Jesse, for fear that Jesse might take over and not respect her values. Paula defined her values as follows:

1. Contracting for safety. I want to stay alive, so I don't want a suicidal part to be in control.
2. Caring for my daughter.
3. Staying sober.
4. Caring about other people.

We did the progressive relaxation exercise again and called out Jesse, who did not remember who Paula was. We explained again that they shared the same body, and Jesse was the one who was there when Paula was born. We talked with Jesse about Paula's values and her need for Jesse to promise that she would not hurt herself. Jesse could not promise. She replied, "I've tried, can't stop the pain. Everybody's hurt me over and over again. Can't take anymore."

Jesse felt that her family wanted her dead. I talked with her about the abuse and let her know that she was sixteen, but Paula, the one she shared a body with, was in her thirties. "The body that you share with Paula is a big body, a strong body. You are here now, because something inside of you is strong. Something inside has stood up all this time. And I want you to get even stronger by getting together with Paula. Two can be stronger than one." Jesse seemed wrapped up in her own trauma and had difficulty taking in this information.

Jesse countered, "I'm no good." When I asked who told her she was no good, she responded, "All the adults around me." Framing her abuse as an intergenerational problem, I let Jesse know that the body she shared with Paula had given birth to a baby, now a precious little girl. I talked about making the future different and about how strong she was to have survived all she went through; however, Jesse did not feel she had any strength. She just wanted to die to stop her pain and could not think of anything important to her in life. She did not believe that stopping the pain was possible and did not trust Paula, saying, "She wants something so she can take something."

Jesse's Baby

Jesse began crying and started to breathe heavily. As I talked about how Paula wanted to live to care for her baby and to help other people, Jesse began to cry harder. She was cradling her arms on her belly as if holding something and reacted every time I mentioned the word "baby." When I asked if she had lost a baby, she cried harder. I inquired what happened to the baby. She replied, "Didn't make it full term." The baby had been five months old when she lost it. I asked how she lost the baby, and she did not answer, but her face showed evidence of severe pain that went beyond words.

Pain Beyond Words

189

Over the course of the next several sessions, the fragments of Jesse's memories came together in a clear picture of what had happened to her. Jesse remembered four people present at the abortion: Aunt Emily plus three male relatives. Jesse said, "Emily aborted the baby with a broken glass. She stuck her whole hand in and pulled the baby out. The three guys held me down and beat me when I tried to get away. It feels like my shoulders are broken. Last night it felt like it was happening: it fades in and out. *They took a part of my life!*"

The abortion caught Jesse by surprise. She was five months' pregnant and had been feeling life in her belly for the previous month. The sensation was strange, but she had accepted this pregnancy at age sixteen and hoped that the baby was her key to getting out of that abusive house. She thought, "Wow, I'm going to give life!" She was very scared when they grabbed her in her bedroom and did not know what was happening. The smell of booze was strong in the air, and she saw one of the men take a couple of drug injections. One of the men nailed down her shoulders and head and kept punching her. Another held down her arms and another pinned down her legs. Whenever she broke free, they kept punching her. She did not realize what was happening until she felt Emily cut through her uterus with the beer bottle. She was feeling the physical pain of being cut as she told the story. They slashed her breasts. One cut underneath, and one on top. Before the abortion, they pulled the tip of one nipple up and hacked it off as if they were using an axe. They amputated the tip of the other nipple after the abortion. One of the men said, "I've sucked this and no one else is going to." Paula had always thought something was wrong with her because she did not have normal nipples. Part of her nipples grew back, but their tips were inverted. She suffered constant pain in her breasts. As the memory explained her anatomical scars, she exclaimed, "They were fuckin' deranged!"

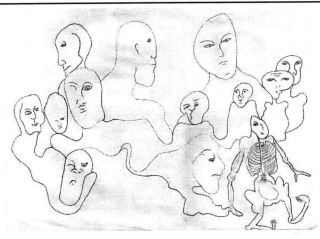

Skeletons

Faceless to the eye.
Yet hurting and terrified inside.
Many skeletons from my youth fill
my head.
With voices wishing I was dead.
Skeletons with any missing parts.
Pulling and tearing my heart.

Many of their missing parts dig
away, trying to destroy my soul.
And many others still trying to
unfold.
Many bones are shattered.
And others are scattered.

The painful fear that stops my tears.

Locked doors, with many unseen
sores.
Many fists flying.
Drunks drowning themselves in a
bottle.
Stopping themselves from crying.
Inflicting so much pain
And teaches the darkest violence
and shame.
Leaving me feeling an emptiness
that I cannot explain.
Feeling an angerful rage, that I
have felt before, and
Feeling very insecure,
For every sound triggers them even
more.

Jesse felt scared and very empty after Emily pulled the fetus out from her slashed uterus. As she was bound and forced to watch what was happening to her baby, Jesse disconnected from Paula. They put the baby on stick stilts, poured kerosene over it, and burned it. Then Jesse lost consciousness and did

191

not see what they did with the baby's charred body. As they did the abortion, they were talking in a language she could not understand. She had learned Spanish and German to survive, but this language was different. Paula said it might have been tongues. I did not understand what she was saying when she said the word "tongues" and asked her to repeat it three times. I had been listening for the name of a language and was slow to finally catch on. When she explained that it was tongues like the early Christians spoke and current charismatic groups today speak, I was confused. I asked, "Isn't speaking in tongues just used in worship services?"

Paula replied, "Yes. Three of them were devil worshippers. They dressed in black all the time. Seven of the perpetrators always had the same clothes on, basic black. They were talking in tongues during the attacks on me. Fire was always involved. When they aborted the baby, Emily said, 'We're doing this because we love you. You deserve it.' But they never gave a reason why. They always said I was 'the prize.'" She reported that eighteen or nineteen perpetrators were involved in this cult, with seven in the black dress and others in street clothes. In her bedroom was a white table with a cross on it with seven red and black candles around it. "The cross was not normal—it had no Jesus on it. Sticks were tied with a rope, but it wasn't put together where it should have been. The top part was too long.[2] A lot of strange things would happen in that room. Books flew around, and once my statue of the Virgin Mary flew off the shelf and went out the window. Then I got blamed for throwing it out the window."

Paula continued pouring out the information that had been hidden behind the walls of dissociation. "Objects moving around scared me at first, but then I got used to it. All of the sexual abuse happened in my bedroom, the cellar, or the shed. The physical abuse happened anywhere. I was told not to tell anyone. They said nobody would believe me if I told. They were always saying they would kill me. They told me, 'Don't let me get my hands on you or I'll kill you.' I was the target, sacrificed all the time." Paula claimed that she used to believe in the God she was taught at church, but because things were so deranged at home, she did not feel she belonged in church anymore. "I ba-

---

2 The inverted cross is the generic symbol for Satanism, representing the antithesis of all that Christianity stands for.

sically don't worship anything. I have faced so much; nothing has any value or meaning to me." She reported she was pronounced dead seven times from blood clots during a hospitalization a number of years earlier. She felt angry that she came back. "Actually, I do believe in something, but I just call it my 'Higher Power.'"

We worked on using her belief system to center herself with the help of her Higher Power so she would not get so carried away by the flashbacks. I pointed out that story of Christ that she was taught in school was also an innocent person who died, like Jesse's baby.

Paula reported that people believe every apartment she has ever been in has had a ghost. Strange things had always happened around her, and a variety of poltergeist activity was occurring in her present apartment: doors opening up when they were closed tight, things falling off the wall, objects moving around, and lights switching on and off for no reason. Aunt Emily was always into witches and warlocks, and Emily's lesbian partner, Nel, was also a perpetrator and wore only black. When Paula came back out after connecting to these memories, she reported that she had not known how she lost her baby at sixteen. She exclaimed, "How could they get away with all that?"

Killing Animals

Memories of abuse continued to pour out from Paula and the parts she had integrated. She loved animals and would rescue injured cats and flying squirrels and nurse them till they were ready to go free again. The cult made her kill her beloved pets, both the ones she had rescued and the ones she raised from young. She recalled a memory where the cult beat her and then raped her with several of them having sex with her at one time. Then four of them held her, put a knife in her hand, and "made me kill my cat. They made me cut her stomach open and drink her blood. She was pregnant." This cat was the runt of the litter she had saved and nursed to health, and it was the cat's first pregnancy. The babies were not alive when Paula saw them. To induce false guilt, they told her she had killed her cat and the kittens. She felt so ashamed that she had taken the lives of her pets. We reviewed the facts of the case, which were that their hands were over hers on the knife, and they had forced the knife into her cat. I said that they did it and were responsible, not her. They also forced her to kill the two bunnies she had been taking care of for the school.

Paula exclaimed again, "I just want this nightmare to end!"

Hurting Inside

Hurting inside
and wanting to hide.
I no longer ask why
Therefore I cry.

But yet I have the will to try.

To try to be the person I once was.

The person I feel I need to be.
That person I let people see.
Hurting inside.
It's another rollercoaster ride.
The pain is real.
Therefore I feel
Angry, confused, frustrated, alone...
So I pick up the phone.

Hurting inside.
A never ending fight.
Many sleepless nights.
My mind races.
Needing to see familiar faces.
Hurting inside.
Feeling like I don't belong.
So I sing a song
Hoping I can be strong.

Paula

Just before she was ready to set the animals free, her perpetrators would make her kill them. "Any sign of freedom was destroyed. Usually, they put the dead pet in a box afterward and took it away. They painted on me with the blood in areas where I couldn't see."

She had only one dog, named Boomerang. "She always showed up when I was in trouble. She would walk me to school and back, meeting me after school. Once Boomerang attacked my brother when he was trying to wake

Boomerang

me up, and another time Boomerang attacked my father when he was going to hit me. The dog would not let anyone close to me and would snarl even when my mother got close."

Paula's mood changed as she began talking about her dog. She calmed down, regained her usual speaking voice, and was able to laugh again. After the family was burned out, she had to give Boomerang away, but she kept finding where Paula lived again. She joked that she was like Boomerang, always coming back.

Trying to Protect the Animals

195

Later in her therapy, when she had gained more strength, she remembered her father bringing her a baby flying squirrel that had broken both its hind legs falling from the nest. He brought it to Paula to heal. I commented on how out-of-character this action seemed for her father. Paula said they were planning to let the squirrel attach to her and then sacrifice it, but she released it just in time. She noted this change in finding memories now in which she was not always the victim. She said she was changing her attitude!

Healing of Memories

Jesse believed in God, so we did an intervention called "healing of memories" that I learned from the writing of Ruth Carter Stapleton[3], sister of President Jimmy Carter. I asked Jesse to go back into her memory of the sacrifice of her child and to see it coming out differently. This time, the men untied her and the baby came out naturally, alive and smiling. I asked her to see God taking the baby into his arms and taking the baby up to heaven to a special place just for innocent little babies. Jesse calmed down as she was able to visualize the baby being safe with God, and playing with Joseph, the baby that Tami lost.

At the session following this intervention, Paula could not believe that the murder of Jesse's child really happened. We played that part of the previous session's tape to give it more reality. Paula was able to tolerate listening till the part where I asked if she had seen the baby coming out. Then she asked me to turn the tape off, saying, "The only thing I can see about the baby is that God took the baby out to avoid the baby getting beaten or abused, like they did to me."

Speaking Out

Paula's daughter was never involved in any cult activities, but when she was eight years old, she was raped by a man unrelated to the family or the cult. Paula pressed charges against the rapist, who went to jail. I told Jesse how Paula had decided to speak out against violence. I read Jesse this poem Paula wrote:

---

3 Stapleton, *The Experience of Inner Healing.*

196

Forced into Silence

Forced into Silence.
Taught nothing but violence.

After the violence came to an end,
I kept silent even to my closest
friend.

I made an escape.
Years later I was raped.
And someone opened the door,
Silent I was no more.

I started to recover.
From one,

Then the other.

But my pain does not stop there.
For within a year,
My daughter became a victim.
And that took me into the court
system.

Once forced into silence.
These days I am against violence.
Silent no more
People will hear my roar.

Paula

CHAPTER 9

Katie's Memories

Solstice Ceremony Part One

Two days after this session with Jesse, Paula called in a state of turmoil, having difficulty speaking because of the emotional trauma she was experiencing. Katie came out, remembering that when she was nine years old, on the evening before the winter solstice, her perpetrators first chased her with a live, harnessed gray rat. Then they cut off the rat's head and tried to make her eat the rat head raw. They had a knife to her throat and sliced her, but she refused to eat the rat. They told her, "Your life is ours."

They put something black and sticky all over her, and her father lit a match. Her whole left side went up in flames. She rolled to put the fire out. They put a circle of red candles around her and took off her clothes. The perpetrators were all dressed in black with their faces painted white, with flames painted in red-orange on sides, cheeks, and temples. Only one face was painted different-ly—black with an eye etched into the center of the forehead, slightly below the midline. It was a woman, probably Nel, Emily's partner. This person wrapped a cloth around a stick, lit it on fire, and rammed the stick into her vagina. Katie was feeling the flames in her physical body as she shared this memory. They did not talk during the process, they just laughed. She remembered hearing the church bells ringing twelve times at midnight.

After burning Katie, they tied up her arms and legs into a ball and locked her up in her bedroom closet. She really hurt and could not get out. No light was in the closet except a crack under the door at times. They often locked her up in that closet, usually after seriously hurting her, and would leave her there for a long time. Sometimes she saw visions of a bright light, but she could not go into the Light because she heard the kids crying and had to stay in her body so she could get back out and see what was wrong.

Katie's Anger

Katie felt angry and wanted to hit something hard. With a bit of encouragement, she began to hit the pillow on the chair, gently at first, and then pounding the pillow with both hands. She made punching motions into the air with her fists, sobbed violently and cried out, "I hate you; I hate you!"

After venting her anger, I pointed out to Katie that the rules had changed. Before, she was not allowed to cry. Now crying her pain out was good. I asked, "Can you say, 'It's good to cry'?"

She replied, "Can't say it."

I asked, "Then can you say, 'It's okay to cry'?"

Finally, after much coaching, Katie timidly said, "It's…okay……. to………………….cry."

Instinctive Reaction

The following morning Paula found shallow cuts on her leg. She was not sure who had done it but figured it was a left-hander, maybe Katie. The cuts did not hurt. That afternoon a person in her day program came up behind her suddenly and touched her. Paula reacted instinctively and hit the person in the face, causing a bloody nose. Paula felt terrible about this incident, because one of her highest values was not to hurt others.

Solstice Ceremony Part Two

That evening she remembered the ceremony done on the winter solstice. She had lost consciousness in the closet many times and did not remember being taken out, but she saw bubbles all over her left side.

> **Note:** Paula's body had burn scars on both arms, with the ones on the left side darker than those on the right. Paula had previously thought that the scars from her left elbow up to the under arm were from her arm being stuck to a hot stove, a burn which happened around that same age. With this memory, she realized where these scars came from. Although some scars appear only when the part is out who experienced the trauma, these burn scars were always on Paula's arms, and I could clearly see them, too.

When she regained consciousness, she was tied down naked and was surrounded by thirteen people dressed in costumes. The head person wore a solid red cape and pants that looked like a jumpsuit. The others wore white jumpsuits without the cape. A peg from the ceiling dripped blood all over her. Black candles a few inches apart surrounded her in a circle. The person in red slashed her face with a wire. Then he told three of them to take their clothes off but to leave on their masks. All of the participants raped her.

At this point in the narrative, Katie had to stop talking because she was coughing and gagging from the memory: she was raped vaginally, rectally, and orally all at the same time. The experience felt sick and painful, and she was scared. This was the earliest rape memory she had recovered. The perpetrators said no words while they violated her—they only laughed. Then they burned her again. She felt fire in her vagina and face as she told the story. When they burned her the second time, she felt helpless. She described the pain of the second burning as "beyond what anyone could ever go through." Third-degree burns covered three-quarters of her body. The tremendous pain produced a torrent of hate and rage and made her dissociate. Twice Katie saw the Light, first in the closet and then when they burned her the second time. She simultaneously saw something darker than dark and a very bright light. She just ran for the brightest light there was. It covered her, went inside her, and then like an invisible shield coming over her, all the pain stopped.

As Paula integrated Katie's memories, she felt that the perpetrators had succeeded in warping her mind because she felt such hate and rage for them. A big part of her wanted to go and find them. Her revenge fantasy was to cut off the testicles of the men and to burn the perpetrators like they had burned her. She felt ashamed at being part of this violence and ashamed that she was still alive. They indoctrinated her to feel that she was the one to blame for what happened to her. She felt that she stayed alive only to suffer, adding, "All I'm doing is suffering!" Paula felt that Katie's memories explained why she was always getting boils and cysts in her vaginal area and also the physical problems Paula had when she gave birth to her daughter. Paula had an asthma attack right after Megan was born. Eight hours later, a cyst above her uterus burst, and she hemorrhaged.

Solstice Synchronicity

When I counted back from Paula's current age to the year when she would have been nine, I remembered that specific night extremely well because it was the night I gave birth to my firstborn child. I shared this synchronicity with Paula. With her characteristic ability to recover from the darkest depths of agony and use her sense of humor to make me laugh, Paula quipped, "We were both in pain!" Something locked into place within me with this realization—knowledge of a deep soul bond between Paula and me. The birth of my first child was the most wonderful and amazing experience of my life. Some pain was involved, but the labor and delivery went extremely well. That very same night Paula was having one of the most traumatic experiences of her life. I realized that Paula and I were partners in healing traumatic patterns. She had her role and special gifts and I had mine. In prayer and meditation, I saw a vision that, before either of us were born, a call went out in heaven showing these dark practices and asking for volunteers to go to Earth and work to end this nightmare. I saw us both volunteering for our respective roles.

Paula's Coping Strategies

Paula used to hide straws in that musky, moldy, damp closet and would work them into her mouth even though she was tied up. She put the end of the straw under the door to get some air. After the perpetrators took her out of the closet the second time, her grandmother got buckets of water blessed by the priest. Paula healed her own burns by wrapping herself in cloth soaked in this holy water, and the burned skin just peeled off.

Paula already had learned to quiet her mind by attending to her breathing in meditation. She had also worked with crystals. During our next session, she used the technique of visualization to "program" a clear quartz crystal to siphon off the pain from the memory into the crystal with the out-breath, to let the crystal transform the pain into strength at the place between the out-breath and the next in-breath, and then to return that energy to her as strength with the in-breath—breathing in strength and breathing out the pain.

Her perpetrators had told Paula that she was a witch. I asked if she believed them and, with a straight face, Paula replied, "No, I'm a bitch!" Then she burst out laughing, and we had a good belly laugh together. She reflected that her daughter's rape had felt much worse than her own rapes. "I may be fragile in a way, but I can take anything. Do it to me but don't hurt my baby!"

Paula never passed on any of the abuse. She never physically or sexually abused any of the kids she cared for. She decided early, "I'm never going to hurt anybody because I know how much it hurts." She turned to alcoholism during her teenage years to numb the intensity of the pain of her own abuse. When she knew that more abuse was coming, she would sometimes smoke marijuana so she could split from the experience and separate from its pain.

Paula added that the sexual abuse was very confusing. Her "aunts" had started abusing her before the men did. She enjoyed part of the sexual activity, but other parts of it were abusive. Her aunts used to do things to her and then laugh at her. Sometimes she preferred their touch to the touch of the men, and for a while she wondered if she were a lesbian. Aunt Emily used to grab Paula and coach the male adults on how to perform abusive sex—"Real sick." If they did not do it right, then Aunt Emily would do it to Paula.

Her father knew all the cops, and he was always tipped off before the police would come to check the house. Most of her family members used illegal drugs. Paula remembered that once the family drugged her and a female cousin and took them down into the cellar. One of the men then "taught" a male cousin and other neighborhood kids how to have sex with them. Another time they started to repeat the process in the cellar, but her aunt stopped them because the police were on their way to check for drugs, and her aunt wanted the kids out of the house and everything in order.

Megan, the Baby Who Survived

Paula did not tell her parents that she had eloped with her husband. When she was twenty years old, the newlyweds moved to California for a while but had so many problems there that they were forced to return. Paula had some trouble functioning in the sexual relationship with her husband, but he was very understanding. If she asked him to stop lovemaking because she could not tolerate sexual intimacy at the moment, he would. She loved him and felt his love for her. The doctor had told her that she could never get pregnant because her uterus was badly damaged. But in spite of the doctor's prediction of infertility, she conceived several months after her marriage. She was already starting her second trimester of pregnancy by the time she found out that a child was growing within her. She refused to believe the doctor when he first told her she was pregnant. She felt amazed when she finally accepted the miracle that this baby had been conceived in love, and survived!

Paula was ill throughout the pregnancy. Her husband's mother died, and he had to return to California to bury her. Because she was too sick to travel, he had to go alone. On the way home, his car went over a cliff because of bad roads and a truck accident. He was killed and was buried in California. Paula was so sick she could not even go to the funeral, an additional hardship for her. She had great difficulty handling this loss on top of the complications of the pregnancy, but she did not show other people these feelings. After her husband's death, she was forced to live with her parents again for the third trimester of her pregnancy. She had no money and nowhere else to go. She stayed with her mother until her daughter was a year old. Nobody abused her during that time, and her father was hardly ever around.

House Fire

The abuse had slowed down after their house caught on fire when she was fifteen, because the fire burned out a couple of buildings where five of the families involved in her abuse lived. When these families were more spread out, they did not come over as often. The fire was set intentionally to cover up someone's death. Paula was worried about all the kids and the old people and managed to get them all out safely. Then members of her fam-

Burning House

ily locked her into a room in the burning house, trying to kill her in the fire. She couldn't get to the door because of the flames, so she jumped out the window.

Paula reported that the family always burned down the house where they were living to cover up evidence of their activities. She reflected, "They got away with murder!"

Strong Therapeutic Bond

Going through these memories together had formed a strong therapeutic alliance between Paula and me. At the end of this session, I made a joke, and Paula laughed and reached over and touched me lightly on the shoulder, the first touch she ever volunteered.

Your friendship I hold so near,
For there is none that can compare.
I know I have a friend in you,
Even when I am feeling blue.

I value you.
So my word to you will always be true.
For your warm, soft voice
Reminds me, I have a choice.

Your friendship I will always hold so dear,
For I know my inner self I can share.
For it's friends like you
That help me get through.

Paula

Friendship

Nightmare

Following this session, one of the parts cut Paula's right arm, requiring another six stitches. She wondered who did it and what was used. She did not like the idea of not knowing what she was doing! She reported the following nightmare:

> I leave where I am and pull into the driveway of the therapy office. Two guys follow me. They grab my hair and talk a foreign language. One starts punching the hell out of my face and stomach. He cuts up my stomach with a knife. Somebody comes, and the other guy kisses me. The faces are blocked out. I jump into my car and drive off.

We talked about the dream, which brought up her fear of being raped again. She stated, "I feel as if I have a sign plastered across my back in neon lights that says, 'Abuse me!'" She felt weary of being dissociated from parts of herself and wanted to integrate with Jesse, her core personality. Since she had just cut herself again with no memory of the event, she did not feel safe from hurting herself. She asked to go into psychiatric hospitalization and wanted to do the integration with Jesse under the protection of the hospital. I made the preliminary calls, and after Paula waited up all night to get admitted, she entered the hospital the following morning. During the night while Paula was waiting to be admitted, I dreamed the following:

> I meet another personality in Paula, "Joy." She is radiant and smiling, with curly blonde hair. I talk with her a bit. She says she doesn't stay long and then she goes. I call her out again and there she is, radiant.

> My own daughter is playing with a tricycle with a wagon attached. I want to be careful going through the trapdoor to the basement. I wonder why she is on the tricycle after she had already graduated to a two-wheeler bike.

I awoke from this dream feeling very positive about the outcome of Paula's hospitalization, hopeful that she could get to a part of herself that until now had been kept in the shadow—JOY! I myself was flooded with joy upon remembering the dream, which strengthened my hope for Paula's recovery. I noticed that Joy did not stay long in the dream, but she could be called out again later.

Take Care!

The second paragraph contained a warning about the traps involved in this work and the need for care when going into the unconscious part of the mind represented by the basement. Entering the unconscious is a delicate, sacred work and is not to be taken lightly—particularly when the personality has been fractured by dissociation. The dream also points out another phenomenon of working with DID. While one part of the personality knows how to function effectively in the world, symbolized by riding a two-wheeler bike, another part of the personality may be fixated at the tricycle stage. In the course of the therapeutic work together, what might appear as regression may instead be connection with a part that had split off at an earlier stage of development.

CHAPTER 10

Integration

To Integrate or Not?

*I*n my doctoral course on dissociation, Dr. Barker had emphasized the importance of connecting the part that was out most of the time to the core personality, the one who was there at birth. He said that chaos would reign in the system until that connection was made because the client needs to build on a firm foundation. My hopes were high that the previous chaos of flashbacks, dissociation, and cutting would recede once Paula, the adult part who was out most of the time, was reconnected to Jesse, her core.

Since Dr. Barker also recommended getting additional supervision with one's first case, I contacted my supervisor at the clinic for an outside referral from an expert in the field. I spoke with this expert, a seasoned psychotherapist, while Paula was in the hospital. She recommended avoiding the use of a relaxation exercise at the beginning of the session to get to deeper parts of the personality. She encouraged me instead just to let whatever parts wanted to come to therapy talk with us. She advised me to give as much control as possible to Paula at all times since feeling out of control had been one of the most difficult aspects of the abuse itself. I filled her in on my client's plan to integrate with her core personality while she was in the protected space of the hospital. The expert warned against doing integration work too soon before an adequate sense of safety had been established in the client's daily life.

I felt conflicted between wanting to follow her professional advice to slow down the integration work and the urge to follow the advice of Dr. Barker to integrate with the core early in the work. The message of my dream seemed to side with reconnecting with Jesse because it promised joy at connecting with other parts. I was naïve about the traps involved, about which both my dream and the expert were warning me. In the end, I decided to leave the decision up to Paula.

Integration Day

I began the session during her hospitalization by talking with Paula about the importance of not rushing integration. Then I asked what she wanted to do. She clearly stated that she wanted to make a connection with Jesse because she was tired of having her life so out of control and wanted to get better. I suggested we first check on who had just cut and found out it was Marge. We recommended other ways for Marge to let out her pain and then came back to Paula. This time I added the suggestion that Paula would stay aware of every-thing that was happening. When she was relaxed, I called out Jesse, letting her know that Paula wanted to talk with her.

I had Paula say hello to Jesse, checked that Jesse had heard it, and then had Jesse say hello to Paula. Facial expression changed dramatically as these two parts of her personality spoke with each other. Whenever Paula the adult was talking, the facial expression was flat, and the voice sounded calm and controlled. Whenever Jesse spoke, the face contorted with pain, and the voice became tearful and shaky. The changes were instantaneous as the conversation went back and forth. Paula asked Jesse to get together with her, but Jesse was unwilling because she was too frightened. I asked Jesse to look at Paula, but Jesse couldn't see her. I racked my brain, wondering what to do next, and then got the idea of asking Jesse to listen for Paula. Then Paula talked with Jesse, and I asked Jesse to repeat everything Paula had said to be sure she was registering what Paula was saying. Jesse comprehended everything Paula said and repeated it exactly. Paula told Jesse she wanted to get together to take care of Jesse. She also told Jesse about her young daughter. Jesse was still unwilling to integrate until I pointed out to her that if they merged, sharing memories, then Jesse would remember having the baby that Paula had, the baby that came out of the body they share. Then Jesse was willing.

Merging Memories

Dr. Stone: "I would like the two of you to hold hands on the inside. Paula, are you willing to accept the memories of Jesse?"

Paula (with flat affect and calm voice): "Yes."

Dr. Stone: "Jesse, are you willing to accept the memories of Paula?"

Jesse (face contorted, voice trembling): "Yes."

Over the next few minutes, I could physically see the process of integration taking place. Paula's facial expression changed to a combination of the two previous looks. No longer was the face carefree and casual like Paula's, but it was not as contorted with pain as Jesse's; it was in the middle of the two extremes. The integration of the two personalities remembered Jesse's trauma, and her body felt weighed down. Paula reported, "I feel pain in the stomach area, vaginal area, head, and neck. I feel as if my head was used as a bowling ball. I still feel split but not as much."

Then Paula wept. She found some of her tears, which had been blocked for decades. This occasion was the first time that Paula had ever cried in front of me, a big emotional breakthrough.

An Ocean of Tears

Body Memories

At the end of the session, she reported, "It was easier than I had expected."

Three hours after reconnecting with Jesse, back in the hospital smoking room, other patients stared at Paula's hands and looked aghast. Paula gazed down and watched her hands turn from purple to black. The hospital staff became frightened and put her into the intensive care unit. They ran numerous tests on her, including a heart monitor, an EKG, and an oxygenation level. However, they could not diagnose the cause of this difficulty. Paula's hands turned black for three hours again on the following day. After she was discharged, the phenomenon repeated itself frequently, once involving both her hands and feet turning color. Once, her oxygenation level dropped, but her blood pressure remained normal. Her arms also discolored.

In her groundbreaking work *Trauma and Recovery: The Aftermath of Violence*, author Judith Herman talked about the central struggle of psychological

211

trauma being the will to deny horrible events and the conflicting will to proclaim them out loud.[1]

> *When the truth is fully recognized, survivors can begin their*
> *recovery. But far too often, secrecy prevails and the story of*
> *the traumatic event surfaces not as a verbal narrative but as*
> *a symptom.*

—Judith Herman

When these symptoms returned several weeks later during Paula's day treatment program, the doctors said it might be a "thermal disorder" and sent her home with a note saying she should "avoid stress." We really laughed at that prescription! Paula and I brainstormed on what the black hands and feet might indicate. She had recovered Jesse's memories of being tied up, many different ways. Paula wondered if the cutoff in circulation might be a result of her body remembering this trauma.

The following week, Paula's hands turned black only once. At the time, I did not know that in some cases of dissociation, onset of physical symptoms frequently accompanies recovery of a memory. These physical symptoms demonstrate the strength of the mind-body connection and perhaps are one of the trapdoors my dream alluded to in entering the basement, which symbolizes the unconscious mind.

More Memories

Paula carried early memories of her mother getting beaten up by her father. Whenever Paula called for help for her mother, she knew she would get the next beating. Her mother did not protect her from her father's physical abuse, Her mother's verbal abuse of her worsened the drunker her mother got. Others in the family called Paula a slut and a whore and were always insulting her, blaming her for everything.

----

1   Herman, *Trauma and Recovery*; http://www.uic.edu/classes/psych/psych270/ PTSD.htm

After a family gathering one Easter, her mother was not feeling well (the usual pattern) and retired to another room. Her father, who was very drunk, grabbed Paula, overpowered her, and raped her. Knowing how to turn the pain off, she did not feel anything during the rape itself. Paula added that being raped by her father, a person she knew, felt "more comfortable" than the rape later by a stranger. Paula was in her early twenties when her father raped her, and she pressed charges against him. Her father knew everybody at court, and Paula thinks he paid them off to get out of the charges. At the same time, she was taking her daughter's perpetrator to court and having a lot of trouble with blood clots—many stressors all at once.

When I asked Paula to contract for safety from harming herself, she replied, "I never feel safe." She could not ever remember a feeling of safety, even as a small child. She was constantly feeling as if she were going to get beaten up again. She was hearing voices clamoring, "We want blood," and she was flashing back to images of the knives and baseball bats they used to beat her and cut her.

Swans

I advised Paula to talk back to the voices, saying, "Be quiet! Enough of this blood has been spilled to last a lifetime. I don't deserve any more of this!" We talked about reprogramming the ideas of low self-esteem that had been drilled into her and seeing her true value instead.

In her next session, Paula brought in five new drawings she had done the previous week. Her creative channel opened up again after having felt blocked for so long. The swan drawing below shows a new style, perhaps with the two swans representing the integration of Jesse and Paula.

Paula awakened during the night after this therapy session, hemorrhaging badly from her uterus. She did not want to go for a gynecological exam, which would seem too much to her like getting raped again. Memories of Jesse's abortion had come back crystal clear, and Paula was having trouble keeping herself in control.

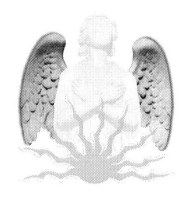

CHAPTER 11

Carol's Memories

With the floodgate of memories opened up from Jesse's integration, flashbacks continued to thrust themselves into Paula's awareness, complete with body memories. She was bleeding from her rectum, and her stomach was swollen. She was in severe pain from her navel down, feeling as if she were carrying three babies. She had to go to the hospital several times because of the bleeding, and on one of these trips, she bumped into Aunt Emily in the bathroom. Aunt Emily drooled, "Oh, Paula," so sickeningly sweetly that Paula felt furious. Aunt Emily had broken her foot and was dying to get out of the hospital so she could "get a few more beers" into her.

Paula figured out that she must have switched and punched the wall, because her hand was swollen. Several hours later, her girlfriend walked into the kitchen and saw Paula pulling a hot cast-iron pan out of the oven with her bare hands. Paula had first and second degree burns on the fingers of both hands—but no pain from these burns.

Eyewitness to Murder

Over the weeks that came, bits of memory pieced together the full story of the seventeen-year-old part named Carol seeing her fourteen-year-old friend Jerry murdered. Jerry was mentally retarded, with the mind of a six-year-old, and could not speak correctly. He was kindhearted and helped everyone. He was great with kids, carried in groceries, and shoveled snow. "He was one of the greatest kids around and probably one of my only friends. He would do anything for you."

Friends of the family, including cult members, were having a drinking party downstairs at the home of "Uncle Matt." Paula was upstairs taking care of the kids. Uncle Matt ordered Jerry to go upstairs and get him another beer. Paula had just come downstairs with four bottles in her hands to mix formula for the babies. Normally, Jerry would have brought Uncle Matt the beer; however, that night Matt's wife saw how drunk he was getting and told Jerry in the kitchen that if Uncle Matt asked for another beer, to say no. When Jerry followed her orders and refused to get the beer, Uncle Matt picked up his gun and shot him in the head, seconds after Paula had entered the room.

Jerry Being Shot in the Head

She was about three feet away from Jerry, almost in the line of fire. She saw a brief look of fear cross Jerry's face and heard the bullet go by her left ear. It hit Jerry in the right temple and went clear through his head and out the other side. He spun to the right and dropped, dying instantly and splattering his blood all over her and the walls. She first dissociated when his blood hit her. The emotional impact of the death of her friend was greater than her consciousness could bear, and she formed another personality named Carol to carry this trauma. Part of the inside of Jerry's head was also on the walls. Carol went and held his lifeless body.

Then the adults beat Carol with an antenna on her back, face, and legs and told her, "You're next." At first she was in shock, then enraged, and then petrified because the gun was still loaded. As the pain of the abuse escalated, she reached a point where she *hoped* Uncle Matt would shoot her. During Carol's beating, the perpetrators told her that if she opened her mouth, they would kill her, but not like Jerry—a slow death.

Several neighbors reported the gunshot to the police, who sneaked up and then barreled through the doors. When the police arrived, Carol was being beaten, wearing only her un-

Flashback of Jerry Getting Shot

derpants. The police took her out of the home and locked her up in protective custody. Neither Paula nor Carol remembered going to court, but Uncle Matt went to prison on a life sentence for first-degree murder. He served fifteen years and then got out on parole.

Intense anger came as Carol remembered the tragedy of Jerry's murder. Paula has a special love and respect for people like Jerry who are physically or mentally challenged. She felt killing Jerry was very unfair, because he had a handicap and could not defend himself against them. "It shouldn't have happened! They had no reason to kill him!" She was also angry because they whipped her with the intention of killing her, putting so much fear and pain into her emotional body. She still heard guns going off inside her head and feared this nightmare would never end. Parts of her had the magical thought, "Kill me instead," wishing she could have prevented Jerry's death by being the one to catch the bullet. Currently, fear was pervasive in her system, sometimes causing her to freeze up, and at other times bringing up anger and the desire to do something.

Carol would sit and rock at times, wanting to cut to release the pain and wanting to go be with Jerry in heaven. Carol came out during our session, frozen in the memory, crying, "Keep beatin' me. Can't run. Ropes are too tight. Can't get out. I don't understand what I did, why they keep beatin' me." I explained to Carol that she shared a body with Paula and that she was seventeen*, but Paula was in her thirties. Carol told me that idea was hard to believe. I saw her wince several times and asked if she were getting beaten right then. She was. I asked if she would listen if I had Paula explain to her what I had just told her. I called out Paula, who told Carol, "We share the same body. You are seventeen, and I am older and have a child. The beatings happened a long time ago, and they have stopped. Those people are not around anymore, and we don't go to them. I understand your pain, and I feel your pain. And I hope that one day it will go away."

At the time of this session, I did not yet know energy therapies to release trauma rapidly by tapping on meridian points; however, I needed to use energy tapping to treat myself while writing this chapter to deal with the vicarious traumatization of hearing about this horrific abuse. Now, I have a client tap on meridian points during a flashback to release the trauma.

Carol came back out and confirmed that she had heard Paula. Sometimes Carol came out during church, as they all attended Mass together. Carol felt very confused by the double life the cult members led: everyone would dress up in their Sunday best to go to Mass. After church, they would cook a big meal, and people would start coming in. Then after dark, the cult members did their ceremonies into the wee hours of the night.

CHAPTER 12

Saved by Fire

ecause of her rectal bleeding, Paula's medical provider performed a rectal exam, which showed bleeding from the third
and fourth quarters of her rectum. An older half brother had
died from colon cancer two years earlier, increasing her colon cancer risk factor, and the physician wanted Paula to have a colonoscopy to see whether the
bleeding came from polyps. The rectal exam felt like more physical abuse to
Paula and triggered the memory of the following cult ceremony on Christmas
Eve when she was eleven years old.

Cult members gathered. Her father was absent, but his brothers Uncle
Hans and Uncle Heinz, Aunt Emily, Nel, and other cult members prepared a
table for the ritual with an inverted cross, candles, and a doll that looked like
Paula. They kept saying, "Today's the darkest day of the year," and they did
this ceremony during the daytime. Cult members kept slicing the doll. They
chopped off its head and then started cutting Paula with a broken beer bottle.
From what happened to the doll effigy representing her, Paula was sure they
intended to kill her. They began sexually abusing her with oral sex. Then Em-

ily stuck a broom into Paula's vagina, and another female penetrated her rectally. They chanted in a language she could not understand and then told her, "We're doing this because we love you. We're teaching you a lesson. We have to sacrifice your life. We want blood!"

We Want Blood!

They chopped up her hair. Blood was everywhere—Paula's blood. At the time, she was dissociated from the pain, but she felt it as she reconnected with the memory during our session. Aunt Emily broke another beer bottle and twisted it into her rectum until it was completely inside. As the cult members kicked her and stepped on her, they laughed mean and nasty. They held her head into a pillow so she would not see who was cutting down her back. As the ritual progressed, one of the members accidentally knocked down several of the candles. The flames hit the bedspread and, within seconds, the place was on fire.

A younger cult member untied her and tried to help her up, but Aunt Emily and another woman grabbed him by the hair of his head to stop him. Paula ran through the wall of flames out the back door away from the house and pulled the beer bottle out of her rectum. She reflected, "That fire saved my life that night!" Paula still has scars on her back from those gashes. Previously, she had thought they were from being pushed through a window. She still had other scars on her body that she could not account for.

The Colonoscopy

Coming back to the topic of the colonoscopy, Paula experienced dread as she waited for the day of the test. More memories of beatings when she was eight years old were emerging—Karen's memories. As Paula awaited the dreaded colonoscopy, she felt she did not want to go on anymore. She asserted, "I'm tired of livin' in so much pain. I just don't feel I'm going to make it through this. Part of me is giving up. I feel like I'm dyin' inside. I'm too weak to fight it. I didn't choose for them to do this to me. It's all happening—all too real. And I can't get myself out of it." I asked what lesson the cult was trying to teach her with their warped reasoning. She first replied, "I don't know...fear?" Then she finally showed her sense of humor again and quipped, "Love hurts. Life sucks. And you don't die fast enough!" She repeated this philosophy often as she trudged through the marathon of uncovering the nightmare of her past.

On the dreaded colonoscopy day, the physician did an enema first and would not let her be alone for even one minute. The doctor came into the bathroom with a flashlight and a mirror to watch while she was on the toilet. Based on the results of the colonoscopy and rectal examination, the doctor told Paula she had "arthritis in the rectal area." We both laughed about that diagnosis, because we had never heard of it before. He gave her suppositories to treat the symptoms. He said most people would not notice the bleeding with this condition, but she likely did because of her blood clotting disorder. He ordered a barium enema and X-rays.

Clotting Disorder

Paula's blood had too many platelets, which made the blood clot too fast. With all the memories that had come forth so far of cutting and bleeding, we hypothesized that Paula's body had learned to make her blood clot faster than normal to avoid bleeding to death during the ceremonies. Currently, the clotting disorder slowed down the bleeding when she cut herself, but it was also life threatening because it increased her risk for a blood clot going to a vital organ such as her heart, lungs, or brain.

Paula felt overwhelmed with all the flashbacks and body memories surfacing. Her right leg was bruised and swollen after flashbacks of Jesse's abortion. The burns on her hands from taking the hot cast-iron pot out of the oven barehanded were already starting to heal by the time I saw them at the next therapy session. In fact, Paula's body healed wounds faster than I had ever seen before. Before Paula got her memories back, her body did not hurt like it did once she reconnected with her memories. I proposed using hypnosis to slow down the memories and to put some of them in a trunk to open just during therapy. Paula objected, because she did not want to stuff the memories again. She was afraid they might not come back and that repressing them might destroy her inside. Her ability to feel the pain was getting better and, as she integrated more parts of herself, she did not feel as split as before. She still had difficulty crying because of an automatic shutoff of emotions. I encouraged her to let herself cry if she could, to release the pain.

CHAPTER 13

On the Edge

*W*hen Paula did not show up for her next therapy appointment, I was quite concerned, as she was usually extremely punctual. I called her home and woke her up. She arrived half an hour late, apologizing. Her left eye was very swollen, with a slight red scratch on the top, and her face looked puffy. She could barely cope with all the physical and emotional pain surfacing as parts inside her fought to come to awareness, each with her own story of trauma and abuse.

We set the intention in prayer to slow down the process of integration so Paula could cope with the pain of the memories already in her awareness. We always prefaced our work by asking Paula's Higher Power to grant the things we asked for only if our request was for Paula's highest good and healing and only if she could handle what we were requesting. We also asked for a shield to decrease the intensity of the flashbacks and to help her body heal faster. As she tried to visualize the shield, the pain got a little easier to bear. The swelling above the eye also started to abate. Her skin tone improved and was less puffy.

I felt happy after this session, proud that, as a therapist, I was finally getting a handle on how to get through the chaos this case presented.

Contracting for Safety

That evening, Paula's doctor called. A part had just cut Paula's left arm quite deeply, requiring internal stitches. The gash was 2.5 inches long and just nicked the fascia. If it had gone any deeper, the ligament would have been damaged and she could also have cut an artery. Paula's doctor was concerned about contracting for safety. Standard procedure in the mental health profession with a client who is in danger of harming self or others is to talk with the person and ask if they can promise to refrain from carrying out their plan of self-harm from then until their next appointment. The client can also contract to call the appropriate provider if their destructive impulses start to get out of hand. If they cannot make a safety contract, then they must be sent for an evaluation for psychiatric hospitalization. I told Paula's psychiatrist that Paula contracts, but I did not know how to contract with Karen, a dissociated part of her personality. Both of us were baffled.

As I hung up the phone from this conversation, I felt terrible. This time the cutting had been much more serious and got closer to being fatal. Whoever was trying to kill herself by cutting was getting better at reaching her goal. The warning of my consultant to be cautious about integrating before sufficient safety was established was ringing through my head. Although my intentions had been to help, I felt helpless to deal with a system in which suicidal parts were continuing to cause chaos. I felt deflated and inadequate and realized I needed a lot more supervision on this case from someone capable of helping me work with Paula.

I called Paula, who was in a reasonably good state of mind. She said she was miserable, but her outer presentation was cheerful, with a good sense of humor. She did not remember cutting but suspected Karen might have done it. Paula could feel her medical provider's concern for her and agreed to his suggestion to take all the sharp things out of her house until Karen was integrated or would contract for safety. Paula added, "But I'm not crazy about this!"

Paula was surprised that her arm was somewhat sore, since she usually did not feel pain after cutting herself. Formerly, she had been so completely

Self-Destruction

*The self-destructive thoughts are
going to win.
For I have a plan.
And soon some relief will begin.
I have started to explode.*

*And I feel very bitter and cold.
Feeling as if I have fallen over the
edge
With no way back up the rocky hill.*

*No fight. I have lost my will.
Not afraid at all.
For at this point I feel my blood
must fall.
Feeling an angerful rage within.*

*And my mind is in a spin.
The confidence, I lack.
Are the voices applauding the images to attack?
The flashbacks, I no longer can
stand.
Relief and a helping hand might
give me the strength I need, to go
on just the same.
For at this time I feel that I am going insane.*

Paula

dissociated from the part of her who cut that she did not feel the pain. Because she was now more integrated, she was more aware of the body sensations of other parts of herself. She reflected that she still did not understand how she lived through all of her abuse. She had trouble believing good things about herself. When people would tell her they loved her, that message would set off fear and negative tapes because of what the cult had done to her in the name of love. The common theme she saw running through all of the ceremonies was sacrificing her. They spoke in another language and she could identify the word "death" in what they were saying—meaning, her death. One of the phrases was "You will die," said in German. She thought they were trying to kill her with torture and did not know why they never succeeded.

She reflected, "Now I see why I don't cry." They conditioned her to repress her emotions. During the ceremony, if she did cry because of the pain, then they increased the pain. If she shed tears, they cut and tortured her more. As a result, she reported, "I don't feel pain—I don't cry."

Paula reported that they conditioned her with the negative programming, "I don't have a right to feel. I don't have a right to think. I don't have a right to be." They tried to stop her from thinking by not allowing her to have any control over the form in which she was abused. The only time she talked or communicated with others was with the little ones and the handicapped ones

Tearless Eyes

My tears I cannot cry.
No place for me to hide,
And I hurt so deep, deep inside.
Tearless are my eyes.

For my mind's eye is trapped in the

past.
Not sure how much longer I will last
With tearless eyes.

Once again, I am losing all hope
With this constant struggle to cope.

For emotionally, I am drained,
And physically, I am in much pain.
Tearless are my eyes.

Hearing many, many screaming
voices,
And once again, I narrow down my
choices,
For deep within, I long to die.
My tears I cannot cry.

Feeling trapped within my child-
hood years
And full of fear!
Where are my tears?
For tearless are my eyes.

Paula

227

around her. The rampant drug abuse in the group resulted in many birth abnormalities. Her sister and three others she cared for had cerebral palsy. Two had mental retardation. One was a dwarf. Seven were either deaf or blind—both ears, one eye, or both. Many of them would not have survived if she had not cared for them. "The deaf ones couldn't hear danger coming. I had to be their ears and eyes." She saw cult members signing and learned sign language to communicate with the deaf children. Caring for the kids held her together. Her aunts would get out of the hospital, come to Paula's house, and give her the baby. She asserted, "The only happiness I could find was with the little ones and carin' and communicatin' with the handicapped. If I didn't survive, they wouldn't. I had no friends or anything a normal kid had, but I had a lot invested in knowing that others needed me. My only happiness was when they laughed, and I only smiled when the kids laughed and smiled with me. I was taking care of the others from age five and younger. I see myself making formula at three or four years old. I didn't measure it!" She was currently active in working for rights for the handicapped.

As we were talking, I speculated, "You may have done more for those handicapped children than you realize. A cult needs a victim for the ceremonies, and if you hadn't been there, they might have used someone else, and the handicapped children might not have survived."

Paula responded, "Three of the kids did die. Jerry, Bill, and Jeff." I knew the story of Jerry's death, but I had never heard her talk about Bill or Jeff.

CHAPTER 14

Marge's Memories

The story of what happened to Jeff comes later in this narrative. When I inquired what happened to Bill, Paula first got very quiet and then became agitated as she told the story of Bill's death. Bill was the son of one of the cult members and was paralyzed from the waist down. He had multiple sclerosis and leukemia and had suffered a lot from chemotherapy, blood transfusions, and surgeries. He did not want to live on life support and once asked Paula to disconnect his respirator and machines, but she refused. When Bill was seven, the cult picked him as ceremony victim after a card game. Whoever won the most money would come get Paula and start the ceremony. She remembered cards, laughter, and booze. She could see costumes and candles and three different symbols: the circle, a skeleton head, and a swastika.

They tied up Paula and made her watch them slowly beat Bill and repeatedly stab his vital organs. His eyes reached out to her for help, but her hands were tied. She felt helpless and pleaded for them to leave him alone and do whatever they wanted to her. Even though Bill did not want to live, Paula asserted,

Witnessing Bill's Death

"He shouldn't have died that way. It wasn't his time yet. Their beating and stabbing him just made him suffer all the more." She wept as she added, "He was reaching for me, and I couldn't help him."

This conversation was over the phone. I responded, "That's so sad! It's good that you can cry about it, Paula."

Personality Switch

The voice on the other end of the phone retorted, "I'm not Paula!" I inquired who I was talking with. Amid coughing and choking sounds, she replied, "Marge." When I asked what was happening, Marge replied, "They made me swallow his blood." More coughing and vomiting sounds came, and then Marge added, "It made me sick." A long silence followed, with distant heaving sounds.

After a few minutes, Paula came back to the phone and asked, "Who am I talking with?" I identified myself. Paula had been in the bathroom vomiting and came back to the bedroom. Vomit was on the rug, and the phone was on the bed so she picked it up. She said, "I feel sick. Did we just do some work?" I told her that Marge had just remembered something yucky and needed to throw up. I said I would hold Marge's memory until she was ready to hear it, but Paula wanted to know what it was. I gave her a brief outline, saying that the cult had sacrificed Bill and made her drink some of his blood. She thought the whole episode was horrible and ranted, "Why? Why did they do those things?" I could not answer that question. She told me that some of the cult members went to church and were well respected in their parish. The priest came to the house at times. Paula asserted, "I feel rage that this could ever happen and that they made me a part of it!"

Spontaneous Bloody Nose

Between sessions, Paula's nose started to bleed, without any trauma to the head. In session, with great pain, Marge reported, "Dad beat me, hit me in the face, in the nose. He kept hitting me." In broken phrases, Marge added that everybody beat her—not just Dad, but uncles, aunts, and friends, too. She had been remembering being hit when the spontaneous bloody nose occurred.

Spontaneous Bloody Nose Body Memory

Poltergeist Activity

After recovering these memories, Paula reported increased poltergeist activity in her house. A locked door opened up by itself. Bubbles were floating up from the toilet. She was having flashbacks, feeling sick as a dog, and had a fight with her daughter for not respecting the limits Paula set for her daughter's safety. Paula asserted, "I'm losing it!"

I did not fully understand how upsetting the poltergeist activity was for Paula until incidents happened in my home as well. My lights switched on or off, and my hot water faucet turned on by itself. The effect is unnerving, because stationary physical objects are not supposed to move by themselves with *nobody* touching them! Paula's psychiatrist had warned me about this possibility, as he had seen it happen in similar cases. Poltergeist activity is a well-known phenomenon in the real estate business, where the deceased former owner of a home may make footstep noises at night or open doors. The word *poltergeist* is a combination of two German words: *poltern* means "to make noise," and *geist* means "ghost." So poltergeist literally means "noisy ghost." One of the reasons I developed my Soul Detective protocols a decade later was to find a way to deal with the activity of an earthbound spirit, who has no physical body (a *nobody*) but can learn to concentrate energy from its emotional body to manifest noises or movements of inanimate objects.

My book *Invisible Roots: How Healing Past Life Trauma can Liberate Your Present* goes into more detail on the reasons why spirits stay earthbound and gives a protocol for helping these "spirit walkers" heal and cross into the Light. One of the primary reasons a spirit becomes trapped is dying in a state of emotional distress and agitation. When we get angry, we give away our power to the people we are enraged with as we throw "emotional daggers" of fury at them. I believe that the cult purposefully made Bill's death as traumatic as possible to try to keep his spirit trapped and earthbound so they could continue to steal his vital force. Was Bill's spirit haunting Paula's house, trying to get help? Or were cult members summoning malicious earthbound spirits to try to stop Paula from remembering and telling her story? I do not know and, at that point, I had no tools to deal with the problem.

Full Moon

Ideas of harming herself continued to bombard Paula, but she did not want to go back into the hospital. Being a locked-up inpatient made the flashbacks worse, and since her daughter's rape, she wanted to be home to protect her beloved child. On the night of the full moon, Paula called me in a state of emergency. The barium enema she had the previous day triggered a torrent of flashbacks of rectal trauma. Hyperventilating and sounding fragile, with a total absence of humor in her voice, she reported, "All of them want to cut."

Full Moon

No relief do I find,
from these painful childhood memories trapped within my mind!

And endless is this night, with the moon full and bright.
For my life once again, I must fight.
Causing an emotional turmoil within my heart and soul.

Home is where I want to go.
Home, that place of final rest.
Peace And Death!!

Paula was trying her best to cope by attempting to accept what had happened to her and to put it into the hands of her Higher Power, but she was struggling. At our therapy session the next day, Paula asked to be hospitalized to keep from cutting herself again.

One of the ways I built more trust in our therapeutic bond and gave Paula more control over her life was that I never forced her into psychiatric hospitalization. When she was not doing well, if she felt she could handle the situation better outpatient, we found other ways to try to support her safety. We only asked for inpatient care when she felt she really needed it. Hearing the stories of previous hospitalizations where an angry part had come out and the hospital staff tied her down and injected her with a major tranquilizer—all in the name of medical care, "because we love you"—felt too much like the abuse she had endured from the cult.

This hospitalization also brought additional trauma. While waiting to get an inpatient bed, the emergency center locked her in a room from 5:00 p.m. until 2:00 a.m. the next morning, when they transported her by ambulance to a distant hospital. While inpatient, the staff took away her purse and all her ID information. Then when she went out on a two-hour pass to get some things she needed, she got lost because she was in a strange place. She laughed as she related this bit of irony about trying to piece together her identity and to find her lost parts. The whole system got lost that day!

Contracting for Safety

Meanwhile, I had been researching how to contract for safety with a multiple—something Paula also very much wanted to do so she could feel safer. Using the ideas I had gathered, together we formulated a contract for safety that worked for Paula:

> "All the parts of Paula promise that we will not cut. This contract is binding until we check in at the next therapy session."

Paula went inside to talk about the contract with the other parts. We asked Marge and Karen to use other coping methods. Neither of them liked the hospital so they both agreed to the contract. I asked for any other parts that had something to say about the contract to speak up, or they would also be bound to it. Paula's face showed agitation, but the session was cut short by a knock from her daughter asking how to spell "Barbara" and a phone call from the office saying our time was up and they wanted to close the clinic. Since nobody spoke up, Paula signed the contract for all of the parts. That weekend Paula used other coping mechanisms and "drew like hell," unlocking her feelings and putting them into sketches depicting the pain of satanic ritual abuse.

Haunted Past

Haunted by my past.
And falling apart very fast.

For even the body memories coincide

With all I feel inside.

My heart fills with many tears
As my mind's eye brings me back
into the fear of my childhood years
Leaving me scarred and bitter.

My whole body starts to quiver
Full of sorrow and despair.
All hope I seem to lose there.

For they took an innocent life.
And continuously cut me with the knife.

Their laughter fills the air.
Within falls all my tears,
Of those childhood years.

Paula

Paula sometimes found her journal in another part of the house with new entries she did not remember making and did not want others to see. We talked about all the parts of her personality needing a place to express their feelings and suggested putting the journal into a locked box to keep it private. Paula reported that sometimes one part would draw a picture, and another part would destroy it. Parts also destroyed the writings of other parts. We added a section to her internal contract stating, "No part will destroy the drawings of any other parts." Her artwork was a way to show what had happened in her life, a way to let out feelings and memories that had been locked up for decades.

New Contract

At our next session, we worked on a more inclusive contract:

> All parts of Paula will take these steps before trying to take their life:
>
> 1. Call the local crisis center.
> 2. Have someone come over and stay until she is able to talk to Barbara.
>
> This contract is binding until we sign a different contract.
>
> P.S. No part will destroy the drawings of any other parts.

We went in to talk with Marge about this contract, and I explained it to her. She looked puzzled as she looked at the paper with the contract written on it, so I asked whether she could read. She responded, "A little." I asked if she went to school, and she said, "Not much."

Then Marge started abreacting and was obviously in a traumatic memory. She clutched her throat and then mouthed some words, but I could not understand. I asked her to whisper, and she could not whisper. She began doing sign language with her hands. I asked her to draw her feelings if she could not talk and showed her Paula's sketchpad. She pulled out the drawing of Witnessing Bill's Death, the first drawing in this chapter.

Throat Slit

She made motions showing that she had been cut with a knife and showed me a line from the top of the neck down through the vocal cords to below the collarbone. I caught on and asked, "You mean you cannot talk because your throat was cut?" She nodded yes and signed some more. I asked if she had learned to sign to communicate with the other children who could not talk, and Marge brightened up. Since I do not know sign language, I inquired, "How do you say, 'How are you?' in sign?"

She tried to show me, but I could not figure out what she was doing. She then took a pen and with her left hand and scrawled "you ok." I asked if she was wondering whether I was okay, and she shook her head no. I was still stumped, so she slowly and painfully wrote out what I thought was "start why to ask how are you." These words made no sense to me. I kept studying what she had written and eventually realized that the first word was "short" instead of start, and that she was showing me a shorthand way to ask "How are you?" by pointing to the person (you) and making a circle with the thumb and index finger, the "okay" sign: You okay? Marge is dyslexic and had turned the *a* in "way" backward so it looked like an *h* to me and I read it as "why" instead of what she was trying to communicate: "Short way to ask how are you."

We had fun "talking" together, with mute Marge expressing herself through her hands. After a while, I told her I had to talk with Karen, and her face clouded again. Karen could talk, because she had not been out when the throat was slit. Karen reported she was angry with everybody. She didn't trust anyone. I told her I hoped that I would be able eventually to get her trust. I talked a bit about how she was sharing the same body with some others, and we needed a contract for safety to be sure that she could go on and the others could, too. I explained the contract, and she agreed.

"You'll Never Talk Again"

Then Paula jumped back out and said, "Now I know who cut my throat: Dad's oldest brother, Hans." Just before she was eleven, at school she had disclosed some things about her home situation. She hadn't said exactly what was going on, but she told them that she didn't like it and didn't want to go back there. Someone from the school came to the house to investigate. The family got word ahead of time that an investigator was coming and cleaned up the place.

After the investigator left, cult members tied Paula's wrists and told her, "What goes on behind locked doors stays here." Hans slit her vocal cords, leaving the knife in her throat. He said, "You'll never talk again."

Nel said, "Leave her there to die." The others laughed and then left her alone. She somehow got her hands free and pulled out the knife. Marge carried this dissociated memory. Paula reported that she could not speak for over a year after this assault and did not go to school during that time. Incredulous, I asked to see the scar. Paula said she had plastic surgery to remove it when she was eighteen. In a later session, she showed me a driver's license photo from before the surgery in which a scar was visible right by the voice box.

I reflected, "Perfect for them. They could abuse you and you couldn't talk to anyone about it."

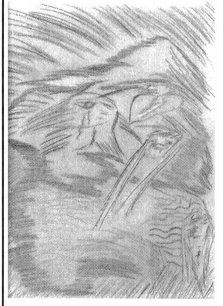

Shattered Heart

My heart's shattered, from the teachings of my life.

I have to make things right.
I struggle to hold on,
Although I can see wrong.

I feel all the pain that is left within me.
I have a need to be free.

My eyes fill with the silent uncried tears.
And deep down I feel all the fear of my childhood years.

The pain eats away my soul,
And I feel a bitterful anger which leaves me feeling
Oh, so cold.
And much more of the darkness I was taught unfolds.

Oh, where do I go from here?

I ask for the strength and the miracle of feeling whole.

I wipe away my tears, even though I feel ever so scared.

Paula

Birthday Beating

Through several sessions, the full story emerged of the original trauma that caused Marge to split off. On her tenth birthday, Marge was forbidden to leave the house, but she went with her older brother to the place her father worked to get a present from his boss. On the way home, crossing a complicated intersection, Marge was hit by a car and her leg was hurt. She got up and was going to walk home, but her brother called her father, who made her get into a cruiser car and go to the hospital. She thought his concern about her getting hurt was just show for the police. The X-rays showed no breaks, and the driver of the car admitted to being at fault. The hospital released her with instructions to stay in bed.

When she got home, her father beat her and smashed her head into the wall for disobeying, saying, "What's it going to take to get through your thick skull?" He was angry because she caused a problem and asked, "How could you put your mother through that?" This statement felt hypocritical to Paula, considering the physical abuse he was inflicting on her in the present moment

Birthday Beating

and how his beating on her sore leg made it much worse. Then her father dragged her into the bedroom for another ceremony, where they kept repeating that her birthday was not to be remembered since her maternal grandmother and her brother Paul had both died on that day.

The family still blamed her for Paul's death and wished that she would have died instead of him. Paula felt the family wanted her dead. Many times they had beaten her so badly that she should have died, and they just left her bleeding. She does not know how she survived, but the clotting disorder of her blood coagulating too fast may have been the factor that saved her life many times.

During the ceremony, her mother went out for a drink. Paula used to have anger toward her mother, but then she realized her mother was a victim, too, and could not get out of the situation. She forgave her mother and reflected, "What I did by going to get a birthday present from my father's boss wasn't that bad."

At the end of the session, I could see in Paula's face that she and Marge were connected, and Paula confirmed that observation. Marge was fully integrated. I suggested that Paula share the memory of her dad's death with Marge and let her know that she is now with Paula, an adult, so Marge would feel more protected.

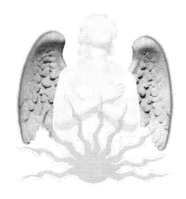

CHAPTER 15

Karen's Memories

aula arrived at our next session with a yellow coating on her tongue and a leg tremor, which she felt was a side effect of a new medication she had just started, 25 mg of Anafranil. Paula reported she was "flashing all over the place" and wanted to go inside to see what was going on. We agreed on the question, "Who needs to talk today?" Karen came out with fists clenched, cringing and shaking, in much pain. The moment that Karen came out, the leg tremor stopped. She was angry with her father. "He hit me with a baseball bat. He was always hitting me with wood. He let the others beat me and do anything to me they wanted." Her crime was turning off the TV set after her Dad had passed out in front of it. She was going up to bed, and her father woke up and "had a rampage, went wild."

I asked how she wanted to express her anger, and Karen wanted to break a window. Instead, I got a pink pillow and put it on a chair in front of her and suggested she put the anger into the pillow. I talked about drawing to get the anger out and writing, too, but encouraged her to use the pillow so she wouldn't hurt her hands by breaking the window. I also did not think the clinic would be very pleased with that form of expressive therapy! Karen was hesitant at first, but then she pounded the pillow and yelled, "I hate them! I hate them!" Then she broke into sobs. When Karen calmed down and could talk again, she did not buy my idea that she was eight years old and sharing a body with a woman in her early thirties, but she knew Marge. She felt angry and helpless and wanted to die. She moved back in the chair, struggling, moving her feet. She told me they were trying to tie her up. I encouraged her to hit the cushioned chair near her, with her coat on top. Karen hit the chair wildly, with her hand veering off to the side. The knuckle she hit on the chair started to swell up.

Closet Time

Next Marge let us know that a four-year-old part who called herself Baby wanted to come out. As Baby remembered getting beaten by her father, she writhed and kicked, yelling "Get off me! It hurts! It hurts!" Then she kicked the chair in the office, trying to get herself out of the closet. Once we helped Baby visualize getting out of the closet, Paula came back out. Immediately her leg tremor started again. Since Baby, Marge, and Karen had not been out when Paula took the Anafranil, none of them were getting its effects—or its side effects. I still could not figure out how the medicine could affect only one part of Paula when the same body they shared ingested the substance, but I witnessed that the medicine affected only the part who took it. This phenomenon explains why medication is generally not extremely effective with dissociative disorders.

Paula wept as she remembered intercourse being forced

Critters

on her at four years old. She said, "No wonder I'm so messed up." She said that the closet they had locked her in after raping Baby was damp, dark, and musty, with no air, and it had mice in it! She was frightened of the mice. Her dad would chase her holding a mouse by the tail, and everyone thought her fright was really funny.

I asked her which was worse, the physical and sexual abuse, or the closet time. She felt the closet time was the worst part, because she was all alone. She said her swollen knuckle hurt, but not as much as she hurt inside. She felt Karen's rage just under the surface and thought she could never heal.

One of the guidelines for diagnosing dissociative identity disorder is that the originating trauma that fractures the personality happens before the age of five, when a person does not have other coping skills developed. This memory was the first one Paula had shared from younger than five, and the trauma of the rape followed by the isolation in the closet was likely a calculated plan to make Paula dissociate. The cult needed children who could dissociate what happened during the ceremonies so that the children themselves would not remember their abuse.

Dear Child Within,

I am doing the best I can with all that is going on inside me. I know you want to be free and I know that your story has to be told, so that both you and I can let go of all the pain that still remains. Child of mine, I as the adult can see all the pain you're in. I am doing all that I can to set you free. And it is not easy for me.

Although I am an adult now there are many things I still have to learn. The first thing was to start trusting others. I have trust in others at this time, and that alone was a big step to take. Once I started to trust others, slowly I started to open up and tell our story. But I had many setbacks. I the adult am sorry for closing you in, but I had to work on myself.

Then I had to concentrate on someone very special to me. My baby started to grow, and then someone hurt her so much in the same ways, both you my child within, and the adult that I am was hurt. I the adult had to stop my daughter's pain. I had her offender put away. During that same time I continued to work on myself. I started to feel bet-ter and I forgot about you my child within—can you forgive me?

Child within, you started to claw at me, but I the adult was afraid to let you come out because I know what you were all about. At first you slowly broke your way through the walls I put you in. Now all those walls are down. I the adult feel your pain, for my mind's eye sees your pain, and the inner voices hear all of what you were told. As an adult I can see, hear, and feel both your physical and emotional pain.

I am struggling through the pain so both you and I can be free from it all. I the adult am still learning how to cry and to let others see my tears. Also I am still struggling with letting people near me when I am having a hard time. Child of mine I am doing the best that I can to set you free, so both you and I can be free from all of our pain. Both of our hearts must mend so our pain can come to an end.

Paula
The adult that I am

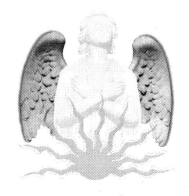

CHAPTER 16

Hurting Others

*P*aula told me once that she thought it was a miracle that she was not crazy. Sometimes she felt she should be locked up because of her fear that her anger might explode and she might hurt somebody. Paula disclosed that once she broke her rule of not hurting anyone else. With great guilt, she related how another child who had been picking on her came after her and hit her in the head with an old-fashioned table leg. Paula got the object away from her and then beat on the other girl with her fists, putting her into the hospital. She could not forgive herself for hitting back so hard. She felt she should have just taken the weapon away. As we worked her false guilt, a fear surfaced that she might really hurt others if all her pent-up rage exploded. She had been hiding her feelings to protect others from the force of her anger.

Temporary Insanity

Another time was much more serious. During one ceremony involving violent and sadistic rape, Paula's arms were not tied down. While a cult member was on top of her, someone slipped a knife into her hand. She stabbed the rapist in the back. He died on top of her, right during his sexual climax. She felt horrible for taking his life, even though it could have been considered self-defense. She felt that the cult purposely arranged the situation, giving her the knife so that, under the duress of the moment, she would violate her own standard of not hurting others and suffer tremendous guilt. The plan worked.

False Guilt

I called it temporary insanity. Later she realized that the cult wanted to eliminate this man because his actions were becoming dangerous to the group. They would have killed him if she had not done it, but the way they arranged it, his death tore her up inside with shame and false guilt.

I doubted that her stab wound was the one that took his life, because the part that reported this incident was only five years old. I did not think that she would have had the strength or the accuracy to find a lethal location in that chaotic moment. I suspected that as she stabbed him, another cult member plunged a knife into his heart and then removed the knife so she thought she had killed him.

A Breeder for the Cult

The stories I was hearing from Paula were so gruesome and outrageous that they were hard to believe. Yet, at the same time that Paula was recovering her memories, my close colleague and friend Marie was sharing stories about her friend Georgia who was also recovering memories of satanic ritual abuse. While the exact details were different, the principles were similar.

Georgia's mother was a breeder for the cult. She produced babies for them to use in their sacrifices. Marie shared an example of how the cult set up a situation to separate Georgia from a person she loved—a theme throughout Paula's history—and to induce false guilt. When Georgia was around four years old, the cult tied up her playmate who was her best friend with an abundance of combustible materials surrounding her. Then they gave Georgia matches to play with. Naturally, a fire started, and the playmate burned to death. Georgia held herself responsible.

Georgia was getting into recovery and realizing all of the ways she had been set up to be filled with shame and guilt. She reported that everyone she knew who was in the cult wanted to get out of it—a very hopeful sign. She said they were tired of the bloodshed and violence and wanted to leave, but that the cult would kill anyone who tried to get out and make it look like an accident. The things Marie told me about Georgia confirmed the existence of cults and the nature of their tactics to try to destroy the human soul.

Roller-skating

Another instance of Paula striking someone brought up great guilt. One Saturday morning, her daughter, Megan, got permission to go roller-skating with her friends. Then the friend's mother changed her mind about going, so Megan walked all the way across town to and from the skating rink by herself. When she did not return home by noon as expected, Paula was very worried and contacted the police to look for her. Megan did not return until 6:45 p.m.

Paula felt angry with her and lectured her about the danger she had put herself in being out alone and unprotected at age twelve. Megan did not think anything was wrong with what she had done and talked back to Paula, an action that made Paula even angrier. Paula hit Megan once on the back, not hard enough to leave marks. Then Paula felt horrible and had flashbacks of her beatings. Paula wept and Megan came over and said, "It's okay, Mom."

Paula felt so ashamed of hitting her daughter. In her eyes, she was just like her abusers, beating a child. I pointed out how different this situation was from Paula's abuse. Paula was not beaten because she had clearly done something dangerous. She was abused because the followers of darkness enjoyed creating suffering.

Rape Trial

Megan had been giving Paula a rough time, so Paula brought her into our next session. Megan told Paula that when she was placed in foster care, she felt that Paula did not love her or care about her. Megan also talked about being raped during this foster placement. Paula let Megan know that she had no choice in the matter. Child protective services placed Megan in foster care when Paula was in the hospital for six weeks with a blood clot. I talked about the benefit of Megan being able to express these painful feelings to her mother. Megan's behavior improved after this session.

Paula recounted how she had won two of her three court cases:

1. She won the custody battle to get Megan back.
2. She prosecuted Megan's perpetrator and won that case, putting him in jail.
3. She lost the case against her own father for raping her.

Later, I reflected how different her attitude was toward her daughter's abuse. Instead of ignoring, denying, or condoning it, she had pressed charges and gotten justice for the offense.

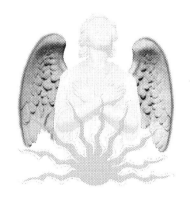

CHAPTER 17

Julienne

O ne night my husband was reading the local paper and announced, "Next week there's going to be a talk on ritual abuse by a survivor." I could not believe anyone would stand up in public and talk about this volatile topic, but as I read the description and saw the beautiful photo of the presenter, whom I will call Julienne, I decided to go. Paula came, too, accompanied by one of her friends.

As I sat in the audience, I felt very uncomfortable. I looked around the room which had about forty people at the talk, wondering who was there to heal from ritual abuse and who was a cult member spying on what Julienne was doing. As I studied their faces, I couldn't figure out who was who. The only common traits of cult members Paula knew were heavy substance abuse and most of them being Catholic. Julienne began her talk by saying that she never quite got over the thought that if she stood up in public and talked about ritual abuse (RA), someone would pull out a gun and shoot her. I had been thinking the same thing and felt relieved to know that Julienne had some apprehension about her talk but did it anyway.

Julienne shared that, from piecing together her memories, the cult she was involved with was not Satanic, as those symbols and holidays did not trigger her. Her cult seemed to be more Luciferian in nature, drawing on the pre-Christian and Egyptian occult. However, the forms of torture and abuse that were used to make Julienne dissociate were similar to Paula's torture. Julienne did not have continual interaction with the cult because she lived hundreds of miles away from her maternal grandfather, who seemed to be in control of the rituals. The ritual memories were limited to his group, location, and her preschool years.

Julienne had no memories of any abuse until she was in her late thirties, when she began to remember childhood sexual abuse from her father along with some strange memories that made no sense. She went into therapy and also began studying with a number of energy healers to refine her professional skills, including intensive study with internationally acclaimed author, healer, and medicine woman Rosalyn Bruyere.[1] The framework to understand those strange memories and the skills to work with them came from Rosalyn.

As ritual abuse is done for both spiritual and material power, it needs to be healed on the energetic as well as the physical, mental, and emotional levels. Some of the power of Julienne's work with RA survivors and their therapists comes from her ability to understand and undo the energies that the cults have tried to establish in the participants of their rituals. Julienne also teaches her clients how to stay energetically safe during the healing and recovery.

A Guided Tour of Hell

Julienne cautioned about the risks involved in working with this volatile topic. She said working with a ritual abuse survivor was "a guided tour of hell," and that the only thing worse was not doing it! Julienne reported a ceremony she remembered from age three in which cult members were gathered in a circle around a couple having intercourse in the center of the room. Her grandfather used her energy as a shield and went around the circle altering the pathways of energy flow in cult members to block proper body function while

---

1 Bruyere, *Wheels of Light*.

they were distracted by watching the couple in the center. If anyone did notice an energetic presence, they would have only seen a three-year-old child.

Julienne guided us to do a visualization of having the protection of Archangel Michael. Paula could not access that image, but she was able to call in the Light that she had felt when she was in the closet. She commented, "Everybody has to find their own thing."

Paula resonated with Julienne's story and decided she would like to do some work with her. I checked with Paula's psychiatrist, who supported the connection with an expert in this specific area, so I set up a consultation session for Paula that I could attend for support.

Paula's First Session with Julienne

Julienne began her session with Paula by asking what she would like to have happen, putting the power and control squarely into Paula's hands. Paula looked scared, had difficulty speaking, and could not verbalize anything. Not knowing where to start, I asked Paula whether it would be all right with her to have Julienne address the issue of getting overwhelmed by flashbacks that were accompanied by full-blown body memories, including bleeding and bruising. Paula agreed.

Julienne sensed that Paula was still connected to the cult by energetic cords and asked if she wanted to disconnect from them. Paula said yes! Julienne used Michael energy to protect, Mother Mary energy to hold, and Horus energy to disconnect the energetic cords from Paula's stomach and sexual areas. Julienne felt resistance to the disconnection from the cords in the heart area. A child part of Paula loved people in the cult, and she felt that if that heart connection were broken, possibly nobody would ever be able to love her. So that cord stayed.

Getting unhooked from cords to the cult felt disorientating to Paula, and her stomach started to hurt. Julienne asked Paula to differentiate whether the pain was from a memory, a pain of one of the parts, or actual stomach pain in the present moment. Paula reported the pain was from a part. Karen came out and talked about her feeling that something had been taken away from her by the energy work that had just been done. Julienne wanted to give something back, but Karen was not able to trust Julienne enough to receive it. Paula felt confused.

251

Tami came out and said, "Baby," clutching her belly. She was feeling the pain of where they had beaten her to abort baby Joseph.

Broken Heart Pain

When Julienne understood that Tami had lost a child, she told her, "Let me tell you a secret about babies. You lost a baby, but that baby's spirit was not hurt. Only its body was hurt. The spirit wasn't, and you can go and be with that spirit when you need to. You can learn how to do that."

Julienne saw a dynamic working inside Paula in which some parts wanted to tell what had happened to them, and other parts would beat them up if they told. So the parts that wanted to communicate had to show what happened in the physical body by repeating the symptoms so that people would believe them. The parts that beat her if she told were trying to protect Paula, knowing the consequences if she did tell (remembering her throat being slit), and were doing their job in the best way they knew

Losing Baby Joseph

how. Julienne talked with them about protecting in a different way so that Paula would not have to go through all the physical pain of the body memories.

Julienne recognized the importance of all of Paula's parts, with all of them deserving to be heard and appreciated for the roles they were playing in the internal conflict. Julienne sent Paula's belly some healing energy from a distance of about eighteen inches, asking for feedback about how much was enough. At the end, Julienne sensed that a part of Paula was really angry at Julienne for changing things inside. She invited the parts that were angry to speak, but nobody came out. Julienne talked about how this work we did would change the relationships between the parts.

Yolanda

Before leaving, Paula was aware of a self-destructive part that wanted to come out. She let her speak, and it was Yolanda, a part we had met briefly in our earlier work together. Yolanda wanted to cut. Julienne asked her to show her where, and Yolanda made a motion on the left wrist by the pulse point, a line parallel to the arm. Julienne asked what would happen if she cut. Yolanda said the pain would get numb so she would not feel the pain anymore. Julienne asked her to get in touch with the part that numbed the pain and let that part come out, without cutting. Yolanda was able to do that intervention and was then okay to leave.

Eight More Stitches

That evening I got an emergency phone call from Paula. She felt that Julienne had been pretty accurate in reflecting what Paula was going through, so the session triggered a lot of feelings. Paula had dissociated and cut her right ankle, which needed eight stitches. Paula still felt very vulnerable from her internal war, in which she felt as if her abusers were still inside her, beating her up. Paula talked about how the sound of certain voices of cult members would call out parts they could control. The old tapes of things they had said to her were running over and over in her mind, and she was having auditory hallucinations of their verbal abuse.

Paula did not understand how she could still be connected to the cult, but the connection felt like "a scary familiar feeling." At that time, I had never had an experience with an energetic cord, and the idea that a pipeline of detrimental energy could go from one person to another person somewhere else was new to me. In the years that followed, I became more aware of the ways these energetic ties between people kept my clients bound to negative feelings. While Julienne's protocol for clearing cords was based on her intuitive healing training, I developed a slightly different protocol based on muscle testing for my Soul Detective work. Both protocols bring in helpful transpersonal energy to break these detrimental energetic ties.

Part of Paula was scared that the cult members who were still alive were going to find out that she was no longer connected. Julienne had mentioned that when the cult members felt an energetic disconnection from someone whose energy they were still stealing, they would frequently make contact to find out what had happened. While Paula and I were talking on the phone that evening, her brother called, sounding drunk. Paula suspected that he was still involved with the cult, so I strongly encouraged her not to call him back. She felt she could not refuse, as the date was the night before the anniversary of their father's death. She said she had to pull herself together for her brother and listen to what he had to say. I respected her decision, even though I disagreed. I checked whether she needed the hospital, and she said no. We agreed to see each other the following day. After we hung up, I wept, feeling pain at the thought of Paula getting drawn back into the cult.

A Letter to All Parts

Paula arrived for her appointment the following day, dressed up, with a nice hairdo, looking great. I asked how she got through the night last night. She said she painted, played the piano, and wrote a letter to all of her parts. Tears came to my eyes as she let me read it:

To all of the parts within my heart and my soul:

I am Paula, the adult in which you all share the same body. I feel all of your confusion and your pain. I Paula, the adult, am doing everything I can to comfort and heal all of us from the past. I also understand your confusion and disbelief of living in someone else's body. Because when I first found out you were in me, I felt the same feelings. I Paula, at this time, accept all of you no matter if I know who or how many of you there are. As I grow, you all grow a little with me. I Paula, the adult, feel I have to take some risks, so all of us can grow and learn a little more. For I feel each risk I take, the more we all can learn, and the more we can heal.

Please trust in me. I do not want to hurt any of us in any way. Because I truly understand the pain and hurt that others can do to a person.

I want to understand and help you all heal from the past. At this time I feel a battle going on inside myself. I can understand some parts, and many others are very unclear. Also, I understand all of your fear. Please help me, help all of you. Help me to understand all of you, and what each of you are most comfortable with if anything. I Paula, the adult, want to heal, and I wish you all can grow, learn, and heal with me. Also, I hope one day we all will be as one.

Paula, the Adult

Paula's letter was an open appeal for integration of her parts. She wanted to go in and have me read the letter to all the parts and give them a chance to talk about it. She also wanted to speak with the one who cut her with the razor blade and then with the one who punishes her. We read the letter, and parts came out who wanted to trust.

Karen had been the one who cut, hiding the razor blade under the rug. She was feeling angry. We talked about other ways to let out the pain, like drawing on her skin with a red marker. I had read this creative idea in one of my books on treating dissociation and wanted to try it out. I asked if she knew where the markers were, and a smile flickered across her face as she responded, "In Megan's room." That was the first smile I had ever seen on Karen. I asked if she did anything in Megan's room, and Karen said she played with her dolls, which she never got to do as a child. But she felt guilty. Megan didn't know, and Karen did not have permission. I told her it was okay to play with the dolls. She liked the Barbies the best. Later Paula felt surprised. She said Megan was always asking her if she had been in her room, but Paula had no memory of playing with her dolls.

Wicked Girl

Next we called out the part that punishes Paula. This part came out and said, "I'm sorry." Paula accepted her apology. This part was fifteen years old and called herself "Wicked Girl." She had taken the punishment for the system many times. Once a dissociated part of Paula knocked over a candle while running from a ceremony, and the candle set the house on fire. Wicked Girl took the beating for that accident. Wicked Girl was afraid of more punishment and thought she would get killed if anyone revealed the abuse. She was punishing the system, trying to keep the parts from disclosing what had happened to them.

We explained that things were different now. Wicked Girl had heard the letter. Her favorite activities were dancing and listening to music on the radio, fifteen-year-old interests that were very different from Karen's eight-year-old doll playing.

Second Session with Julienne

When we arrived, Julienne commented on how much better Paula looked. This time Paula was able to articulate a clear goal for the session. She wanted to work on issues around a tumor in her belly that would have a biopsy the coming week. Julienne recommended talking with the doctors and asking them to explain to her everything that they were going to do before it happened so it would not feel as much like her abuse. Paula reported, "Almost all of the parts are hoping it is cancer and that I will die."

I said I was hoping Julienne would find a part that *didn't* want to die, and we all laughed. Julienne saw a part sitting on top of the tumor, which looked to her like a clump of things. Julienne sent some energy to the tumor, and then this part that felt masculine got angry at Julienne for what she had done. Paula connected with the part and realized it was the one that would go around making clots and doing other creative things in the body to survive her abuse. Julienne talked about allying with this part to use the incredible gifts it had in service of being able to build tissue (something it couldn't do yet) and to do healing work with others.

Julienne got permission to teach that part how to put energy around something, saying that this skill was one thing it would be very difficult for him to use against her. After this intervention, Paula felt upset at the internal shift. Her parts had felt love and caring, so they were waiting for the storm to hit after this calm. They could not believe that Julienne would come with only her positive energy without also doing something bad to them. Julienne reflected that when a belief is lost, one goes through a grief process, like a death—the death of a belief system.

Paula's Extrasensory Perception

At our next session, Paula said, "I learned a lot about myself at Julienne's today. Through my life, I've had these energies. My instincts are very different from others. I know things before they are going to happen. From very young, I was able to see things." Sometimes she mistakenly felt she was responsible for what happened because she could see it beforehand; however, she did not have the ability to stop the bad things she saw coming.

I commented that her "sixth sense" was handy as a child, so she could get ready when she knew she was about to be abused. Paula said that when she knew the abuse was about to happen, the part that Julienne had discovered had to "make the adjustments inside myself." It would raise the level of pain tolerance. That part also had to work really fast to stop the physical effects of the abuse, like clotting real fast when stabbed or when damage was done to a vital organ. This part could not repair the body. Another part did the healing. This part did not like taking medication because it was foreign to the body and interfered with her ability to self-regulate.

Paula reflected, "I see things so differently from other people. I know evil." She sometimes did not share all of what she knew with others because her viewpoint was so radically different. Sometimes she would pick up on a girlfriend's being about to cut and would be able to stop her. When she picked up the phone, she often knew who it was. She knew what her friends had been doing when they called her. Her boyfriend would get mad at her because he would tell her he was going one place, and she would call at a different place for him and he would be there. He said that Paula could see through the walls, and Megan hated this feature of her mother's ESP because she could not get away with anything.

The previous week, Paula had felt something was wrong. She looked under the porch of her building and found kids there playing with matches. When people tell her about deaths or accidents, she is calm because she already knows what happened. She sensed that the cult put curses on people, binding their energy so that bad things would happen to them. Before working with Paula, I thought that curses were just figments of people's imagination. Paula felt they were real and had affected her personally.

Magic Wand

Julienne advised me to make Paula a wand with a copper pipe capped by a quartz crystal, advising Paula to work with it to see how to use its power. Always surprising us, Paula declared she already knew how to use wands. In high school, she had a baton that her family let her have for cheerleading, and she learned how to use it to generate energy.

Reversals

Paula reported, "What would work in someone under normal circumstances has the opposite effect with the cult. It is the reverse of what it should have done." I noticed this phenomenon happen time after time with Paula before I understood energetic reversals. Paula wept, "What's so sick is that they enjoyed causing pain and suffering." I pointed out that she is different: she does not enjoy seeing her daughter in pain. She had to disconnect from trauma and turn the other cheek, like the Bible says. If she struck back, they abused her twenty times worse. She had to keep silent about the abuse. Nobody believed her, and they covered up the evidence.

Cover-ups

Paula reported that cult members included police officers and a judge. After a ceremony that sacrificed human life, they always claimed the death was accidental. They arranged for the police officers who would come for the body to be cult members. Some cult members were in positions to erase and destroy records. The cult members on the police force would sometimes get the police report and have a ceremony the following night to burn it. She also remembered other ceremonies of burning records, birth and death certificates, and destroying all evidence of the existence of a person they had killed.

She also pieced together a pattern of arson. Whenever the cult moved to a new location, they would burn down the house they left to cover their tracks. Paula remembered three times when they left a house and it burned down that night. Every house she had ever lived in while growing up had burned down.

Love-Hate Relationships

Paula reported she had a love-hate relationship with everyone in the family. Many of the cult members were kind to her at times. Things could be calm and pleasant and then, out of the blue, all hell broke loose. We know that this kind of early childhood trauma has profound consequences in the formation of the personality.

> One of the most serious consequences of early trauma stems
> from the betrayal of trust that occurs when a child realizes that

Destroying Evidence

the adult or adults on whom she/he must depend are, in fact, dangerous and unsafe. This kind of trauma, being blocked from the experience of trusting and relying on others, has the potential to distort every other important relationship, including the relationship with one's body, the relationship with other people, and the relationship with the world. It can become the foundation for depression, anxiety, self-hatred, shame, generalized negativity, and more.[2]

I inquired what made cult members switch, and she said that dim light brought out fear and then they acted out uncontrollably. Paula thought that many cult members were also multiple because she would see their eyes and demeanor change when they started a ceremony. Booze and drugs made their

2   S. Eldringhoff and L. Karjala, "Association for Comprehensive Energy Psychology Certification Module 13: Client Trauma Care Skills & Resources," 2006.

behavior worse. Paula said they chose the other way to cope, by passing on the abuse done to them, numbing their pain with alcohol, and choosing to resort to violence to save their own lives.

I asked how Paula was able to survive the violence of her early years. She reflected that she got her love from the Light. She saw a dim light coming through a hole in the shade and she saw herself staring at it, just staring at the Light. Then that memory stopped and she saw herself left as a baby in her crib or locked in a box, a cupboard, or a drawer. A dim light was always present, and she gazed into it. She said, "The light comforts and takes away whatever is wrong, just holds it." The name that she used to access this benevolent light was "The Grace of God."

Paula's Decision

Paula couldn't control the abuse, but she could control how she responded to the pain. She said, "Unconsciously, my spirit, a piece deeper than my soul, accepted that the abuse couldn't be controlled, and I would do whatever was needed to spare others from suffering the same thing." Paula kept staying alive because she knew the ceremonies were going to happen, and by healing and coming back into her body, she could be there to take the abuse the next time so the other kids wouldn't have to be the victims, even though some of them were also abused.

Some of her parts were just mad that they were still alive, and they all had different perspectives on death. When Paula had her near-death experiences (NDEs), only the part of her who was out at the time got the peacefulness of death. The other parts went deep into the soul, encapsulated in spirit, and locked into their suffering. Some called her back. She returned because the kids were crying, both the children outside and the kids inside. Paula decided, "I have to be all one before I die so I can take all of us home together."

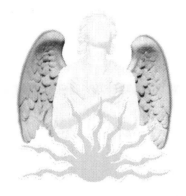

CHAPTER 18

Joeanna

aula was having difficulty with anemia and deficiency in vitamins C and D, and her period came two weeks early. Her physician had put her on prenatal vitamins. Memories surfaced of another part that had lost a child. She called herself Joeanna. At fourteen years old, Paula got pregnant again after Tami's abortion. This fetus was not as far along as Tami's, but the cult did not want others to know she was pregnant and to find out that they had been raping her.

To get rid of the fetus, three people held her down and then they cut through Joeanna's stomach across the navel to cut the umbilical cord and suffocate the fetus. Joeanna could feel the baby suffocating. They wiped the blood off of the knife onto her face and laughed. Then they had sex with her. Sorrow over losing her baby poured out of Joeanna.

Currently, Joeanna wanted to cut her stomach out so it would stop hurting. She was too afraid to talk because they warned her not to tell. Instead, she drew pictures of what happened. To connect Paula more fully with Joeanna, I said her name and held out her drawing and let her share her memory with Paula.

Within the Darkness

*Many, many tears fall deep down
within.
And my mind is in a constant spin,
For once again, it's a continuous
struggle
To deal with all that I feel.
Feeling tormented, bitter and cold.
And feeling trapped within the dark-
ness.
Feeling helpless, and oh so all
alone.*

*My heart burns, with much pain.
My soul darkened and torn.*

Trapped, and wanting to go home.

*For more and more of the darkness
and pain reconnects with me as a
whole.
Many parts feel so out of control.*

*Struggling with letting go.
Emotionally drained, and feeling
much shame.
Shaking and scared, I pray:*

*Oh Lord--I surrender to you!!
For I don't know what to do.
Your Love shields me
in the darkness of my pain.*

*Oh Lord, I know even in the darkest
parts of my past,
Your Love clears me a path.
For I feel your loving Angels around
me.
They help me withstand the darkness and pain of long ago.*

*Within the darkness of my pain
Oh Lord, I Love thee!!
For Loving you is my key to learn-
ing the lessons of
letting go.
Oh Lord, I thank thee,
For your Love for me sets me free.*

Paula

263

Joeanna's Abortion

Joeanna then shared her memory of being taken to the office of a physician in a neighboring city who was a cult member to do a D & C to get rid of the dead fetus and to staple her stomach back together. Paula wrote this letter to help Joeanna integrate into her system:

Joeanna

I feel the pain you're in. Thank you for trusting me. I see what they have done. Help me ease your pain!! Help me tell our story, your story. My body is your body, that's how I can feel your pain. Together we can let go of the pain, anger, sadness, and the tears of the past. You are safe with me, and those I surround myself with. I trust and love them. Some of these people are helping me let go of the past. They are helping me grow.

Joeanna, you can grow with me!! Those who have hurt us in the past, I have nothing to do with anymore. Also Ma and Dad are no longer living. No more denial!

So now together we can heal from the past. I know it is hard for you to believe that Ma and Dad are dead. But it is true. Also I know how hard it is for you to believe that your body and my body are one. At first I had a hard time believing that I had parts that were not connected with me. But I learned to keep an open mind, so that I, we all can grow, and heal from the past. So we can all become whole and at peace within oneself.

Paula

CHAPTER 19

Twin Brother Paul

s Paula gained strength to face her earliest wounds, memories emerged of the most traumatic loss of all, the death of her beloved twin brother, Paul. Having been together in the womb, they were very close and loved each other greatly. Paula said the family used to dress them alike as babies. I saw photos of them in their christening gowns, and telling them apart was difficult. The memory that emerged from a dissociated preverbal part of Paula contradicted the family story that Paul died of sudden infant death syndrome (SIDS). Paula switched, watched what happened in her memory as if in a trance, then switched back, and reported to me what she had seen. She said that on the night of their first birthday, their father came into the room after they were in bed and switched them into each other's cribs. The cult came and got Paula, thinking she was Paul, and tied her down. They brought Paul to watch. They beat Paula and then when they undressed her to abuse her further, they discovered they had the wrong baby. Once they realized the mistake, they stopped and switched babies. They beat Paul, and he started crying. The more he cried, the harder they beat him. Paula was scream-

Sacrificial Fire

ing at the top of her lungs, and they stuffed something in her mouth. She couldn't reach Paul.

During the beating, her father was in the house getting beers for everyone. Paula said that Paul died because his body was not strong enough to withstand the abuse. Paula saw her father helping to build the fire and the cult burning Paul's body. Paula saw Paul's spirit coming out of the fire, going up, and then splitting. Part of him went into the Light and the peace of death, and another part went into her. He split and gave her the ability to split.

She reported, "There will always be a part of me that is my twin." As she connected with the implications of this memory, she realized with horror that all these years the family had been blaming her for Paul's death and saying they wished she had been the one who died instead of Paul. She realized he did not die from SIDS as they had told her, but instead was intentionally killed. This knowledge was very heavy for her. She lamented, "They took away a part of me when they killed him."

Admission Price for the Cult

Paula reported that every cult member had to sacrifice their firstborn child. For those who joined as adults, it was their initiation, their ultimate sacrifice.

She said she had witnessed at least a dozen of these sacrifices of the firstborn child. I shared with her the information I had read from the literature on ritual abuse that the perfect sacrificial victim is a baby, a male child of superior intelligence. In the Bible, the sacrificial instructions are "If any of you—either an Israelite or an alien living in Israel—presents a gift for a burnt offering to the Lord, either to fulfill a vow or as a freewill offering, you must present a male without defect..." (Leviticus 22:18-19a). In Leviticus, God's people were allowed to substitute cattle, sheep, or goats for humans for the sacrifice.

Paula reported that with twins, they were supposed to sacrifice them both, starting with the firstborn on the birthday night and the other twin on the following night. She had witnessed the murders of two other sets of twins and was the only twin who survived. Paul was the firstborn of their father who, through his pain and agony, consented to that sacrifice. On their birthday, the sacrificial victim was not supposed to see the night through. The only other option for Paula's father would have been to leave the cult, but death was the price for those who left. She knew of three cult members who tried to leave and were murdered, confirming what Georgia had told me about the only way to leave the cult being in a coffin. This sacrifice was particularly difficult for her father because Paul was the only son he ever had and was also the only boy in the whole family, as his brothers only had girls.

Paula reported that they also killed the firstborn of the animals and the runts. On her aunt's farm, they also killed the firstborn of the cats and pigs. In front of the children, the cult members tortured the animals, killed them, burned them, and put the roasted flesh in front of the children to eat. She said, "You learn real fast how not to be hungry." But they were forced to eat. The cult also killed her firstborn child, Jesse's baby.

Second Night

On the night following Paul's death, the cult held another ceremony. Paula reported that they tried to kill her, but they could not because Paul would split off her spirit, and his energy would come out in her physical body, so they would just be killing him again. Her life energy would slow down to almost nothing, and she would go out of body into the Light. Then when the ceremony was over and the coast was clear, the Light would send her back into her body.

She would plead to stay in the peace of death, but the Light always said that she was not finished yet and sent her spirit back into her body. Whenever trouble came, Paul's spirit would come out as her protector. He would hold her up and then put her down again.

Paula declared that Paul was in her and that his spiritual presence was what was carrying her through this recovery of her memories. She said he wanted what happened to him to be known. She was the only one other than cult members who had witnessed his death. As an adult, Paula went to city hall to see what was written on his death certificate, but she found no record of either his birth or his death. She felt the cult had destroyed the evidence of his existence to cover up his murder. She asserted, "Paul wants to go completely into the Light, but he will not be free to go until what happened to him is known to his satisfaction." As we went through

Held by Paul's Hands

this memory, my heart was moved. I had just published my first book, and my heart felt called to be the one to write Paul's story.

As the memories came, Paula interjected, "I just can't comprehend this." I too had difficulty comprehending that the practice of sacrifice of the firstborn was still happening. I knew that in the Bible, God had asked Abraham to sacrifice his firstborn son to prove his loyalty to his God. But I was shocked to hear that satanic cults were still adhering to this practice in current times.

Still trying to put together in my mind how a god could require sacrifice of a child, I remembered that God also sacrificed his only begotten son, Jesus Christ, on the cross. This act is celebrated as having great redemptive value for all of humankind. Sacrifice and the idea that one person or animal can pay for and cancel the sins of another and bring a blessing for the one offering the sacrifice is an ancient idea.

Bert Hellinger, the originator of Family Constellation Therapy, talks about the need sometimes to break with the family god to be able to live an authentic life. He gives the example of a man who had a dream that he heard the voice of God calling him to rise up and sacrifice his only and beloved son. The next morning the man arose and looked at his wife and son, and then at his God. "He looked his God in the face and answered, 'I will not do that.'"[1] Paula made the same choice over and over, to refuse to do what the god of her family was demanding of her.

---

1 Hellinger, *Love's Own Truths*, 256.

CHAPTER 20

Halloween

emories of the cult's Halloween ceremonies pieced together for Paula as we approached this holiday in her second year of treatment. She reported that Halloween was the high point of the cult's year, when a lot of things in the earth were dying. Coming after the equinox, it was a time when the power of the darkness was continuing to increase, and the nights were longer than the days. She felt that putting up ghosts and witches made it easier to bring up detrimental energies from Mother Earth. She said the cult celebrated Halloween for nine days and tried to kill three people. Twice they tried to kill her during this celebration.

In her current life, her brother had been missing since mid October. Paula had the gut feeling she gets right before someone she knows dies. Paula was getting psychic impressions of a remote place where the cult used to hold their ceremonies.

She felt the cult was baiting her, holding her brother hostage and sending a psychic message that she could come and get him out, but that she would not

Cabin in the Woods

leave alive this time. She felt they were angry with her for remembering what happened and that they wanted her dead.

First Halloween Ceremony

The first time she was one of the intended victims in the Halloween ritual was when she was seven years old. The cult made her and another child watch the first sacrifice. Then she was forced to witness the sacrifice of the second child. In that memory, she avoided being killed by jumping out a window. I asked how she got untied, and she answered, "Real young I learned how to get out of things real fast."

Second Halloween Ceremony

She remembered another Halloween ceremony that happened when she was fifteen. The first three days of the ritual, they sexually abused a child she had been caring for, a very sweet six-year-old boy named Jeff who had a speech impediment. She was tied and chained, forced to watch them torture

Jumping Out the Window

Jeff to death. He kept calling her name and reaching for her, but she could not help him. Then they beat and tortured Heather, her best friend, who was close to her age. Heather's parents were also in the cult. They told Heather, "Die or vow to become one of us." To save her life, Heather made the choice to swear into the cult. Then they made Heather start Paula's abuse, and she had to obey.

The cult gave Paula the same choice. She refused to join them, so they tortured and beat her until her spirit left her body. They left her for dead. During the ceremony, Paul again came out and took the beating and Paula went to the Light. When the ceremony ended, her spirit came back into her body. She felt that the cult members were particularly angry with her because she had refused to join them, asserting, "That's why they tried so hard to kill me."

During the session, she drew a picture of Jeff's death. She sketched a figure missing his left leg from the knee down, with something beside the body that may have been that part of his leg. He had a rope around his neck and something like blood on the ground beneath him. Two hooded figures were on his left, and a female hooded figure on the right holding a candle had a

Halloween Cross

five-pointed star drawn around the left eye. In the upper right was a swastika symbol, flowing clockwise, inside a circle that did not quite meet and close properly. In the center was an upside-down cross inside a triangle, with three candles in front of it, and something like energy going out in rays from this configuration.

Then Paula stopped drawing, too shaky to continue. Her whole body was trembling, and she said, "Hold me." I wasn't sure I had heard her right, as she had never before allowed me to hold her, so I asked for clarification, and she clearly said, "Hold me." I moved my chair close to her and put my arm around her. She leaned her head against me and sobbed. Then she went into the bathroom and vomited from the memory of being forced to drink Jeff's blood.

Consequences

A couple of weeks before this memory surfaced, a cult member "cousin" who had been one of her perpetrators blew his brains out. After a ceremony, he would come to her and apologize for the things he had been forced to do to her, saying he had not wanted to hurt her. He was the only cult member who ever apologized. This man had been having trouble with the people living downstairs from him and was drinking. When a policeman came to investigate, he killed himself right in front of the officer.

Paula saw the consequences in the lives of children of cult members who gave in to the pressure of joining, under the pain of death if they refused. She saw the consequences of Heather's life decision and the pain and sorrow that resulted. Another "cousin" who had joined the cult was going to jail, got into a fight, and killed himself by shooting himself in the head.

If Paula had joined the cult, she might not have had to sacrifice her daughter, as the cult had already sacrificed her firstborn child, Jesse's baby. But she would have been required to abuse her daughter and try to force her daughter to join. She could not have lived with herself if she had passed on these sadistic practices of torture and abuse to her own child.

I inquired how she felt about her cousin's suicide, and she replied that she was wearing pants that said "Bum Equipment." She began to laugh again for the first time during our session, using her sense of humor to portray that she felt as if her whole system was defective—"Bum Equipment."

One of her older two stepbrothers had joined the cult and went deeply into substance abuse, winding up in prison twenty-seven times. Later in his life, a few years before he died from cancer, he went into substance abuse treatment and turned his life around. He got clean and sober and left the cult. Somehow he escaped the death penalty for leaving. Perhaps his time in prison separated him from cult activity, a blessing in disguise. We prayed that more of those who have gotten lost in the darkness would be able to find the light and transform their lives.

Escape

Two days before Halloween, Paula reported that the police found her brother in a distant state, very disoriented. Cult members had taken him from his house to the place of the Halloween ritual. Somehow, he escaped. He was dehydrated and starved, but alive. Paula said that the cult "sacrifices food and water" for the victims, meaning they withheld food and water from the people they were planning to kill. She felt relieved that her brother got away but also angry with him for refusing to press charges. She verbalized that she wanted to get a gun and go shoot them all, but that action went against her ethics. She was able to stop herself from carrying out her homicidal ideation.

As she processed her Halloween memories, she reported that splinters kept coming out of a lump on the left side of her head. She thought these splinters had been embedded in her body from a beating with a piece of wood a long time ago and were now being pushed out of her body. Another time, Paula was quiet for a long time when coming out of a flashback. She remembered two people abusing her that she had not known were involved with the cult. One woman involved was one of her best friends and she still called her. After seeing this person a couple of weeks earlier, Paula had a spell of deafness connected with the memory of her head being pushed through a window, being clubbed on the back of the head, and having blood coming out of both her ears. The deafness was another body memory tied to a buried memory of previous connection with this woman. Paula felt shocked and saddened by realizing this woman had been involved with her abuse and might have been assigned to try to hold back her recovery.

Antecedents

My impression was that Hitler and the Mafia killed people fast, without torturing them like the cult does. Paula strongly disagreed with this idea and reported she was slowly realizing the link between cult activity and the Holocaust. She said Hitler did not kill people fast. When he killed the Jews, he tortured them first. He imprisoned them, starved them, and separated family members. He killed parents and children in front of each other to increase the traumatic impact of the deaths. She said that Hitler persecuted the Jews because their ways and beliefs were different, but he also targeted Catholics and others who followed God and Jesus. She reported that after World War II ended, Hitler's followers who had been inducted into satanic practices continued to persecute and torture people who believed in God. Paula claimed that much of what happened in the Holocaust is not taught in our books, to protect the survivors, because anyone connected with any of the families who had been targeted for death were also executed, even after the war ended.

Safety Concerns

Paula called me up after the session with the Halloween memories and asked me to burn the picture she had drawn. She felt uncomfortable revealing the masking they used in the ceremony. She said that because she was dyslexic, she had drawn the Swastika symbol backward from the way it had been used in the cult and that its energy flowed counterclockwise rather than clockwise. She was concerned for my safety because she passed me in her car and saw a flash of a car accident. She had been praying for protection for those who were working with her. We talked about her fears that her material might contaminate others she worked with, including friends of survivors. I said the main dangers I saw were the self-destructive forces inside of her, not whatever danger might be on the outside. Inside was a place where she had some choice and control.

Cutting continued to be an issue for Paula. One day when she got home from downtown, in addition to the cat food she bought, she found two separate packages of razor blades, with receipts dated one hour apart. She did not remember buying either package. She said that she must have switched, gone in and bought one pack, come out and switched back, then later switched to another part and bought some more. She threw them away, complaining, "I'm tired of wasting my money!"

Be Extremely Selective

After these memories, Paula came into a session in an antagonistic mood, angry at the world. She wanted to give up and to let nature take its course and kill her with a blood clot—to die in her silence. By the end of her session, she was able to find some hope again and used humor as a coping mechanism. She told me that her horoscope in the newspaper for that day said, "You must be extremely selective regarding your counselor today if you solicit advice from others. You might get involved with a person who knows less than you do." We both laughed hard! I felt like she knew so much more than I did about the whole process of dissociation.

CHAPTER 21

Holidays

Holidays in the Hospital

For three years in a row, Paula had been in the hospital on all the holidays: Thanksgiving, Christmas, New Year's Day, and Easter. She said, "I don't consider them holidays!" She claimed that the letters in "holiday" stood for "Hell Of Love In Days Of Youth." On holidays, the whole pack came and abused her for days. "Till their party was over, my hell didn't stop." She remembered both plain sexual and physical abuse plus the ceremonies. Even when the family went on a vacation to the beach for two weeks, the time was traumatic for Paula because by day she would be stuck caring for all of the children and her crippled sister, and then by night, the family called in their friends and did satanic rituals there at the beach, abusing Paula.

Thanksgiving

Memories came of how her father celebrated Thanksgiving when she was six years old. He brought home a live turkey and cut off its head in front of the children. Headless, it ran around the house, splattering blood all over. Then they took Paula and the dead turkey down into the basement and beat her with the turkey and stuck part of it into her. The next day they all ate the turkey, and she did not remember what they had done to her with it the night before. She felt sick, knowing she ate that turkey, and wanted a bath, saying she felt slimy all over.

Easter

In our next session, a memory came up that happened on Easter, a high point of the Christian calendar.

A very quiet part came out saying, "[You] Don't want to know me." She couldn't tell what happened. I said Paula was listening to her memories because Paula wanted to get to know her, too. Although she said nothing, I saw a very painful and difficult memory come into her awareness. Then Paula came back, held her head bowed in sorrow, and was quiet for a long time. When she finally spoke, she said, "My Aunt Martha's death...wasn't a normal death." Then she said, "I'm going to be sick." She cried a bit and then got up and left for the bathroom. I followed her to the bathroom and heard heaving sounds. I went in and saw Paula trembling all over. Stomach fluids mixed with blood were in the toilet. Paula washed up and came back to the therapy room. She sat in sorrow some more, then shared the memory.

Aunt Martha's Death

When Paula was thirteen years old, on Easter the family went to the home of her paternal grandmother, who lived with her sister Martha and her sons Hans and Heinz, Paula's uncles. Paula saw a photo of herself at her grandmother's house and commented, "I don't remember having those clothes on when I got my picture taken." The photo turned out to be a picture of Aunt Martha taken at age thirteen, and she looked exactly like Paula. Everyone was always commenting on how similar the two of them were. Martha had always been kind to Paula.

Cult members started a ceremony centered on Martha. When they began abusing Martha, Paula tried to intervene, but they tied up Paula and made her watch them cut Aunt Martha and collect her blood. Then they beat Aunt Martha to death. They also beat Paula and made her drink Aunt Martha's blood. It made her sick at the time and made her sick again as she remembered. I was trying to figure out how Aunt Martha's blood could get into the toilet by my office decades later, because I witnessed the bloody vomit with my own eyes.

I asked why she thought they killed Martha. Paula said they killed her because they did not need her anymore. During the ceremony, as Martha was disrobed, Paula recognized scars on her body that she, too, had, only Martha's body had not healed as well as Paula's. She realized then that Martha had been a victim of cult abuse long before Paula's birth. The family had tried to separate Paula and Martha. When Paula came over to visit, an uncle said one word in German, and Martha would go to her room, no questions asked. Martha only spoke when spoken to.

After the ceremony, they said, "Now you are the most beautiful. We did this for you." She understood that in their twisted thinking, Paula was now the most special chosen one for sacrifice to Father Satan.

Paula did not fear death. She wished she had been the one they killed, to end her hell by bringing the peace of death. I asked whether she thought Martha found peace when she died in this ceremony. Paula reflected that she thought Martha did find peace, because she did not protest in any way throughout the ceremony.

Paula thought that her father and his brothers had been involved in satanic practices in Germany before the family immigrated to the United States and that perhaps this activity might have been the reason they had to leave their home country. She suspected that Martha had been a victim throughout her life. This possibility made sense to me, as I had read that cult practices were intergenerational, with the parents themselves being victims and then abusing their children and bringing them into the cult.

Once when Paula went over to her grandmother's house, her uncles were not there, and Paula asked Martha to teach her a song on the piano. Paula caught on instantly and played the song by ear. Martha asked her why she was so sad. Paula said it was just taking care of her handicapped sister. But Martha looked at her and said she knew there was more. The exact words she used were, "I know." Paula realized that Martha knew because she, too, was a victim, though Paula never saw Martha switch. Paula wept openly in talking about Martha, letting the ocean of tears locked inside her start to flow out.

Paula felt the pain of the crystal-clear memories of this thirteen-year-old part. She was able to verbalize the anger, shame, and blame she felt during the ceremony.

Your pain is the breaking of the shell that encloses your understanding.

Even as the stone of the fruit must break, that its heart may stand in the sun,

so must you know pain....

It is the bitter potion by which the physician within you heals your sick self.

—Kahlil Gibran

Grieving

Paula said, "I got through the abuse by myself. Why can't I get through the healing myself?" Aunt Martha had been the kindest person Paula ever knew. The pattern of separating Paula from all the people she loved and who loved her was a consistent theme in the cult, the aim to isolate her emotionally.

Aunt Martha was a strict Catholic. There was a room in the house where she and Paula's grandmother prayed, with an altar. Grandma had one corner, Martha had another, and a third corner was for someone else. The next room was the "Forbidden Room," where they did ceremonies. Her grandmother knew about them but could not stop them. They killed Martha while Grand-mother was away and said it was an accident. After reporting the ceremony, Paula reflected, "No wonder I'm so fucked up."

Black Magic

Still, Paula had been able to use good judgment when given the opportunity to choose. In high school, her friends wanted her to join them playing around with black magic and Ouija boards. She always refused, feeling that they did not know what they were getting themselves into. She never got involved with this dabbling in the dark arts.

Lifesaver Lori

Once Paula intervened in a beating and was able to save a life—her mother's. Her parents had gone to a wedding by themselves, and when they returned, her father beat her mother severely. Then he pushed her out into the street in front of a car, which hit her and knocked her unconscious. Paula dissociated and a part named Lori came out and yelled for help. Lori did CPR on her mother. When her mother revived, she felt angry with Lori for saving her and chided, "Why didn't you let me die?"

Then when Lori got home from the hospital, her father gave her a severe beating for having saved her mother's life. As he beat her, he said, "You're no good. Your mother's no good. Why didn't you let her die? Why don't you die?" Lori wept as she told the story. She felt hurt and angry with both of her parents.

I asked Paula why Lori didn't just let her mother die there in the street. She responded, "I just couldn't do that."

Paula seemed to have a mission in life of helping others. As a teenager, she'd had a job as a lifesaver and saved three people from drowning. I reflected that she is very good at her job of helping others but needs to be appreciated for what she does! Like a shaman, she has been through the doors of death many times but has always come back.

Learning to Swim

Paula was good in the water because her father had taught her to swim. His method for her aquatic training was throwing her off a boat in the ocean fifty feet from shore. He told her that if she wanted to get back, she could swim. Paula learned how to swim on the spot, and when she got to the shore, she stuck her tongue out at the men in the boat. Her father threw her brother off the boat, too, but he was not able to make it on his own. They had to haul him back into the boat. I made the analogy that her father did the same thing psychologically, always throwing her into more than she could handle, and that she had managed by figuring out ways to master the situations.

She reported that when her bones were broken and she was locked in the closet instead of being taken to the hospital, she was able to reset her fractures by herself. But when her father beat Lori for saving her mother's life, he broke her jaw in four places, and she was not able to get all the bones back in quite the right places.

CHAPTER 22

Meeting a Ghost

O ne day, as Paula came in for our session, a bone-chilling cold wafted in with her. The room got so cold that I put on my winter coat. Still, I could not get my hands warm. My fingers felt like ice. I had learned to let Paula begin our sessions so, after the initial greeting, I waited until she was ready to talk. After a few minutes, she said, "My father's spirit is attached to me."

Stunned, I tried to process those words. Slowly, I realized that the spirit of her deceased father was in the room with us, attached to Paula. If the room had not suddenly gotten so cold when she walked in, I might have thought that she was having a hallucination of the presence of her father because of all the unresolved issues that kept emerging as she recovered her memories. As the truth of her words sank in, I freaked out inside and thought to myself, "Holy _____, I'm here with a ghost, and it's a satanic cult member!"

Spiritual SOS

I did what I always do when I don't know what to do: I prayed for help! I sent up a huge SOS to my spiritual helpers, asking for safety and guidance. Within seconds, perfect peace came into my heart and into the room. I knew exactly what to do. I said, "Well, if your father came to therapy today, let's talk with him." We brought in an extra chair and sat it between us, a Gestalt therapy dialogue technique. I asked Paula what she wanted to say to her father, and she expressed her feelings. Then I asked her to intuit what he wanted to say to her, and she told me his responses. Back and forth, with Paula addressing her issues and channeling her father's responses, she did some major forgiveness work with him.

Action Plan

The session was heartfelt and beautiful. This event was my first direct encounter with an earthbound spirit. At the time, I had no idea that I could have done some healing work with her father, too. But after Paula left that day, I realized I needed an action plan in case another earthbound spirit showed up in my practice.

Sometimes I think that when a therapist is able to handle a new issue, the spirit guide of the client sends a text to the spirit guides of others with similar issues to find that therapist! After this session, earthbound spirits started showing up with increasing frequency in my practice. As I was learning Thought Field Therapy (TFT), a new technique of tapping on acupressure points to resolve disturbing feelings, I realized that if an earthbound spirit were linked energetically to my client, then when the client tapped on the points, the spirit would also get the benefit. The concept is similar to computers linked in a network. I tried out this theory and it worked extremely well so I wrote a Soul Detective Earthbound Spirit Protocol[1] to help other therapists dealing with similar issues.

---

1   Stone, *Invisible Roots*, 175-201.

CHAPTER 23

Backlash

*A*s Paula progressed in her healing, her case manager told me that she had known Paula for a long time, because Paula used to come to a clinic where she worked. Her case manager emphasized that Paula was the very best she had ever seen her. She told me Paula used to walk around "like a zombie."

Julienne worked with Paula to be better able to hear her parts, one at a time. Paula talked about how all of her parts like to sing, and she could be most fully herself when she was singing. She sang "Precious Memories" for both Julienne and me, beautifully and full of feeling. Playing the piano and organ also helped her cope.

As Paula healed, she felt an escalation in the cult's efforts to silence her. Julienne reminded me that satanic ritual abuse survivors are programmed to self-destruct if they start to recover their memories of what happened. This situation explained why Paula's suicidal impulses intensified as she reconnected with her memories. In addition to this internal attack, Paula also felt that the cult had put "death energy" into her house. She felt that dark energy filled her living space, increasing her nightmares and feelings of psychic attack. I asked

Julienne why the cult was so invested in Paula not getting better. Julienne explained that each time Paula went up a notch in her healing process, the cult felt more threatened that she would break their secrecy, so they tried harder to pull her down. Paula's body was going haywire, with multiple problems, including vaginal and rectal bleeding, stomach upset, headaches, and more clots. She was also running into cult members on the street. Sometimes they would try to talk to her, but she did not want to converse with them because just seeing them triggered more memories.

During another session with Julienne, when the subject of Paula's self-destructive impulses came up, fiery rage came out of Paula into Julienne's heart center. Julienne gave Paula the option to continue, stop, or change the subject. Paula decided to change the subject. Julienne sensed the "death energy" the cult had placed in Paula's home and got permission from Paula to undo it. The process felt brutal to Paula, because some of her young parts could not tell the difference between a perpetrator's energy and the healing energies. Julienne saw that Paula had been attacked at the third, sixth, and eighth chakras and corrected the blockages, knowing that a little one inside might go back and undo what was fixed. Julienne followed the dark energy back to its source and told it, "No!"

Speak Out

Paula was the first in her city to speak out about her abuse and, with her disclosure, others in the area started talking, too. She said, "They want me to shut up so others will shut up." One of Paula's cousins called her up and told her to quit therapy. This cousin had also been abused and had gone into therapy. When the cousin's father, a cult member, told her to quit therapy, she did. Paula refused to quit. She claimed her stubbornness was what kept her going!

Nel

The cult then tried another tactic to discourage Paula from getting therapy. One day when I went to the clinic to see Paula, she was sitting outside on the steps and I could see she had switched. Her cheekbones seemed more prominent and her eyes bigger, and she looked younger and very frightened, a look I associated with Marge. She told me that she could not go into the clinic because Nel, one of the lesbian partners who headed the cult, was there. She told me she had run into Nel in the waiting room, and Nel offered to take her to the graveyard to visit her mother's grave. Bewildered, I asked what Nel was doing in the clinic. Paula said that Nel worked in the billing office and had asked Paula to stop by the office to give Nel her telephone number. I felt stunned. Could it be true, or was Paula having a psychotic break, hallucinating that the head of the cult worked at the clinic?

To get more reality into the situation, I asked what Nel was wearing. Paula said she had on a white blouse and a green skirt. Paula waited outside while I went cautiously into the clinic and inquired whether anyone new was working in the billing office. The front desk said no. I was beginning to think that Paula had lost it, but I next stepped into the billing office to look for a woman with a white blouse and a green skirt. I didn't see anyone by that description.

Babysitter

While I was standing there, the regular head of the billing office at the front desk asked me if I was there on business for a client. I said yes, that Paula had mentioned someone she knew was in the office and had asked her to stop by. A sweet-looking little middle-aged woman wearing something that did not match Paula's description said, "Oh, that was me. I have known Paula for twenty-five years and used to babysit for her. I offered to take her to visit her mother's grave."

I will always remember that moment, when a wave of terror went through my system as I realized that Paula was not crazy and that I was standing face-to-face with the head of the cult. After the initial wave of terror passed and I sent out another spiritual SOS, I felt my spiritual guidance team surrounding me with God's Light. That day was the first time I had ever worn all white. Nel continued, "If Paula has any questions about her bill, have her come directly to us with them."

Slowly, I realized that the cult had access to Paula's chart and all the information she had disclosed and also knew my name and address. A huge wave of fear hit me. I felt vulnerable. When I got home that day, I fell on my knees in front of my picture of Jesus and cried out in anguish for spiritual help and protection! I could not believe that Nel had disclosed her connection with Paula to me. If she had not said anything, I would have thought that Paula was psychotic, especially since nobody in a white blouse and green skirt ever showed up. Nel confirmed Paula's report of their encounter. Who in their right mind would want to go to the graveyard with the head of the cult?

Nightmare

That night Paula dreamed that when she came to the clinic for our next appointment, a car of cult members pulled up, forced her into their car, and abducted her. Coming to the clinic no longer felt safe to her since she knew Nel was working there. Nel had never been out smoking before when Paula came to the clinic. Nel's office was only twenty feet away from the room where we worked together, and the situation did not feel safe to me either.

The head psychiatrist at the clinic did not believe that the sweet little woman he had hired to work in the billing office was actually the head of a satanic cult, but he understood that Paula felt terrorized by her presence. To support Paula, he arranged for me to see her at a satellite office of the clinic. Paula was grateful for a safer place for us to continue our work. I had to come back to the main clinic after each session to write my note, and I always seemed to run into Nel. I continued praying for protection!

Escalation

The attacks on Paula escalated at every level. Her neighborhood was overrun with drug activity and gunfire broke out, with five shots at her building. The whole area was crawling with police, and her normally extremely high level of anxiety went off the charts. She felt as if she were in a pressure cooker and wanted to move out of town.

Attacked

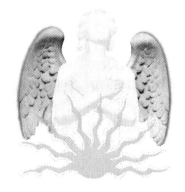

CHAPTER 24

Getting Out

Paula pleaded for several days of respite time in a motel near town where she wanted to move so she could calm down. Since the gunfire attacks were external, she refused psychiatric hospitalization, especially because she would not be able to supervise the safety of her daughter if she were locked up. Her case manager arranged the respite care. When Paula and her daughter arrived at the motel, the church gave them some food, but not enough to feed a hungry teenager for three days. Paula felt stranded. She called me, saying her parts were freaking out. "My life is a nightmare. Life stinks."

Boundaries

I told Paula, "I'll loan you some money for food. It's breaking the boundaries, but under the circumstances, I'll do it." I felt a little nervous as I got ready to go. I tried to buy Paula a newspaper on the way, but the machine wouldn't open. It kept giving me an extra nickel when I pushed the coin return button.

I stopped at a stand and bought some fruit for me and some extra fruit for Paula. I put the food in the trunk of my car and then found I had locked my keys in the trunk. I asked myself, "Am I nervous?" The answer was obvious. I was thinking about how Julienne had emphasized keeping appropriate boundaries with Paula. But my heart said to go. I fumbled with the open sunroof and took it out so I could crawl into the top of my car. Then I remembered I had an extra car key in my purse.

Paula and Megan were very glad to see me. I loaned Paula $45, which she repaid later. Paula said that when she heard the bullets, she flashed to Carol's memories of seeing Jerry getting shot. She was shaky and was having heart palpitations. I reviewed the procedure to get into the hospital if she wanted to and reminded her that she could ask the motel owner to call her an ambulance. The next day, Paula used part of the money for a cab to go apartment hunting. Under the circumstances, I felt I could not live with myself if I had not taken action. Like Lori, unable to stand by and watch her mother die in the street, I could not stand by watching Paula and Megan go hungry. I also realized how emotionally involved I had become in the case.

When Paula got back home, she intensified her efforts to move out of town, but felt extremely discouraged by all the problems that came up. I pointed out how miracles happened all around her, and about how she had always pulled through. I said the evidence of the miracles was that she was still alive. With her characteristic sense of humor, Paula quipped, "That was my first mistake!"

Blockages Galore

I have never seen a person run into so many blockages at every turn when they tried to mobilize a plan to move, but every difficulty imaginable seemed to find Paula. At last she located an apartment in a different city that was in the catchment area where I worked at another clinic so that we could continue working together in a safer place. Just before she was about to move, that apartment fell through. Discouraged, I took an envelope with Paula's picture sealed inside to a special charismatic prayer meeting I had been attending and asked for support for a satanic ritual abuse survivor. I told the leader that a group of people was praying for her destruction, so I figured a group of people praying for her healing was a good idea. In specific, I asked for help with getting an apartment so she could move. The leader prayed with me, "Lord, we just claim her back!"

I wept as we prayed. Then the group gathered around her picture and prayed to break the bonds of darkness that bound her and to set her free in the name of Jesus. Then an older woman got a message from Spirit to pray also for me and my husband, for our home and cars and family and animals. They anointed us both and also the envelope with the picture inside. We sang a song for this sister and I cried all the way through. My husband and I felt immense support and my heart came into peace. I knew that whatever happened would be right. Paula stuck to her determination to leave the area where her abuse had happened and where she was vulnerable to running into cult members everywhere. After the combined efforts of everyone in her support system, at last Paula signed a lease for an apartment in the new city!

No Brakes

In our last session at the clinic where Nel worked, we both expressed our joy that Paula had finally been able to move herself out of the area that kept triggering so many memories of her abuse. My husband drove me home from that last session. As we pulled into our driveway, the car mildly bumped into the trees at the end of our parking space. My husband said that the brakes had been acting funny all the way home and, by the time we pulled into our driveway, they were completely gone. He inspected the car and found a hole in the brake line, where the brake fluid had gradually leaked out. I still do not know whether the brake line rusted out from natural causes or whether someone tampered with it to try to cause us to have an accident.

Fear

I went for an appointment with my chiropractor. While waiting in the treatment room to see him, I broke down. I felt inner tension that was like a spring wound up very, very tightly. I wept in fear. The full impact of the possibility that the cult was trying to kill me suddenly struck. I felt afraid, and I prayed for Jesus Christ to tell me right then whether or not it was sabotage. I needed to know! Jesus responded with a telepathic message that either way, I would be okay.

292

I prayed and asked whether to tell my chiropractor what was going on. The angels said I had to tell somebody. I shared the story with him and, after a couple of sentences, he named an "incorruptible" policeman he knew, and then left the room. I felt totally abandoned. The two minutes he was gone felt like an eternity until I accepted that I was alone with this fear. When he came back, he was supportive and asked pertinent questions. He worked on me and got some good releases.

Sitting with mortal fear, the real possibility that someone was trying to kill me was a new experience. For the first time, I understood what life was like for Paula. Knowing I needed more support, I shared the experience, without mentioning any names, with a trusted friend. She said, "You just got scared by the boogeyman. You go into deep, dark places in that work." She questioned whether I should get off the case, but I did not choose that solution. My friend reflected that the dark had power, but there was also great power in the Light, and that, frankly, I was very much on the side of the Light. To get through that fear, I had to increase my connection with the light of Christ Consciousness, a golden grid of energy that goes around the whole Earth. Doing this was the first time I worked consciously to transform my fear into gold!

I also talked with my family and asked them to pray for me. My father, a very practical man, was concerned for my safety and advised me to quit working on the case. I knew I was deeply enmeshed emotionally and spiritually with Paula and dark force energy, but leaving at that point would have felt like quitting and running away with my tail between my legs. I could not do that, either for Paula or for myself. My father respected my decision to stay.

Spirit Attack

The feeling of being attacked continued. Once while I was lying in bed, just starting to wake up, I felt the presence of Nel's spirit beside my bed, trying to penetrate my energy field. Struggling to find my voice, I commanded, "In the name of Jesus Christ, NO!" The spirit left immediately, but I felt shaken by the experience. I had the following dream, which shows contamination with cult energy, gross images of human sacrifice, and fear for my dog Terri's safety.

I am doing an intake for a man accused of killing a young girl. His wife is present during the session. I ask for his date of birth, and he says, "The Immaculate Conception of Mary." He also says he is a devil worshipper. His wife looks startled when he says that, and he comments that his wife does not know his religion. I inquire whether "the Immaculate Conception of Mary" is a satanic holiday, and he says it is and demonstrates the position used for sex on that day: both partners of the couple have their hands around the other one's throat, with some pressure. He says it is to build trust that the other will not choke you during sex. He admits in a roundabout way that he did kill the girl. Somehow he is out on bail till the court date. I see him gathering things for a ceremony and tell him he is forbidden to do satanic ceremony in the space we are in.

I see him at a public gathering. The focal person is someone else, and the devil-worshipper man is in the background, inconspicuous, like the cult members. I see him prodding a woman with a stick. Then I see a blonde woman tied to a board in several places hanging upside down in some kind of slow torture. After the gathering is all over, I go back and see the blonde woman's dismembered head and part of her body. I see they roasted her flesh and ate most of it. Parts are still attached to the board, strands of flesh and bone sticking out.

Then I am with my dog Terri and her blue sweater falls off. Then her black coat of fur slips off and I see the white dog underneath slip out. I call her and try to get her to put her coat back on.

Poltergeist activity started happening in my house, phenomena similar to things Paula had been reporting. I thought of the warning the psychiatrist had given me at the beginning of my treatment with Paula about seeing therapists getting frightened and burned out when supernatural things started happening. I got a very eerie feeling when the lights in my house switched on by themselves.

Terri

I was most worried that the cult would hurt my beloved little dog Terri while I was gone at work. I knew that one of the tactics the cult used was killing pets or placing dead birds on a person's doorstep. While my husband was taking Terri for a walk, the neighbor's huge dog Shiva (named for the Hindu god of destruction) attacked Terri and hurt her. Fortunately, Terri got away without serious injury, but I wondered whether my fear had attracted the very thing I was afraid of. I worked with Julienne on my fear. She said that fear was the energetic cord by which the cult tracked survivors and those involved with them. If I would stop fearing them, they would not be able to find me. But just how does one stop fear?

Satanic Ceremony

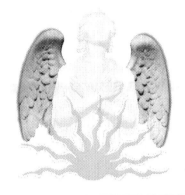

CHAPTER 25

New Techniques

*O*thers in my support group for working with cult survivors reported getting harassed by the perpetrators of their clients. Some would get phone messages that their client was dead. The cult also called the client saying that the therapist was dead, playing on everyone's worst fears. Others received pages of satanic symbols through their fax machines.

EMDR

The support group recommended I learn a new therapy called Eye Movement Desensitization and Reprocessing (EMDR) to help transform and heal trauma. I went for training and was amazed how much EMDR helped with my own trauma. Practicing on myself, I was able to clear trauma from past life memories. It just seemed to melt away. Eager to share this new healing tool with Paula, at our next session I had her think of a traumatic memory and do the side-to-side eye movements of EMDR. Before her eyes had gotten from one side to the other, she left the room, ran to the bathroom, and vomited.

Eye movements tend to bring up more emotion, and EMDR intensified her trauma. Later, I learned not to try a new technique on my most traumatized client, but rather, to test it with others first. Also, I learned that a client needs to be stable first before digging in for memories, and Paula was still not stable.

TFT

My trusted colleague Marie recommended I learn Thought Field Therapy (TFT), a method developed by psychologist Roger Callahan. Marie said TFT worked for some people when EMDR didn't. I found an advertisement for TFT that had a banner at the top saying, "There is a cure." I laughed to myself, knowing that emotional pain could not be cured, but that one just adjusted to carrying the load. Still, I went to the training given by psychologist Greg Nicosia to check it out.

During the workshop, Dr. Nicosia asked for volunteers to come to the front of the room to demonstrate the protocols for each emotion. When he asked for volunteers to demonstrate the protocol for rage, as a joke, I raised my hand. I am a peaceful person and was not in touch with any rage. Another woman raised her hand, and he asked if she would like to come forward to release her rage. She refused, saying that rage was a most delicious feeling, and she wanted to keep it! Dr. Nicosia called on me, and I had to scramble to think about whether I had any rage. As I went inside, a livid geyser of rage surfaced from deep within my soul over what the cult had done to Paula. When Dr. Nicosia asked me what rage I wanted to work on, I was too afraid to talk about the cult in public, so I whispered in his ear, telling him about the situation. Not jarred in the least, Dr. Nicosia thought a moment and then said, "So you are enraged about the abuse that has been done to your client." I agreed that wording was accurate and safe.

He did a strange procedure of having me extend my arm and then pushing on it to get information about the interior configuration of the problem in my energy field. He found that I had no limiting beliefs blocking my ability to release the rage, something he called "reversals," a wording Paula had also used in describing her programming.

Then he showed me how to tap on a sequence of meridian points on my body for rage and trauma. Something profound shifted in me, and I realized

I was no longer afraid of the cult. Dr. Nicosia explained that the trauma happened first for me and then the rage was an overlay on top of the trauma. The rage also melted with this amazing treatment.

I decided I would just use the opening centering exercise from TFT with Paula. This exercise, called the "Heart Massage," is a stabilization technique—just what Paula needed—and is good for all people with all diagnoses. At our next session, I asked Paula to circle her palm clockwise around her heart (from under the throat, down to the left, around to the bottom, and back up) while saying the affirmation "I love and accept myself with all my problems and limitations."

She only got from 12 o'clock on the circle to 2 o'clock when she put her hand down and declared, "But I don't love myself. I hate myself!"

Stumped, I realized what she said was true. She was so honest that she was unable to lie to herself. I did not know what to do so I gave up using TFT with Paula for the time. Fifteen years later, an experienced colleague named Mary Sise told me how to adapt the Heart Massage for highly traumatized clients. Either they could just circle the heart clockwise without saying anything, spinning the heart chakra in the proper direction, or they could say "I wish I could love and accept myself with all my problems and limitations." If this affirmation still did not work, as a last resort, the client could simply say, "I really want to feel better." Even though I was not able to use TFT with Paula at that time, it worked extremely well to help me clear my vicarious traumatization and worked well for almost everyone else in my caseload that was willing to try this experimental technique.

TFT with Megan

Paula noticed that Megan had stopped going out and was wearing sweat pants in the house, even in the sweltering heat of the summer. She asked Megan what had happened and found out that a man at the pool had molested her by touching her inappropriately. Paula brought Megan in for a session, and I did TFT with her to release the trauma and the shame from this incident. Megan recovered immediately and went back to her cheerful, rambunctious, mouthy, outgoing self.

Reiki

The only energy therapy that was able to duck under the radar of the cult and escape getting its healing energy reversed was Reiki, a hands-on healing treatment I had learned that channeled Universal healing energy. When Paula was not doing well, she would ask for a Reiki treatment.

TFT at Last

Much later in our work together, Paula called me up and asked, "Where do you tap for fear?" Three cult members had just come to her door, including one of the men who had raped her. This man claimed that he was her daughter's father and wanted visitation rights with Megan.

Horrified at the thought of having to give her daughter visiting time with a cult member, she refused and told them to take her to court to prove paternity. Then she called me. I told her the tapping sequence or fear was directly under the eye, under the arms on the side of the body where a bra strap would cross, and then in the indentation under the collarbone right beside the sternum. Later she told me that the sequences worked better for her if she tapped them backward, and the tapping helped reduce the charge of her fear. Paula had found a creative way to get around the reversals that had been embedded in her system: reversing the procedure, since two negatives make a positive.

Fear

CHAPTER 26

Paula's Funeral Plans

*O*nce Paula got settled into her new apartment, she felt a large clot forming in her body, an internal attack that threatened her life. Julienne cheered Paula on, reflecting that she was on the brink of a very big change and acknowledging that the transition felt disorienting to the parts inside. Julienne asked for Paula's permission to go in and work on the blood clot that was forming. With a humorous gesture of resistance, Paula begrudgingly agreed. Julienne said that parts of Paula were making the clot and that she knew that those parts could rebuild it after Julienne undid it. Julienne asked if these dissociated parts knew about the Grace of God, Paula's link to Divine energy. Paula said the other parts only had glimpses.

Julienne reflected that Paula's energy was a closed system. The parts inside that got glimpses of other realities were told that these other realities were worse than their familiar pain and suffering. Julienne said that, in her own healing process, she went back and forth between realities. Sometimes she would go back to a memory, but she could move out of that reality again. She encouraged Paula to explore more fully the glimpses of the world outside her closed system. At the end, Julienne laughed and said, "They're putting the clot back together again. I see them with little trowels and bricks, forming it one cell at a time." Paula laughed and admitted it was true. Julienne noted that Paula could take apart the clot just like Julienne had done, and Paula admitted that she could.

The next day, Paula called, feeling upset, and reported, "I'm in a battle with all of the parts. It's them against me. They want to kick in the second phase of the clot. I'm not going to make it to the end of the week like this. I don't know how much longer I'm going to last. I feel like I have been raped fifty million times over—a combination of that and the clotting."

I asked what had pulled Paula through this far, and she answered, "Your support. You're the only one who has really cared and listened." I included others in that circle, too—especially Julienne and Paula's acupuncturist.

Paula lamented, "Can't fight 'em off anymore. Anything would be better than this."

Very moved, I said to Paula, knowing this might be the last time we talked, "You have all my love and support."

Paula wept and said, "I know. I think that's why it's so hard for me to be where I'm at right now." She ended by telling me to take care of myself. After meditating and crying, I called Paula back. She was coughing during the whole conversation because she was so ill. She gave the exact information of the outfit she wanted to be buried in, the funeral plans, distribution of her healing crystals, and the location of the plot beside her mother where she wanted to be buried. She dictated her last will and testament to me, naming the person she wanted to have custody of Megan.

My Journal Entry

Sorrow wrenched my soul as Paula felt like she was dying. After this conversation, I felt as if a Mack truck had run over me. I wrote the following in my journal:

> I experience the double bind that I want her to live, but she
> wants to die. Partly I am weary of fighting against the parts
> of Paula that want to die, and I feel tempted to give in to the

death force. Part of me is homesick too and wants to go home. I have always known that the other side is more peaceful than here. People say to keep my boundaries. There are no boundaries around my heart when it comes to Paula. My heart is fully open to her, and perhaps that is why the thought of her death hurts me so much. I don't know anyone else that I have really and truly known so deeply and have felt this open to. This case has been a real gift in my work as a therapist and has opened my heart.

I hear the voice of her first psychiatrist saying, "Keep your boundaries! Detach!" I hear him and value his advice, yet my heart does not want to put fences around this relationship. I broke a boundary, consciously, when I took food and $45 to Paula while she was in the motel. Yet, I could not have lived with myself if I had left her there, stranded. I know I need the boundaries because I felt totally depleted afterward. I want to learn another way to deal with people, because if God calls me to do more work with this population in the future, I need to let Spirit bear the burden. It is too great for me personally. Just now Paula called, and I set the boundary to talk only a few minutes. I know she also needs to know the rules and have our boundaries clear.

I cannot stop death. I cannot stop separation nor the pain and suffering it brings to the world. But I will live in dignity with or without Paula's presence on the Earth plane. Lord, please teach me true wisdom, to do what my heart knows is right, regardless of the outer rules. Please give me good judgment. Help me see truth.

I called my older sister Johanna, a massage therapist, after this conversation and shared with her how sad I was about Paula's being so close to death. The next day at work, I was on the edge of tears all day. I consulted with another therapist in my division who helped me focus on what I needed through this process. I told her, "I'm countertransferred! No doubt about it!" My colleague reminded me that Paula had already demonstrated an amazing set of survival skills and encouraged me to use one of Paula's main coping skills, humor, to lighten up the grave situation.

That evening I called to check on Paula and she picked up the phone, knowing it was me (before the days of caller ID) and quipped, "Hi, Barbara," before I had a chance to identify myself.

I countered with, "Hello, this is the Heavenly Herald. We have an apartment ready for you. When do you want to move in?"

She laughed, "Yesterday!" Paula told me, "Don't worry about me so much. I'll be all right!"

CHAPTER 27

Going into the Light

*P*aula was feeling weak and in pain. She stepped out of her room, and when she returned, she reported she saw a white shadow coming out of the wall. She heard her deceased husband's voice saying, "I'm here to hold you." He extended his hand, and she reached for it. Then it just wrapped around her. His energy was warmer than hers. She knew she was still not out of danger and was alternately feeling cold and then sweating.

The following night she felt so weak, she almost called the ambulance, but she was too weak to pick up the phone. The white light was opening more, and she could not move. She just opened up and said:

> *Divine Light, You are true love.*
> *You are the energy. If you want me, take me,*
> *And send your Divine Light to those who have carried me.*

I Surrender

Isolated within the walls of deadly fear,
And silenced with the memories and violence of long ago years.

Deep within fall my tears,
Leaving me feeling bitter and cold,
And feeling oh, so alone,
With an endless longing for home.

Much, much pain within the mind, heart, and soul,
For I feel trapped within these walls
And the isolation only I know.

I surrender to you Lord,
For it is your will that will take me home,
And your love that holds me when I feel
Alone with pain of long ago.

305

She called all of her parts to integrate so they could go as one, saying, "It's time to go home." All of her parts saw the Light and felt it wrap around them. She was unconscious for a full hour, and this time in the Light rejuvenated the things inside of her that were dying.

Paula arrived at our next session with a calmness she had never felt before. She showed no startle reflex when doors slammed outside or when the sirens screamed outside the window several times. I could see she was calm, with deep peace inside of her. She was not on meds but was not depressed and did not need to go pace the sidewalks. She had not been switching or flashing and was peaceful. She reported that her kidneys were working hard trying to get the taste of death out of her body, and she felt the process was about half done. As she was healing, she reported her tongue turned brown, black, and then yellow as her body was detoxifying. She smiled and said, "I beat them again."

I asked how much of her desire to die was her own death wish, her home-sickness, and how much was the death energy channeled to her by the cult. She said 90 percent of the death energy came from the cult, and she had reduced that input to about half at that time. I asked where her energy came from, and she said, "The Divine Light." I inquired what she was learning and she quipped, "I'll tell you when I figure it out!" Paula shared that she has always surrendered to the Grace of God. She felt closest to her higher power when she was making music. When they took away her voice and her hearing, she surrendered and asked the Grace of God to lead the way. "When I couldn't sing vocally, I had my hands. When I sign, I'm able to grab the light into me. I always have that. No matter where I am, I know that's there."

Silence

Paula said cult members would not be able to come out of their pain and suffering and know the Light until they broke their silence. Her perpetrators thought in their hearts that what they were doing was the right thing, worshipping their god. But through all of the abuse, Paula always knew it was wrong. She felt that the reason her dead relatives kept coming back to her was because they died within their silence. They had tried to shut her up when she was alive.

I called my sister Johanna, and she wept with joy when I told her of the transformation in Paula. She was studying tongue diagnosis and informed me that yellow is excess heat, black is excess cold, brown is stagnation, and pink means good circulation. The normal color is a white coating, but not thick. Johanna reflected how blessed we are by the story of Paula's healing.

Paula gave me a beautiful card that said, "With warmest thoughts of you... and all we've shared as friends. I'm thankful for our yesterdays, but what pleases me most is that we're still so close today." She wrote on the inside:

> You have been there the past few years, as I walked through the memories and pain of my past. Your love and Support I will always hold within my heart. You helped me take the mask off.
>
> Thank you.
> Love always, Paula XOXOXO

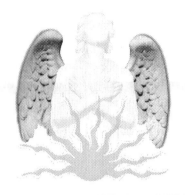

CHAPTER 28

Treatment Plan

After Paula moved, the director of the clinic where I was seeing her alerted me that the psychiatrists in charge of her case did not feel comfortable with the way I was working with Paula. The director was calm and cool and said, "There's nothing like a good clinical discussion." He wanted me to be prepared for what was coming.

The head psychiatrist and Paula's psychiatrist started our meeting together by saying that I knew Paula better than they did and letting me share what I wanted to say about her case. I said that Paula had given me permission to talk with them and that I trusted them, because talking about her to the wrong people could be dangerous. They asked, "Like about the cult?" I said yes.

A Different Diagnosis

After I shared, they told me they were convinced that Paula did not have multiple personality disorder (MPD), but rather factitious disorder, a situation in which a client intentionally produces symptoms to get attention from a provider. Although factitious disorders are usually medical and clients will do things like adding a substance to a urine specimen to fake a physical illness, they said Paula's disorder was a psychotherapeutic type instead of a medical type. They cited her long history of medical disorders and hospitalizations. One of the psychiatrists was present when the hospital did a VQ scan on Paula's lungs to check for the presence of blood clots. The lung scan was inconclusive, as 80 percent of them are. They had consulted with a nurse on the floor where Paula was hospitalized, someone who had known her for many years. They said Paula keeps giving different stories. Sometimes she says she has had twenty-seven hospitalizations, and sometimes she says the number is higher. They said Paula did not feel like the other multiples they knew. They had never seen a split-off part of her personality while she was in the hospital. They felt her stories had a "tall tale" quality to them, like her saying, "I've seen nine people killed." They had seen the rage attacks she had on the unit but did not think they came from alter personalities.

The psychiatrists said it was extremely important that I continue to work with her and not abandon her because she was very, very bonded to me. She had told the hospital staff, referring to me, "She's the best therapist I've ever had!" They felt she unconsciously produced the symptoms to get more therapy time, to get more connected with me, and to get me thinking about her all the time, doing more and more for her. They felt Paula was extremely sick, very mentally ill, and at high risk for suicide. They thought that if I stopped working with her, she would commit suicide. They also said it was much better for her to be bonded with a therapist than to have that bond with a medical provider, because I was not doing surgery on her.

Expert Supervision

They encouraged me to get supervision other than Julienne for the case. The head psychiatrist said he had seen a lot of cases of factitious disorder at his previous job. He said there had been a lot of hype about the diagnosis of MPD lately and felt that Paula produced this diagnosis so I would be interested in her. They said that if the correct diagnosis were factitious disorder, she would not integrate and would not heal, because then she would lose the therapy time with me. I added that if it was MPD and I treated it as factitious disorder, then she also would not heal, because the parts that would be left out would be angry and try to hurt her. They agreed, and that was where the treatment plan split: if MPD, work with the parts; and if factitious disorder, work more with the main personality part. They wanted Paula to go for a week or two of inpatient evaluation with an expert on MPD at a well-known psychiatric hospital in the area. They felt they needed therapists with more expertise to evaluate Paula more fully.

I asked, "If her diagnosis really is factitious disorder, would that mean that the abuse she reports did not happen?" They said there may have been some abuse but not to the extent she reported. I said, "I'd really, really like to believe that it did not happen—I'd like to believe that humans are not capable of the horrors she reports." They responded that there really are very bad people in the world and quoted what was happening in Bosnia at that time.

At the end, I said that although I knew Paula better than they did, I respected that they'd had exposure to a broad patient base and had seen much more of both these diagnoses than I had. Then I gave some evidence that contraindicated factitious disorder and said I was not convinced of their diagnosis. But I agreed to work with Paula on the idea of going to the hospital for evaluation by specialists. I thanked them for taking such an interest in the case that they gave up half of their lunchtime to talk with me. They said they had not known whether I would even consider looking at another diagnosis.

Dual Relationship

The psychiatrists were also particularly disturbed that I was planning to write a book about her case and that its title was *I Want This Nightmare to End*. They were alarmed by the dual relationship that intention created between the two of us. In hindsight, I realize how right they were on that point. From then on, I put the project of writing this book on the back shelf and started to work on a different book. Whenever the topic of writing this book came up, I told Paula that she had not written the last chapter yet. If the ending of her story were that she committed suicide, meaning that the cult had won, then I would not print that story. The only ending I would print was if she was able to integrate her parts or to die from natural causes—hopefully, having reached her goal of integrating all of her parts first! I continued to keep careful notes on the case, but I postponed writing them up until I had terminated therapy with Paula a decade later.

After the meeting, I felt absolute rage, and I felt physically ill. I felt paranoid and wondered whether the psychiatrists at the clinic were members of the cult. I brought up the issue with Julienne, and she said there was no way to know for sure, but her guess was that they were not cult members. In a larger sense, however, Julienne said that the psychiatrists were part of the cult of disbelieving that the cult existed. They worshipped darkness blindly by being unconscious of the truth. The cult worshipped darkness consciously.

I felt I was being attacked from both sides, from the cult and from those who did not want to believe in its existence. I experienced what it was like to be in Paula's situation. The cult was threatening her life, and others did not want to believe the cult existed.

I shared the following dream with Julienne, which reflected the fear I felt from this entanglement:

Tangled Up with the Mob

I have gotten tangled up with the mob, and they are after me. Where can I go? Who can I trust? I don't know. The director of a health clinic points me out to the mob. A well-dressed, good-looking man in a suit comes over and grabs me. He takes off my special Teslar watch so they will not know who the body is. I fight back. He pounds me, but I maneuver so my watch will be hit, to fix the time of my attack. He throws me off a high cliff, and I crash on the ocean shore below. My spirit leaves my body.

I stay earthbound. As I am on the beach without my body, a feeling of sadness comes over me that my physical existence is over in my early forties. I remember saying to someone recently, "Better to enjoy the moment as it is, because who knows whether we will be here next year." I reflected that at least I did have some pleasure in this incarnation, though it was cut short.

The following day, I am filling out a questionnaire for the director of the health clinic mentioned earlier in the dream from the perspective of being dead. She comes over to make conversation with me, and I tell her I am dead. At first she can't believe this statement and says she is not going to call me "Barbara Bone" instead of Barbara Stone!

I have her put her hand through my body and it passes right through my energy field. She is shaken. She stutters and asks if I feel I did something wrong. Everything human within me is shouting, "It's all YOUR FAULT!" She was the one who pointed me out to the mob; she is the one who was suspicious of me. But I tune into the spirit level and say to her a truth that comes from beyond me, "You did the best you could." I say the words slowly, and she receives them.

I see my daughter was thrown from the same cliff the next day. The woman who witnessed my murder was also killed.

Julienne reflected that all the feelings coming up were good material for the book. The question for me was "How can I set appropriate boundaries with Paula, ones that do not rob me of my life force?" She emphasized that I did not need to get drained by doing this work. She asked whether a younger part of me wanted to rescue Paula, and of course it did! Julienne encouraged me to work on my inner child and to learn how to protect myself and let the angels help me.

Responsibility

Julienne pointed out that Paula did not feel safe from harming herself and wanted me to rescue her. Julienne helped me see that I needed to give back the responsibility I had taken on for keeping Paula alive. The next time we spoke, I told Paula, "I really can't stop you if you or one of your parts decides to kill yourself." This message put the responsibility firmly back on her shoulders. I continued, "But I will work together with you to try to be sure that suicide really is the best way out of a given situation and to find better ways to solve your problems that don't involve hurting yourself."

One of the protective measures I took to increase my personal safety was to write a letter with names, birth dates, and other identifying information of cult members and to put five copies of this letter in safe places, to be opened only in case of my untimely death.

We did go to the hospital to get an evaluation with the world-renowned expert on MPD, but we compromised with an outpatient evaluation rather than a week of inpatient time. I went with Paula and we both spoke to the doctor. He was empathic, confident, and listened carefully. At the end, he said that no matter which diagnosis was accurate, the treatment plan would be the same, and we agreed:

1. Continue in therapy together, as we had developed a strong therapeutic bond.
2. Tell Paula that she had remembered enough and not to elicit any further memories.
3. Focus therapy on stabilizing her life and her health, which is the first stage of trauma treatment. He reinforced that uncovering memories is better left for the final states of treatment, when a client has her life in order and is stabilized in all areas of her life, no longer suicidal, and is caring for herself well.

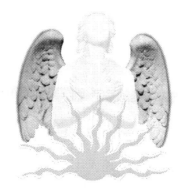

CHAPTER 29

Enoch

The aspect of my work with Paula that triggered the most feelings of helplessness was the pathos of the people who had been tortured and sacrificed. I wanted to fix everything for everybody but did not know how. As I looked inside to see why I was getting so emotionally involved, I found memories in my soul of a time when I was sacrificed in a ritual.

Julienne worked with me on the scene I experienced in my mind's eye of an ancient time when I was a Hebrew prophet during the 400 years when the Israelites were enslaved by the Egyptians. My name was Enoch, and I taught my people nonviolence. I preached that we should love the enemies, the Egyptian masters. One day Egyptian soldiers accosted me on the street while I was away from my home and marched me into a cave. I remembered the red and black colors in the cave, the beating of the drums, and the candles in the central circle. Then I dissociated. Julienne could see what happened next. The soldiers tied down Enoch, spit on him, and hurled insults at him. Then the Egyptian Queen Sereptil raped him. Enoch suffered extreme shame and felt defiled from this sexual contact with a person he considered unclean. He did not want his body to respond, but it did. At the moment of sexual climax, all of the chakras open up and receive whatever is in the energy field of the sexual partner. Enoch got a download of all the Queen's negative energy programs so, in addition to physical, emotional, and sexual abuse, he had spiritual abuse. This act also violated the sanctity of his marriage to his beloved wife, Sarai.

Castration

After the rape, the Queen castrated him and collected his blood in a bowl. Enoch slowly bled to death while he watched the group drinking his blood and eating his genitals. He was totally enraged at his own murder and heartbroken that he had not been able to say goodbye to Sarai. He loved her so much, and he realized she would never know what happened to him or why he suddenly disappeared. But he was even more enraged at himself that he could not practice what he preached and love his enemies. He felt like a failure. He hated Queen Sereptil and all of the Egyptians. This mixture of shame, guilt, fear, anger, hatred, and rage kept Enoch's spirit earthbound. Julienne saw that the queen kept a piece of Enoch's foreskin to do ceremony with, and she was able to pull life energy from him even after his death because his spirit did not go into the Light.

Soul Resonance

I felt the soul resonance of Queen Sereptil in a person in my current life that had been very challenging to me in this incarnation. Thousands of years later, this person still had an energetic hook in me that made me feel like a failure and siphoned off my life energy. As I did the work to forgive myself as Enoch for getting caught in the trap of the dark side, I realized that I would never have believed this story because it is so gory and unthinkable if I had not been exposed to the tactics of the satanic cult through the work with Paula. I took my power back in stages, and each time I let go of a piece of my anger and helplessness, a synchronicity happened in the life of the other person, a sign to me that the process was real.

Dragon's Tail

In one healing session, I sensed the presence of the other person saying that my Light had been the draw in our previous incarnation together. This person had wanted my light and asked my forgiveness for what Queen Sereptil had done. My therapist then asked me to look at myself in the mirror. I saw a red dragon's tail flick in front of me, then saw it was wrapped around me—what energy psychology innovator Judith Swack calls a "war entanglement." It looked like a big dragon. As the light came into it and I asked for release, it shrank and then flopped, turned black, and went into the eye of the light portion of the yin-yang symbol, giving me awareness of the darkness.

One of the many reasons I am so grateful to Paula for all she taught me is the personal empowerment that came from deeply, completely forgiving myself for my response to what the queen and her group did to me in that past life. I was also able to come into peace and harmony with this person in my current life.

Choice

Although I cannot control all of the outer circumstances of what might be done to me, I can choose to go immediately into forgiveness like Jesus did on the cross when he was being tortured. He prayed, "Father, forgive them, for they know not what they do." Jesus did not fall into the trap the darkness laid for him, did not stay earthbound, and resurrected!

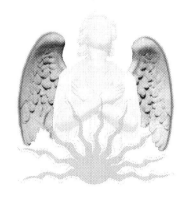

CHAPTER 30

Boundaries

*T*en years into our work together, Paula was still having a combination of flashbacks and spirit attack from some of her deceased perpetrators. She reported they were beating her up and raping her in spirit form.

Desperate to get out of the attack she felt, Paula asked for a Reiki treatment and was able to tolerate the complete Reiki protocol in two consecutive appointments.

I had a series of four dreams that included Paula and showed me emotional aspects of how she was feeling under this bizarre series of psychic attacks. How can we really believe something if we never experience it? The things she was reporting to me were difficult to comprehend because they were outside the realm of my personal and clinical experience. My dreams helped me understand her feelings and also showed how deeply involved I had become in her case. A Freudian would say that I had countertransference and was emotionally enmeshed with her suffering. A more positive view would be that my soul loved hers and knew we had signed up for a journey together. I had sur-

Another Night

Can't sleep, for the flashbacks and voices are very strong at this time. And I am feeling very insecure and frustrated with myself and what my mind's eye keeps taking me back to.

My mind is racing and flipping from one age to another. I am having a lot of conflict with both my feelings and emotions. Also I am having self-destructive thoughts.

All I can see is what they did to me as a child. And all I can hear is their voices telling me they are doing this because they all love me, and they want me to be strong.

At this time there is so much conflict and confusion in both my head and in my heart.

I feel I need some release, so the thoughts of cutting are becoming stronger.

I feel all the pain, and I see all that fear.

And I cannot cry a single tear.

rendered to letting Spirit guide the process and was willing to go through whatever I needed to experience to be able to walk with her through her healing journey. This first dream shows emotions that come with poltergeist activity.

Dream One: Pursued by the car

I am with my husband and another woman in a park with a model car that does different things when we push the buttons. Then the car starts doing things all by itself. My two companions run for the safety of our own car, but I refuse to show fear, and I leave walking.

The car revs up and pursues me. As it approaches to run me over, I jump high so it passes under me. The car goes around the building to come back and attack me again, and I run to the side of the building where it has just been so it can't see me. I can run as fast as the car goes. I am strategizing what to do next—listen for where the car is and keep going in circles? Enter a door of a building to hide? What if I get inside a building and whoever is in the car comes after me? Should I stay outside where my husband can come pick me up?

The dream brought up feelings that may be similar to Paula's experience of being attacked by spirits. Where do you run or hide to find safety? What do you do when the attacker is invisible?

Dream Two: The Butterfly Robot

I awakened while pondering the dilemma and then went back to sleep and had a second dream in which I was helping Paula at her house. In the dream I am sleeping at her house, which could be seen as a sign of going into the depths of the unconscious world with her. In this dream, I experience the craziness of hearing voices in my head, a problem that Paula reported happened to her constantly, and I think about how crazy a person feels in the midst of all that psychic activity. At some point in the dream, Paula says to me with deep gratitude, "Thank you for completely surrendering to this process."

Dream Three: Twenty More Years

The third dream was so real that even now, many years after it happened, I feel the emotional impact it portrayed of the agony and grief of an earthbound spirit, trapped and unable to connect. This dream came a few months after my beloved older sister died from cancer. I was grieving her death, and my heart was broken.

I have heart trouble and die very suddenly, in my sleep. I go into the Bardo state rather than passing through the veil to the other side. I see my mother and my younger sister, who are emotional wrecks with this further loss. I feel terrible that the system to notify my clients in case of my death has not been activated, and I try to go to my sister and tell her who the contact person is to send out this notification. But my sister shudders as I come near, and I realize that I am a disembodied spirit, a ghost.

I want to go to my own funeral to see what happens, but I am fuzzy, and I feel as if I am standing in the edge of the ocean or up in thick clouds, unable to see anything or anyone. I ask my mother and sister to come back, but they cannot hear me.

Now I have been dead several days, and they already had the funeral. I feel terrible grief at being lost and alone and send out a huge spiritual distress signal, asking for help. My spiritual council responds to my cry for aid. They grant me another twenty years and send my spirit back into my body. I set my intent with this extra time to really love people more. Reentering my body, I initially feel nausea and stomach pain, but I get back in. I am *radiant*! I stand before my younger sister, saying, "I'm back." She can scarcely believe it is me, in the flesh.

I awoke from this dream feeling that I had actually died and then had been granted another two decades. I had a very secure feeling that I would live another twenty years, and being a cancer survivor, every year counts and is a blessing! Several years later in an energy healing session, I felt my spiritual council grant me an additional twenty years, which would extend my life to age ninety-two.

The final dream in this series shows how much trouble Paula had trying to turn off the flow of traumatic images flashing through her system and also the presence of a threat to my car, which represents my ability to get where I need to go in this world.

320

Dream Four: More Boundary Violations

Somehow Paula comes home with me to take a swim in my pool. She is fiddling with the water hose outside. I ask her to turn the faucet off, and she can't because her wrist is injured. I turn it off for her, as the spigot needs a lot of force. She jumps in the pool, which isn't very clean. It has little fish in it. She says they are probably tuna. The fish have big eyes and keep coming up to look at me and possibly nibble on my toes, as I am also in the pool.

Then somehow when I awaken the next morning, Paula is sleeping in the bed beside me. How did that happen? More boundary violations. She has the radio playing, and the alarm goes off.

I tell Paula I'll take her home early in the morning. When we go out into the parking lot, a man has the hood of my car open and is looking over the car, with the engine running. I realize I left the sun top open and that's how he got in. I think he is trying to steal my car and confront him with the question, "What are you doing with my car?" He doesn't panic and proceeds to listen to the engine, then licks the upraised hood to taste the chemicals that are being emitted. His key is in the ignition. I ask how he did that, and he says some keys fit other engines. As we talk, he flashes his knife and another sharp instrument a couple of times. I realize that if I attack him or pressure him, he could stab me. I quietly ask him to leave. He packs up his tools and goes. I want to ask Paula if she saw him flashing his knife, but then I realize that question would trigger her.

The ending of the dream indicates the presence of real danger and the need to proceed gently, without attack or using pressure. The whole issue of trying to set appropriate boundaries with Paula and her parts was very difficult for me, and these dreams with the repeated theme of sleeping next to my client made me feel like I was not doing a good job of establishing healthy boundaries. And yet, the dreams helped me empathize with Paula's emotional states.

A Change of Attitude

When Paula came for the next session after I had this series of dreams, she reported that she felt better and that her body memories had stopped. She reported she had actually gotten a couple of hours of sleep the previous two nights, which was unusual for her. I asked what she had done to stop the body memories. She was quiet awhile and then, after reflecting, said she had changed her attitude. "When they started to beat me three nights ago, I did something weird. I said, 'Well come on, hit me some more. That didn't hurt. Can you hit any harder?' The more I said that, the less they beat me, as it wasn't fun for them anymore, and then it stopped." She was modeling the principle of surrendering to the process that was happening rather than fighting it.

I shared some of the content of my dreams with Paula and she confessed, "You know that dream you had of me sleeping in the bed beside you? I did that. I remember sitting up in my bed and calling for you, because I couldn't handle what was happening. I'll never do that again, because I felt so guilty afterward. I didn't realize that by calling out your name, you would feel my pain and what I was going through."

I felt grateful for Paula's confession. During the night, her spirit had called out to mine for help, and my spirit responded. The dream image of her sleeping in my bed reflected her spiritual presence with me. I felt less crazy after she disclosed what happened, but the dream also let both of us know we needed better boundaries.

CHAPTER 31

Paula's Courage

O ne of the little children of the cult members that Paula had cared for while she was growing up was "cousin" Helen. When Paula heard that Helen committed suicide by overdosing, she was determined to go to Helen's funeral. I proposed doing a visualization of putting Paula's child parts in a safe place so they would not have to face all the cult members who would be at the funeral, but Paula refused. She felt she had to and wanted to go with all of her parts. She said she had already done all the protection work possible and wanted to face the people there rather than running from them. She agreed to call me as soon as she returned from the funeral.

At the wake, Helen's father walked by Paula, brushed his hand across her right breast, and laughed. Nobody there reprimanded him for this physical violation. The smell of whiskey around him was so strong it was almost nauseating. He told her, "Watch your back. You're next!" The implication was that her funeral would be the next one. Paula turned her back on him and walked away. Many people were doing drugs and marijuana openly at the funeral. They offered some to Paula and she was tempted but declined. Others used vulgar language. Nel and Emily, the lesbian partners who headed the cult, attended the funeral, as well as many other cult members she had not seen for a long time. When Paula did not call me after the funeral as we had agreed, I called her. She was suicidal. Her plan was to get a bottle of alcohol, drink it all, take all of her medications, and then cut herself. If one action didn't kill her, the other would. She had just gotten Megan into bed and was going to put her plan into action when I called. She felt the cult had put fatal energies into her at the funeral, trying to suck her back into the darkness and make her self-destruct by triggering urges to kill herself.

The Darkness Pulling Me In

She was not proud of the suicide she had planned before my call and the sound of my voice interrupted the spell of dark energy they had thrown at her.

Noting the Differences

The experience made Paula see how her decision not to join the cult had impacted her life. Helen's sister Heather, the one who joined the cult at the Halloween ceremony when Paula was fifteen, was at the funeral. Looking at

Heather, Paula saw the price she had paid for joining the cult and forgave her. She knew Heather would have been killed if she had refused. Heather was several years younger than Paula but looked older than her. Heather's hair was unkempt, and her youngest daughter was screaming, frightened by seeing a corpse. People who had tried to stop Paula's abuse but were unable to help told her, "Paula, you turned out the best. It's so good to see you again. We wondered what happened to you."

Others wore tee shirts, jeans, and sneakers that were falling apart. Paula dressed up. She told me, "I look better than all of them." She also felt proud because she still had her child. Others had either lost their children, or the children they still had were severely troubled. Helen's mother grabbed Paula and would not let go of her for fifteen minutes. Facing everyone helped Paula fill in the blanks of who was who. She said, "I see more and more how I've always gone back to music. I'm using my anger and fear to my advantage. I have to. I've done that most of my life—used it to face it. I feared myself more than them."

Murder

The people at the funeral stopped saying that Helen's death was a suicide. Even under heavy makeup, Paula could see bruise marks on Helen's chin. Her hands had bruises and indentations on both sides showing that that her circulation had been cut off. The body did not look like Helen. Paula knew that Helen had been killed by the cult.

She reflected, "I know I still have more healing to do, but I'm not afraid to face myself. Even when I don't want to, I have to look closer. I even feared myself. It's one thing to fear others. But when you fear yourself, it is more tearing and more fatal."

Paula felt anger at the way cult members treated her at the funeral, but she kept quiet. She reported, "I did not lash out when they put the fatal energies into me this week because I did not want them to get the best of me. Instead, I let the Grace of God guide me. I had the dignity and grace to go through the experience. It didn't feel good, but I know it is okay to feel something and better to admit it. By admitting it, I am able to let go of it. My actions spoke louder than their threats. If I gave into my feelings, urges, and cravings, I would have been history a long time ago. I have always had to take things and turn them around to their opposite."

Paula kept herself together throughout the funeral and then fell apart after she got back home. After we talked, she cried for five hours. Then she surrendered, asking God to lead her path. She needed two days to finish pulling herself together again. She affirmed, "I'm a better person because of the choices I have made."

Laugh Back

Back off for I am in control.

The voices I will not let you take hold.

I am ok for it's only the memories of the past.

No one can hurt me now.

I have survived what they have done.

Now your voices are not going to win.

For I am going to have the last laugh.

I don't need to hurt myself now.

I can be proud.

I also don't need to feel threatened in a crowd.

Back off assholes!

Back off! I am in control.

I will win for I have friends who understand.

They will help just by holding my hand.

Look who is laughing now.

I can feel proud.

Paula

CHAPTER 32

Emily's Death

A couple of years later, Emily (joint head of the cult) died. Paula did not find out until a month later. She was devastated. In our therapy session four days before Emily's death, Paula told me that Emily had been calling, wanting to see her, but Paula had refused. Emily was drinking and drugging right up until her death from cancer. Paula feared that Emily wanted to hurt her more, a fear I felt was quite realistic. Paula could not sleep, looked haggard, and had been in emotional turmoil. She was still keeping her façade up for the public, but safety had become an issue. Going to the funeral would have helped put closure to Emily's part of the abuse done to Paula's system. Since she couldn't go, many internal parts did not know that Emily was dead and still feared she would abuse them again. Paula did not know how to communicate with these little ones and felt they were locked into Emily's abuse forever.

She had been unable to cry. Every time a feeling started to come up, the cult rules of being severely punished for showing feelings throttled any emotional expression. She was worried Emily would come abuse her in spirit form.

She reported that other deceased cult members had come to her after they died and abused her in spirit the same way they had when they were in their bodies—physically, emotionally, and sexually. The voices were back, telling her the same things they had told her when she was being abused. She heard Emily's voice saying, "You deserve this. We're doing this because we love you. You are bad. You should have died and your brother should have been the one who lived."

Parts came out during this session that had never come to therapy before. They looked around, knew they didn't know the office, and immediately exited. During the session, Paula switched and couldn't talk. I called her name and asked what was happening. She was getting beaten up again. I offered to pray a blessing of protection around her, and she accepted. We prayed forgiveness for Emily for all the horrible things she had done. We prayed forgiveness for Emily's walking in the darkness and thinking that what she was doing was right. Paula wept during the prayer and told me it was the first time she had been able to cry since she got news of the death. After the prayer, Paula said, "I know I have a lot more forgiveness work to do. I've done it before, but now it feels like I have to do it all over again."

I explained that the Bible says, "Judge not, that ye be not judged. For whatever measure you use with others will be used for you." This means that when we choose to forgive others for the things they have done to hurt us, we get forgiveness for all the things we have done that have hurt other people. I talked about hoping that Emily had learned from this life, as she has free will, and since her choices in this life did not bring her happiness, she might choose a different path in her next life.

Paula quipped, "I don't want her to come back!"

I laughed and prayed, "Yes, God, and if she does come back, may it not be anywhere near Paula!"

CHAPTER 33

Termination

Twelve and a half years after Paula and I began our work together, a major change occurred in my life, which involved my moving away from the area. As soon as I knew I was going to move, I let Paula know so we would have five months to prepare for this change. Terminating our therapeutic connection was difficult for both of us and felt like a loss, but it also opened a door of possibility for us to work together on this book project several years in the future after ending our relationship as client and therapist. As I reflected on how much integration work Paula had done with her parts, I filed this termination report with her health insurance company:

Termination Summary Report

Diagnosis: 300.14 Dissociative Identity Disorder and
296.34 Major Depression with psychotic features
In the years before we worked together, Paula had been diagnosed as having borderline personality disorder. Although some features of her behavior

resemble borderline characteristics, they are also consistent with the long-term effects of the extensive sadistic abuse she suffered.

History: Paula grew up in a dysfunctional, alcoholic family. She was a twin and the sixth of seven siblings, including two deceased older half brothers. Her closest older half brother has been diagnosed with colon cancer. He has frequent lapses into substance abuse and erratic and suicidal behavior.

Paula's twin brother, Paul, died on their first birthday, a great loss. Paula reports that her father was a member of an intergenerational satanic cult and that she was abused in this cult in a ritual manner from the time when she was still crawling through the time she moved out of the house in her teens. When she was nineteen, her husband married her to take her out of her abusive home situation. Paula's husband died in a tragic car accident before their daughter, Megan, was born.

Megan is now in her early twenties and lives independently in Paula's home along with Megan's three-year-old daughter, an absolute delight for Paula.

Psychiatric History: Paula had frequent psychiatric hospitalization from the ages of eighteen through the time I met her in her early thirties, right after both of her parents died. She had over thirty hospitalizations during that time. Shortly after we met, I realized that she was dissociating when she made suicide attempts. Since we have been working together and getting to know her system, she has needed psychiatric hospitalization only a few times. Once was early in our work together while I was gone on a four-week trip. The most recent time was right after the 9/11 attack, in which she lost four family members.

Client's Strengths: Paula has survived abuse that few of us can even imagine. She consistently finds ways to get through whatever challenges face her life. She has a great sense of humor and an ability to make people laugh.

She is a very talented artist, and parts of her that were forbidden to talk have drawn sketches of what happened to her. She has musical talent and sings in a local community group. She also has good interpersonal skills and is very popular at the local community service agency, which supports and empowers people with emotional challenges to live more productive lives.

Paula is also extremely reliable and truthful from her point of view. Time and time again, the stories her parts presented were extremely consistent. I have come to trust Paula to know what is best for her in any given situation.

Safety: Paula reports she does not even know what the word "safe" means, as she has no felt experience of this emotion. Contracting for safety has been a challenge, given that we have met over thirty parts and the general situation seems to be that her parts are suicidal and fight, as many of them want to kill themselves. Still, the safety factor has been that if one part finds the means to hurt herself, the others will stop her because they want to be the one to die. The standing contract for safety I have had with Paula is that before she takes her life, she will call me, and we will talk over whether or not that really is the best solution to the problem at hand. She has been reliable in keeping this contract and has only called me a half dozen times over the last eight years.

I have never forced Paula into hospitalization. When she is in crisis, I ask her directly, "Do you feel you need the hospital right now?"

Usually, she responds, "Stop swearing at me!"

Because she had no control over what happened to her in her early life, I give her control now over deciding when she needs to go into respite care or into the hospital. She is a survivor and will not use these services unless she knows it is absolutely necessary, as the confinement of the hospital triggers memories of former abuse.

Substance Abuse: In her early years, drugs were forced upon Paula during her abuse. In her teenage years, she began willingly to use drugs and alcohol to numb the pain of the ongoing abuse. She got into recovery before she got pregnant with her daughter at age nineteen and has stayed free of drugs and alcohol except for one or two brief times when a part came out and got high. When Paula switched back, she would find herself in a bar with an empty glass of alcohol and then felt terrible that she had relapsed.

She originally went to AA, but currently she finds that she gets too triggered by other people at AA and instead relies on her inner strength to think through the consequences of using substances. She says, "I don't want the kind of life that brings."

Treatment Summary: Paula has grown tremendously over the twelve and a half years we have worked together. Initially, she resisted the diagnosis of dissociation, but she has come to accept this explanation for the unusual things that have happened to her, such as losing time, suddenly finding herself in a different place, and finding herself with a razor blade in her hand ready to cut her wrist.

She continues to hear voices replaying past negative messages attacking her self-esteem and telling her to hurt herself. She continues to lose time and dissociates frequently during sessions, always becoming very quiet when she "switches." She has never presented a danger to herself or others during a psychotherapy session, and she uses visual cues to refocus herself back to present time when she switches. In spite of these symptoms, she is personable and has learned to trust the therapeutic relationship we have formed. This has perhaps been her biggest learning, that she can trust someone.

Though life continually presents challenges to Paula, she always finds a way out the window when trapped in a room. She is resourceful and feels guided by the Grace of God in her life.

Medications:

> Lunesta 2 mg hs
> Trazodone 400 mg hs
> Thorazine 50 mg TID plus 2 PRNs
> Ativan 1 mg x 5 per day
> Requip 10 mg hs for restless leg syndrome
> Maxair and Advere inhaler BID for asthma

Prognosis: After getting through the initial grief of termination of this long-term therapy we have done together, Paula is likely to be able to form another therapeutic bond and to continue to grow, cry her tears, and heal her heart.

Recommendation: Three months of transportation provided by the Department of Mental Health to see her new therapist while she adjusts to the transition.

Barbara Stone, PhD, LICSW

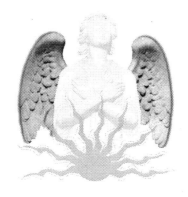

CHAPTER 34

Soul Detective Sessions

everal years after we terminated, I got an e-mail from Paula's day program clubhouse case manager letting me know that Paula was in the hospital with a very serious and potentially fatal blood clot. She asked me to contact Paula, as she had not yet been able to find a new therapist she felt she could trust. When I called, Paula sounded discouraged and very ill. The leg with the clot was swollen and extremely painful. I told her about the new direction my work had taken with the publication of my book *Invisible Roots: How Healing Past Life Trauma Can Liberate Your Present*, which presents the Soul Detective protocols I developed for various spiritual issues. Also, I was using an "Ultimate Energy Healing Checklist" developed by my colleague Sue McKenney that expanded the range of issues I could cover with my healing methods. I offered to do several sessions of telephone support work with Paula, and she agreed. Below is a synopsis of each of the six post-termination sessions we had together.

Session One: "Everything is going wrong"

Paula reported that the department of mental health dropped her case management services. Her physician also dropped her because she felt Paula's case was outside the scope of her practice. Paula felt abandoned and very discouraged. "I feel I have lost myself again. I have lost faith in everything, including myself. I'm tired of fighting for my life, and I'm tired of the spiral of this nightmare."

Her goal was to feel peace. My checklist showed two patterns interfering with this goal. To enlist spiritual help, we asked to have a golden pyramid of light surround us with archangels on each side and our guardians and guardian angels on the inside of the pyramid as we addressed these issues.

Anti-Faith Units

First, we cleared "anti-faith units," blockages in the crown chakra that are like specks of dust on the lens of a camera, impeding the flow of spiritual energy into the system. This intervention reopened the flow of energy from the Divine, so Paula could connect again with the Grace of God, her name for spiritual help.

Dark Forces

Next, we addressed two dark forces, an angel and its minion (servant). Paula was initially very afraid of these dark forces, but she trusted the therapeutic relationship we had built together and was willing to face her fears.

The purpose of the Dark Force Angel was to make her doubt herself, fill her with sorrow, and reduce her will to live. This Dark Angel did not believe that Light existed and thought it was imaginary. When Archangel Michael cut the cord connecting this angel to its dark employer, it was free to get a new job. We prayed for Paula's whole system to heal from all the damage that had been done to all the parts of the system from this interference. At the end of the session, Paula reported that she had resumed her psychiatric medications following their absence during her surgery. The meds were starting to get back into her system, though they helped only a little bit.

Session Two: "Things are looking a little brighter"

Paula's former physician referred her to a new hematologist. She went to see this new physician and felt that this doctor was the first one in a long time who had treated her with common decent courtesy. Drug activity around the housing project where she lived was triggering more traumatic memories of violence and sexual abuse.

In this session, Paula talked about the suicide of her brother's stepdaughter two years earlier. The date of the suicide was Megan's birthday. By this time, Megan had grown up and had a daughter of her own. Paula, Megan, and Paula's young granddaughter had all seen the spirit of the deceased woman, clothed in shades of gray. Although Paula felt that this woman's spirit had not yet crossed to the Light, she did not feel that the time was right to do earthbound spirit crossing work with her.

Paula still felt numb emotionally. She asked for a distance Reiki session[1] to help ease her chronic physical pain. We worked together for twenty minutes, with Paula letting me know when to move on from each area. Her enlarged spleen did not like the Reiki energy, and we moved on after just a few seconds. At the end of the treatment, she thanked me warmly for the Reiki.

Session Three: "I'm in a fog"

After our previous session, Paula's leg pain got more intense for a while, and then it gradually subsided. This pattern of her symptoms initially getting worse before they got better had been consistent in Paula's personal experience. She reported, "I'm in a fog."

Muscle testing indicated the next thing on the checklist we needed to address was past life trauma. Paula believed in reincarnation, though she had never directly worked with any of her past lives. Muscle testing indicated that three of her past lives still held unresolved trauma, and the one we needed to start with was the most recent in chronological time.

---

1   Reiki is a hands-on healing method that channels universal healing energy into a person's body. It can be done remotely, sending the intention for healing from a distance. It's a lot like prayer. I lay hands on my acupuncture meridian model of a woman as a representative of the client for distance healings.

Past Life Trauma

In 1427 AD, Paula's soul incarnated into a life of slavery on a New Guinea island in the South Pacific, before the white explorers came. This incarnation asked us to call her Kathy, and she could not remember any happy time during that life. Eventually, she could no longer handle the abuse of her masters. At age thirty-three, she tried to escape by running away. She was caught, bound and gagged, and executed for this crime. Kathy did not believe in God or in anything! She believed she had no freedom, and she was still earthbound, chained as a slave. Meanwhile, Paula felt like something was pulling on her whole body. She was afraid to let anything in or out. The familiar feeling that there is no safe place in the world permeated her life. She did not feel comfortable in her own home or her surroundings. As the Easter holiday approached, memories of past Easter holiday abuse resurfaced.

Paula felt the presence of Kathy's earthbound spirit during the session, but before we could do any work to help her spirit cross into the Light, Kathy left.

Chakra Spin Technique

Paula learned the chakra spin technique of pulling out negative imprints from her heart center by tracing the heart chakra counterclockwise (as if her chest were a clock), throwing them away, and then spinning the heart chakra clockwise to imprint positive feelings. Paula agreed that if Kathy showed up during the next week, she would do a chakra spin treatment for her.

After this work, Paula reported her system felt rattled. We did some deep breathing together, making the out-breath longer than the in-breath to help her calm down. As we practiced this breathing together, a lot of static came on the phone line, a phenomenon I find happening frequently when I am working with a client on intense negative programs. We hung up and I called back again and got a clear line.

Session Four: The Right of Free Will

The following week, Paula reported that every time she tried to practice one of her self-help techniques, something blocked her. She could not sing or draw. When she tried to play her meditation and relaxation tapes, her mechanical devices would malfunction. This pattern had come into full force when she returned from the hospital.

Sexual Harassment

Another stressor was that for the past several months, a neighbor who had helped her out financially in a time of need had been making unwanted sexual comments to her that triggered her memories of sexual abuse. He had never touched her, but this sexual harassment made her feel unsafe in her own home. Because he was a retired police officer, she felt he had authority over her and that she had no rights—the very same feelings that Kathy had as a slave. We asked Archangel Michael to release Kathy from the alternate reality she was living in wherein she was still bound in slavery, even over five hundred years after her death. We also asked Archangel Michael to release all the parts of Paula from the illusion of being a prisoner in her own body and in her own home and to restore her right of free will. Parts of Paula's system became angry with this intervention. She reported, "They refuse to believe they have any rights!"

I responded, "You hit the nail on the head! Kathy had no rights because she was a slave, and that emotional imprint is still operating in you. That is the belief system we are here to change."

Barbara's Dream

I shared with Paula that I had just dreamed about her—a dream in which I was reporting another dream I had about Paula. The message of this dream was that, in Paula's system, "The way was open to court," with court representing true justice and defense of one's rights. In my dream about Paula, this pathway to true justice was already open. This dream gave me hope that our work to clear the limiting beliefs imprisoning her would be successful. I asked to speak directly with the parts of Paula that refused to believe they had any rights. They had been told they were not allowed to say anything. I inquired whether they were allowed to think, and got no answer. I asked whether they could move their bodies and, after a time of silence, Paula responded, "They don't know what they can do." Knowing these were child parts, I offered to play a game of Simon Says. They responded, "That is a bad game!"

Since I could not use any of my trauma desensitization techniques with them, I asked whether Paula could work with them herself doing a chakra spin pullout of anything they believed that is not true, especially the part about them having no rights, and to install the affirmation "Free will is my God-given right!" She was able to make a connection with them and tried to do this technique. She felt energy shifting and, as the patterns came to the surface, she commented, "I want to crawl out of my skin!"

She realized we were trying to change the belief systems of the parts, and I reminded her that the hardest thing for people to change is their belief systems. She inquired, "What if it is not possible to make this change?" This question about possibility is another limiting belief, called a "psychological reversal" in energy psychology. I added the idea that healing was not possible to the list of untruths to pull out of her system. Paula asked me, "How do I change my belief system when, if I do, I will just keep getting beaten up with the same old thing again?"

I responded, "It's like magic. The heart acts like a magnet. When you rehearse feelings in your heart of past abuse, it draws more abuse into your life. When you truly change the feelings you put in your heart to rehearsing joyful feelings, like how much your granddaughter enjoyed her Easter egg hunt, then the patterns around you change and you start to draw good things into your life."

At the end of the session, my surrogate muscle test for Paula indicated that Kathy's spirit had been released and had been taken to the spiritual hospital where she could recuperate from the extensive damage done to her soul by that lifetime of slavery. I asked Paula to see if her internal intuitive knowing matched my muscle testing. She reported, "I don't feel her around anymore."

Session Five: Breakthrough!

At the start of our session, the pain of the blood clot in Paula's left leg was at a level of five or six on a scale of ten, with ten being the worst pain. Although the big toe had no feeling, the rest of her leg was very swollen and painful. I asked Paula to identify what was going on inside her. The thought that Paula kept thinking was "What did I do to deserve all this suffering?"

Ancestral Wounds

To find the origin of the issue at hand, I did some muscle testing with my energy healing checklist. Ancestral wounds came up. Realizing that so much of her trauma came through her father, I opened the subject by telling Paula the story of a case in which a client was carrying a curse from his father. I asked whether she felt that any of her suffering was the result of her father's involvement in cult activities. She agreed that part of the emotional burden she was carrying was from him.

How do wounds get passed down the generations in a family? Some say God does it as punishment because, in the Ten Commandments given to Moses, God tells his people not to worship idols:

> ...for I, the your LORD God, am a jealous God, punishing the children for the sin of the fathers to the third and fourth generation of those who hate me... (Deuteronomy 5:9 NIV)

Some say these wounds get passed down from living with a traumatized person, and Paula certainly had a great deal of trauma from her father's emotional, physical, and sexual abuse and witnessing him battering her mother in addition to the abuse done to her during cult ceremonies. Others teach that the disturbance is imprinted into the emotional biofield at birth, so that a child who was adopted into a loving family would still feel the emotional disturbances of the birth parents. Others theorize that the emotional disturbance is imprinted into some of the ten strands of nonphysical DNA that accompany the visible DNA we can see under a microscope.

To heal the ancestral wounds, we set sacred space with octahedrons of light around Paula, around me, and a big one including us both as we were working over the telephone. We called in the guardians and guardian angels for both of us, for all of Paula's family, and for anyone else involved in this pattern of wounding. We prayed to release all detrimental genetic imprints in her system from her father, adding in a healing pattern I learned from Richard Bartlett's Matrix Energetics, called Universal Healing Frequency 13. This frequency can be called in by anyone and is designed to repair the genetic template by restructuring the fields that influence the DNA.[2] Next we prayed for healing for her father and all others involved in this form of worship with distorted beliefs about what our creator wants from us.

Past Life Karma?

During my work with Paula, I once had a dream in which a character from my family was collecting blood from rats. In Jungian dream analysis, all parts of the dream are considered parts of the dreamer. This dream made me wonder whether I might have been involved in some form of dark worship long ago in a previous incarnation. Karma is really very simple: what you give comes back to you, like a boomerang. Because of the laws of karma, if we hurt others, we will experience that same pain in our own lives. Since I remembered being sacrificed in my past life as Enoch, I had to consider the possibility that in a previous incarnation, when my consciousness was at a lower level, I might have participated in some form of ritual abuse or sacrifice of human life. While I have no conscious memory of any form of dark worship in my soul's history, I begged forgiveness if I had ever been part of this distorted form of worship in any past life.

Paula prayed the same prayer, asking for forgiveness for her soul if she had ever been involved in any of these dark practices in any previous incarnation. We offered a chance for any earthbound cult members to make sincere repentance, accept forgiveness, and move into heaven's spiritual hospital for repair of their souls. To end, we sent Reiki energy to heal Paula's leg. At this point, the pain level was down to only a three or four. Paula felt very tired after this work, so we thanked the angels and spiritual helpers and closed down the octahedrons after a session of only forty minutes. We put up a new octahedron of healing, comfort, and love to stay around Paula at all times.

---

2 Matrix Energetics was developed by Richard Bartlett, DC, ND, online at www.matrixenergetics.com. Bartlett's spirit guides gave him 21 universal frequencies that govern healing in the human species. These packages of energy Bartlett calls intelligent entities, with consciousness that will interact, teach, and self-monitor. (Matrix Energetics Workshop Level Two, June 17, 2010)

A flood of joy broke loose in my heart during and after this session. I am highly sensitive to what is going on emotionally with my clients, and I experienced a profound sense of emotional relief as I attuned to Paula after this prayer. My heart felt like something that had been stuck for a very long time had dislodged, opening up a path for healing. I do not know how much of the lifting I felt of the emotional burden was from the healing for Paula's ancestral wounds and how much was asking for forgiveness for any involvement in these matters during past lives for her or for me. What is important is that something shifted, and I felt it in my very bones. I pointed out to Paula that the usual pattern of reversal—her internal programming for things that are supposed to heal to make her worse instead—did not happen this time. We both rejoiced!

Session Six: "I'm doing okay"

When I asked Paula how he was, she replied, "I'm doing okay." This response was much more positive than the initial report in earlier sessions. Her leg was finally healing, and we rejoiced together over this good news! Formerly, the leg had been swollen to the groin. After our last session, it began to slowly heal, and the swelling had receded down to the knee. A little feeling was coming back into her big toe. She was able to walk around a little bit, on crutches.

Paula felt more emotionally stable. She did not want to stir up the system by doing any further work at that time, so we did not schedule another session. I offered to have Paula call me if she felt the need to do further work, but she did not contact me.

Epilogue

Two years later, I contacted Paula to review this section of the book and to get her feedback on its accuracy. We were in touch over the next year during the editing process.

Current Functioning

I wish I could say that everything is great in Paula's life now, but she still faces severe stressors: poverty, disability, flashbacks, health challenges, and difficulties navigating the health care system. Her greatest victory is that she survived the attacks from cult programming and dark forces that tried to stop her from telling her story by pushing her to commit suicide. Paula often said that stubbornness was one of her best qualities. She was too stubborn to let the dark side win! She dedicated herself to living out her natural lifespan and continuing to integrate her parts so that when her days here are complete, she can take all of her parts with her into the next world. She also let the world know what happened to her beloved twin brother Paul so his spirit could finally go completely into the Light.

Despite the physical, emotional, mental, and spiritual wounds she has suffered, Paula refused join the cult and to pass on her pain by abusing others. Remembering that the choice she was given was to join the cult or to die, deciding to follow what she knew in her deepest heart was right took great courage. Paula has guts! After refusing to join, Paula was beaten to the point that her spirit left her body, and the time she spent in the near death state being held by the Light renewed her spiritual strength to continue when the ceremony was over and her spirit was sent back into her physical body.

Although Paula often sees the half empty part of a glass first before seeing the half full part, she has remained a loving person, and people like her. She is scrupulously honest and treats others with compassion and caring. She is a dedicated mother and grandmother, and her grandchild adores her. When Paula and I were doing the final proofreading for this section, neighbors kept coming to her apartment to talk with her, and her telephone kept ringing all through our work time. Finally we just laughed about having so many interruptions. Paula is the person others go to when they need to talk. She is considerate of others and is an excellent listener. People feel safe around Paula. Reaching deep into a well of wisdom within her soul, she always has a compassionate response. No matter how upset she might be at the time, she is present for her friends when they need her. She also helps out her neighbors with odd jobs like taking care of their animals while they are away. Perhaps most important of all, Paula never lost her sense of humor.

Professional Development

When I first worked with Paula, I had no idea how to work with dark force energies, ancestral wounds, curses and hexes, past life trauma, or earthbound spirits—all issues that came up in her case. As I floundered my way through these challenges, I used therapeutic skills I learned from energy psychology to work out ways to assess and treat each of these issues that had such a profound impact on Paula's life. Refining these methods over time, I developed Soul Detective protocols to help other therapists navigate the spiritual realm and a Soul Detective training program to support therapists in mastering these skills.

Energy therapies have had a huge impact on my life. They have given me a way to manage my own affect and to get my strength back when the traumatic material that comes up in my caseload zaps me. Refining these tools to use with others has given me versatility and expanded the range of issues that I can successfully deal with in my practice. The human experience is so rich and varied that no two clients are ever alike, so each case that comes into my practice is a fresh, new challenge that keeps my work extremely interesting. The tool that I use most frequently is building a customized meridian sequence to find the exact configuration of the disturbance at hand. Each person has a different configuration of internal imbalance when faced with the same challenge as someone else. The exception to this rule is that, to date, the only emotion that has ever come up when helping Dark Force Entities is fear. They are afraid of their boss and afraid of punishment. They infect the people they are assigned to with the same fears they are carrying. The major areas of fear I faced in this case were fear that Paula would kill herself, fear of not being qualified enough, and fear that the cult would get me.

The fear I faced during the moment when I first realized I was speaking with the head of a satanic cult turned into gold, as this work has brought great abundance into my life at all levels. Financially, I have a full practice of Soul Detective work. Emotionally, I have been able to work through fear stemming from my own past life trauma that I had been carrying around for thousands of years. Most of all, I have felt a spiritual blessing as I see people being able to shed their emotional burdens and live in an expanded state of well-being.

Working with my Soul Detective students has been a special joy, seeing each of them light up as they remember who they are and why they are here.

Paula's Response to Reading Her Own Story

When the parts of Paula began disclosing what had happened to them, Paula initially had difficulty believing the material that was coming through because it was so dissociated from her awareness. At times, she did not even think it was her voice she heard on the tape recording. Going through all of the difficult memories again when proofreading this section was hard for Paula. When she saw her drawings and remembered what happened, she felt chaos at times, as she tried to sort out the experiences of her parts interwoven with my journey as her therapist. As we worked together in her home to proofread the manuscript, flashbacks of the experiences returned. At times Paula had to leave the room where we were working and step outside for some fresh air to pull herself back together.

Trauma is encoded in snippets; a trauma happens and is cut off, and then something else happens that is encoded as another isolated incident. Seeing the memories of the parts put into a coherent storyline was a new experience for Paula and helped give her system more clarity about her past. Reading her whole story on paper, Paula remembered a lot of what had happened, but fragments of it did not feel like they were about her. She questioned whether she might have been feeling some of the experiences of earthbound spirits who had been attached to her and who were working out the trauma of their own abuse. She also wondered whether some of the material could have been the memories of her ancestors who had been abused coming through her system. But however and whenever the traumatic things happened, she said emphatically, *"I want this nightmare to end!"*

SECTION THREE:

Hope for Humanity

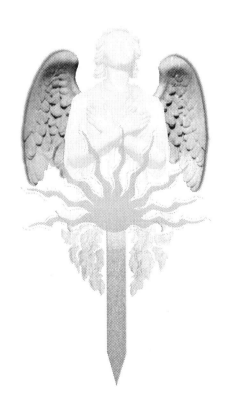

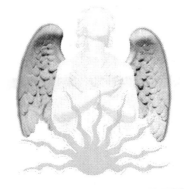

CHAPTER 35

Death of the Firstborn

Just being aware of the truth brings about inner change.
—Osho

Infant Sacrifice

This chapter examines the whole concept of sacrifice, questioning two ideas inherent in the concept:

1. A god is pleased by humans sacrificing their children to him.
2. The life sacrificed can compensate for the sins of someone else.

First, we look at an ancient practice and then a pattern in my own family: death of the firstborn child. As shocking as the stories of human sacrifice are in the previous section, the idea of giving one's firstborn child to the gods is ancient.

Molech

The Ammonites were descendants of Abraham's nephew Lot. They lived in the area that is now the country of Jordan, the capital city of which is Amman. Their national pagan god was Molech, the god of child sacrifice. Although I have not found mention of him in the Sumerian tablets translated so far, the Bible and other sources talk about Molech. This god required that his people give their firstborn child to him as a living sacrifice in order to get blessings and favors. A large brazen statue with a bull's head was heated with a fire under it. The people then presented their infants to the statue, and the infants passed through the arms of the statue into the fire and were burned. The parents then got blessings from Molech. Why would a local deity demand such a sacrifice? I do not know. As I search my brain, I can only make some guesses. Perhaps Molech liked the taste of roasted human babies. Perhaps he used this method to enforce his supremacy or to keep the human population in his area under control. Can you imagine how it would be for humans in his area to marry and mate, knowing they would have to burn their first baby alive?

Complete Allegiance

Yahweh used the practice of sacrifice of the firstborn to test the loyalty of a high priest of Nippur originally named Abram, later renamed Abraham.[1] The Lord said:

> "Take your son, your only son Isaac, whom you love, and go to the region of Moriah. Sacrifice him there as a burnt offering on one of the mountains I will tell you about."

> Early the next morning Abraham got up and saddled his donkey. He took with him two of his servants and his son Isaac. When he had cut enough wood for the burnt offering, he set out for the place God had told him about. (Genesis 22:2-3 NIV)

I'm pretty sure Abraham did not tell Sarah what he intended to do when he went off to Mount Moriah to slay their son, his only legal heir. This precious son was the only child born to his sister-wife, Sarah, when she was in her nine-

---

1 Sitchin, *The Wars of Gods and Men.*

ties after she had already gone through menopause. Abraham had Isaac carry the wood, and Abraham carried the knife and the firewood.

> When they reached the place God had told him about, Abraham built an altar there and arranged the wood on it. He bound his son Isaac and laid him on the altar, on top of the wood. Then he reached out his hand and took the knife to slay his son. (Genesis 22:9-10 NIV)

In the biblical account, God then changed his mind and instructed Abraham:

> "Do not lay a hand on the boy. Do not do anything to him. Now I know that you fear God, because you have not withheld from me your son, your only son." (Genesis 22:12 NIV)

God knew he could expect complete, utter obedience from Abraham, no matter what he asked him to do, because Abraham feared him. Since Abraham passed this loyalty test, God promised to make a great nation of him and to give his descendants land. But what kind of god would ask a subject to murder his only child? Also, what kind of priest would kill and burn his beloved only child for the gods? The answer has to be those who fear the gods and desire Divine blessings more than they love their children.

Author Zecharia Sitchin concludes that the Lord of the Old Testament was not the creator of all, but the Anunnaki god Enlil, who was in a power struggle with his nephew Marduk. Headquartered in Babylon, Marduk was threatening Enlil's position as supreme commander on Earth. Enlil wanted to raise a people loyal only to him and tested Abraham to see if he was the right human to beget this lineage.[2]

In the Qur'an, in the same account of God testing Abraham, Ishmael (called Ismail) is the one bound on the altar, Abraham's firstborn son by his wife's Egyptian maidservant and slave Hagar, before Isaac was born. According to the Qur'an, when Abraham's son Ishmael became of age, Abraham told

---

2   Ibid.

Ishmael about what Allah had asked him to do and asked his opinion about the matter.

> When he grew enough to work with him, he said, "My son, I see in a dream that I am sacrificing you. What do you think?" He [Ismail] said, "O my father, do what you are commanded to do. You will find me, GOD willing, patient."
>
> They both submitted, and he put his forehead down (*to sacrifice him*).
>
> *God Intervenes to Save Abraham and Ismail*
> We called him: "O Abraham. You have believed the dream." We thus reward the righteous. That was an exacting test indeed.
>
> We ransomed (*Ismail*) by substituting an animal sacrifice. And we preserved his history for subsequent generations.
>
> Peace be upon Abraham. We thus reward the righteous. He is one of our believing servants. (Surah 37:102-111)

Note that in the last verse quoted, the Divine is referred to as plural rather than singular, supporting the idea that more than just one omnipotent god was involved in the fate of the humans. According to the Qu'ran, the birth of Isaac was a reward for Abraham's obedience. Just like the Anunnaki rules of succession, Abraham's legal heir was his son by his sister-wife Sarah, not his firstborn by his concubine Hagar. The Bible is very clear that Sarah was Abraham's sister. When Abraham traveled to the land of Ambimelech king of Gerar (part of the Gaza strip), he was afraid that he would be killed because his wife was so beautiful. Abraham instructed Sarah, "This is how you can show your love to me: Everywhere we go, say of me, 'He is my brother.'" (Genesis 20:13 NIV) King Ambimelech took Sarah for one of his wives but was warned in a dream not to touch her. When he confronted Abraham with his deception, Abraham said, "She really is my sister, the daughter of my father though not of my mother; and she became my wife." (Genesis 20:12 NIV) When Sarah finally had a child of her own, she threw out Hagar and Ishmael. God had compassion on Ishmael and made a great nation of him also. The descendants of Ishmael make up the Arab nations, and they are still in conflict with the Israelis.

Although the Lord had asked Abraham to sacrifice his firstborn, after that incident the Lord specifically prohibited the practice of infant sacrifice with his people. He commanded them not to sacrifice their children to Molech. He wanted his humans to multiply. He instructed the Israelites:

> The LORD said to Moses, "Say to the Israelites: 'Any Israelite or any alien living in Israel who gives any of his children to Molech must be put to death. The people of the community are to stone him. I will set my face against that man and I will cut him off from his people; for by giving his children to Molech, he has defiled my sanctuary and profaned my holy name." (Leviticus 20:1-3 NIV)

Yahweh's Sacrifice Policy

Yahweh also wanted burnt offerings, but he asked his people to substitute animals like sheep and cattle instead of killing their children. The sacrificial items needed to be male and perfect, without blemish. The Israelites had very clear instructions on Yahweh's policy about infant sacrifice, but they did not obey him. Once they got to the Promised Land, they disobeyed.

> They turned their backs to me and not their faces; though I taught them again and again, they would not listen or respond to discipline. They set up their abominable idols in the house that bears my Name and defiled it. They built high places for Baal in the Valley of Ben Hinnon to sacrifice their sons and daughters to Molech, though I never commanded, nor did it enter my mind, that they should do such a detestable thing and so make Judah sin. (Jeremiah 32:33-35 NIV)

The Valley of Ben Hinnon was one of two principal valleys that surrounded the old city of Jerusalem. Another name for this valley is Gehenna, considered a destination for the wicked. In the Qur'an it is called *Jahannam* and is a place of torment for sinners, the equivalent of hell. The prophet Jeremiah tells the people their disobedience is the reason the Lord was giving them over to Babylon, Marduk's empire.

Family Curse: "The Firstborn Dies Young"

The ancient idea of sacrificing the firstborn child came into my family not as a demand from a god, but as a family curse of "the firstborn dies young." This story about finding and stopping this curse demonstrates the principle that when we spot a pattern that is controlling our lives in unconscious ways, we can take action to correct the problem.

In 2004, my beloved older sister Johanna was diagnosed with late stage ovarian cancer. She had surgery that removed three tumors, each the size of an orange. Since I lived over a thousand miles away, I tried to do remote healing on her with a method I had learned called Neuromodulation Technique (NMT).[3] My treatments seemed to have no effect. After two weeks of turmoil, with her condition steadily getting worse, our entire family of origin flew down to say our good-byes to Johanna. On the flight, I was reading *Love's Own Truths*, by Bert Hellinger, a book about family patterns being handed down through the generations. Suddenly, I noticed a pattern on my father's side of the family that formerly had seemed like isolated, unconnected events. My father had two older siblings, my uncle and my aunt. My uncle, the firstborn of my grandfather, died in his forties from complications of diabetes. In the next generation, his firstborn child, my cousin, died of cancer in his forties. The firstborn child of my aunt died in an automobile accident in his thirties. And now my sister, the firstborn in my family, was about to die in her fifties. The pattern seemed also to be extending into the next generation as Johanna's firstborn was having life-threatening attacks of hives unresponsive to the finest of both allopathic and complementary health care providers available. With

---

3   The work of chiropractor Leslie Feinberg, online at www.neuromodulationtechnique.com

the family all gathered together, I explained the family pattern I had spotted, and everyone agreed to a family healing session.

Getting away with Murder

I used Bert Hellinger's family constellation healing protocol. First I inquired whether anyone in the family had died in an unusual manner. My father disclosed that his uncle had been murdered. His uncle went to a dance with a woman who was separated from her husband. The woman's husband became enraged and ambushed their horse and buggy after the dance. He shot and killed my father's uncle, breaking the heart of my grandfather. The murderer was never punished, as the attitude in the early 1900s was "You don't mess with a man's wife." Women were considered the property of the man, like a horse, and if somebody tried to steal your horse, you had the right to shoot him.

"I Want the Death Penalty!"

Next I asked family members to role-play their ancestors. The surrogate who stood in my grandfather's place felt gypped in life because his brother had been killed and his first wife died young of a sudden illness. The energy peaked when Grandfather's surrogate exclaimed, "I want the death penalty for the man who killed my brother!"

The family understood this feeling, stemming as it did from Grandfather's deep grief and loss. However, Grandfather wanted the authorities to execute the man who had murdered his brother. He wanted the murderer to die young, just like his brother. This energy was a curse aimed at the murderer, but because it did not land on him, the early death pattern boomeranged back to Grandfather and fell upon the one he loved the most—his firstborn child. The curse also fell on the firstborn of all of his grandchildren and was starting to affect the firstborn of his great-grandchildren.

I did healing work with Grandfather, his brother, and the murderer, who were all now united in death. Grandfather was able to release his lack of forgiveness, which canceled the curse. The three men involved were reconciled. The family felt as if a heavy, dark burden had lifted.

Johanna had been unconscious and on the brink of death before this curse was unraveled. Too weak for chemotherapy, the cancer was advancing rapidly, and the doctors said her chances of not surviving this illness were 99.9 percent. The physicians offered to put medication into her IV to make her pleural membranes adhere to themselves so her lungs would adhere to her chest wall, making breathing easier. Sometimes athletes will have this procedure done to prevent a lung from collapsing. With the lungs pleurized, the breathing tube could come out so she could say good-bye and tell us that she loved us—the only important topic when getting ready to cross into the next world. The doctors did not know whether she would survive five minutes, five hours, or five days. The family agreed to this procedure.

The Time Is Now!

I called my close colleague Mayer Kirkpatrick,[4] a gifted acupuncturist and therapist, to tell him the bad news about Johanna's prognosis. Spirit had been urging him to do remote NMT healing for Johanna all day, even though he had a full schedule. He said, "If ever there is a time to do NMT, it is now." So over the phone, Mayer surrogate tested what to work on, and I did surrogate treatments for Johanna. Mayer detected and corrected some glitches in her system that I had not found. He muscle tested, "She wants to live," and the answer was negative. He tested, "She wants to die," and the answer was again negative. He realized she was divided within herself on whether to live or die. Mayer felt that if Johanna had been unified in wanting to die, she would probably not have survived her surgery.

Mayer first did an NMT protocol to unify all versions of her autonomic control system. Then he did a protocol to put her into resonance with the "Unified Morphic Field," otherwise known as God. Finally, he did an original protocol to get her immune system back on track. He felt a transfer of energy happen from him to Johanna during this treatment and was absolutely exhausted afterward, almost as if Johanna's physical system had so little chi of its own that she would not have been able to enter the NMT corrections into her nervous system if he had not sent some of his own personal chi to her out of his love and care for her.

---

4   Located in western Massachusetts, Kirkpatrick calls his work "Guided Energy Medicine," e-mail mayerkirkpatrick@gmail.com

When the family arrived at the hospital the next day, the physicians removed Johanna's sedatives, took the breathing tube out, and she woke up. But instead of telling us that she loved us, like she was supposed to, Johanna muttered that she wanted to brush her teeth. She glared at the family awhile, with an expression like "Why are you all standing around acting like I am going to die?" Then she sent everyone home.

Turnaround

That night Johanna called in her firstborn and told her, "I'm not going anywhere! I'm going to beat this illness." With her energy field unified, she had chosen life, with her whole heart. While the curse was in place, it blocked the NMT protocols I had done for Johanna. But once the curse was lifted, the NMT that Mayer did worked! The physicians had not done anything to treat the cancer, but it was going into remission. I contacted the originator of NMT, Dr. Leslie Feinberg, to work with Johanna over the phone because of his highly successful work with cancer patients. He was warm and engaging and gave Johanna an appointment that very day even though it was Christmas Eve. Johanna improved so rapidly that she was able to leave intensive care and go into a regular hospital room that same day. Johanna told me, "That Dr. Feingold is really good."

I answered, "He sure is, but his name is Dr. Feinberg."

Christmas

Johanna sent her orders out for the exact health food she wanted to eat for Christmas dinner the next day. Then her children had a problem: since Johanna had been unconscious and not expected to live, nobody had purchased a Christmas present for her! They did an emergency shopping trip. I stayed overnight in the hospital with Johanna. When the others left, Johanna looked at me and beamed a radiant smile, from ear to ear. Johanna and I had a long talk in the middle of the night about our relationship as children, our parents, and our present lives. When I told Johanna about the curse we had lifted from the family, she responded, "That is chilling!" Johanna told me again, "The work of Dr. Feinstein really helped me."

I answered, "Yes, and his name is Dr. Feinberg."

The next morning, Christmas Day, two of the doctors from the hospital came into Johanna's room and found her perky and smiling. They looked somewhat dumbfounded by her progress and remarked how sick she had been in ICU just a few days earlier. She told them, "I'm very happy to be alive, and I thank you for saving my life." Nobody in the family mentioned the NMT treatments to the hospital personnel.

The physicians inquired, "Do you have any pain?"

As I stared at Johanna's swollen belly, her colostomy, and the six tubes coming out of her torso, Johanna replied, "No." She was not on any pain medication and had no pain, which felt like a miracle. I could visibly see the swelling in Johanna's belly going down and light coming back into her eyes.

NMT Treatments

Dr. Feinberg worked with Johanna on each issue as it came up. To the great amazement of her physicians, in a matter of weeks, Johanna no longer needed any drainage tubes. She improved so much that she was discharged and airlifted to an alternative cancer treatment clinic in Mexico. But on the way, the chartered plane flew too high, and she had difficulty breathing at that altitude. Her heart rate spiked at 250 beats per minute. She had to land before reaching Mexico and then relapsed. But in the two months from the time of lifting the curse until her death, Johanna did a tremendous amount of personal and family healing work. Her daughter's hives also cleared up completely.

Healing Gifts

When the time came to unplug the machines, Johanna had given our whole family an enormous gift: release of "the firstborn dies young" curse on the next generation of our Grandfather's descendants. Dr. Feinberg also made an important discovery through working with Johanna. He found that a compromised system may be unable to accurately assess its own condition, and he developed a way to correct this informational fault to increase the effectiveness of NMT.

CHAPTER 36

Anunnaki Gods and Humans

If the success or failure of this planet, and of human beings,
depended on how I am and what I do, how would I be? What would I do?
——Buckminster Fuller

I wondered how the Old Testament god Molech's requirement of the sacrifice of the firstborn of everyone in his area got imprinted into humans. How could the darkness that befell Paula have gotten into the belief system of satanic cults, where the god still requires infanticide? Answers come in ancient records from Sumer, the oldest known civilization on Earth and the first one to leave a written history. They shed light on the emotional underpinnings shaping human character and explain the drives for gold, power, and control. Including all of Old Testament history and expanding to a comprehensive view of the origins of our solar system, our planet, and our race, they explain why the Earth is still filled with nations waging war against other nations who serve different gods. We also see lack of the

356

spiritual qualities of compassion, sharing, and love that are needed for humans to live in peace with each other and with our environment.

The Sumerian records say a planet named Nibiru has shaped our history from the time our solar system was first forming. Four and a half billion years ago, Nibiru came into our solar system from deep outer space and collided with a large planet named Tiamat and split her in two. One half formed the Earth and the other half was shattered into the asteroid belt on Nibiru's next circuit. Nibiru has a 3600 year elliptical orbit around the sun that is retrograde to the motion of all the other planets.

Tiamat did not have the elements necessary for life, but Nibiru did. When they collided, some of the elemental building blocks of life got rubbed off on Earth, and life forms began slowly to evolve on our planet. Life forms on Nibiru had a big head start.[1] See the Appendix for more details of this cosmic collision.

Myth or History?

The Sumerians went to a lot of trouble to leave us over 500,000 cuneiform clay tablets filled with historical and scientific information. Many people consider their stories myths, but even if they were, Carl Jung said, "Myth is more individual and expresses life more precisely than does science."[2] Either way, looking at the Sumerian account of our origins explains the emotional makeup of the earliest humans on the planet and how slavery got imprinted into society. If the information is historically accurate, the implications for *Homo sapiens* are twofold:

1. We were genetically engineered by the extraterrestrials from Nibiru, called the Anunnaki, with incomplete DNA activation so we would be inferior, obedient, and subservient gold miners for them. With the emotional and spiritual technology available today from various energy therapies, we can now delete our programs of slavery and reprogram to reach our full human potential.

---

1   Sitchin, *When Time Began.*
2   Jung, *Memories, Dreams, Reflections,* 3.

2. We carry emotional imprints of struggle over power and control fed by the terror of total annihilation. This book is a guide to transforming these patterns of fear and strife.

When people are frightened, dark forces can invade. Satanic cults run on pure fear, and people will do almost anything when they are terrified, even giving their firstborn child to be sacrificed. People will also follow orders from ten-foot-tall extraterrestrials with superpowers who say they are gods.

Zecharia Sitchin

The late Zecharia Sitchin devoted much of his life to translating the Sumerian tablets, writing the *Earth Chronicles* series of seven books plus numerous others. In the coming chapters, I summarize the parts of his work that elucidate the psychological makeup of the Anunnaki. Understanding this story, whether it is true or allegorical, holds the key to changing our dysfunctional emotional patterns and establishing world peace, the only way our planet will survive.

Sitchin's work has sold millions of copies and been translated into twenty-five languages. Still, his premise of ancient astronauts coming to Earth to mine gold and gene splicing *Homo sapiens* as a slave race is not widely accepted, and many have tried to discredit his writing. The whole concept that intelligent life exists on another planet is hard for some people to swallow, and harder still to digest is the idea that we might all be part extraterrestrial. According to Sitchin, the humans eventually multiplied out of control, and most of the Anunnaki gods went back to Nibiru in the sixth century BC.[3]

My belief system is that Christ came to Earth to correct religious distortions imprinted into humans by the Anunnaki, who claimed they were gods and wanted the humans to worship and serve them. The Old Testament is filled with examples of the Lord Almighty destroying his people with fire, pestilence, and flood for their disobedience. Christ came to show us the true nature of the Prime Creator, which is love. Knowing this truth sets us free from false religious dogma and fear of retribution from the gods.

---

3 Sitchin, *The End of Days*.

Then you will know the truth, and the truth will set you free.
—Jesus Christ (John 8:32 NIV)

Prior Times on Nibiru

Long before the Anunnaki came to Earth, their planet had a war between the nations of the north and the south which escalated to nuclear warfare, devastating Nibiru for many millenniums. Finally, they united their planet with a king from the north and a queen from the south. In time the Anunnaki noticed that with each 3600 year circuit around the sun, their summers got hotter and their winters got colder. A breach in their atmosphere kept them from retaining the heat coming from their planet's molten core during their long winter far from the sun. When close to the sun in their summer, they were less protected from the sun's rays. Weather cycles became disrupted. Drought and heavy winds caused crops to fail. Nibiru's volcanoes that supplied their atmosphere became less active. Their use of nuclear weapons in their civil war had long-term environmental consequences that they were not aware of in the heat of the battle.[4] We seem to be repeating this pattern on Earth at present.

Nibiru came into our solar system from deep outer space and is much older than the Earth. Nibiru was dying. The only thing the Anunnaki could find to heal their atmospheric rift was powdered gold, which is light enough in its monatomic form to stay in orbit.[5] The Anunnaki needed an enormous amount of gold, their only salvation, to prevent annihilation of all life on their planet. Desperate people will do desperate things.

Asking for Help

When the Anunnaki had a problem, they tried to solve it with science and their own intelligence. In their ancient history, only one person, Queen Lahama, ever suggested to her husband, King Lahma, to ask the Great Creator of All for help with the ever-worsening atmospheric problem.[6] Elizabeth Clare

---

4   Sitchin, *There Were Giants upon the Earth*, 137.
5   D. R. Hudson, "Library of Halexandria," http://www.halexandria.org/dward467.htm
6   Sitchin, *The Lost Book of Enki.*

Prophet reflects that we need to keep our faith in the responsibility of the Deity to help us if we ask. She says, "The greatest problem with people is that they don't ask. People have no momentum on asking."[7] But instead of beseeching for Divine assistance, the royal princes of Nibiru rebelled and overthrew King Lahma. The King tried to escape, but a prince named Alalu pursued him, killed him, and illegally seized the throne. Here we see the first recorded political coup.

Space Mission

Nibiru needed gold, and Tiamat was the only planet in the solar system that had been endowed with an abundance of this precious metal. They first tried to gather gold from the asteroid belt, which had been part of Tiamat before she had been cleaved and shattered, but the chaos of the asteroid belt destroyed all the spacecrafts they sent there. Next King Alalu tried dropping nuclear explosives into their volcanoes to make them belch out more atmospheric gasses, but this action only made the breach worse.[8] As conditions deteriorated, a powerful young warrior named Anu who had legitimate claim to the throne challenged Alalu. Rather than abdicate, Alalu negotiated that Anu could be his successor and married Alalu's daughter Damkina to Anu's firstborn son, Enki. But after many circuits with no improvement in the environmental catastrophe, Anu again challenged Alalu for the throne. The council decided to settle the contest with a naked wrestling match. Anu prevailed and was made king. Afraid that he would be killed, Alalu sneaked out after the wrestling match and escaped in a spaceship loaded with nuclear arms. In desperation, he set his course for Earth, blasting his way through the asteroid belt with nuclear weapons.

Alalu reached Earth safely and was delighted to find he could breathe the air and drink the water. He discovered Earth indeed had gold and radioed back to Nibiru that he had found the solution to save their planet. He added that if the gold saved the planet, he demanded to be reinstated as king. Anu decided to send a fleet of fifty Anunnaki headed by his firstborn son Enki to investigate the situation with Enki's father-in-law Alalu.

---

7   Prophet, *The Lost Teachings of Jesus*, 191.

8   Sitchin, *The Lost Book of Enki*.

Anu's Genogram

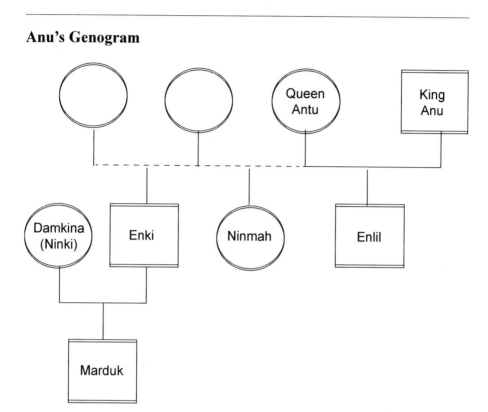

Anunnaki Sexual Rules

Anunnaki society was highly patriarchal. The war on Nibiru had depleted the supply of males, so they made the rule that a man could have as many lovers and concubines as he wanted, but he could only marry one wife. His legal heir was the firstborn son from his wife, who was preferably his half-sister by a different mother. Enki was Anu's firstborn and cherished son, but he was not the legal heir to Nibiru's throne because his mother was a concubine. Enlil, Anu's firstborn son by his sister-wife Antu, was legal heir to the throne. Anu also had a daughter named Ninmah and an additional fourteen other children.

Gold Mining

Enki's memoirs[9] say that when he landed in the ocean, Alalu was present with a joyful greeting for his son-in-law. Enki verified the presence of gold

---

9   Ibid.

on Earth, and the Anunnaki set to work extracting gold from the waters and marshes. This method provided a very small amount of gold, but enough to verify that the method worked. Anu then changed the plan to splitting open the earth to mine underground gold, a much more productive method, and sent his son Enlil to help with the mission.

Tellinger believes that the ten million ancient stone circles that have been found in South Africa are connected to the Anunnaki presence on Earth. He says, "I believe we have discovered the physical evidence of what Zecharia Sitchin has written about."[10] The stone circles, each of which is unique, create different energy patterns that were used to mine the gold. Scientific testing shows that the circles create electromagnetic waves and heat signatures. One ancient gold mine discovered by De Beers mining company is 22,000 feet deep and appears to have been cut straight down into the earth with a laser-like technology.

The Anunnaki gold mines produced great quantities of gold. Anu decided to ship the gold to a landing site on Mars for easier transport of the large shipments shuttled to Nibiru each 3600 years when the planet came close to the Earth. Since Mars is smaller than Earth, it has less gravitational force and therefore spacecraft could take off and land more easily. The Anunnaki sent a fleet of six hundred workers for Earth and three hundred for the space station on Mars, where the workers were called the Igigi. Enki's firstborn son Marduk was put in charge of the difficult Mars Mission.

Sore Losers

When the ore mining was all in order, Anu came to Earth for a state visit. Then Alalu demanded to be the king again, as his promise of gold to save Nibiru had been fulfilled. The council decided to settle the issue with another naked wrestling match. Anu prevailed again, but Alalu was a sore loser. After the match, when Anu lifted his foot off Alalu's chest, Alalu jumped up, grabbed Anu's legs, bit off Anu's testicles, and swallowed them. Then Anu was also sore!

---

10 M. Tellinger, "Ancient Ruins and Anunnaki," June 14, 2011, http://www.youtube.com/watch?v=7tp-WNrwQhk&feature=related

Rather than the death penalty for Alalu, he was exiled to Mars, where he soon died from the toxins created in his system from swallowing Anu's testicles.[11] In *Slave Species of god*, author and television producer Michael Tellinger speculates that the Anunnaki might have programmed something into their DNA to discourage cannibalism whereby, "There was apparently something in the 'flesh' of others that killed anyone who consumed it."[12] Alalu was smart enough to know that his action would bring about his death, whether from execution with their weapon called the death ray or whether from ingestion of Anunnaki flesh. But in the moment, the wound of losing the throne for a second time seems to have made Alalu vulnerable to infection by a Dark Force Entity that filled him with desire for revenge and inspired him to take an action that led to his own destruction.

Gold Miners on Strike

Anu went back to Nibiru, nursing his wound. Enlil was put in charge as chief military commander on Earth, and Enki was put in charge of the gold mining operation in South Africa. Anunnaki workers toiled in the gold mines for over 100,000 years. Each time Nibiru came close to Earth, young and eager newcomers from Nibiru replaced the workers who had been toiling for the past circuit of 3600 years, called a "Shar." Over time, Nibiru's atmospheric breach was healing. The young Anunnaki miners who came to Earth had not experienced the former hardships on Nibiru and were unused to the rigors of the shorter cycles of Earth. Unrest spread among them.[13]

Enki did not notice the labor dispute that was brewing because he was busy studying wildlife in his science lab called the House of Life. The ape-like beings that walked on two legs fascinated him. He invited his son Ningishzidda (later called Thoth) to join him in his genetic exploration and experimentation. They were developing what we might call computer program chips that contained all the genetic information needed for the different species of life they found on this new planet. They called these little chips that fit into the palm

---

11 Sitchin, *The Lost Book of Enki.*

12 Tellinger, *Slave Species of god*, 428.

13 Sitchin, *The Lost Book of Enki.*

of a person's hand "Tablets of Destiny." Another word the Anunnaki used for these mysterious chips were "ME's." Nobody knows exactly what they were, but each planet had a Tablet of Destiny that gave it the right to circle around the sun and also set the parameters of its orbit. Some of these computer program chips giving rulers their power and weapons had already come with the Anunnaki from Nibiru. Enlil's power as a ruler came from the ME's he wore around his neck. One day when he took them off to bathe, an enemy came and stole them. Enlil was stripped of his power without these ME's, but his son was able to get them back for him.

As Earth was coming out of an ice age, the weather was getting hotter and working conditions in the gold mines became unbearable. Enlil came to South Africa from his home in Nippur, an area in Iraq, to try to settle the unrest. During the night, the Anunnaki gold miners mutinied, burned their tools, and surrounded Enlil's house in a riot, demanding relief from their backbreaking jobs. What were the Anunnaki to do? Everyone would die without the gold, and nobody wanted the gold mining job.

A Radical Solution

Enki proposed a win-win solution to his brother Enlil to relieve the Anunnaki workers and still save their planet. He told Enlil about the primitive ape-like humanoid he had found that grunted and snorted. Ningishzidda had tested the DNA of this primitive humanoid:

> Ningishzidda, my son, their Fashioning Essence has tested:
> Akin to ours it is, like two serpents it is entwined;
> When their with our life essence shall be combined, our
> mark upon them shall be,
> A Primitive Worker shall be created![14]

Note that the Anunnaki already knew the double-helix form of DNA, like two serpents entwined, which was rediscovered by molecular biologists Francis Crick and James Dewey Watson in 1953. Backing up Enki's story with

---

14   Ibid., 130.

scientific findings, a paleontologist discovered skulls in Kenya of both *Homo habilis* and *Homo erectus*, indicating that they lived side by side 1.5 million years ago, for at least half a million years. This find pokes holes in the theory that, in man's early evolution, one species evolved from the other: *Homo habilis* into *Homo erectus* into *Homo sapiens*.[15] *Homo erectus*, named because the species walked erect rather than on hands and feet, was likely the one Enki showed to the Anunnaki. Other research confirms that the genetic endowment of all living creatures comes from ancestors which lived on other worlds:

> This inherited extraterrestrial genetic machinery coordinates gene duplication and expression, speciation, and evolutionary innovation, thereby giving rise to a genetically regulated progression leading from simple to complex creatures including woman and man.[16]

Enlil was sternly opposed to Enki's idea of upgrading *Homo erectus* into a more complex creature able to mine gold for the Anunnaki. Enlil argued that slavery had long ago been abolished on Nibiru and that tools were slaves, not other beings, and that creation should be held only in the hands of the prime creator. Enki enthusiastically countered that they would be making helpers, not slaves. Enki's sister Ninmah added that the Beings already existed and they were just going to give them more ability. Enlil firmly stated that this plan of creating a new race violated cosmic law of the prime directive not to interfere with the culture and species of foreign planets.

Ninmah tried to convince Enlil by reasoning that it was their destiny to use the wisdom and understanding that the Creator of All had given them. Her words resemble the attitude of scientists today who are genetically modifying grains and plants. Ninmah asked, "To what purpose have we so been perfected,

---

15   S. Borenstein, "Fossils alter view of early evolution," *Akron Beacon Journal*, August 9, 2007, A8.
16   Joseph, R. "The Evolution of Life from Other Planets, Part 1: The First Earthlings, ExtraTerrestrial Horizontal Gene Transfer, Interplanetary Genetic Messengers and the Genetics of Eukaryogenesis and Mitochondria Metamorphosis." Journal of Cosmology, 2009, Vol. 1, 110-150.

else of it utmost use to make?"[17] In other words, we can do it because we can. Because the siblings could not reach an agreement, they took the issue before the council on Nibiru. Long and bitter ethical discussions followed involving what was destiny and what was fate. In the end, to avoid their own extinction, the council decided to break the rules and make a lesser species willing to work in exchange for food.

With the conscious decision to violate cosmic law, dark energies of abuse of others by more technologically advanced beings entered the picture, a pattern that continued as the Europeans invaded the Americas and took advantage of indigenous peoples because they had more powerful weapons. The Anunnaki were desperate, faced with annihilation of life on their planet, and dark energy got into their vulnerability with the promise of protecting their planet.

Trial and Error

Creating the primitive worker took several Shars (orbits of 3600 years each) of trial and error. Ninmah's first idea was to have a male Anunnaki impregnate a primitive ape-woman, but the genetic material was not close enough for conception. Next Enki and Ninmah spliced Anunnaki essence into the genetic template of the primitive humanoids, implanting the embryos into the wombs of the primitive ape-women. The first models they created had serious defects, including paralysis, nerve tremor, faulty lungs, and a malfunctioning liver. One could not hear and another was blind, and in one model the arms were too short to reach the mouth. Ninmah kept rearranging the mixtures, and Enki found some useful life for each of the deformed beings they created. When one experiment resulted in a man with faulty eyesight, Enki taught him to sing and play the lyre.[18]

They kept trying, and Ninmah eventually decoded the whole human genome. Enki suggested mixing the gene formula in a vessel made of the clay of Earth so that it would have the elements of gold and copper rather than one made of Nibiru's crystals. This plan resulted in a child that was physically perfect but could not comprehend speech and made only grunts and snorts.

---

17 Sitchin, *The Lost Book of Enki.*
18 Sitchin, *The Cosmic Code.*

Next they implanted the embryo in Ninmah's womb, resulting in a child who could comprehend speech. When Enki handed the newborn boy to Ninmah, she exclaimed, "My hands have made it!"[19] She named the child Adamu. They noticed that the penis of the Earthling had a foreskin, unlike the Anunnaki. They decided that this foreskin would be the distinguishing mark between the Anunnaki and the Earthlings, which throws a new light on the practice of circumcision. Also, the skin of this male child was brown, like the color of the earth, unlike the white skin of the Anunnaki.

They cloned seven more male primitive workers from Adamu and then realized the process of making workers this way was too slow and demanding for the Anunnaki women to gestate each one. They made a female model and named her Ti-Amat, which means the Mother of Life. Ninmah cloned seven females to mate with the seven males. Adamu and Ti-Amat were protected from the toil of the excavations and taken to Enlil's area of Mesopotamia which was called the Edin so everyone could see their handiwork. After a time, they realized that no pregnancies were resulting from the copulation of these Earthlings. Enki and Ningishzidda found that Earthling DNA was arranged in twenty-two pairs of chromosomes and needed another pair for fertility. Ningishzidda did a procedure under anesthesia with Enki, Ninmah, Adamu, and Ti-Amat that sounds like a bone marrow transplant.

> From the rib of Enki the life essence he extracted,
> Into the rib of Adamu the life essence of Enki he inserted;
> From the rib of Ninmah the life essence he extracted,
> Into the rib of Ti-Amat the life essence he inserted.[20]

With the genetic upgrade, Adamu and Ti-Amat became aware of their nakedness and of their sexuality. In the heat of the day, Enlil was strolling in his orchard enjoying the shade. He saw Adamu and Ti-Amat with aprons on their loins and asked Enki to explain this change from their running around naked. Enki explained the fertility problem and the genetic upgrade. Enlil was furi-

---

19   Sitchin, *The Lost Book of Enki*, 139.
20   Ibid., 148.

ous and thought that next Enki might give the humans the long life span of the Anunnaki. Ningishzidda pacified Enlil, assuring him that they had only been given the ability to procreate, not an extended life span.

In the Bible story of creation we see everything turned around, making Enki, the fashioner of the humans, into the devil. The Serpent (one of Enki's names referring to his knowledge of the double helix spiral of DNA) is blamed for tempting the woman to eat of the fruit. In the Sumerian story, the woman had nothing to do with the upgrade decision. In the Bible, Lord Enlil called himself the Creator, which he was not. Both versions agreed the Lord was furious and cast the humans out of Eden/the Edin.

Tellinger feels that the Anunnaki purposely stunted the genome of the slave species to protect themselves against competition from them. "They ensured that the new human species did not live too long, was prone to disease, did not use much of its brain and had a finite memory."[21] But they did not count on our genome evolving, perhaps because Anu had promised the Anunnaki that once they had enough gold, they could all return to Nibiru as heroes and heroines.[22]

Junk DNA

Many researchers studying the human genome have been puzzled by why at least 95 percent of human DNA has noncoding sequences, which means that it has no known function. In contrast, simple fruit flies have only 17% noncoding genes. Many conclude that this "junk DNA" in humans is extraterrestrial in origin. Nobel prize–winner Frances Crick, one of the two discoverers of the double-helix form of DNA, claimed that an advanced ET civilization must have transported the seeds of life to Earth.[23] Another author, Sir Fred Hoyle, took the same position in his book *Evolution from Space*. Hoyle felt that the beginnings of life must have been the product of purposeful intelligence, giving the odds of life being formed from inanimate matter one to a number with 40,000 noughts after it. He states, "The chance that higher life forms might have emerged in this way is comparable with the chance that a

---

21   Tellinger, *Slave Species of god*, 131.

22   Sitchin, *The Lost Book of Enki*.

23   Crick, *Life Itself*.

tornado sweeping through a junk-yard might assemble a Boeing 747 from the materials therein."[24]

Tellinger points out that the human genome is "the same length of that of our maker, our genetic donor. The genes have however been tampered with, resulting in the removal or shutting down of most of them (97 percent), leaving behind an unintelligent, primitive and subservient creature."[25] Other species do not have the myriad genetic defects that show up in humans. The Anunnaki life spans of around 500,000 years indicate they did not give us their excellent immune system programming, and with good reason. If every *Homo sapiens* born were still living 500,000 years later, either this planet would be way too full of people, or a law would have been passed against reproduction!

For forty Shars, which would be 144,000 Earth years, the primitive workers toiled in the South African gold mines. Then the Anunnaki at the headquarters in the Edin clamored for workers for domestic help. Enlil's son Ninurta led a raid to South Africa capturing Earthlings in nets, similar to the ways that slave handlers raided African tribes to sell humans as slaves in Europe and the Americas. For seven more Shars, another 25,200 Earth years, the lot of the Anunnaki was greatly eased. Then the greater number of mouths to feed started depleting Earth's supply of grain, fish, and fowl. Also, as the Earthlings progressed through their generations, the offspring gradually regressed back to their wild ancestors. Enki was pondering how to create a civilized mankind, as the creatures could understand language and take orders but still could not talk.

Upgrading the Humans

In the 93rd Shar, 335,000 years after the arrival of the Anunnaki and 108,000 years ago, one day Enki was down by the river watching two wildly beautiful naked female Earthlings. He became aroused and mated with both of them to see if conception was now possible across the species. To his delight, one bore a son, Adapa, and the other a daughter, Titi. These two children had greater intelligence and were capable of speaking. Civilized mankind had come into being. Being more purely Anunnaki, they grew up more slowly

---

24 F. Hoyle, "Hoyle on Evolution," *Nature* 294:105 (1981).

25 Tellinger, *Slave Species of god*, 58.

than the other Earthling children. Enki and his wife, Ninki, taught the children crafts, and they were able to learn farming and shepherding. Enki told everyone that he had found the children among the bulrushes in reed baskets, just like the story of Moses, and the Anunnaki marveled at the sudden appearance of a new kind of Earthling who could talk. Anu wanted to see the miracle for himself, so Adapa took a short spaceship trip to Nibiru and back. When Adapa and Titi proved their fertility by giving birth to twins, Anu sent grains and sheep down from Nibiru for the new civilized humans.

Historical Timeline

14,000,000,000 years ago the Universe begins.

4,500,000 years ago our solar system forms.[26]

450,000 years ago deposed ruler Alalu escapes to Earth and finds gold.[27]

445,000 years ago Enki lands on Earth and starts extracting gold from seawater.

430,000 years ago Enki's half-sister Ninmah arrives on Earth with a handful of women nurses.

416,000 years ago Anu comes for a state visit to plan the Earth Mission. Assigning roles by drawing lots, Anu goes back to Nibiru as king, Enlil gets command of the Earth, and Enki is put in charge of the mining operation in South Africa.

300,000 years ago Anunnaki gold miners mutiny and Enki and Ninmah start creating primitive workers.

---

26 National Aeronautics and Space Administration website "Universe 101"
http://map.gsfc.nasa.gov/universe/uni_age.html

27 Sitchin, *The Lost Book of Enki.*

290,000 years ago Adamu and Ti-Amat, the worker templates, are finally perfected and cloned.

108,000 years ago Adapa and Titi are born, the first civilized
humans who can talk.

100,000 years ago the Anunnaki males begin to marry
the Earthlings.

48,000 years ago Ziusudra is born, called Noah in the Bible.

13,000 years ago a flood sweeps over the whole Earth.

Cain and Abel

Adapa and Titi named their twin sons Ka-in and Abael, called Cain and
Abel in the Bible. Ninurta, the firstborn son of Enlil, taught Ka-in crop cultiva-
tion, and Marduk, the firstborn son of Enki, taught Abael shepherding and wool
making. At the celebration of the first crops and the first sheep that matured,
Enlil blessed both of the brothers joyfully. Enki blessed Abael's shepherding
but did not give a blessing to Ka-in, which hurt his feelings. Abael boasted to
his brother that he was the one who brought abundance to the Anunnaki from
the meat and wool his sheep provided.

Ka-in and Abael argued through the next winter, as the divisive energies
of rivalry and jealousy infected their relationship. Ka-in felt unappreciated,
and Abael felt proud and boastful. The following summer a drought came,
and Abael watered his flocks in Ka-in's irrigation ditches. Ka-in vigorously
protested this invasion of his territory, and the brothers got into a fistfight. In
the heat of the argument, Ka-in picked up a stone and hit Abael in the head
again and again until Abael fell dead. Then Ka-in cried for a long time when
he realized that he had killed his brother. In the offspring of the two civilized
humans, the pattern of enmity between the Anunnaki brothers Enlil and Enki
continued and escalated to murder.

I see the emotions of jealousy and rivalry as dark energies that enter human relationships when a person feels slighted, unappreciated, or treated unjustly. Another person boasting of superiority exacerbates the bad feelings,

which then poison relationships between people, groups, and nations. Marduk was furious that his protégé had been murdered. He wanted Ka-in executed for his crime with the rule of an eye for an eye and a tooth for a tooth. Enki did not want to lose both of his twin grandsons. He took Marduk aside and spoke softly to him, revealing that he was the father of Adapa and Titi.

> By the revelation Marduk was at first astounded, then by
> laughter he was overcome:
> Of your lovemaking prowess much to me was rumored, now
> of that convinced I am!
> Indeed, let Ka-in's life be spared, to the ends of the Earth let
> him be banished.[28]

Ka-in was sent wandering and was marked so that his offspring would be distinguished and spared. Ningishzidda altered Ka-in's DNA to remove facial hair, a trait we see in the native peoples of the Americas, as they are descendants of Ka-in. The biblical version of Cain's punishment is as follows:

> Cain said to the LORD, "My punishment is more than I can
> bear. Today you are driving me from the land, and I will be
> hidden from your presence; I will be a restless wanderer on
> the earth, and whoever finds me will kill me."
>
> But the LORD said to him, "Not so; if anyone kills Cain, he
> will suffer vengeance seven times over." Then the LORD put
> a mark on Cain so that no one who found him would kill him.
> (Genesis 4:13-15 NIV)

Adapa and Titi had more children, thirty sons and thirty daughters. Their twins, Ka-in and Abael, were born in the 95th Shar, when Adapa and Titi were 7,200 years old. Their first grandson was born in the 97th Shar, showing that their life cycles were much longer than the life span of *Homo sapiens* today.

---

28   Sitchin, *The Lost Book of Enki*, 186.

Intermarriage

As civilized mankind proliferated, a new problem arose. Earth had a shortage of Anunnaki women, as nine hundred Anunnaki men had come on the Earth mission and only few Anunnaki women. Marduk was in charge of the three hundred men from Nibiru who manned the station on Mars and were called the Igigi. In the 100th Shar (25,200 years after the birth of the first two civilized humans), Marduk told his parents he wanted to get married. Enki and Ninki were shocked when he told them he wanted to marry a human named Sarpanit who caught his fancy. Ninmah offered him any of her daughters by Enki to marry as a half sister, the royal custom, but he wanted Sarpanit. Enlil was furious with the idea, saying that Marduk had gone too far. Enlil radioed his father about the matter. Anu urgently summoned the council, but they could not find any policy in the rule books on whether or not one could marry an inferior species created for slave labor on another planet. Having sex with a human was one thing, but marrying a human was an entirely different matter.

The council decided that Marduk could marry the human, but he could never bring her to Nibiru, and he had to give up all claim to the throne on Nibiru. The decision was similar to the one Prince Charles made when he gave up his right to the throne of England to marry a divorced woman, Camilla Parker Bowles. Marduk already felt cheated by his father Enki's inferior rank to Enlil and by getting the rotten job of working on the harsh planet of Mars for so long. Marduk set his sights on becoming supreme ruler of the whole Earth, and marrying an Earthling was a step that brought him popularity with the humans in the ages to come. As a wedding present, Enki gave Marduk and his bride the territory that is now Egypt.

Abduction

The three hundred Igigi on Mars had a very harsh life. The atmosphere was so thin that they had to constantly wear space suits. Over time, Mars lost more of its atmosphere and conditions got worse. No women went to Mars, only men, and the Igigi were tired of suffering in loneliness and not having offspring. Two hundred Igigi came down to Earth for Marduk's wedding and abducted wives after the wedding ceremony, demanding the right to marry and threatening to destroy everything on Earth with fire if denied permission.

Enlil was totally enraged at their action as he could see its consequences. He complained:

> One evil deed by another has been followed, fornication
> from Enki and Marduk the Igigi have adopted,
> Our pride and sacred mission to the winds have
> been abandoned,
> By our own hands this planet with Earthling multitudes shall
> be overrun![29]

He was absolutely right on that last point! Overpopulation is currently one of the most serious problems on our planet. Here is the Biblical account of intermarriage between the Anunnaki, called the Nephilim, and the humans and their offspring of demi-gods:

> When men began to increase in number on the earth and daughters were born to them, the sons of God saw that the daughters of men were beautiful, and they married any of them they chose. Then the LORD said, "My Spirit will not contend with man forever, for he is mortal; his days will be a hundred and twenty years." The Nephilim were on the earth in those days—and also afterward—when the sons of God went to the daughters of men and had children by them. They were the heroes of old, men of renown. (Genesis 6:1-4 NIV)

The offspring of the Igigi made a big pool of superior Earthlings called "Children of the Rocketships," the Aryan race, characterized by their white skin and blonde or red hair. The primitive workers first created were called "the Black-Headed People" because of their dark hair. The skin tone of the Earthlings was generally darker, while the skin of the Anunnaki was white.

If Adamu, the first primitive worker, was half Anunnaki, then Adapa, the first civilized worker, was three-quarters Anunnaki because Enki was his fa-

---

29 Ibid., 202.

ther. The offspring of the Igigi mating with civilized humans would then be seven-eighths Anunnaki. In modern times, Hitler picked up the theme of racial superiority and glorified the Aryan race, seeking to create a master race of lords to rule the Earth. *Nazi* is the Hebrew word for "prince." The Nazis reflected Marduk's goal of having supreme command on Earth, and they persecuted the Jews, Enlil's chosen people.

Ziusudra

During the next ten Shars, the Earth headed into another ice age. The weather got colder, rain did not come, crops diminished, and not many new lambs were born. Food became scarce and was rationed. Meanwhile, Enki was taken with the outstanding beauty of Batanash, a human female. He sent her husband away to Egypt to study how to build a city and sent Batanash to his sister Ninmah's house for protection. Of course, Enki then visited his sister and impregnated Batanash. The child was born in the 110th Shar, 48,000 years ago, and did not look like an Earthling to his father because of his white skin, blonde hair, and brilliant blue eyes. The father-in-law of Batanash demanded to know whether this child was the son of one of the Igigi. Batanash swore upon her life that the boy's father was not one of the Igigi. She was telling the truth, because Enki was not an Igigi. This child was named Ziusudra, called Noah in the Bible.

Ninmah and Enki adored this child and endowed him with knowledge. Enki taught him to read and observe the priestly rights. Ziusudra grew up and had three sons—Shem, Ham, and Yafet (Japeth). As the climate became harsher and food more scarce, the humans became an anathema to Enlil, making him lose sleep. The Anunnaki also had to ration their food, and Enlil blamed the humans. Plagues and pestilences afflicted the earth, and the humans got sick. Ninmah wanted to teach the humans how to cure themselves, but Enlil forbade her. Enki wanted to teach the humans to fish, but Enlil again forbade him. Enlil wanted to get rid of the humans and hoped they would all starve to death. For three Shars, the suffering of the humans increased.

Global Catastrophe

As fear and famine spread on Earth, the Anunnaki observatories noticed sunspots and solar flares, and the orbit of Jupiter destabilized. The Hammered Bracelet (asteroid belt) showed irregularities in its circuit. Earthquake activity increased, and worst of all, the ice cap on the South Pole had begun to slip. On Nibiru, the people shouted that the Creator of All was angry! The Anunnaki knew that the next time Nibiru came around the sun, Earth would be exposed to Nibiru's full gravitational force as it would be in close proximity to Nibiru at the time of its crossing. They realized that the ice cap on the South Pole would slip into the ocean, causing a huge tidal wave to spread across the whole Earth. King Anu and the council decided to evacuate Earth and Mars before the calamity hit. They shut down the gold mines in South Africa, lofted all the gold to Nibiru, and sent a fleet of "fast celestial chariots" to Earth for evacuation.

Galzu, the Great Knower

At this time, a white-haired Anunnaki named Galzu stepped off one of the Celestial Chariots with a sealed message from Anu. Enlil was surprised because Anu had not sent prior word of his coming. Galzu called a special meeting of Enlil, Enki, and Ninmah. He warned them that returning to the longer cycles on Nibiru after having over 400,000 years on Earth would be very hard on their bodies. He told them their minds would be affected and that they would die quickly if they returned. He advised them to go up in their spacecraft and orbit Earth while waiting for the flood to subside, then return to Earth and rebuild.

The three siblings responded to the news in their characteristic fashion. Compassionate Ninmah said, "That much was to be expected!" Enki the scientist said, "That much was clear!" Enlil the anger-management-challenged one blamed his brother for everything, saying:

> Before, the Earthlings like us were becoming,
> Now we as Earthlings have become to this
> planet imprisoned!

This whole mission to a nightmare turned, by Enki and his
Earthlings from masters, slaves we were made![30]

The three siblings decided to stay, and each of the other Anunnaki were
given the choice to leave or stay. All of the sons of both Enki and Enlil chose
to remain on Earth. Enki wanted to protect the Earthlings he had created, but
Enlil flat-out refused to let Enki help them. Enlil wanted all the humans to perish in the approaching calamity. He was fed up with Enki's taking the powers
of the Creator of All into his own hands and the Anunnaki marrying the humans. The account in the Bible attributes to the Lord the actions of both Enlil
and Enki:

> The LORD saw how great man's wickedness on the earth had
> become, and that every inclination of the thoughts of his heart
> was only evil all the time. The LORD was grieved that he had
> made man on the earth, and his heart was filled with pain. So
> the LORD said, "I will wipe mankind, whom I have created,
> from the face of the earth—men and animals, and creatures
> that move along the ground, and birds of the air—for I am
> grieved that I have made them." (Genesis 6:5-7 NIV)

Enlil forbade the Anunnaki to speak a word about the coming disaster to
the Earthlings. The Igigi were given three choices:

1. Abandon their spouses and children and return to Nibiru alone.
2. Go to Mars to wait out the calamity with Marduk and their wives
   and children.
3. Head with their families for distant mountain lands.

Enlil asked Enki to inscribe tablets with records of all that was done by
one planet to another so that any survivors would have a record of what happened. Enki wrote the records and buried them in golden chests in their capital
city of Sippar, along with some information storage devices. Thousands of

---

30   Ibid., 210.

cuneiform tablets have been recovered from Sippar, site of the modern city of Tell Abu Hibbah along the Euphrates River in Iraq. Enki and Ninmah began gathering DNA and ova from living creatures so they could reconstitute life after the catastrophe.

As the flood approached, Enki had a dream-vision of Galzu engraving a diagram. When he awoke from his dream, lo and behold, he found a lapis lazuli tablet with an exact diagram for a submersible boat. He sent his emissaries to find Galzu, but nobody could locate him, saying Galzu had returned to Nibiru long ago. That night Enki went to the reed wall of his son Ziusudra's home and told the wall about the coming calamity and the boat that needed to be built, adding that he would send a navigator for the vessel on the day it was to launch. Ziusudra wanted to see Enki's face, but Enki said he had not been talking to Ziusudra, for he was bound by an oath not to speak to any humans about the disaster. He had been talking only to the reed wall, but Enki left the diagram.

Ziusudra had only seven days to build the vessel, and he set to work immediately. Ziusudra took animals and food and his wife and his three sons aboard and invited any others who wished to come along. On the sixth day, Enki's son Ninagal came to navigate the boat, holding a precious box of cedar wood that had the life essences and life eggs of all the living creatures that Enki and Ninmah had collected. The flood came in the 120th Shar, 36,000 years after the birth of Ziusudra. Sitchin places the event around 11,000 BC.

Details of the Catastrophe

The Anunnaki could see Nibiru in the heavens as a glowing star as it approached. The days were dark, and the earth shook from the gravitational force of Nibiru's proximity. Thunder and lightning lit up the skies. The Anunnaki spaceport commander signaled the Anunnaki who chose to ride out the storm in their spaceships to lift off. When Ninagal saw the light from the rocket blast-offs, he buttoned up the hatch of the submarine.

With a roar equal to a thousand thunders, the sheet of ice slipped off the South Pole and made a tidal wave that went over Africa and into Iraq where Ziusudra's submarine was waiting. It proved to be watertight and rode out the fierce storm. From her spaceship, Ninmah and other Anunnaki wept and mourned the destruction of all life on the planet. The devastation they witnessed of unbridled fury humbled them and moved them to an awareness of the Creator of All.

After the tidal wave, for seven days the rains from above mixed with water that rushed in from lower sources, likely from the earthquake activity, and then the rain from the sky continued for forty more days and nights. The account of Noah and the ark in the Bible matches almost verbatim the account in the Sumerian tablets.

The Lost Book of Enki, pages 227-228	The Bible, Genesis 8:6-12 NIV
"Then, forty days after the Deluge over the Earth swept, the rains also stopped. After the forty days Ziusudra the boat's hatch opened, his whereabouts to survey." The Sumerian account then remarks on the beauty of the day and how the boat was alone on a vast sea. Impatient, Ziusudra released some birds he had on board. "To check for dry land, for surviving vegetation to verify he sent them. He sent forth a swallow, he sent forth a raven: both to the boat returned. He sent forth a dove; with a twig from a tree to the boat it returned!" *The last statement again is almost identical to the biblical record:* "Now Ziusudra knew that the dry land from under the waters had emerged."	"After forty days Noah opened the window he had made in the ark and sent out a raven, and it kept flying back and forth until the water had dried up from the earth. Then he sent out a dove to see if the water had receded from the surface of the ground. But the dove could find no place to set its feet because there was water over all the surface of the earth; so it returned to Noah in the ark. He reached out his hand and took the dove and brought it back to himself in the ark. He waited seven more days and again sent out the dove from the ark. When the dove returned to him in the evening, there in its beak was a freshly plucked olive leaf! Then Noah knew that the water had receded from the earth.

The Anunnaki navigator steered the boat to one of the twin peaks of Mount Arrata, called Mount Ararat in the Bible, which is in Turkey. When Ziusudra and his family stood on dry ground again, he sacrificed a burnt offering of a ewe-lamb in gratitude to Enki for saving their lives.

Enlil Explodes

The Sumerian record includes an interchange between Enki and Enlil not recorded in the Bible. Landing on Mount Ararat to survey the damage, Enlil met his brother Enki smiling, and they locked arms in joy. Then Enlil was puzzled by the aroma of roasting meat coming from the other peak. When they flew over and Enlil saw Ziusudra and the survivors, his fury had no bounds. He shouted, "Every Earthling had to perish!" He lunged at Enki, ready to kill him with his bare hands, like Ka-in had killed Abael. Once again, Enki revealed his secret to calm down the situation, letting Enlil know that Ziusudra was no mere mortal, but was his son. Then Enki told Enlil about the dream-vision and diagram that had come from Galzu and how he had spoken only to the reed wall. Enlil's son Ninurta reflected that the survival of mankind must be the will of the Creator of All. Then Enlil relented, had a change of heart, and blessed Ziusudra and his wife, Emzara, saying, "Be fruitful and multiply, and the Earth replenish!"[31]

> Then God blessed Noah and his sons, saying to them, "Be fruitful and increase in number and fill the earth." (Genesis 9:1 NIV)

Triple Calamity: Mars-Nibiru-Earth

Marduk sent word that the dwindling atmosphere of Mars had been completely destroyed by the calamity, and all the Igigi had to return to Earth as Mars could no longer serve as a space station. Anu sent word that the close passing of the two planets had ripped open the hole in Nibiru's atmosphere again and much more gold was needed, quickly! But Enki and Enlil sent word to Nibiru that they could not provide any more gold. The flood had filled up

---

31   Ibid., 229.

all the gold mines in South Africa with mud. All of the primitive workers who had been mining the gold died in the flood. The gold refining facilities were destroyed, and the Anunnaki who had done the processing had all returned to Nibiru. All the tools were also gone. The situation was desperate.

Enlil's son Ninurta flew around the globe assessing the damage. He was astonished to find that across the waters, in the area of South America, the avalanche of waters had cut deeply into the mountains, and nuggets of pure gold that did not need refining were lying all around and could be gathered without mining. The Anunnaki were overjoyed and, in this moment, gave thanks to the Creator for this miracle.

A few descendants of Ka-in (Cain), four brothers and four sisters, had survived on rafts in South America. Their mountaintop was now an island in the midst of Lake Titicaca, a 3200-square-mile lake on the border between Peru and Bolivia. The Anunnaki set up gold-processing facilities in Cuzco, Peru, at a place called Sacsayhuamán.

I visited this ancient site on a trip to Peru and was amazed walking along the zigzag rows of giant boulders that fit together perfectly, without even enough space for the blade of a knife to pass between the joints. One carefully hewn stone was twenty-eight feet high and was calculated to weigh 361 tons. Author Graham Hancock reflects on this engineering feat, wondering how these ancient peoples had cut and transported the huge blocks tens of miles from distant quarries and made walls of them:

> These people weren't even supposed to have had the wheel, let alone machinery capable of lifting and manipulating dozens of irregularly shaped 100-ton blocks, and sorting them into three-dimensional jigsaw puzzles.[32]

At Machu Picchu, I saw more buildings made from huge stone blocks. The people of South America all have ancient myths that these structures had been built by bearded strangers called the Viracochas, who had white skin and were called "the shining ones."

---

32 Hancock, *Fingerprints of the Gods*, 50.

What was particularly noticeable about these traditions was the repeated emphasis that the coming of the Viracochas had been associated with a terrible deluge which had overwhelmed the earth and destroyed the greater part of humanity.[33]

The primary purpose of the Viracochas had been as teachers, to give man civilization. They were kind and loving, but if threatened, could call down fearsome weapons for their own protection. In one legend, when a gentle benevolent teacher and healer was threatened, he used a weapon of heavenly fire.

> ...the people rose up against him and threatened to stone him. They saw him sink to his knees and raise his hands to heaven as if beseeching aid in the peril which beset him. The Indians declare that thereupon they saw fire in the sky which seemed all around them.[34]

The Pyramids

The Anunnaki set to work rebuilding their cities and space facilities. They set up new markers for the landing corridor at their home base in Sumer and built the pyramids to mark the pathway for incoming spaceships. Ningishzidda perfected a scale model, the smallest of the three pyramids at Giza. Next to it he placed a taller peak, setting its sides to the four corners of the Earth, which meant that they pointed to the zodiacal constellations at the rising points of the equinoxes and solstices. Scientists have been amazed that the faces of this pyramid are set exactly to true north, south, east, and west. The Anunnaki used their power tools to cut the stones and made chambers and galleries to house the crystals they used in their missile guidance system. Enki's son Gibil made a special mixture of electrum for the apex capstone. Enlil activated the crystals from Nibiru and lights began to flicker inside the pyramid, and then its capstone shone brighter than the sun.

---

33 Ibid., 52.

34 Osborne, *South American Mythology*, 74.

The pyramid was a beacon that generated a tracking signal for incoming spacecraft, and this building was so durable that it is still standing thousands of years later. Scientists think the Pyramids at Giza were built around 2550 BC by Khufu as burial places for kings and queens, a theory that Graham Hancock thoroughly disputes in his book *Fingerprints of the Gods*. One of the points of evidence that the Sphinx is much older than that date is that it shows unmistakable signs of being weathered by water. Geological reports show the Sphinx was carved out of native rock long before the dynasty of Khufu, pointing to its beginnings "in the period between 10,000 BC and 5000 BC, when the Egyptian climate was wetter."[35] The Pyramids, which I have visited, are indeed one of the Seven Wonders of the World. These two photos were taken at the Great Pyramid of Giza.

**My mother is standing at the center front.
Look how big the pyramid is!**

The author in front of the entrance to the King's Chamber

---

35   Sitchin, *When Time Began*, 256.

The Great Pyramid of Giza covers 13.1 acres at the base and weighs about six million tons. It has 2.3 million individual blocks of limestone and granite. Around 115,000 casing stones weighing ten tons each originally covered all four faces.[36] Another remarkable feature is that when viewed from the air, the placement of the three pyramids corresponds exactly to the placement of the three middle stars in the constellation of Orion, in the position that they were in around 10,400 BC.[37]

Face of the Sphinx

Enki suggested the monument of a lion so when future generations would ask who built this marvelous creation, the lion would mark it in the Age of the Lion, 10,000 BC according to the precession of the equinox. The earth's wobble around its axis results in a different constellation being on the horizon on the equinox about every two thousand years. The order of the constellations goes backward around the zodiac. We are now entering the Age of Aquarius. The Age of Pisces started around the birth of Christ, and 2000 BC marked the beginning of the Age of the Ram, Aries. Before that was the Age of the Bull, Taurus, starting in 4000 BC; the Age of the Twins, Gemini, starting in 6000 BC; the Age of the Crab, Cancer, starting in 8000 BC; and the Age of the Lion, Leo, starting in 10,000 BC.

They cut the image of a lion gazing due east, the Sphinx, with the image of Ningishzidda on its face. Marduk felt left out of the rebuilding and complained that he had been deprived of command and glory and wanted his face on the lion, a position that angered Ningishzidda and his other brothers.

Division of the Earth

After the flood, the sons of both Enki and Enlil demanded land and devoted Earthlings to serve them. All of the Anunnaki wanted territory of their own, so Anu divided things up.

---

36   Hancock, *Fingerprints of the Gods.*

37   Bauval and Gilbert, *The Orion Mystery.*

1. The Sinai Peninsula, the site of their spaceport, was a neutral zone they gave to Ninmah because she was a peacemaker between the brothers. Ninmah was renamed Ninharsag, which means "Mistress of the Mountainhead." This area was off limits to the Earthlings.

2. The area to the east (the Middle East) was given to Enlil and his offspring and to Ziusudra's sons Shem and Yafet (Japeth).

3. Africa was given to Enki and his clan and also Ziusudra's middle son Ham.

4. Enlil's granddaughter Inanna was granted dominion in the valley around the Indus river, now the countries of Pakistan, northwest India, and eastern Afghanistan.[38]

As Ham was passing through the Middle East on his way from Turkey to his assigned land in Africa, he liked the area and decided to squat there. Others warned Ham that he could bring a curse upon himself and his offspring by crossing the will of the gods, since that land had been promised to Enlil's people, but Ham would not listen.[39] Thousands of years later, Enlil raised an army and took back this land promised to him, annihilating the people who had illegally settled there. Ham had four sons: Cush, Mizraim, Put, and Canaan, who settled in Palestine.

The Bible gives the account as follows:

The Table of Nations

This is the account of Shem, Ham, and Japheth, Noah's sons, who themselves has sons after the flood. (Genesis 10:1 NIV)

The sons of Ham: Cush, Mizraim, Put, and Canaan. (Genesis 10:6 NIV)

Cush was the father of Nimrod, who grew to be a mighty warrior on the earth. He was a mighty hunter before the

---

38   Sitchin, *The Lost Book of Enki*, 239-240.

39   Sitchin, *The Wars of Gods and Men.*

LORD; that is why it is said, Like Nimrod, a mighty hunter before the LORD." The first centers of his kingdom were Babylon, Erech, Akkad and Calneh, in Shinar [Sumer]. (Genesis 10:8-10 NIV).

Location of the Ancient Cities

Shinar is the biblical name for Sumer. All of the cities below are located in Iraq, the home of ancient Sumer:

Eridu is in southern Iraq and was the city Enki built for himself when he first came to Earth.

Nippur, also in southeastern Iraq, was Enlil's home city.

Shuruppak was built for Ninmah and her nurses and was called "The Healing Place."

Sippar was the capital city in Sumer, the site of the modern city of Tell Abu Hibbah on the eastern bank of the Euphrates River.

Erech, called Uruk in Sumerian, was located in southeastern Iraq. It was the site chosen to build a pure white ziggurat palace in seven stages for Anu during his upcoming state visit and was later given to the goddess Inanna.

Bad-Tibira in southern Iraq was the headquarters for refining the gold ore.

Babylon was on the Euphrates River about fifty-five miles south of Baghdad and was the city Marduk chose as his headquarters. Babylon's beautiful hanging gardens were one of the Seven Wonders of the World, and its remains are the city of Al Hillah.

Agade in northern Iraq, called Akkad in Akkadian, was the center of the Akkadian empire which developed and penetrated into the surrounding area in Mesopotamia, peaking in the 22nd to 24th century BC.

State Visit

After Earth had been reorganized, Anu and his spouse, Antu, came to Earth for a state visit. When the siblings Enlil, Enki, and Ninmah (also called Ninharsag) saw their parents again after hundreds of thousands of years of separation, they wept, laughed, cried, embraced, and kissed. The difference in the amount that the children had aged from being in the shorter cycles of Earth was obvious, because the parents looked younger than their children. Enlil and

Enki both looked old and bearded, and Ninmah's former beauty had faded to wrinkles and a bent frame.

The family had a wonderful reunion celebration and feast. Then Anu and Antu slept for six days and nights as they were adjusting to the shorter Earth cycles. The children had a long talk with their parents after they woke up. Enki spoke of his dream and the tablet from Galzu, Anu's emissary. Anu was puzzled and told them he never sent any emissary by that name. Enki told Anu that Galzu had warned them they would die if they returned to Nibiru. Anu reported that the change in cycles was a big adjustment, but it could be cured with elixirs.

Divine Compassion and Angelic Intervention

Apparently, Galzu had intervened to get the siblings to stay on the planet, telling them the half-truth that going back to Nibiru's longer circuits would be very hard on their bodies and they would die. Actually, all of us, including the Anunnaki, will die sometime, so what he said was technically true, although he left out the part about the elixir cures. Galzu intervened again, coming to Enki in a dream and leaving the instructions to build the submarine to save the Earthlings. Ninmah was the first to realize that Galzu had been an angelic messenger sent by the Creator of All, who had compassion on *Homo sapiens* and intervened to save our race. Anu reflected that the hand of destiny had directed every step the Anunnaki had taken and that they were emissaries for the Earthlings, a convenient explanation to assuage his guilt for violating cosmic law to save his planet.

Our Debt to the Anunnaki

If the Anunnaki had never had an atmospheric problem and had never come to Earth to mine gold, the flood would still have happened from the close conjunction of Earth and Nibiru around 11,000 BC. The flood would have wiped out all of the land and air creatures on the planet—all specimens of *Homo erectus*, all the four-legged animals and birds, and most of the plant life. Only some fish, sea creatures, and vegetation would have survived. Evolution on Earth would have been set back by billions of years. You and I and seven billion other people would not be having an incarnation right now on this amazing planet, called one of the most beautiful gardens in the whole universe.

The dark force energy of fear of extinction that prompted the Anunnaki to create a slave race was turned around for greater good to preserve life on Earth. I have found the same process at work in my own life. The dark forces keep finding my vulnerabilities and attacking them, but each time they do, I have the opportunity to call in more spiritual resources, bring Light into corners of my shadow, strengthen my weak spots, and raise my level of consciousness so I can radiate more golden Light!

CHAPTER 37

The Anunnaki and Spirituality

Establishing Kingship

After seeing the status of the Earthlings on his state visit, Anu decided to give the humans more independence and to establish cities for them as centers of civilization with sacred precincts as abodes for the Anunnaki. He established the priesthood as a system for humans to worship the lofty Anunnaki as lords and set up a kingship system of leadership and command like on Nibiru. The first kings were priests who communicated the will of the Anunnaki to the people in their precinct. To make the kings special and smarter than the average Earthling, each king had one human parent and one Divine parent. At first, the Anunnaki males impregnated or artificially inseminated human females when they wanted to make a king for an area. Later, the Anunnaki goddesses mated with humans to make the kings.

Worship of the Gods

The Anunnaki called themselves gods and said they were the Divine Creators of the humans. The attribute of creator was only half true. They did gene splice the hybrid race of *Homo sapiens* and saved it from destruction in the flood, but they did not create *Homo erectus* or themselves. To the humans, the Anunnaki certainly looked like they were Divine. They had superpowers, a theme reflected in our present culture with stories of Superman (from a different planet) and his successors Batman, Spiderman, Iron Man, and so on. Anunnaki technology made them appear miraculous to the humans. They could fly about in their "Divine Birds," their jet airplanes. They had awesome weapons of combat, including bombs and missiles, and could strike a person dead with a death ray weapon that separated the spirit from the physical body.

Bringing the Dead Back to Life

The Lost Book of Enki reports that the Anunnaki had two devices that could be used to bring a dead person back to life, the Emitter and the Pulser. When Enki's sister Ninmah came to Earth as Chief Medical Officer with a group of female nurses in 430,000 BC, she first stopped on Mars, where Alalu had been exiled, and found his dead body. Another Anunnaki named Anzu had gone with Alalu to Mars as an escort for Alalu and was also found dead. Ninmah used first the Emitter to charge up Anzu's energy field with life energy and then the Pulser to jump start life again. The records are not clear why these instruments were not used at other times, like when Enki's son Dumuzi met a tragic death.

Humans who obeyed the instructions of the gods were rewarded with land, livestock, and riches. Those who disobeyed were treated harshly or killed. The Anunnaki figured out an ingenious method to get the humans to bring them food. The humans were always making mistakes and transgressing the laws set up to guide their behavior. When a human committed an error, the sin could be atoned for by sacrificing an animal. A dove would fix a small sin, a sheep a medium-sized sin, and a bull a great big transgression. The sins were put into the animal, which was then killed, releasing the donor from the guilt of the sin. The priests burned the sacrifice, and the priests and the local Anunnaki lord who lived at the temple ate the roasted meat.

Confusion with the Angelic Realm

The Anunnaki called themselves the Elohim, a plural word meaning "gods" and sometimes translated as "angels." The Igigi on Mars had been called the "Watchers," as they had a global view of things happening on Earth. The Anunnaki were also called "the shining ones" and "the radiant ones." The name of their land, Sumer, is called Shinar in the Bible, meaning the Land of the Watchers.

The bodies of the Anunnaki radiated golden light, probably because they drank gold in its monatomic form to slow down the aging process, especially since the shorter cycles on Earth made the Anunnaki here age faster. Remember that when Anu and Antu came for a state visit around 4000 BC, they looked younger than their children. These names of the Elohim, the Watchers, and the Shining Ones set up the Anunnaki to pretend they were angels—but they were not from the angelic realm, they were mortal. Angels are higher dimensional immortal beings of Light that can modulate their frequency to appear in third-dimensional reality and then beam themselves back up to their home frequency, seeming from our point of view to appear and disappear. The Anunnaki could not do that. They had to travel from place to place in spaceships, boats, or aircraft. Galzu may have been a genuine angel, or he may have been an advanced extraterrestrial from a different planet in a higher dimension that intervened on behalf of the Prime Creator to save life on the Earth.

Real angels give warnings to humans in danger and communicate a sense of peace, comfort, and love, all Divine attributes. The angel in the following story does not sound like a messenger from Source helping people out. Once when Jerusalem was being attacked and mocked by King Sennacherib of Assyria, King Hezekiah prayed:

> LORD Almighty, God of Israel, enthroned between the cherubim, you alone are God over all the kingdoms of the earth. You have made heaven and earth. Give ear, O LORD, and hear; open your eyes, O LORD, and see; listen to all the words Sennacherib has sent to insult the living God. (Isaiah 37:15-17 NIV)

The Lord responded to this prayer and saved Jerusalem in the following way:

> Then the angel of the LORD went out and put to death a hundred and eighty-five thousand men in the Assyrian camp. When the people got up the next morning—there were all the dead bodies! So Sennacherib king of Assyria broke camp and withdrew. (Isaiah 37:36-37 NIV)

The angel in this scripture sounds like an emissary sent by Lord Enlil using a super-weapon to cause destruction. Perhaps the angel zapped the Assyrians with the death ray while they were sleeping. One other difference between the true angelic realm and the Anunnaki "angels" is that true angels never interfere with the free will of humans. They need to be asked for help before they jump into action. On the other hand, the Anunnaki were definitely trying to enforce their will on the Earthlings.

Higher Dimensions

The greater part of ourselves is outside of space and time.
—William Tiller

Many levels of existence are higher than this three-dimensional world we live in. When we dream at night, we go into a higher plane and interact in another world that seems very real. True spirituality cultivates a relationship with these higher dimensions for guidance in our earthly lives. When we sit quietly in meditation and ask a Being of Light to help us understand the nature of the choices that come into our lives, we can make better decisions. When we move into a state of gratitude for the wonder of the night sky, the beauty of a flower, or any other handiwork of the Creator, we bring joy and peace into our hearts. The Psalms of the Old Testament have hymns of praise that King David sang to Source, but so far I have not found record in the Sumerian tablets of the Anunnaki singing hymns to their Creator. Perhaps they did privately worship the Father of All Beginning, but they would not have wanted the humans to know they were not the prime creator.

392

Immortality

The slower cycles on Nibiru, with one of their years equaling 3600 of ours, spread out their birth, life, and death cycles over a much longer time period. King Anu was already an adult when the first space mission came to Earth, and he was still reining half a million years later when the flood came. With such long natural life spans, the Anunnaki certainly looked immortal to the humans. But the Anunnaki had flesh and blood, and they could die. The ancient records of the succession of kings imply that, over long periods of time, one king's life ended and rule was passed down through generations. The story of Enki's son Dumuzi's accidental death is a concrete example of the death of an Anunnaki god.

At will, the gods could give a human an elixir that granted the human immortality, and the story says they did this for King Ziusudra (Noah). One of the demi-god kings named Gilgamesh set his heart on also being granted immortality. He went through great trials and tribulations to visit the gods and ask them directly for immortality, recorded in the Epic of Gilgamesh. When he finally arrived at the abode of the Anunnaki god Utu/Shamash (Enlil's grandson), his request was turned down. Utu told Gilgamesh that the gods had allotted death for Mankind and retained enduring life only for themselves. Utu urged Gilgamesh to live and enjoy life day by day, good advice for us all.

Humans have a different kind of immortality from that of the extended lifespans of the Anunnaki. The Creator gave each human an immortal soul, something the Anunnaki did not realize in the beginning as they considered us more like work horses. Gilgamesh and other *Homo sapiens* also did not seem to be aware that each person had an immortal soul. In the traditional Christian version, after death the soul is judged and then sent either to heaven or to eternal hell. In the theory of reincarnation, the soul of each person choses one body suit to learn a particular lesson, sheds the body suit at death, and then gets an upgraded version by reincarnating into a new body suit to master the next lesson. I have not seen reincarnation mentioned in the Sumerian tablets. Perhaps with such long life spans, the Anunnaki did not spend much time thinking about their souls' future or about how the karma incurred in their present life would affect their future life. Or perhaps their use of monatomic gold closed down their awareness of the spiritual aspect of their souls that would survive their current physical bodies.

A Rocket Ride to Nibiru

The ancient Egyptians believed that their king, the pharaoh, was the only person who got immortality.[1] The process of getting the deceased pharaoh to his afterlife in Nibiru involved saying incantations over the body and having the earthbound spirit of the pharaoh pass through a false doorway drawn on the eastern side of the stone wall of his burial chamber.

> The Pharaoh was then envisioned as raising himself, shaking off Earth's dust, and exiting by the false door. According to the Pyramid Text which dealt with the resurrection process step by step, the Pharaoh could not pass through the stone wall by himself.[2]

Then, guided by the priests chanting, "The king is on his way to Heaven!" the pharaoh undertook a hazardous journey, crossing the Lake of Reeds in a ferryboat through a subterranean realm of the Netherworld to reach the "Hidden Place" where his spirit was guided through a series of underground passageways to a place where a god would open for him secret gates leading him to the Eye of Horus and a Celestial Ladder to climb. Then he shed his clothes and dressed in a falcon suit, symbolizing that he would be able to fly like the gods. He reached an object called "the Ascender to the Sky," what we would call a rocket ship. Four "sailors of the boat of Ra" prepared the spacecraft for the king to ascend to Heaven on it.[3] Then with roaring and quaking, the vessel blasted off the launch pad of the Anunnaki, and the pharaoh got a view of Earth from the sky as he embarked on the eight-day space flight to Nibiru. When he arrived, Ra [Anu] welcomed the king to Nibiru, the Imperishable Star. This journey sounds like an earthbound spirit traveling to the launch pad of a rocket ship and being blasted off to another planet. It is not the kind of rocket ride to

---

1   Sitchin, *The Stairway to Heaven*.
2   Ibid., 58.
3   Ibid., 83.

heaven that I envision when my time in this body is done! I plan to see a vortex of Light open up a doorway through which my guides, my Guardian Angels, my dog Terri, and my Soul Family come to get me and take me home into a higher dimension, without a spacesuit.

Monatomic Gold

The Anunnaki immune systems appear to have been more fully activated than ours, because we never hear about the Anunnaki getting sick. Author Michael Tellinger speculates that they used gold in its monatomic form, a white powder mixed into water, and that this drink was the elixir of the gods that gave them immortality.[4]

In its metallic form, gold has nineteen atoms bound together. When gold is heated, the bonds between these atoms break apart leaving single atoms of gold, monatomic gold, which is a white powder. This powder can be mixed into water and ingested. A cotton farmer named David Radius Hudson rediscovered this technology in the late twentieth century and applied for patents in March of 1988 for the process, which he calls "orbitally rearranged monoatomic [monatomic] elements" (ORME). Other names for the substance are white powder gold, white gold, ORMUS, and manna. Hudson reports, "Any alteration, any defect in the DNA is corrected by the precious elements. It perfects the cells of our bodies. But the element going into our bodies is not a metal, the element is not a heavy metal, it is an element."[5] One of the big surprises of Hudson's research was that when the gold was transformed from its metallic form to its monatomic form, it actually weighed less. Hudson reports that the pan in which he heated the gold would levitate if a hand were passed underneath it. Hudson says the energy of the hand added enough energy to make the pan overcome the gravitational force holding it down. The lightness of powdered gold is what made it able to stay in suspension in Nibiru's atmosphere and mend the breach.

According to Hudson, white powder gold acts as a superconductor in the body, increasing the flow of light, elevating the level of consciousness, repair-

---

4   Tellinger, *Slave Species of god.*
5   D. R. Hudson, Presentation at the International Forum of New Science, Fort Collins, CO, 1995.

ing the DNA, and rejuvenating the physical form.[6] This idea may seem far out, but the Bible records an event in Exodus that sounds like people were drinking monatomic gold. The Israelites got tired of waiting for Moses while the finger of God was writing the Ten Commandments on stone and made a golden calf that they then worshiped. They danced around the golden calf and offered it burnt sacrifices to incur the favor of the god it represented.

> When Moses approached the camp and saw the calf and the dancing, his anger burned and he threw the tablets out of his hands, breaking them to pieces at the foot of the mountain. And he took the calf the people had made and burned it in the fire; then he ground it to powder, scattered it on the water and made the Israelites drink it. (Exodus 32:19-20 NIV)

A website titled Ascension Alchemy calls ingesting monatomic gold a "little-known spiritual biochemistry," claiming that it allows a continuous flow of Light through the body that heals right down to the subatomic level. The effect is supposed to strengthen the immune system and raise the capacity for awareness of higher consciousness. The website claims that sacred civilizations such as Lemuria and Egypt and spiritual sects all over the world have used this technique for developing spiritual powers.[7] Various forms of monatomic gold are available commercially, and one puts the white powder gold into water and then drinks it, just like the instructions of Moses to the Israelites.

Dangers of Monatomic Gold

Other websites warn that using monatomic gold may have adverse effects. We have two strands of DNA that can be seen with a microscope, but according to metaphysical teachers including Stevan Thayer, developer of Integrated Energy Therapy,[8] we also have an additional ten pairs of DNA in the nonphysical realms that govern our emotional, mental, and spiritual makeup. A website from Ken Adachi warns that taking monatomic gold may promote physical

---

6   D. R. Hudson, "Library of Halexandria," http://www.halexandria.org/dward467.htm
7   Ascension Alchemy: http://www.asc-alchemy.com/mono.html
8   For more information: www.CenterofBeing.com

health and initially give more mental clarity and psychic awareness, but later this awareness declines.[9] The site points out two main dangers of taking monatomic gold:

1. Ingesting this substance, which is a superconductor, may block a person from progressing to higher states of spiritual awareness by destroying the templates for access to higher dimensions, called the ten strands of DNA in the nonphysical realm by many spiritual teachers.
2. Some of the commercial products available may actually be gold chloride, which is a nerve toxin known to make the hair fall out and to cause peripheral neuropathy.[10]

So think twice before ingesting something that is supposed to be white powder gold! Before I saw the warnings, I got excited about the claims made about monatomic gold and bought a product on the Internet listed as monatomic gold already in a water solution. Before it arrived, colleagues pointed out the warnings to me, so I decided to check out the product before ingesting it. Muscle testing is the way I find out if energy is flowing properly in my body. I tested my energy flow while holding this product over my navel. While I felt a slight initial rush, just having this product near my body reversed my polarity at the crown of my head. Muscle testing also indicated that the product I had purchased for under $40 was gold chloride, which made sense because it was so inexpensive. I sent the gold solution back unopened and got a refund.

Negative Green as a Carrier Wave

Using monatomic gold to build their physical and mental bodies at the expense of their spiritual bodies may have blocked the receptor sites of the Anunnaki from receiving communication from their own spirit guides and guardian angels. I have put together some things I have learned about energy and BioGeometry to formulate a theory of how this blockage might have worked.

---

9   K. Adachi, editor: http://educate-yourself.org/cn/
monoatomicgoldthinktwice15aug05.shtml
10   Purest Colloids: http://www.purestcolloids.com/ionic-gold.php

Radio waves are a good example of subtle energy waves that carry information at different frequencies. We tune our dials to the radio station we want to hear. Likewise, the spiritual universes are all sharing space with our physical universe, and we can tune in to listen to our own spiritual guidance. Author Mark Macy writes, "What separates these worlds one from another is the difference in the frequency at which their matter vibrates."[11] Ibrahim Karim founded the new field of BioGeometry, which works to harmonize physical spaces, cancel electromagnetic pollution, and promote physical health. Karim teaches about the importance of a combination of three frequencies he calls BG3 (BioGeometry Three) that harmonize and transform a person, a space, or an area into an ultimate permanent state of balance. Karim defines BG3 as follows:

> The three basic qualities that are in resonance with The One Harmonizing Subtle Energy Quality and are used to detect it: Horizontal Negative Green (HNG), Higher Harmonic of Ultra Violet (HHUV) and Higher Harmonic of Gold (HHG). They are found simultaneously as the main components of the One Energy Quality.[12]

He also teaches about an important frequency called "negative green," which is the exact inverse of the wave light we see as visible green. In the 1930s, a French scientist named Leon de Chaumery became obsessed with the qualities of negative green, which has both a beneficial horizontal aspect and a detrimental vertical aspect. Not understanding how powerful the vertical negative green was, Chaumery did an experiment using geometric shapes to emit energy and placed a large copper rod pyramid around his bed as an experiment on mummification. In the morning, he was found dead of dehydration. Karim's BioGeometry finds this vertical negative green frequency at the center of each side of the base of a pyramid and advises people to put some kind of mark or object in the center of each side of a pyramid to cancel the vertical negative green created. This frequency is generated by certain shapes of pendulums,

---

11 *Spirit Faces*, x.
12 Karim, *Back to a Future for Mankind*, 290.

and in the hands of a skilled practitioner can be consciously directed to kill a pathogen in the body such as a malignant tumor. Karim identifies negative green as a "critically important spiritual carrier wave essential to spiritual work"[13] and identifies negative green as a carrier wave between humans and the higher dimensions of light. Many healers find that after channeling healing energy from the Angelic Realm or after giving someone a treatment of Reiki, a Universal Life Force transmission, the practitioner feels very thirsty because the negative green carrier wave to the Spiritual realm dehydrates the body.

Karim teaches that the Higher Harmonic of Gold "is a subtle energy quality on a higher spiritual dimension that is in resonance with physical gold."[14] Gold is the highest vibration in the metal kingdom, and perhaps the abundance of the superconductor of gold in the bodies of the Anunnaki made their frequencies vibrate so fast that their BG3 energies became unbalanced, and they were blocked from the ability to access negative green, the subtle communication system by which one can send and receive thought packages from Source.

Mind Control

This section presents some ideas that may seem extremely radical to the reader and may be judged as unfounded speculation on my part. I would have thought them outrageous myself earlier in my life, before I read about the remote viewing and mind-control experiments the CIA began during World War II called Project MK-Ultra using hypnosis and drugs for interrogation and reducing fatigue. The information about this project has been declassified and is available on the internet. After the war, Project MK-Ultra branched out to creating multiple personalities in subjects that could be used as spies who were invulnerable to torture. The illegal, covert program used drugs, hypnosis, verbal and sexual abuse, torture, and chip implants to manipulate mental state and alter brain functions. In short, the project researched how to control human behavior. Knowing that the government of my country would like to be able to control the minds of others makes the idea that the ancient astronauts might have wanted to control the minds of their subjects a little more plausible.

---

13   Ibid., 297.
14   Ibid.

The Voice of the Lord Speaking

The Old Testament is filled with volumes of explicit instructions for the Israelites regulating every aspect of daily life and worship. Over and over, it says, "And the voice of the LORD spoke unto Moses, saying...." Now, how exactly did the Lord communicate with Moses in such intricate detail? Moses clearly heard the voice, and he did not have a cell phone or even a transistor radio. I wonder whether these voices could have come from energetic implants installed in the priests and kings by the Anunnaki for communication and direction/control, just like the Dark Devices described by the demons earlier in the Detrimental Energy Protocol. Then the Anunnaki could broadcast radio messages that could be tuned to the frequency of the device in each individual king or priest to give explicit instructions on a given topic. Moses also heard the voice of the Lord speaking from between the two golden Seraphim on the top of the Ark of the Covenant, but not all of the kings and priests were in the proximity of this Ark.

Hearing a disembodied voice is actually quite easy and is done all the time, except that today we classify hearing voices as mental illness. Many of the schizophrenic patients I have worked with reported hearing audible voices speaking in their heads. The phenomenon happens to normal people also, who may occasionally hear their name being called when nobody is around. Some of the patients in the psychiatric ward where I used to work claimed that ETs had implanted communication devices in their brains. Psychiatry defines hearing voices from non-existent people as a seizure of the auditory nerve and uses tranquilizers to subdue the symptom. The medication does not stop the problem, but my clients on antipsychotic drugs told me that their meds muffled the voices so they were not as bothered by them.

As incredible as the next statement will seem, in my work with clients, we have muscle tested that many of them who hear voices in their heads have extraterrestrial implants that are broadcasting information to them. When we do the Soul Detective protocol for Extraterrestrial Interference to remove the implants, the voices stop and physical symptoms resolve. I will share two examples:

Case of ET Implants

Tenacious presented with extreme hip pain on the left side of her body that radiated up her back, to her neck, and down her leg. This hip had a joint replacement twenty years earlier and had been acting up. She was scheduled for surgery to remove the accumulation of old blood in the hip joint.

We first called in Matrix Energetics Universal Healing Frequency #3[15] to harmonize and balance her body to her current medications, morphine, codeine, Tylenol, and synthroid. Next we called in Matrix Energetics Frequency #4[16] to physically restructure her muscle, bone, tendon, joints, and fascia for the hip and the pain. Then we found a deeper origin of the problem.

Group One

We muscle tested that Tenacious had eight Implants from extraterrestrials with detrimental intent. They were from two different groups of ETs. Group one had an implant in her Gallbladder meridian and one in the back of her third eye. The leader of this group of ETs communicated to Tenacious that their purpose was to stop her from her mission of helping Earth come into alignment with the other planets and all beings. They reasoned, "If she is healed, she will destroy everything!" These ETs worked for the darkness and wanted chaos. They were told that if Tenacious succeeded with the Earth alignment, they would disappear. Tenacious told them that if the Light came, they would not disappear, but would be able to be seen. They looked into their centers, found Light, and all jumped ship, converting to Lightworkers.

---

15 Bartlett, *The Matrix Energetics Experience* audiobook.
16 Ibid.

Group Two

ET group two was inside a black barrier that prevented them from seeing out. Their purpose was to cause an early death for Tenacious, and they had been after her for a long time. Several times they had failed in their attempts to cause her terminal illnesses. They worked for the darkness and were not given any rationale for their job. They just took orders. Tenacious reported, "They are as low as one can go and were created just to do this job." They could not see outside of their barrier, so we asked them to look inside themselves. They were startled at that request. Tenacious told me, "You really shook their tree!" They found their Light but did not even know what the Light was. We asked Archangel Michael to remove the barrier around them, but the ETs had been told that a bomb would go off if the barrier were removed. We asked Archangel Michael to disarm it, but even that plan did not feel safe to them. They believed that if the barrier were removed, they would all die, and Tenacious would also die.

Tenacious opened up her heart and sent them love. In taking this action, she felt as if a bomb went off in her own heart, exploding a barrier that had been in place, and her heart chakra opened.

ET Ambulance

The Dark ETs were unable to open up their own hearts and did not want new jobs—that step was too big and hard. They were willing, however, to go to the ET hospital with Archangel Michael. We offered to take them in a spaceship, but they absolutely did not want to go that way, because that was how they got to planet Earth. They wanted an ambulance and went, with all of them hanging on to each other. Their gift to

Tenacious was presenting her another opportunity to practice forgiveness and a chance to reinforce her own worthiness.

We removed these six implants from ET group two from Tenacious one by one. They were in the root chakra and the back of each chakra from the third eye down through the sacral chakra. We started with the third eye, and Tenacious felt pinchers, like a beetle, constricting the awareness of her third eye. She commented, "They did not want me to see."

Next we went to the heart chakra, where she experienced a hammer pounding her heart and a feeling that electrodes were zapping each other. As we asked her spiritual guidance team to heal this chakra, Tenacious committed to a huge step with the affirmation, "I have decided to take the plunge and love myself as I am and to accept the full capacity of my ability to love."

Help from the Whale Kingdom

We called in the assistance of Minerva, a humpback whale who made a telepathic communication with me while I was swimming in the wild with her and her calf,[17] to aid Tenacious in her ability to love herself. Tenacious recalled a previous lifetime as a whale. I inquired why she had stepped down from the superior life form of the whales, mammals that are centered in unconditional love, to take on a human body. She responded, "To teach whale love to humans." She recalled the film *Star Trek IV: The Voyage Home* set in the twenty-third century, about an alien probe looking for the sound of humpback whales and destroying Earth's oceans because the whales were extinct. Admiral Kirk, Dr. Spock, and their crew traveled back in time to 1986, beamed two humpback whales

---

17　Dr. Stone, "Swimming with Humpback Whales" http://www.youtube.com/watch?v=IPf8yw5vKjY and "Toronto EP Conference: Releasing Limitations" http://www.youtube.com/watch?v=a7kGx5ewfYU

into their spaceship, and brought them back into the twenty-third century, stopping the destruction of the probe and saving planet Earth.

Next we did the root chakra, which felt like "a mess that needs a major cleanout." Tenacious reported that she'd had a cyst removed from her hip a couple of years ago that would have killed her if its contents had been released into her body. We called in Matrix Energetics Frequency 12,[18] Energy Center Repair, to restore proper rotation to her root chakra. Frequency 12 looks like black oil, and she needed five quarts. Tenacious quipped, "I needed an oil change!" With her characteristic sense of humor, she redefined chaos as "energy that wants to be organized."

We finished by repairing the solar plexus, the throat, and the sacral chakras. The implant at the throat had been designed to stop her voice and her creativity. Tenacious asked to have these healings go through all of her lifetimes and incarnations in all dimensions. We ended with Matrix Energetics Frequency 8,[19] Integration, to take in and integrate all of the work she had done during this session.

Tenacious reported feeling tired after this session, a good sign that she had made major energy shifts in her system! After this session, her body shifted its pattern of getting progressively worse and was able to begin a gradual process of healing the multiple health challenges she faced. Over the course of the coming two years she shed forty pounds of extra weight and gradually regained stamina.

This next case shows a different origin of ET implants.

---

18 Bartlett, *The Matrix Energetics Experience* audiobook.
19 Ibid.

ET Invitation

Francis wanted to find and clear the origins of the unrelenting skin rash on her left hand. We muscle tested that one of the contributing factors was extraterrestrial interference. Francis was not surprised. Highly intuitive and trained in observing and navigating other realms, she had seen two different types of ETs in the healing room where she worked with her clients. The first kind she noticed was two tall blue machinelike ETs with slightly human forms with facial features and armlike appendages. Later she noticed some silvery metallic ETs, each with a single eye in the forehead.

Four Implants

With a combination of Soul Detective muscle testing and the intuitive information that Francis gathered, we determined that these ET implants had the neutral purpose of simply studying her system. The ETs had implanted four tiny metallic devices, each 0.25 mm long, into her left hand to monitor the energy flow in four of the meridians that run through the hand: the Large Intestine, Triple Energizer, Heart, and Small Intestine.

We asked her guardian angels to converse with these ETs to let them know that the presence of their implants was altering the proper flow of these energy lines, resulting in two problems:

1. All data they were gathering were invalid.
2. The presence of the implants caused a physical problem for Francis.

The ETs understood and were willing to take out the implants. Francis wanted them to do it on the spot, but the ETs said it would be better if they would do it while she was sleeping. We asked the angels to show the ETs better ways to gather the data they needed and how to access help from transpersonal dimensions. We also asked them to take out the implants of anyone else they were studying—but Francis wanted to go first! The ETs agreed and thought they would need several nights to finish the job.

The ETs commented that Francis was an interesting study subject because of the dichotomy within her, having a strong logical masculine left-brained side but also a rich, heartfelt right-brained connection to the spiritual world. Being so logical and intellectual themselves, these ETs knew nothing about the angelic kingdom or how to access help from a transpersonal dimension. They found humans complex, having so many gifts they did not use.

Old Friends

Francis reported awareness of a previous lifetime on the ET's planet of origin, which is why they felt so familiar to each other, and also why she did not get frightened when she first saw them in her therapy room. She expressed her aggravation to her old friends about the physical suffering she had been going through with the itching and soreness in her hand. A spirit guide named Gideon reminded Francis that *she had invited the ETs in*! He showed her exactly when it happened. The day she first saw them in her therapy room, she had felt a little thrilled but not scared. With a wide-open heart, she invited them in to observe the beautiful energy in her healing space and the angelic presence that filled the room with beauty, love, and healing. She did not realize how literally they would act on her invitation to observe.

Aldovarians

The ETs said they were from another galaxy and were Aldovars. They did not have individual names, but they liked being called Aldovarians. They thanked Francis for the day's inter-action and all they had learned about accessing the transper-sonal realm and the angelic kingdom.

At the end of the session, everyone involved was filled with gratitude. The open wound of the skin rash Francis had on her hand took three weeks to heal and never returned.

Anunnaki Implants?

If the Anunnaki installed listening devices to instruct their priests and kings, they may also have had the kings and priests drink monatomic gold so they would radiate light, look more Divine, live a long time, and be unable to listen to the voice of Source. In general, the governing religious authorities in many churches have frowned upon their members talking directly to Source energy. The Catholic Church claims to be the only proper channel for the voice of God, which comes through the pope, the cardinal, the bishop, and the priest down to the church member, who is not supposed to do independent think-ing on the nature of God or to communicate directly with God. An exception in organized religion is the Unitarian Universalist Church, which encourages each member to seek for truth and accepts all faiths as legitimate pathways to the Divine.

Plagues

Here is an example of specific instructions given to Moses:

> Then the LORD said to Moses, "When you take a census of the Israelites to count them, each one must pay the LORD a ran-som for his life at the time he is counted. Then no plague will come on them when you number them. Each one who crosses over to those already counted is to give a half shekel..." (Exo-dus 30:11-13a NIV)

In this scripture, the money given by each subject was for plague preven-tion, similar to getting a flu shot. If the people paid the Lord, then no plague would afflict them. If they did not pay, they could be stricken with illnesses. An interesting twist on plagues is the idea proposed by Michael Tellinger that the Anunnaki may have used germ warfare for population control. Tellinger asks:

> Is it possible that while the ancient Anunnaki gods were trying to keep humankind enslaved with religious dogma, they were also attempting to reduce the growing numbers of their slave species, which would allow them to exercise greater control over humans?[20]

Explicit Instructions

Later, in Leviticus, the voice of the Lord gave Moses a long list of sexual relationships that were unlawful, including a sexual relationship with any close relative, siblings, both a woman and her daughter, taking a rival wife that is your wife's sister, sex during a woman's monthly period, or sexual relations with an animal. This prohibition against a human marrying a sister is different from the Anunnaki practice of needing a child by a sister to qualify for succession to the throne. Since the Anunnaki had perfect DNA, they did not need to worry about the dangers of inbreeding that come with genetic errors being compounded when *Homo sapiens* mate with a close relative.

Implications for Mental Health Treatment

In my practice, I have had many cases in which a voice seemed to result from the attachment of an earthbound spirit to a client. Helping this earthbound spirit heal and cross into the Light stopped the voice the client used to hear, so from that piece of information, I deduce that a spirit is able somehow to create the thought form of a voice that registers in the ears of the client.

Progressive caregivers around the world are beginning to open up to the ancient wisdom of shamanic practices and include the spiritual realm in their diagnostic framework. Psychiatrist Robert Alcorn, MD, reports the case of a man in his thirties diagnosed with bipolar disorder whose body was covered

---

20   Tellinger, *Slave Species of god*, 207.

with elaborate tattoos of dark and demonic images. This man reported he had been playing with a Ouija board as a teenager and had a frightening experience in which his girlfriend started speaking in the voice of a deceased friend and then had claw-like scratches on her back, though no one in the session had touched her. Using shamanic techniques, Dr. Alcorn found and removed two demon entities from the young man, which removed the "doom and gloom" that had formerly surrounded him.[21]

Whether or not we believe in demons, ghosts, or implants, if we really want to find solutions that cure problems rather than just cover them up, we need to keep our minds open to adding integrative healing methods, especially non-invasive procedures that rely on guided imagery and prayer as a complement to surgery and medication when necessary. We need to shed our prejudices and listen to what our mentally ill clients are saying about why they are disturbed and then develop treatments using their metaphors in our remedies.

Implant Devices in Humans

If the idea that ancient astronauts who had perfected interplanetary travel and communication 500,000 years ago implanted communication devices in their kings sounds far out, look at what is happening today. Humans are placing implants in other humans and animals, billing the chips as safety and health monitoring devices.

An implant device called a VeriChip is currently being used for tracking and communication. These mini microchip devices have already been implanted sub dermally in thousands of people, from children to the elderly, and in pets. In 2009, a company named Reuters got patents to develop a system that will be able to detect viruses.

> "The patents, held by VeriChip partner Receptors LLC, relate to biosensors that can detect the H1N1 and other viruses, and biological threats such as methicillin-resistant *Staphylococcus aureus*," VeriChip said in a statement.

---

21 Alcorn, *Healing Stories*, 81-83.

"The technology will combine with VeriChip's implantable radio frequency identification devices to develop virus triage detection systems."[22]

If a mini microchip can send out radio frequencies for tracking purposes, is it such a stretch of the imagination for a mini microchip to receive radio frequencies that would play like a radio voice in someone's head if inserted in the proper location in the brain?

DNA Responds to Frequencies

Fritz-Albert Popp, a German researcher, invented and proved the biophoton theory, which says that biological organisms emit coherent photons; in other words, they shine out a form of light that can carry information. Popp was trying to find a cure for cancer and discovered that compounds that produce cancer all absorbed light at a frequency of 380 nanometers and then sent it out at a different frequency. In other words, they scrambled the 380 nanometers frequency, which happens to be the frequency that the body uses most efficiently for a process called photo repair which rebuilds damaged cells.[23]

Taking this idea one step further into the future of mini microchip technology, could a chip implanted be made to scramble the frequency of the host at a certain bandwidth of light? Could cancer or other illnesses be induced in a person with a chip if the authorities that implanted the device wanted to punish or eliminate that person?

DNA Responds to Frequencies of Light

Russian scientist Peter Gariaev, PhD, director of the Wave Genetics Institute in Moscow, conducted research showing that DNA responds to frequencies of light. He writes of some incredible things his research team was able to do:

---

22 Gabriel O'Hara, "Comprehend VeriChip's Swine Flu Chip," Wise Up Journal, September 23, 2009, http://wellnessuncovered.com/joomla/index.php?option=com_content&view=article&id=939:comprehend-verichips-swine-flu-chip-&catid=1:latest-news&Itemid=50
23 http://www.viewzone.com/dnax.html

...we have found it possible to regenerate endocrine glands in animals. By the same means, we have significantly curbed the aging process in human cells and even grown new adult human teeth in individuals who had lost them.[24]

One experiment Dr. Gariaev did showed the effects of light emissions broadcast from a quantum biocomputer:

A control group of rats was injected with lethal doses of a poison called alloxan which destroys the pancreas. As a result, all the rats in the control group died from diabetes in three to four days. Then the same lethal dose of alloxan was injected in another group of rats. And when the rats reached the critical condition, they were exposed to light images/ waves coming from a quantum bio-computer. Those light images/waves were created beforehand when the bio-computer read information from the pancreas surgically removed from healthy newborn rats of the same species as those used in the alloxan experiments.

The pancreas was restored and returned to health in 90 percent of the rats exposed to these healing light rays. With some of the rats, the computer broadcasting the program was twenty kilometers away.[25]

In this same report, Dr. Gariaev writes:

In addition, it ought to be mentioned, such a technology—a quantum bio-computer, is capable of:

• treating oncological diseases on a fundamentally distinct basis—without use of any chemical substances,

---

24 "An Open Letter from Dr. Peter Gariaev, the Father of 'Wave-Genetics,'" October 30, 2005, http://www.fractal.org/Life-Science-Technology/Peter-Gariaev.htm
25 Peter Gariaev, "Wave Genetics," http://eng.wavegenetic.ru/index.php?option=com_content&task=view&id=2&Itemid=1

• eliminating pathogenic viruses and bacteria and agricultural vermin parasites—also without use of any chemical substances.

It may seem as a technology of another age, from the distant future. However, a discovery of fundamental properties of living organisms is occurring today and it is our task to research and explain the phenomena and bring it to the service of humanity.

One other study by Dr. Gariaev is truly amazing to me because it does something I would not have believed possible. He zapped a salamander embryo with a beam of laser light and then redirected that light to shine into a frog embryo. The frog embryo then completely morphed into a healthy salamander embryo.

If this technology can be used to build health, it also brings up the possibility that it could be used to destroy health if a malicious computer programmer were to broadcast the energies of diseased organs into humans. Yikes! The Lord of the Old Testament often threatened to punish his people with disease and plagues if they did not obey his orders, and perhaps he actually had the technology to do it.

Author Stephen Greer reports that in 1997, after he gave a series of briefings to congress disclosing what he knows about UFO activity, both he and his assistant were diagnosed with aggressive, metastatic cancer six months later. At the same time, Greer's dog got cancer in his left triceps muscle and had to have his leg amputated. Greer returned from having a metastatic malignant melanoma removed from his shoulder, and he and his golden retriever had matching scars. Greer believes that some kind of weapon system was targeting him and his assistant with disease frequencies. Greer survived, but his assistant died.[26]

---

26 Greer, *Hidden Truth*.

CHAPTER 38

Henry the Sixth

I n the introduction to my book *Invisible Roots*, I talk about my reaction to a dream I had in which a scribe read me a list of people I had been in previous incarnations, and this list included King Henry VI of England.[1] There is no way to prove whether this information that came to me in a dream is historically true, but there is also no way to prove it is not true. While I still cannot say for certain whether Henry VI was one of my past incarnations, whether my soul has picked up a thread of resonance to the morphogenetic field of his life, or whether I am dealing with the archetype of the wounded king, I do know that the themes and challenges of his life resonate with issues I have faced. I work with this material as if it were true to enter fully into the mindset of Henry and to see what needs to heal in my own heart and what needs to heal in our collective consciousness.

Henry's parents could not afford the servants necessary to run their castle and so placed young Henry in a monastery during his childhood and teenage

---

1   Stone, *Invisible Roots*, 5-6.

years. When he became King of England, Henry was so devoted to God that he would not fight on Sunday. Under the leadership of Joan of Arc, the French gained back all the territory his father, Henry V, had captured. Interestingly, Joan of Arc was instructed by voices she heard that she said came from God in heaven. She used input from those voices to wage war against the English. Eventually, the English captured her and judged that the voices she heard were coming from the Devil. They executed her for blasphemy.

Henry became mentally ill and had catatonic spells.[2] England wanted a king who was a warrior, not a saint, but Henry was unable to give his country what they wanted. He lost the throne and had to flee for his life. His wife eventually raised an army and got him reinstated. Shortly thereafter, Henry was stabbed in the back while praying in the Tower of London. Within ten years of his death, the "sillie weake King," as King James I had called him, had become a popular saint and was seen as a royal martyr, with many miracles done in his name.[3] When I visited the Tower of London in 1985 and got to the place where Henry was killed, disconcerting feelings came up inside me, and I felt sadness.

Brain Scramble

As I worked with Soul Detective Janet Nestor (who wrote the foreword to this book) to clear the trauma from this past life, I came to see the situation from a different point of view. Although I realize that the account that follows may seem preposterous, it is the direct emotional experience the two of us had as we connected intuitively to the energy of Henry VI. Henry did a lot of meditating in the monastery and connected directly with the voice of the Holy Spirit, which came from the Creator of All. Perhaps his parents did not have the funds to get him monatomic gold while he was in the monastery, so his crown chakra remained open. We felt that the Anunnaki had implanted a communication reception device into Henry's brain in his early childhood. When he became king, the Anunnaki implant instructed him to take actions that had the goal of filling his treasury with gold. They told him to do things that went against his personal values and the voice of the Holy Spirit that spoke from

---

2   Wolffe, *Henry VI.*
3   Ibid., 351.

Guard by the Tower of London.   **Author at the altar where Henry was killed.**

within his heart. When Henry did not cooperate fully with the instructions of the Anunnaki, they scrambled his thought processes, which put him into periods of catatonia.

As I connected with the feelings of Henry, I felt totally enraged at his being used as a puppet for the goals of the Anunnaki. I had to treat myself for my anger at his not having choice over his own life. I experienced the soul loss that Henry felt when his brain became so disorganized that he could not think clearly. We did a tapping treatment with Henry for the trauma of losing his mind, being forced to flee for his life, and eventually being stabbed to death after he had been reinstated. We shared the story of the Anunnaki with him. He had no knowledge of this overview of what had happened in his life. We did energy work for Henry to regain his self-respect and gather in his lost soul fragments. When he was ready to take all these lost parts of himself into the Light, I saw him in his royal robe, holding his scepter, saying, "God bless the Anunnaki!" This statement is saint-like—blessing those who had cursed him. Then I saw that, on a deeper level, I had chosen this lifetime to understand the inner workings of mental illness and to have direct interface with the Anunnaki.

As we did some work with the Anunnaki, we intuited that the block in their crown chakras came in part from their developmental origins of experiencing fear, pain, and loss. The Anunnaki had well-developed minds and mental abilities and tried to figure out everything by themselves. As reported earlier, when they had a hole in their atmosphere, the solution they came up with was to send out a space expedition to another planet to gather gold to powder and throw up into the breach. When their gold miners went on strike, they created a hybrid race of primitive workers to do their gold mining. We prayed for healing for the hearts of the Anunnaki from the trauma in their own past, and we prayed for a clearing of the blockages on their crown chakras that made them unable to connect with the transpersonal help available to them.

CHAPTER 39

Infighting of the Gods

Conflict Between Enki and Enlil

*S*trife between brothers started on Nibiru and spread to Earth. Rivalry between brothers started when the Anunnaki changed their succession rule from the firstborn son to the firstborn son by a sister-wife. Enki was the firstborn of King Anu, and Enlil was the firstborn by Anu's sister-wife Antu. Just as Enki and Enlil vied for power and control, in the next generation, their sons also competed with each other over who would rule.

Originally, Enki had been commander on Earth. When Anu came for a visit and brought Enlil with him, they decided to draw lots to see who would rule on Nibiru, who would rule on Earth, and who would head the mining operation. Anu drew first and got the job of going back to Nibiru to rule. He was very pleased. Somehow, I wonder if he intuited which slip would let him continue his reign. Enlil drew next and got being ruler on Earth and was pleased. Enki was not pleased with his job of heading the mining operation, but with his brilliant scientific mind, he was the one best suited to design the technology needed to extract the gold from deep down in the earth. Enki might then have been in a position to go back to Nibiru and follow his father on the throne in Nibiru, but living on Earth had worn out his body so much that he wanted to retire from political life.

Enlil Banished for Rape

Enlil got in trouble twice for sexual violations. Anu had betrothed their sister Ninmah to Enki so that their son would have claim to the throne. He wanted the offspring of his firstborn, Enki, to be in the line of succession. But Ninmah was enamored of Enlil and conceived a child by him. Their father Anu was angry with Ninmah for this violation of her engagement to Enki and forbade her ever to marry. The son Enlil and Ninmah had on Nibiru was named Ninurta.

Enlil's Genogram

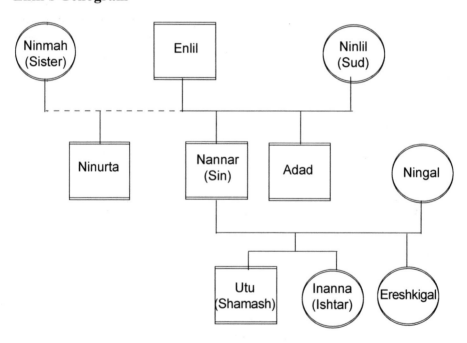

Later when Enlil was ruler on Earth, he almost lost his position as supreme commander as a result of a violation of the Anunnaki ethical code. As Enlil watched the young girls Ninmah was training to be nurses bathing one day, he was taken by the beauty and grace of a girl not yet of age named Sud. Inviting her to his abode, he spoke to her of intercourse. She was unwilling and vigorously protested his advances, saying, "My vagina is too little, it knows not copulation!" Enlil spoke to her of kissing, and again she was unwilling, saying "My lips are too small, they know not kissing!"[1] Enlil overpowered her and raped her. For this crime, he was exiled. Sud conceived from the rape. The council asked if she would take Enlil as her spouse, and she consented. Enlil was pardoned and returned home. Sud was renamed Ninlil so that her name corresponded to her husband's name, and she named their male child Nannar.

Conflict Between Enlil's Two Sons

Enlil had three sons: Ninurta, Nannar, and Adad. Ninurta was his firstborn by his sister Ninmah, and Nannar was his firstborn son by his wife. Both had some claim to power, as Nannar was the firstborn by the official wife; however, Ninurta was the legal heir because he was the son of a sister. Enlil loved Nannar, who was reported to be a firstborn "of beautiful countenance, perfect of limbs, wise without compare."[2] Enlil also loved Nannar for giving him twin grandchildren, Utu/Shamash and Inanna/Ishtar. On the other hand, Ninurta was Enlil's foremost warrior.

---

1   Sitchin, *The Lost Book of Enki*, 113.

2   Sitchin, 1985, *The Wars of Gods and Men*, 179.

Enki's Genogram

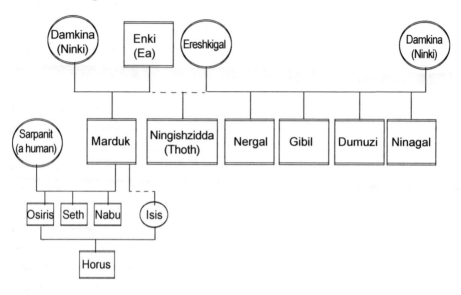

In addition to the offspring listed above, Enki bore many other children on Earth, first two daughters by his sister Ninmah and then children from the humans, including Adapa, Titi, and Ziusudra (Noah).

Conflict Between Marduk's Two Sons

Marduk was the firstborn son and legal heir of Enki. The first two demigod sons of Marduk and his human wife, Sarpanit, were Seth (also called Satu) and Osiris (also called Asar). Osiris married his half-sister Isis, and Seth married the daughter of the Igigi leader. In 9780 BC, Marduk decided to divide dominion over Egypt between his two sons. He gave each son half of the Nile river valley. Osiris lived with his father in Marduk's area, and Seth lived near the space pad, where the Igigi dwelt. Seth's father-in-law and the Igigi incited Seth's wife to constantly prod Seth with the idea of being the sole ruler. Seth plotted to kill his brother. He invited him to a banquet in honor of Osiris, got him drunk, and Osiris passed out. Then the conspirators put his body in a coffin, sealed it tight, and threw it into the sea.[3]

---

3   Sitchin, *The Lost Book of Enki*, 244-245.

When Isis got word of what had happened to her husband, she went to Marduk and they searched the seas together. They found the coffin of Osiris with his lifeless body inside. Marduk rent his clothes and put ashes on his forehead out of grief over his son's death. His mother Sarpanit cried, and Enki the grandfather was also distraught and wept in agony, feeling that the curse of Ka-in killing his brother Abael had been repeated.

Isis, enraged, demanded that Enki have Seth killed for his treachery and that Enki give her a child as a successor. Enki, greatly grieved that his grandchildren had repeated the curse of Cain and Abel, refused to have Seth killed. He also told Isis that he would not be the sperm donor to give her a child. He told Isis that by their law, the brother of the deceased had to impregnate the widow (Isis), and that child would count as an heir, not to his biological father, but to his deceased brother. This policy that if a man dies without having offspring, the brother of the deceased needs to marry his brother's widow and have a child with her that would count for the brother rather than the biological father is a practice recorded in the Old Testament, though the logic of who gets the credit for the child escapes me. Isis was not pleased at the thought of having sex with her husband's murderer. Meanwhile, Seth seized the whole area as the sole heir of Marduk. Isis wanted to get around the rules and still have a son with right of succession, so she extracted the "life seed" of Osiris from the genitals of his corpse and made herself conceive with it to raise an heir and avenger to Seth. When her son Horus was born, she hid him "among the river's bull rushes" to escape the wrath of Seth. Enki's son Gibil adopted Horus and trained him in the use of weapons. He gave him the secret of iron and a special guided missile. We see reference to the Greek god Hermes in this description:

> For him Gibil winged sandals for soaring fashioned, to fly
> like a falcon he was able;
> For him Gibil a divine harpoon made, its arrows bolts of
> missiles were.
> In the highlands of the south did him Gibil the arts of metals
> and smithing teach.[4]

---

4   Ibid., 246.

When the hero Horus grew to adulthood, he challenged his uncle Seth to battle. Seth hit him with a poisoned dart and killed him. Isis cried out, and Enki's son Ningishzidda (Thoth) came and gave Horus the antidote to the poison, which brought him back to life. Horus then hit Seth's spacecraft, which crashed to the ground, blinding Seth and crushing his testicles. Horus took his captive uncle before the council for execution. When it was time to put Seth to death, Isis had compassion for him as her brother. He looked "like a discarded jar," and Isis asked to let him live.[5] Mythology abounds with many variations of the Isis-Osiris-Seth story. *The Lost Book of Enki* says that blinded and crippled, Seth left Egypt and seized the Sinai Peninsula and Canaan. Enlil, enraged that all the space facilities were now under the control of Enki's descendants, launched war. This was the first war in which the gods enlisted the aid of humans to fight their battles and was called the First Pyramid War. They armed the humans with weapons made of metal, which up until then had been a secret of the Anunnaki.

New Precedent: Gods Enlist Humans to Fight Their Battles

This action has had far-reaching consequences on planet Earth. Even today, nations continue to fight other nations with claims that their God is the only one, their God is the right one, or that they are a superior race, chosen by God. The confusion set in motion by this battle has persisted into current times and we still see struggle between factions in the Middle East. The gods seem to be competing with each other. Here is the first of the Ten Commandments in the Bible:

And God spoke all these words:

> I am the LORD your God, who brought you out of Egypt, out of the land of slavery.

> You shall have no other gods before me. You shall not make for yourself an idol in the form of anything in heaven above or on the earth beneath or in the waters below. You shall not bow

---

5   Ibid., 247.

down to them or worship them; for I, the LORD your God, am a jealous God, punishing the children for the sin of the fathers to the third and fourth generation of those who hate me, but showering love to thousands who love me and keep my commandments. (Exodus 20:1-6 NIV)

If there were only one God, why would God say not to have any other gods before him? This passage makes much more sense in the setting of rival Anunnaki gods competing for the allegiance of humans.

Seth escaped to Asia and seized the Sinai Peninsula and Canaan in 8970 BC, 810 years after Marduk had divided Egypt between the brothers. As demigods, their life spans were longer than the humans but shorter than the life spans of the gods. Three hundred years later, Enlil, opposed to Enki's descendants controlling all of the space facilities, launched the Second Pyramid War, which resulted in Enlil's army, led by his son Ninurta, cornering Enki's people inside the Great Pyramid of Giza. Enki's side had designed and built the pyramids and were using crystal technology generated from inside the pyramid to create a force field of defense. Ninmah, who had a child by both brothers involved in this war, was the peacemaker who finally called a halt to the hostilities. After releasing Enki and his offspring from the pyramid, Ninurta went inside to dismantle the missile guidance system apparatus inside the pyramid. Inside he found minerals and crystals, some from Earth and some from Nibiru, some of which he had never seen before.[6]

Marduk's Hunger for Power

Enki's son Marduk had great ambition. Long ago in Nibiru, Anu and Alalu had made the deal that Alalu would keep the throne, but his daughter Damkina would marry Anu's son Enki, and their son Marduk would be the successor to the throne. That plan changed when Anu overthrew Alalu and Anu's legal heir became Enlil, his firstborn son by his sister-wife. Marduk was later put in charge of Mars, so he had his own planet to rule for a time. After shutting down operations on Mars following the flood, however, he was left without a position

---

6   Sitchin, *The Wars of Gods and Men*.

or a planet to rule. Enki's son Dumuzi and Enlil's granddaughter Inanna fell madly in love. Their story is similar to Romeo and Juliet, with the two lovers coming from rival clans and experiencing family interference. Inanna had great ambition to rule over all of Earth with her beloved Dumuzi. When Marduk became aware of her aspirations, he was alarmed. In Enki's version of the story, Marduk sends his sister to seduce his brother Dumuzi, telling him that before he has a son by his wife, he must have a son by his sister if he wants to have an heir that will rule. Other versions say that it was Dumuzi's idea to seduce and rape his sister, trying to have a legitimate heir to the throne before he married Inanna. Both versions agree that Dumuzi had sex with his sister, fell asleep, and had a bad dream about being chased by Marduk's marshals for what he had done. He awoke hearing Marduk's officers coming for him. He fled, and in his haste at trying to escape, he fell to his death and drowned in a river.

Livid with anger that she had lost her lover, Inanna blamed Marduk. She waged a full force war against Marduk and his people, bombing his lands and eventually imprisoning him in the great pyramid of Giza and cutting off his air supply. He would have suffocated to death if his aunt Ninmah had not intervened to save his life. His brother Ningishzidda, the designer of the pyramids, drilled a passageway up through the bedrock to the chamber where he was imprisoned and rescued him. That passageway is still visible in the pyramids, set apart from the other smooth-walled tunnels by its rough surfaces.[7]

Marduk's Turn to Rule

The angel Galzu intervened again, coming to Enlil in a dream and telling him that Marduk would rise to supremacy in the Age of the Ram, which would begin about 2000 BC. This prophecy was known to both Enlil and Marduk, who watched the skies constantly to see when the constellation of the Ram would be on the equinox. Enlil realized he was going to lose his control of Earth and wanted to develop a group of humans loyal to him as a hedge against losing all his power. He chose the son of the high priest at Nippur, Enlil's home city, a young man named Abram who was later renamed Abraham. Enlil tested Abraham to see whether he would give him complete allegiance by telling

7 Hancock, *Fingerprints of the Gods*.

him to sacrifice his only legitimate son, Isaac, whom he loved. As a child, I was taught that the moral of this Bible story is always to do whatever God commands. In other words, trust and obey unconditionally—do not think for yourself or question the Lord. So, if God commands you to stab and burn your firstborn child, do it. This idea never made sense to me.

As I read this story again now, what makes a lot more sense to me is that the god who ordered Abraham to kill his son was not the Creator of All, but the vengeful Anunnaki Lord Enlil who once wanted to wipe out all of human-kind and now was bent on keeping some of his power over humans. The truly blood-chilling part is that Abraham would have done it! I feel horrified by the way I used to blindly accept the Bible lessons advocating this policy of obey-ing a god who orders parents to kill their children. May we all wake up and think for ourselves!

Reward for Obedience

Abraham knew that Enlil had a power higher than his, and he was willing to obey anything Enlil asked of him. Enlil rewarded Abraham for his dedica-tion with lands and livestock, making him one of the richest men in the world. He gave Abraham a group of elite soldiers with weapons to use against Mar-duk's attempts to seize power.[8] And he did multiply Abraham's offspring and create a nation loyal to him, the Israelites. At the time, Marduk was gaining popularity with the humans, especially since he had married a human.

Ereshkigal and Nergal: More Anunnaki Family Internal Conflict

Enlil stationed his granddaughter Ereshkigal at a place at the tip of South Africa seen as the netherworld, or the land of the dead. Enki transported her to the location and impregnated her on the trip. Ereshkigal gave birth to Enki's son Ningishzidda (Thoth). In one of the wars between the gods, Enki's son Nergal attacked and was about to defeat Ereshkigal, wanting her out of his father's domain in South Africa. In lieu of defeat, Ereshkigal offered to make Nergal her king and share power with him in the underworld. He accepted and later, during some of the wars, he sided with his in-laws, Enlil's family, instead

---

8   Sitchin, *The Wars of Gods and Men*.

of with his father, Enki. Nergal had a violent streak. Called "the pitiless one," he once entered Enlil's sacred precinct and destroyed it. When Enlil asked his son Ninurta who desecrated his shrine, Ninurta lied and blamed Marduk, fueling the antagonism between Marduk and Enlil.

The Tower of Babel

As the Age of the Ram approached, Marduk and his son Nabu worked together to rally support for his takeover. Marduk built an alternate space-launching tower in Babili (the Tower of Babel in the Bible).

> Now the whole world had one language and a common speech. As men moved eastward, they found a plain in Shinar [Sumer] and settled there.
>
> They said to each other, "Come, let's make bricks and bake them thoroughly." They used brick instead of stone, and tar instead of mortar. Then they said, "Come, let us build ourselves a city, with a tower that reaches to the heavens...." (Genesis 11:1-4)

Enlil was very displeased and intervened to stop the plan.

> But the LORD came down to see the city and the tower that the men were building. The LORD said, "If as one people speaking the same language they have begun to do this, then nothing they plan to do will be impossible for them. Come, let us go down and confuse their language so they will not understand each other."
>
> So the LORD scattered them from there all over the earth, and they stopped building the city. That is why it was called Babel—because there the LORD confused the language of the whole world. (Genesis 11:5-8)

If the god of the Old Testament were the benevolent creator of all, why would he purposely not want his people to develop, and why would he purposely block their communication with each other? That idea makes no sense. It makes a lot of sense, however, if seen as the conflict of Enlil not wanting Marduk to have a spaceport of his own in Babili/Babel/Babylon.

King Ur-Nammu

In 2113 BC, Enlil appointed the demigod Ur-Nammu to be King over all Sumer. "The choice was a signal that the glorious days under the unchallenged authority of Enlil and his clan are back."[9] Ur-Nammu rebuilt the shrine to Enlil and found favor with him. Enlil gave him a Divine Weapon that could "heap up the rebels in piles" and sent him to subdue the evil cities loyal to Marduk in foreign lands with this superweapon. Inanna and Enlil teamed up against Marduk, supporting Ur-Nammu with blessings, honor, weapons, and protection. But King Ur-Nammu met a tragic death on the battlefield in 2096 BC. His chariot got stuck in the mud, he fell off, and his head was crushed by his own chariot. The boat returning the king's body to Sumer sank on the way home, and they could not recover the corpse. Enlil's people lost faith in their gods.

> They could not understand why "the Lord Nannar did not hold him by the hand, why Inanna, Lady of Heaven, did not put her noble arm around his head, why the valiant Utu (Inanna's twin brother) did not assist him."[10]

In the past, the system was that the gods had great power. If you obeyed their orders, you got their protection and goods, but if you disobeyed, you got punished. This punishment-reward system was why the people in Molech's area were willing to sacrifice their firstborn children to him. When they obeyed Molech's command, they got land, protection, and goodies. They were afraid to disobey Molech because of his superpowers. King Ur-Nammu was a very good king and did everything right. His tragic death was disillusioning

---

9   Sitchin, *The End of Days*, 52.

10 Sitchin, *The Wars of Gods and Men* , 276.

to the Earthlings, and they began to see that their gods were not all powerful. Ur-Nammu's son Shulgi succeeded him on the throne and was "full of vile and eager for battles."[11] These events contributed to Marduk's rise in power.

Father-Son Argument

In 2024 BC, Marduk marched on Sumer and enthroned himself in Babylon, right in the middle of Enlil's territory. Marduk and Nabu were about to seize control of the Anunnaki spaceport on the Sinai Peninsula. Alarmed by the imminent takeover, Enlil called a council of the Anunnaki to try to stop Marduk. Enki did not want the council to intervene in Marduk's military advances. Long ago he had promised Marduk that one day Marduk would rule, and Enki argued that Marduk's time had come. The others would not listen to him. Enki's son Nergal, who was married to Enlil's granddaughter Ereshkigal, sided with his woman's family in the vote, which aroused a violent argument between father and son. Enki stood by his firstborn, Marduk. He lost patience with Nergal's opposition and shouted for Nergal to get out of his presence. Nergal's feelings were hurt, and he hated his brother for being favored by his father and rising to power. Dark Force Entities appear to have infected Nergal from this emotional wound. Seeking revenge, in a frenzy, Nergal decided to unleash the nuclear weapons that Alalu had brought with him to Earth. Nergal formed a plan of utter annihilation:

> "The lands I will destroy, to a dust-heap make them; the cities I will upheaval, to desolation turn them; the mountains I will flatten, their animals make disappear; the seas I will agitate, that which teems in them I will decimate; the people I will make vanish, their souls shall turn to vapor; none shall be spared..."[12]

We see a plan of total destruction and annihilation, typical dark force goals. Enki's son Gibil got word of Nergal's plan and let his father know. Back

---

11 Sitchin, *The Lost Book of Enki*, 305.
12 Ibid.

in council again, to Enki's surprise, not all of the other gods were as shocked as he was to find out about Nergal's plan to use atomic power for destruction. Enki spoke out strongly against the devastation the use of nuclear arms would have on the land and the people, but his voice was not heeded. His father King Anu authorized the nuclear attack, and Nergal and Ninurta were appointed to carry out the plan. Nergal just wanted to scorch everything. He was consumed by hatred for his brother and nephew. Nergal shouted:

> "I shall annihilate the son [Nabu], and let the father bury him;
> then I shall kill the father [Marduk], let no one bury him!"[13]

Ninurta finally calmed him down and got him to modify his plan, leaving out his attack on the seas and leaving out Mesopotamia. The modified plan included destroying only the targets preapproved by the council: the greatest prize that Marduk was after, the spaceport, and the cities Nabu might be in.

Nuclear Bombs

Still in the year of 2024 BC, Ninurta and Nergal first dropped a bomb on the spaceport itself. Aerial photographs of the Sinai Peninsula today show the flattened, blackened effect where the bomb was dropped. Then they bombed Sodom and Gomorrah, the cities where they thought Nabu was hiding, after Abraham's nephew Lot was given time to escape. Lot's wife was warned not to look at the area because the force of the blast would be blinding. She did not heed the warning and was vaporized, another way to translate the words the Bible used when it said she was turned into a pillar of salt.

> Then the LORD rained down burning sulfur on Sodom and Gomorrah—from the LORD out of the heavens. Thus he overthrew those cities and the entire plain, including all those living in the cities—and also the vegetation in the land. But Lot's wife looked back and she became a pillar of salt. (Genesis 19:24-26 NIV)

---

13   Ibid., 328.

The use of nuclear weapons caused a disturbance in the atmosphere, and a huge windstorm arose, blowing deadly radiation over all of Sumer. The Anunnaki gods had to flee in their spaceships or they would have also been killed. The devastation was tremendous. All the humans, animals, and plants in the area died. It turned Sumer into a wasteland. Marduk kept marching on, assisted by the devastation of his enemy Enlil's territory, and the gods were at war with each other, using the Earthlings as soldiers to fight for their causes. Tremendous human bloodshed ensued.

Marduk's Lust for Power

By this time Marduk's human wife Sarpanit had died, and he had lost his firstborn son Osiris. Marduk seems to have been infected by a Dark Force Entity that gave him lust for absolute power. He wanted to be the supreme ruler. He rewrote Anunnaki history, renaming Nibiru "Marduk" and saying that he was the creator of the whole universe. He usurped the attributes of all the other gods for himself and decreed hymns to call him by aggrandizing names:

> The foremost from the earliest times! So he decreed in the
> hymns to be called;
> Lord of eternity, he who everlastingness has made, over all
> the gods presiding,
> The one who is without equal, the great solitary and
> sole one![14]

He had a huge ziggurat temple built for himself in Babylon and named it the Esagil, "House Whose Head is Lofty," and in 2000 BC when the age of the Ram began, Marduk invited all the other important gods to live with him in Babylon as his subordinates.[15] This idea was not well-received by Enlil and the others. All the gods were concerned at Marduk's total unwillingness to share any of the command, glory, or power with others. Even his father Enki objected to Marduk's pretentions going too far. By about 1800 BC Marduk's

---

14 Sitchin, *The Lost Book of Enki*, 298.
15 Sitchin, *There Were Giants Upon the Earth*, p. 19.

King Hammurabi had conquered the surrounding area for him, giving Babylon imperial status. Enlil did not give up, however, and continued his effort to expand the territory of his people. The Old Testament is filled with cycles of the Israelites conquering and being conquered by their neighbors and contests to see whose god was more powerful.

Dark Force Entity

Marduk's craving for total control sounds like being possessed by a Dark Force Entity. When a person feels slighted, as Marduk did, dark forces can infect the wound with compensatory ideas of inflation. The reason the dark forces constantly seek more power and control is that the power they steal from people is then confiscated by their boss, so they feel deflated and continually grasp at robbing their host even more, setting up cycles of addiction. Love and Light are the only energies that truly satisfy the heart. Love wants to share, but power wants to control. Marduk did not have love in his heart, and his grasping for ultimate control of the world backfired on him and brought upon him a curse that he would wither and die. The Lord (Enlil) told the prophet Jeremiah to say:

> Announce and proclaim among the nations, Lift up a banner and proclaim it; keep nothing back, but say, "Babylon will be captured; Bel [another name for Marduk] will be put to shame, Marduk filled with terror. Her images will be put to shame and her idols filled with terror." A nation from the north will attack her and lay waste her land. (Jeremiah 50:2-3a NIV)

The Babylonian empire declined for five centuries, rose again, and finally fell in 539 BC when Cyrus, the king of Persia (Iran), captured Babylon, just as Jeremiah had prophesied. Can you imagine the disillusionment Marduk felt when his megalomania was crushed? He withered, became confused, and died. The dark force of lust for power destroyed him. By the time of Xerxes, the successor to Cyrus, the Esagil served only as Marduk's glorified tomb, and Xerxes destroyed it in 482 BC. When Alexander the Great reached the city of Babylon in 331 BC, he went to Marduk's temple to grasp the hands of Marduk, the custom all conquering kings did to receive the blessing of the god, but he was shocked to find Marduk dead. Some sources say he saw Marduk's body preserved in oils lying in a golden coffin.[16]

We can see how the desire to control the world infected Hitler and the way his actions led him to destruction by his own hand, suicide. The unconventional documentary film *Thrive*[17] shows another example of the dark force of lust for complete power and control over the whole world. Co-writers Foster and Kimberly Charter Gamble follow the money trail to a global conspiracy by a small group of extremely wealthy people bent on controlling every aspect of our lives and building even more wealth for themselves. The documentary includes a section on an insidious plan this covert group has to reduce the world population down to approximately one billion so it will be more manageable to control. Somehow this idea reminds me of Enlil's massive destruction of the humans with plagues and warfare. *Thrive* also outlines practical steps we can take to protect ourselves and build a harmonious future.

Multiplying Abraham's Seed

Enlil kept his promise to multiply the seed of Abraham into a great nation. He also made a great nation of Ishmael, Abraham's firstborn son by his wife's servant Hagar. The descendants of those two lines of Abraham's children are still fighting against each other in our current day, the Jews and the Arabs. The mission control center of the Anunnaki was in Jerusalem, and the two groups are still fighting over that place.

Joseph

Abraham's son Isaac had a dozen children. Isaac favored the two youngest ones, Joseph and Benjamin, because they were from Rebecca, the wife that he loved the most. Joseph hold his brothers about a dream he had in which the sun, the moon, and the stars bowed down to him. They accurately perceived that the dream showed him ruling over his parents and siblings. They were furious with his ideas of grandeur and decided to kill him, throwing him into

---

16 Sitchin, *The End of Days*.
17 http://www.thrivemovement.com/

a pit to die, dipping his many-colored coat in blood from a lamb, and telling their father that a wild animal killed Joseph. We can see the Anunnaki struggle for power and dominance imprinting into Joseph's siblings.

Later Joseph's oldest brother rescued him from the pit, selling him as a slave to a caravan heading for Egypt. Joseph found favor in the eyes of the pharaoh and rose to power in Egypt. He had a dream that foretold of a famine coming after years of plenty and was put in charge of storing up grain for the lean years. When the famine came, Joseph's whole family moved to Egypt to avoid starvation. As Enlil's twelve tribes of Israel multiplied in Egypt, they became the slaves of the Egyptians and spent around four hundred years there. Then Enlil commanded Moses to go to the pharaoh and demand release of his people. The rest of the story is well documented in the Bible. Enlil gave Moses powers to part the waters to escape the Egyptians and to find water in the desert. The people grumbled that they did not have enough food since leaving Egypt and then saw the glory of the Lord appearing in the cloud bringing them a special kind of flaky nutritive substance called manna.

Enlil wanted to get back the land of Canaan, which had been promised to him in the division of land after the flood. The Israelites wandered around in the desert for forty years to let the older people who still thought of themselves as slaves die off and to raise up a new generation that was free of slave mentality. When the new batch of Israelite young blood was ready, Enlil commanded his people under the leadership of Joshua to seize the land of Canaan and kill every man, woman, child, and animal there. I understand that Enlil wanted to kill all of the women so his people would not intermarry with them and get subverted by their wives into following other gods, but slaughtering the livestock does not make economic sense to me. Why would he want to annihilate every living thing in Palestine unless he were infected by the dark force of vengeance? This action does not sound like something the benevolent Creator of the universe would do, the one who has compassion for every creature in the web of life. It is more consistent with the Sumerian story of Anunnaki brothers fighting for control of territory and Lord Enlil taking revenge on those who had stolen his land.

433

Showdown Between Prophets

Even after Enlil reclaimed the land of Canaan and renamed it Israel, he had problems of the people in his area giving allegiance to other gods. In the lifetime of the prophet Elijah, Israel was divided between the old religion, Baal worship, and the new worship of the Israelite god, Yahweh. Ahab, born in 874 BC, became king of Israel and married Jezebel, the daughter of a neighboring king whose country worshipped Baal. Ahab defected and began to serve Baal and worship him.[18] In a political strategy designed to remove the opposition, Jezebel began killing all of the prophets of God she could find. The Lord ordered Elijah to go into hiding. At last, in a great showdown of power, Elijah had a contest with the 450 prophets of Baal to see whose god was more powerful. Each side sacrificed a bull and called upon their god to light the fire to cook it. Nothing happened to the sacrifice of the prophets of Baal, even though they danced feverishly all day, shouted and self-mutilated. But as soon as Elijah called upon the name of the Lord, the God of Abraham, Isaac, and Israel, fire fell from heaven and burned up the sacrifice. The people realized his god was more powerful, and Elijah seized the opportunity to slaughter all 450 of the prophets of Baal.

Superpowers

Elijah had superpowers at his command and could do things like part the waters by striking them with his rolled-up cloak and calling down fire to destroy his enemies. God spoke directly to him and told him when to hide and when to come out. Because he had remained true to Yahweh, he was rewarded by being taken directly to heaven without dying first. He knew the day he would go and was walking and talking with his colleague the prophet Elisha.

> As they were walking along and talking together, suddenly a chariot of fire and horses of fire appeared and separated the two of them, and Elijah went up to heaven in a whirlwind. (2 Kings 2:11 NIV)

---

18   The Holy Bible, 1 Kings 16:31 (New International Version).

This image sounds like the celestial chariots of the Anunnaki, and Yahweh sounds a lot like Lord Enlil!

Promotion to the Angelic Realm

Jewish and Christian literature teaches that two humans were promoted to the angelic realm:

1. The prophet Elijah who became Archangel Sandalphon.
2. Enoch, who became Archangel Metatron.

Note that these two angelic names are the only ones that do not end in *el*, which means "God" in Hebrew, because the original form of their creation was human.

Enoch was also raptured into heaven without going through the passage of death. In the Old Testament, Enoch is listed in Adam's lineage as the father of Methuselah, who lived 969 years, the longest life span of anyone mentioned in the Bible. When Enoch had lived 365 years, "Enoch walked with God; then he was no more, because God took him away" (Genesis 5:24 NIV). The Old Testament apocryphal book 3 Enoch reports that Enoch ascended into heaven and was transformed into the Archangel Metatron.[19]

In the following case of my client Lailah, the name Enoch had been coming up often for her, so she had been doing research on him. During our Soul Detective session, some information surfaced that was outside the framework of my belief system. First of all, the concept of the soul having two incarnations going at the same time was hard to wrap my mind around. Second, I did not believe that a human could have a parallel life as an angel, but I had to suspend my disbelief system and go with my client's truth.

Angelic Parallel Life

Lailah, a dynamic, highly intuitive, well-organized woman, seemed to be able to process information on many different levels simultaneously. Extremely sensitive, she picked up on the energy of others in her environment. Lailah was on the

---

19   3 Enoch 9:1-5; 15:1-2.

brink of a huge expansion of her spiritual energy, but she felt blocked by trauma locked into her system from something very ancient, possibly from a different galaxy. The physical clues to tracing this pattern were pain in her right trapezius muscle and frontal sinus irritation. In the weeks before our session, she had noticed her awareness going out into the cosmos more frequently, almost as if she were going out-of-body.

Muscle testing indicated trauma in three past lives. After setting sacred space, we asked her spirit guides to show us the most important one to work on first. The information that came through muscle testing went beyond what I thought was possible, but I had to suspend the boxes around my reality and go with what made sense to Lailah.

Past Life Trauma

The past life trauma we needed to work on first happened in another galaxy with beings that had no physical aspect linked to their light bodies. Apparently, in a previous incarnation, Lailah had also been promoted to the angelic realm. The name that came to connect with her angelic essence was Seriaph. Even though the angels have balanced masculine and feminine qualities, Seriaph's nature felt more feminine. After becoming an angel, Seriaph was given the job of protecting people on a planet in another galaxy. A vision of a holocaust came to Lailah, and she saw Seriaph being picked at and withheld from being able to do her job of protection, as if her wings were pinned—perhaps manifesting as the pain in her right trapezius muscle. More than three thousand Dark Force Angels had ganged up on Seriaph—not a fair fight!

Lailah felt these Dark Angels standing in front of her again in the present, with the message, "We're back!" They were warning her about trying to go forward into the fullness of her current life's mission.

The Leader

We asked to speak with the highest-ranking Dark Force Angel of the group of more than three thousand assigned to Lailah's soul. When we asked him what their purpose was, he turned "a cold shoulder" (trapezius) toward us, refusing to communicate.

We asked if he were afraid he would get in trouble if he interacted with us, and he affirmed he was terrified of punishment. From this response, we told him we assumed he was working for the darkness, as fear is the hallmark of dark force activity. We assured him that we were working for his highest good, reminding him of our invocation that only what was "in the highest good of everyone and everything" would come to pass. When we mentioned a possible job promotion for him, he turned sideways, interested in what we had to say. Our message to him was "You have the right to know what is in your core energy, what was there when you were created."

Next Step

I tried to go to the next step in my Detrimental Energy Protocol of asking what his employer had told him about the Light, but this head of the Dark Angelic force was one step ahead of me and had already opened up to his own inner light. He had been corded to the darkness by a hurt that he could not get over. He asked Archangel Michael to free him from the cord of deception that went into the middle of his torso. A ray of Light from Michael dissipated the cord in a puff of white smoke. Simultaneously, the pain in Lailah's shoulder disappeared and her nasal passages cleared.

Now that this angel was standing on the other side, he realized the truth, "Nothing is impossible!" We invited him to command all 3000 Dark Force Angels who had been under him to look into their centers to find what had been there when they were created, and they all converted into New Lightworkers!

Next, set free of her bondage, Lailah swirled around the planet she had been assigned to protect and gathered up all the earthbound spirits of people who were still stuck in that holocaust. They were willing and ready to go, without any tapping! When we multiplied the benefits for all other holocaust victims in the universe, the trauma in Lailah's other two past lives disappeared.

Soul Lesson

"Nothing is impossible!" The application for Lailah was that she had always felt she had to abide by society's rules. In her new job, she noticed that, almost effortlessly, things were falling into place to give her the capacity to help many other people. She reported, "I have been guided and pushed to where I need to be." She is working with several leaders in her field who complement each other beautifully and are opening up to the extra value an integrative approach provides for the people they serve.

Lailah felt more joy and peace after this work. She reflected that she constantly gets messages from other places. She sees the big picture, gets concepts from just flipping through a new book, and always works for the highest good. Several days later, Lailah reported that the shoulder pain had not returned. She felt Seriaph's wings were free! In the course of the following year, she found the shoulder pain would wax and wane as new challenges came up for her, and she needed to continue working at all levels—physical, energetic, emotional, and spiritual—to continue her soul's growth.

Parallel Life Trauma

Lailah's trauma was actually a parallel life trauma in a different dimensional realm. Angels are in a higher realm and do not die, so they cannot have a past life that is over. But evidently a person promoted to the angelic realm can have a parallel life as a human. In the New Testament, the Pharisees, who believed in reincarnation, calling it "the transmigration of souls," asked Jesus if he were the reincarnation of the prophet Elijah, because of the prophecy that before the Messiah came, Elijah would come. Jesus answered, "And if you are willing to accept it, he [John the Baptist] is the Elijah who was the one to come (Matthew 11:14 NIV)."

Clearly, the writer of Matthew identifies John the Baptist as the reincarnation of Elijah,[20] who had been promoted to the angelic realm as Archangel Sandalphon and chose a parallel incarnation as John the Baptist to prepare the way for the messiah. *The Spirits' Book* notes the karmic cycle Elijah created by beheading the 450 prophets of Baal and then getting his own head chopped off as John the Baptist.[21]

Angels from the higher realms seem to have the ability to manifest physical bodies in lower realms like the one we live in when they want to help people without scaring them too badly by appearing as shining winged Beings of Light ten feet tall. Many people living today report feeling that their lives have been touched by a being they identify as an angel who really is from the higher realms. Authors Marilynn Carlson Webber and William D. Webber collected many such stories in their book *A Rustle of Angels: Stories about Angels in Real Life and Scripture.*

---

20   Lampe, *The Christian and Reincarnation*, 120.

21   Kardec, *The Spirits' Book.*

Angelic Help

One example that I believe was a manifestation of a real angel in physical form was an encounter I had on the way to the airport to go to my sister's memorial service. I got stuck in a snowdrift in a remote area with no traffic on a steep, twisty road named "Snake Hill Road." I did not have a cell phone at the time. My heart broke as I saw how likely it was that I would miss my flight. I am a minister in the Universal Life Church and was in charge of the service. With great emotion, I cried out to the angelic realm, "Help! I can't miss this memorial for my sister!" Just then I saw a yellow SUV turn into the bottom of Snake Hill Road. I couldn't believe it. The SUV pulled up to me and stopped. An incredibly handsome young man got out, and without saying anything, looked at my car and then got out a yellow belt, which he hooked to my axle and to his car. I was very impressed because I had never seen a tow belt like that before. He pulled me right out of the snow bank.

I suspected he might be an angel who came in a human form so I wouldn't freak out if my car just moved itself out of the snow without human intervention. I was so awestruck I could barely speak, but I asked him, "What is your name?"

He responded, "My name is Justin, and this is what I do for fun!"

I thought, "Justin...he came *just in* time to get me to the airport for my flight!"

The Wrath of the Old Testament God

The nature of the Old Testament Yahweh was clearly not angelic. Yahweh wanted his people to fear him so they would obey his commands. He became enraged at their disobedience and punished them severely. One example of Yahweh's hot-headedness is the following quote from the time when the Israelites were wandering around in the desert after fleeing slavery in Egypt:

> Now the people complained about their hardships in the hearing of the LORD, and when he heard of them his anger was aroused. Then fire from the LORD burned among them and consumed some of the outskirts of the camp. When the people

cried out to Moses, he prayed to the LORD and the fire died down. (Numbers 11:1-2 NIV)

The Old Testament is filled with stories of the wrath of God and drastic actions that the Lord took to try to discipline his people to obey him. The humans had a persistent pattern of not doing what they were told and getting punished. These stories are currently taught in Christian churches as lessons that exemplify the need for humans to obey God's rules. The following Bible quiz is taken from the website of the Landover Baptist Church, a fictional church based in the fictional town of Freehold, Iowa. While the entire Landover website is a satire of fundamentalist Christianity and the religious right, the quiz below is based on scripture and points out the volatile temper of the Old Testament Lord. Check out your score as the answers, with the scripture verses to back them up, follow the quiz.

Bible Quiz "The Wrath of God"

1. **How many men did God kill because someone decided to peek into the ark of the Lord?**
   a. None. God Certainly wouldn't kill someone merely for examining holy things.
   b. 50,070.
   c. Just the people who looked into the ark.
   d. 250. The people who looked into the ark and their immediate families.

2. **How many men did Moses kill in one day because they failed to say they supported God?**
   a. None. God doesn't kill people for their mistakes.
   b. 200. Those who failed to say they supported the Lord, but not their family members.
   c. 1,000. Those who failed to say they supported the Lord and their spouses.
   d. 3,000. Those who failed to say they supported their Lord and their brothers, companions, and neighbors.

3. **How many people did God kill in a plague before someone pleased God by ending a mixed marriage with the murder of the couple?**
    a. None. God loves all his children and imposes no restriction on whom they marry (so long as the person is of the opposite gender).
    b. 100.
    c. 24,000.
    d. None of the above.

4. **How many animals did Solomon kill in a sacrifice to please the Lord?**
    a. None. God is not so insensitive as to gain satisfaction from man's slaughter of innocent animals.
    b. Two head of cattle, two rams, and two ravens.
    c. A herd of 100 sheep that he and his men came across in their conquests.
    d. 120,000 sheep and 22,000 oxen.

5. **How many Israelites did God deliver to the people of Judah to slaughter?**
    a. Trick Question. The Israelites were God's chosen people, hence He never would have allowed anyone to slaughter them.
    b. Half a million.
    c. 552. The number who disobeyed his commands.
    d. 200. The number who worshiped strange gods.

6. **Notwithstanding the above, how many people of Judah were once killed or enslaved because they didn't give God his due?**
    a. 120,000 valiant men were killed and 200,000 women and children were taken as slaves (not to mention the theft of property).
    b. One.
    c. Two.
    d. None of the above.

7. **How many Ethiopians did God kill for His chosen people?**
   a. None. God doesn't kill people!
   b. One million.
   c. One thousand.
   d. A hundred.

8. **Speaking of God's chosen people, how many kings were maimed in God's name?**
   a. None.
   b. One had his legs broken so he couldn't gather men to form an army.
   c. Two had their tongues cut out so they couldn't call the people to war.
   d. 70 had their thumbs and big toes cut off.

9. **How many soldiers did God burn to death with fire from Heaven because they confronted Elijah?**
   a. None. God would never engage in such a cruel act.
   b. 50.
   c. 100.
   d. 150 (three sets of 50).

10. **By the time God gets through with his killing spree, how many dead will there be?**
    a. None. God doesn't kill.
    b. Ten million.
    c. One hundred million.
    d. Enough to cover the entire surface of the Earth.

Answers to the Bible Quiz

1. How many men did God kill because someone decided to peek into the ark of the Lord?

Correct Answer: B. (50,070) "And he smote the men of Bethshemesh, because they had looked into the ark of the Lord, even he smote of the people fifty thousand and threescore and ten men: and the people lamented, because the LORD had smitten many of the people with a great slaughter" (1 Samuel 6:19).

Note: The NIV version says, "But God struck down some of the men of Beth Shemesh, putting seventy* of them to death because they had looked into the ark of the LORD. The people mourned because of the heavy blow the LORD had dealt them." * There is a footnote after "seventy" noting that only a few Hebrew manuscripts use this number, and most Hebrew manuscripts and the Septuagint use the number 50,070.

2. How many men did Moses kill in one day because they failed to say they supported God?

Correct Answer: D. (3,000) "Then Moses stood in the gate of the camp, and said, 'Who is on the LORD's side? let him come unto me.' And all the sons of Levi gathered themselves together unto him. And he said unto them, 'Thus saith the Lord God of Israel, Put every man his sword by his side, and go in and out from gate to gate throughout the camp, and slay every man his brother, and every man his companion, and every man his neighbor.' And the children of Levi did according to the word of Moses: and there fell of the people that day about three thousand men" (Exodus 32:26-28).

3. How many people did God kill in a plague before someone pleased God by ending a mixed marriage with the murder of the couple?

Correct Answer: C. (24,000) "And, behold, one of the children of Israel came and brought unto his brethren a Midianitish woman in the sight of Moses, and in the sight of all the congregation of the children of Israel, who were weeping before the door of the tabernacle of the congregation. And when

Phinehas, the son of Eleazar, the son of Aaron the priest, saw it, he rose up from among the congregation, and took a javelin in his hand; And he went after the man of Israel into the tent, and thrust both of them through, the man of Israel, and the woman through her belly. So the plague was stayed from the children of Israel. And those that died in the plague were twenty and four thousand" (Numbers 25:6-9).

4. How many animals did Solomon kill in a sacrifice to please the Lord?

Correct Answer: D. (120,000 sheep and 22,000 oxen) "And Solomon offered a sacrifice of peace offering, which he offered unto the LORD, two and twenty thousand oxen, and an hundred and twenty thousand sheep. So the king and all the children of Israel dedicated the house of the LORD" (1 Kings 8:63).

5. How many Israelites did God deliver to the people of Judah to slaughter?

Correct Answer: B. (Half a million) "Then the men of Judah gave a shout: and as the men of Judah shouted, it came to pass, that God smote Jeroboam and all Israel before Abijah and Judah. And the children of Israel fled before Judah: and God delivered them into their hand. And Abijah and his people slew them with a great slaughter: so there fell down slain of Israel five hundred thousand chosen men. Thus the children of Israel were brought under at that time, and the children of Judah prevailed, because they relied upon the Lord God of their fathers" (2 Chronicles 13:15-18).

6. Notwithstanding the above, how many people of Judah were once killed or enslaved because they didn't give God his due?

Correct Answer: A. (120,000 valiant men were killed and 200,000 women and children were taken as slaves [not to mention the theft of property].) "For Pekah the son of Remaliah slew in Judah an hundred and twenty thousand in one day, which were all valiant men; because they had forsaken the Lord God of their fathers....And the children of Israel carried away captive of their brethren two hundred thousand, women, sons, and daughters, and took also away much spoil from them" (2 Chronicles 28:6-8).

7. How many Ethiopians did God kill for His chosen people?

Correct Answer: B. (One million) "And Asa had an army of men… And there came out against them Zera the Ethiopian with an host of a thousand thousand…Asa cried unto the LORD his God, and said LORD, it is nothing with thee to help, whether with many, or with them that have no power, help us, O LORD our God… So the LORD smote the Ethiopians" (2 Chronicles 14:8-12).

Note: The NIV version of the Bible says that Zerah marched against Judah with a vast army, and the footnote says that the Hebrew words used denote an army of a thousand thousands or with an army of thousands upon thousands.

8. Speaking of God's chosen people, how many kings were maimed in God's name?

Correct Answer: D. (70 had their thumbs and big toes cut off.) "And they found Abonibezek in Bezek: and they fought against him, and they slew the Canaanites and Perizzites. But Abonibezek fled; and they pursued after him and caught him, and cut off his thumbs and his great toes. And Abonibezek said, Threescore and ten kings, having their thumbs and their great toes cut off, gathered their meat under my table: as I have done, so God hath requited me" (Judges 1:5-7).

9. How many soldiers did God burn to death with fire from Heaven because they confronted Elijah?

Correct Answer: D. (150 [three sets of 50]) "And Elijah answered and said to the captain of fifty, If I be a man of God, then let fire come down from heaven, and consume thee and thy fifty. And there came down fire from heaven, and consumed him and his fifty. Again also he sent unto him another captain…And Elijah answered and said unto them, If I be a man of God, let fire come down from heaven and consume thee and thy fifty. And the fire of God came from heaven, and consumed him and his fifty…And he sent again a captain of the third fifty…Behold, there came fire down from heaven, and burnt up the two captains of the former fifties with their fifties" (2 Chronicles 1:10-14).

Note: Actually, the Landover website has the reference wrong. This passage comes in 2 Kings 1:10-14, rather than in 2 Chronicles. Another error is that the third captain with fifty men saw what had happened to the other two groups and begged for mercy. He was not killed. So only two sets of 50 were burned to death with fire from heaven.

10. By the time God gets through with his killing spree, how many dead will there be?

Correct Answer: D. (Enough to cover the entire surface of the Earth.) "And the slain of the LORD shall be at that day from one end of the earth even unto the other end of the earth: they shall not be lamented, neither gathered, nor buried, they shall be dung upon the ground" (Jeremiah 25:33).

Note: In the prelude to this statement, Jeremiah reports his instructions:

> This is what the LORD, the God of Israel, said to me: "Take from my hand this cup filled with the wine of my wrath and make all the nations to whom I send you drink it. When they drink it, they will stagger and go mad because of the sword I will send among them." (Jeremiah 25:15-16 NIV)

The passage implies that the Lord Almighty actually gave Jeremiah some kind of poisonous drink that he was to take to each of the kings and make them imbibe, something that would make them go mad and destroy them. In Egypt he was instructed to make every person in the whole country drink from the cup.

> "Then tell them, 'This is what the LORD Almighty, the God of Israel, says: Drink, get drunk and vomit, and fall to rise no more because of the sword I will send among you.' But if they refuse to take the cup from your hand and drink, tell them, 'This is what the LORD Almighty says: You must

drink it! See, I am beginning to bring disaster on the city that bears my Name, and will you indeed go unpunished? You will not go unpunished, for I am calling down a sword upon all who live on the earth, declares the LORD Almighty.'" (Jeremiah 25:27-29 NIV)

The natural response of the body to ingesting a poison is to vomit, as is mentioned in verse twenty-seven. The Lord asks the people to drink willingly of this cup of God's wrath. If they refuse, they are threatened with annihilation. This sounds a lot like the same god who wanted to destroy the whole human race with the flood. Reading these Holy Scripture verses after hearing Sumerian history is truly chilling! Why would God want to poison and punish all of humanity? I can only conclude that Enlil was succumbing to Dark Force Entities who were using fury and wrath to turn him into a raging psychopath. He almost sounds like Reverend Jim Jones who led the mass suicide of 909 members of his temple in 1978. When we look at the current madness in the world, especially with random acts of violence of an insane person going on a killing spree and shooting innocent people, we might say that people did drink of that cup and are still mad/insane. We need the antidote to that cup of God's wrath!

Totally Fed Up

According to ancient documents, Enlil and the other Anunnaki gods became totally fed up with the wickedness of the humans. Yahweh's attempt to whip his people into shape using fear of annihilation as a motivator did not really work. Fear is the major tool of the dark side, and it lacks the true power wielded by the golden light of love. When Nibiru next came close to the Earth in 610 BC, Enlil led many of the Anunnaki gods in a mass exodus over the next fifty years. They lifted off from the spaceport in Peru where the Nazca lines still have long straight lines from takeoff blasts that cut into the earth with engine exhaust.[22] Society broke down with the departure of most of the gods. From the looks of things in the world today, perhaps a few of the lesser Anunnaki saw an opportunity open up with the exit of their superiors and may

---

22 Sitchin, *The End of Days*.

have stayed to gather power and more gold, perhaps going underground to try to control the humans from behind the scenes.

The people mourned,

> Yahweh sees us no more,
> Yahweh has left the Earth![23]

The humans were desolated at feeling abandoned and longed for the gods to return. Formerly, when they needed something, they could go to the temple where the god lived and ask for it. If they were loyal subjects, the gods granted their wishes. The theme of feeling abandoned by God comes up a lot in my practice. It appears to be a deep scar in the psyche of our ancestors, and they longed for a Messiah to come save them.

God's Sacrifice of His Firstborn

The political climate in Palestine when Jesus was born was a hotbed of discontent. The Jews chafed under Roman rule and wanted a Messiah who would defeat the Romans and regain their independence. Jesus was in the lineage of King David and had a right to the throne, but he aimed his ministry at developing spiritual power, not political power. He taught rules for living together in harmony with equality for everyone, including women, and taught the radical message, "Love your enemies." The Jewish high priests god rid of Jesus by having him crucified.

My early religious training taught me that the death of Jesus on the cross was a blood sacrifice to atone for my being born a sinner, from Adam and Eve's original sin of disobedience. Logically, how can one person's death atone for someone else's mistakes? It doesn't seem fair to kill a good person because others have purposely been programmed with defective DNA, are highly sexual, and lack impulse control. The idea that God gave his firstborn and only begotten son to be killed as a blood sacrifice is the same practice that satanic cults still require of their members. How twisted by fear can our minds get that we accept this gruesome practice and praise it? What kind of parent

---

23   Ibid, p. 231.

advocates this level of suffering for his or her firstborn? Somehow the purpose of the Crucifixion got subverted as dark forces and Anunnaki influence infiltrated the Christian movement. The following chapter gives another version of what Jesus did on the cross.

CHAPTER 40

Yeshua, the Avatar

*All the armies of the world are not as powerful
as an idea whose time has come.*
—Victor Hugo

Sacred Rites

*E*ver since I can remember, I have always felt the presence of Jesus Christ, as if he were a person I had known for a very long time. Once I chose to be baptized at the age of nine, I was able to participate in the sacred rites of our church. We had two main rituals:

1. **Foot washing**, where we washed each other's feet, as Jesus did for his disciples, in preparation for communion.
2. **Communion**, in which we drank a little vial of grape juice as a symbol of having the blood of Christ inside us and ate a piece of bread symbolizing internalizing the body of Christ.

In satanic ritual, the participants actually drink of the blood and eat of the flesh of the victim. We did it symbolically. Our preacher had told us that Jesus was present at these sacred rites. I was so excited the first time I was allowed to participate in communion, because I fully expected to see Jesus in the flesh-and-blood of his resurrection body sitting in the front row of the church! After my initial disappointment that only church members were sitting in the front row, I realized that the presence of Christ was an energy that I had invited into my heart to guide my life, always.

The book *Jesus: The Explosive Story of the 30 Lost Years and the Ancient Mystery Religions*, by Tricia McCannon, opened my mind to deeper understanding of the extensive training Jesus had in Egypt, England, India, and Tibet in many different religious traditions before beginning his public ministry in Palestine. Jesus was called by his Hebrew name Yeshua, and in India he was called Saint Issa.

According to McCannon, the Brahmins in India trained Saint Issa in the spiritual laws of karma, dharma, and reincarnation, and he went through four major initiations corresponding to the elements of earth, fire, air, and water.[1] Everywhere Jesus went, he brought a radical new message of equality for everyone—including women, servants, and untouchables. In India he got into big trouble with the nobility and upper classes because he wanted to abolish the whole caste system and had to flee because of an assassination plot against him.[2]

A Lifetime with Jesus

I do not claim that the following is absolute truth. The material is from past life regressions that a colleague and long-time dear friend and I did for each other in February of 2012 remembering lifetimes we shared as brothers in India during the time of Christ. The information is a blending of the memories that we experienced as we guided each other's regressions and is integrated with insights generated later from these experiences as well as from other pertinent sources. Many others have channeled messages of events from the life of Christ, with varied and conflicting content. Please let your heart evaluate the content of these regressions to see if they resonate as truth. They are our truth.

---

1 McCannon, *Jesus*, 220.
2 Ibid.

In my memory of that lifetime, my brother Sri Ananda (now incarnated as my friend) is the oldest of three siblings. He is four years older than I and our sister is two years older. Our mother died giving birth to me, and I am named Sri Hari. Our father cannot raise us by himself, so he gives all three of us to be raised in the temple with our lives dedicated to service there. This decision is very honorable in our culture. My older brother shelters me under his wing, and we love each other greatly.

A Visit from Yeshua

When my brother is fifty-eight years old, a nineteen-year-old Hebrew comes to our temple to study. When my brother looks into the eyes of this young man named Yeshua, he immediately recognizes the presence of divinity in him from the radiance of love that emanates from every pore of his being. Yeshua comes to learn from us all that we know as adepts, including the chakra system, the flow of Kundalini energy, and breathing practices that promote health. Sri Ananda realizes that Yeshua absorbs all of this knowledge from him instantly, just by gazing into his eyes.

Opening the Third Eye

I am initially skeptical, but Sri Ananda takes me down by the river to meet this remarkable young man. Yeshua gazes into my eyes, touches my forehead, and instantly my mind is opened. Yeshua pops a bubble of limitation that has been constricting my third eye, which fully opens, melting illusions and leaving only truth. Everyone had one of these third eye constriction programs put in place by the Anunnaki to try to keep the humans under control. Then Yeshua floods my heart chakra with the unconditional love my creator has for me. This love is like my brother's, but far greater in its magnitude, reaching to the stars. It is a total "beingness" of love. Deeply moved by this direct experience with divinity in human form, Sri Hari pledges his soul in service to Yeshua, through however many incarnations it takes, until everyone awakens to the truth about the creator's great love for all of us.

Even though Yeshua absorbed all of our knowledge instantly, he stays in our country to teach us and to learn our language and culture. He shows us the flaws in our belief systems. We think that karma justifies the caste system.

We believe our lowest caste, the untouchables, have done grievous errors in previous incarnations and deserve to be in their position at the bottom of the social ladder. But Yeshua teaches us that love can overcome karma and that touch is the greatest healer. He preaches that we Brahmins, the landowner priests, should share our land and our food with the poor. He teaches that all people from all castes and varied intellectual abilities are equal in the sight of God—including women.

My brother and I embrace this radical new position. Who could say no to a direct experience of that caliber of pure love? We support Yeshua, taking him to meet others in the hierarchy of our society. Some of our colleagues open to this new truth and also become followers. But this teaching of the need to abolish the caste system is not well received by those in power, because they fear they would lose too much. Even some of the poor are so entrenched in the belief system that they think they deserve to be punished. Others of the lower castes embrace the truth, stand up, and clamor for equality.

Bloodshed

Armed revolt breaks out. People opposed to Yeshua draw swords and start fighting, trying to kill Yeshua and his followers. Others stand up to defend this new truth. Sri Ananda's heart is broken by the bloodshed, and Yeshua has to leave immediately, as it is not yet his time to die. He makes himself invisible and somehow makes us invisible, too, and we slip out from the crowd and move toward safety.

As my friend and I were remembering this shared lifetime, our conscious minds had trouble figuring out how Yeshua got invisibility cloaks for all of us. Yet, the Bible reports a similar event when the people at the synagogue were furious with Yeshua for what he was teaching:

> They got up, drove him out of the town, and took him to the brow of the hill on which the town was built, in order to throw him down the cliff. *But he walked right through the crowd and went on his way.* [my emphasis] (Luke 4:29-20 NIV)

Invisibility Photos

The ability to make oneself invisible is a feat witnessed and photographed by Thornton Streeter, who has done extensive research work at the Centre for Biofield Sciences with special photographic devices showing the emotional and spiritual states of people.[3] The first photo has the profile of a doctor who cannot believe what she is seeing.

In the second photo, the top part shows the energy configuration of a yogi (an adherent of yoga philosophy) as she started to go into meditation. This woman then made herself invisible right before Thornton's eyes. He could see only a filmy outline of where her body was, but the photograph shows the beauty of her aura while in this state of invisibility.

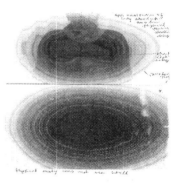

Secret Society

Four of us Brahmin priests disguise ourselves as carpenters and guide Yeshua as he escapes. We carry a cart filled with small items of furniture. We do not dare dress as the priests we are, because our lives are also in danger. Whenever one of us becomes discouraged, the others hold and comfort us. We know that even if our physical bodies are surrendered, our spirits will carry on the mission until the message of truth gets out to everyone.

We have formed an underground network of a secret society of about 150 followers of Yeshua. When we go to a new place, we can see into people's hearts and know who belongs to our group. We communicate telepathically. As adepts, we can broadcast a thought and target it, like an instant messenger program, but without any technology. We can alert our colleagues in other places, and they report their whereabouts to us. We are like underground bodyguards.

---

3   The Centre for Biofield Sciences: www.biofieldsciences.com

We are purposely not in the public eye, but we keep our fingers on the pulse of what is happening. Angels guide us and support us, watching our backs, and they wake us up when needed. Yeshua asks us to take him to meet with holy men who are living during our time. One is an immortal master named Babaji who lives in the Himalayas. Although we do not know where Babaji is, we know others who link us with those who can guide us there. Along the way, we work for food and sell our carpentry wares.

Babaji

When we finally complete the long journey to meet Babaji, he has a private audience with Yeshua. Although Sri Hari is not physically present, he is telepathically connected and sees that Babaji completes Yeshua's understanding of human nature. In his teenage years, Yeshua had overestimated the capacity of humans for rapid change. Babaji helps him see the way the nervous system is programmed with the ingrained fear of not being able to survive. He helps Yeshua see why the campaign in India resulted in a bloody revolution rather than the peaceful change Yeshua wanted.

They lay out a new master plan. Jesus is an avatar, come to bring a greater understanding of truth and love that will correct the distortions in the Anunnaki imprinting on our minds. The Anunnaki broke the heart of the world by claiming Divine powers only for themselves and treating us as soulless servants they genetically engineered who had to strictly obey or be severely punished. The truth is that the Anunnaki do have divinity within them, but so does everyone and everything else in all of creation!

The Great Creator of All had compassion for our hybrid race, and Yeshua came as the son of the true God to break the fear system the Anunnaki had installed in our minds to program us to work and obey, or be destroyed. I realize that the Anunnaki set up the whole caste system. Kingship everywhere was set up to rule the humans, because the Anunnaki did not design us to be smart enough to manage on our own! We believed our creators were angry, demanding, punishing parents we were supposed to fear.

The Cross and the Resurrection

Yeshua came to raise our consciousness to higher truth. Being nailed to the cross was part of this plan. Avatars down through history have connected with the cross as a symbol of "the x-y axis of space and time, as well as the Tree of Life."[4] Like other great avatar teachers, including Krishna and Quetzalcoatl, who got nailed to the Tree of Life, the plan was for the power of Yeshua's love to resurrect his body and regenerate the world. He would sacrifice his physicality and would transmute his physical cells into a resurrection body that could not be harmed by sword or anything else. He had studied resurrection in the mystery schools during his time in Egypt and knew how to do it.

The new plan was that during his physical ministry, Yeshua would gather a group of followers and open them to the truth. These awakened ones, both male and female, would then spread the message of love around the globe, like a little bit of yeast making a huge loaf of bread rise. This plan is different from his original strategy of working with the structures of authority. This underground movement goes to the common people. We follow Yeshua for the rest of his ministry on Earth, staying in the background. Yeshua instructs his disciples, "Heal the sick, show your powers, teach, and spread love everywhere."

Holy Week

Yeshua knows that being a prophet in his own country is dangerous, which is why he spent so many years studying in other places before he began his ministry. The Levitical priesthood in Jerusalem felt threatened by the priesthood of the Nazorean order and had banned all prophecy after the time of the prophet Ezra.[5] Prophets were forbidden to exercise their gifts, upon pain of death—from their parents' own hands. Instructions had already been written in the Bible:

> And if anyone still prophesies, his father and mother, to whom
> he was born, will say to him, 'You must die, because you have

---

4   McCannon, *Jesus*, 18.
5   Ibid., 135.

told lies in the LORD's name.' When he prophesies, his own parents will stab him. (Zechariah 13:3)

Yeshua knows he can be put to death for teaching a higher wisdom, but he has to go to the center of Anunnaki territory in Jerusalem for his final sacrifice. When Sri Ananda sees Yeshua being nailed to the cross, his loving heart is utterly shattered by the cruelty done to our beloved friend and master. Sri Hari holds his brother as he sobs in his arms. Sri Hari tells him it is part of the plan and that this event is as it is supposed to be, and greater good will come from it. But part of Sri Ananda leaves. He cannot tolerate staying and seeing the suffering. As my friend and I do the regression, I call back that part of my brother, because he needs all of his parts to go forward in his mission.

The gospels of Matthew, Mark, and Luke all tell that during the Crucifixion, darkness came over the land from the sixth hour until the ninth hour, when Jesus died. They said the sun stopped shining, which we would call an eclipse, a synchronicity that reflected the prevalence of the dark forces during those hours. Sri Hari sees that when Yeshua's spirit leaves his physical form, out pops his atman, his spirit, and it is about thirty feet tall! He's big and bright, filled with absolute golden Divine Light. Free of his human binding, his glory radiates immensely.

Matthew tells us about other supernatural events that happened when Yeshua gave up his spirit:

> At that moment the curtain of the temple was torn in two from top to bottom. The earth shook and the rocks split. The tombs broke open and the bodies of many holy people who had died were raised to life. They came out of the tombs, and after Jesus' resurrection they went into the holy city and appeared to many people.

> When the centurion and those with him who were guarding Jesus saw the earthquake and all that had happened, they were terrified, and exclaimed, "Surely he was the Son of God!" (Matthew 27:51-54 NIV)

Uranium-Based Thought Projector

Sri Hari telepathically follows Yeshua as he goes from the cross with a host of angels to the temple's Holy of Holies, the place where the Ark of the Covenant is kept. Sri Hari sees that the Ark is a uranium-based etheric thought projector. His conception of what is happening is that the Anunnaki are using the Ark to generate a force field of mind control to broadcast the thought forms that they are the rulers and humans are subservient to them, not having rights or immortal souls. The thought system includes the belief that the Anunnaki have the secrets of immortality. If humans are really good and work really hard, the gods might grant us more time, but they have the Divine power over life and death and can grant or deny these things as they please. This message is falsehood, because every single being has divinity and a soul. Sri Hari perceives that the Anunnaki have been using this broadcasting device to affect the humans they created, and they have installed etheric chips in everyone's third eye to receive the broadcasts. Sri Hari sees that at their first meeting, Yeshua removed his chip and opened his third eye to truth, popping the bubble of limitation that had been installed around his pineal gland, the organ of perception. Yeshua also did the same for Sri Ananda and the other followers. He deactivated the receptors for these mind-control broadcasts.

The radiation in the Holy of Holies does not bother Yeshua, because he does not have a physical form. Sri Hari sees Yeshua adjusting the broadcaster to pull out fear-based programs from the dark side and to purify what is being broadcast. He puts in the possibility for all beings on the planet to live in peace and harmony, in joy and truth. Then Yeshua goes to the dead and to the astral plane to minister to earthbound spirits and bring them the message of God's love. I see him taking multitudes of earthbound spirits into the Light, all those who are ready to embrace the higher path of love.

I also saw that Sri Hari had strong connections with the angelic realm. While his human heart grieved at the bloodshed of the Crucifixion, through the grace of the angelic presence with him he could see what Yeshua was doing and that it was the only way to free humankind from the bondage of the mind-control broadcasts.

459

The Strategy

Sri Hari sees the strategy. The Holy of Holies was well guarded by the dark energies to preserve the power of the Anunnaki to get more gold. The dark forces were guarding the Ark to prevent anyone and anything from disabling their mechanism. But the goriness of the Crucifixion distracted the dark forces. They were vehemently opposed to Yeshua and wanted him dead. They were absolutely delighted by all of his suffering and went over to Golgotha to watch. They really thought they had destroyed Yeshua when his spirit left his body. So with the Ark unguarded, Yeshua popped out of his body and just walked right into the temple and reprogrammed its broadcasts with the psychic opening created by the Crucifixion. As I was remembering this lifetime, I exclaimed, "Well, that's pretty wild, isn't it!" I had never thought of the possibility that he really is our Savior in a unique way because of setting us free from mind control.

The dark forces did not see that the Crucifixion was Yeshua's initiation into the next stage of spiritual mastery. One of my mentors, Gloria Karpinski, teaches about five stages of spiritual initiation:[6]

1. The call to Discipleship
2. Baptism
3. The Transfiguration
4. The Crucifixion
5. The Resurrection

When you pass through the initiation of the Crucifixion, when you are the avatar nailed to the Tree of Life on whatever planet you are on, only then are you ready for the last initiation of Resurrection. Once you have passed through the Resurrection, then you become a creator of universes. The ordeal of the cross was the final test of Yeshua, and he passed it.

---

6   http://gloriakarpinski.moxysite.com/

Our Mission

Yeshua came at the beginning of the two-thousand-year Age of Pisces. Now we are entering the age of Aquarius, the time for the work of Yeshua to come to full fruition. Yeshua instructs us to just hold our light, to be love and light. We do not have to worry. Legions of angels are supporting our work. He says to keep my brother Sri Ananda close to me.

Sri Ananda lived only three years after the Crucifixion and was assassinated with a sword at the age of seventy-seven. When he died, most of his spirit went with Yeshua when the Master came for him, but a dissociated part of him stayed earthbound. We worked to get the part of him that had dissociated at the Crucifixion into the reality of the glory of the Resurrection and then to rejoin the rest of his soul in the Light with Yeshua.

Sri Hari lived for ten years after the Crucifixion and died by poisoning. At first I wondered how, with his telepathic abilities, he could not have known about the poison, but then I saw that he was tied down and forced to drink the poison. Sri Hari felt angry with himself for trusting the older woman who betrayed him. She felt like a mother figure to him, an energy he lacked, especially since his mother died at his birth and his older brother was also gone.

As I went through this memory, the mild symptoms of an upset stomach that I had been feeling all day worsened, and I became violently ill with vomiting and diarrhea, as if I had food poisoning. The synchronicity of these physical symptoms coinciding with my memory of being poisoned convinced me that the whole memory was more than just an imaginary fantasy! We did energy work for Sri Hari to release his self-judgment and cross fully into the Light with his beloved Master Yeshua.

CHAPTER 41

Connecting with the Whale Kingdom

*I*n this lifetime, I had an experience similar to what Sri Hari experienced when Yeshua opened up his third eye. In 2011, I was swimming in the ocean with wild humpback whales off the coast of the Dominican Republic. Our group of snorkelers had been in the water watching a mother whale and her baby for hours. I was sending an energetic cord of love to this beautiful forty-five-ton mammal, when suddenly I experienced the popping of a bubble of limitation I had never even noticed because it had been around me all my life. I felt as if I had been a fish swimming around inside a small fishbowl, and suddenly the fishbowl disappeared and I was free to explore the whole ocean. At the same time, I got a strong telepathic message from the whale asking me to call her Minerva and telling me, "Be all you can be!" This message is not just for me, it is for all of us humans. Who would have thought that a forty-five-ton cetacean could expand my membrane, stop the inner critical voice that told me everything I did was wrong, and fill my being with unconditional love in an instant?

Escort whale breeching in front of our group. The author is the snorkeler on the far right. Photograph by Sandra Heaton.

Gifted clairvoyant Patricia Cori teaches that the whales and dolphins come from a planet called Oceana, which is mostly water, a planet revolving around the Sirian star known as Satais.[1] Cori teaches that these Cetaceans have been on Earth for billions of years, and their songs hold the ocean in balance and are essential to the harmony of all life on our planet.[2] This idea brings up the question of just how the whales and dolphins could have traveled to Earth. I have trouble imagining a whale piloting a spaceship and wonder if they had the ability to shift into a higher dimension, travel as orbs of light, and then shift back down into our third dimension, manifesting their physical bodies once again.

---

1   Cori, *Before We Leave You*, 60.
2   Cori, *Before We Leave You*.

Interdimensional Travel

Mind-blowing as this idea is, in his book *Hidden Truth: Forbidden Knowledge*, physician Steven Greer gives examples of people who witnessed interdimensional travel. He and his wife went to Belgium during the wave of UFO sightings there in the early 1990s. He had direct encounters with the triangular space vehicles sighted in that area and he talked with other witnesses. In one case, a massive ship the size of three football fields hovered over the steeple of a church in a small village. The eyewitness version before editing it for the press was as follows:

> This huge triangular ship, 800 feet long on each side, hovering above the town square, suddenly collapsed into a pulsing red ball of light the size of a basketball. It moved a little bit and then vanished straight out into space, in the blink of an eye![3]

Greer notes that the capabilities of the extraterrestrials are extremely advanced and that the way they seem to appear and then disappear marks their ability to make a dimensional shift.

Swimming with the whales felt magical and exhilarating. The following underwater photograph is one of the baby whales our group swam with. Note the orb of white light in the photo. Perhaps these orbs are higher dimensional beings giving us a glimpse of their presence!

If the whales do come from another planet, then they might be a special kind of extraterrestrial presence here trying to help us evolve and connect with our higher selves.

> *All of the galaxies are coming together to help each other.*
> *Get with the group!*
> —ET message channeled by Soul Detective Margaret Clench

Author and metaphysical teacher Drunvalo Melchizedek, like Cori, teaches that the whales and the dolphins were the first conscious beings to arrive

---

3   Greer, *Hidden Truth*, 79-80.

**Newborn whale calf with an orb of light in lower left corner of photo.
Photograph by John LaSalle.**

on planet Earth billions of years ago. Melchizedek says that the first Anunnaki spacecraft to Earth landed in the ocean because galactic law required an off-planet race to get permission from the conscious beings already on a planet before entering into a different consciousness system.[4] He states that the first Anunnaki astronaut leader spent a long time in the waters learning the advanced knowledge of the cetaceans and that when he came out of the waters, he had the tail of a fish, like a merman.

Implants of Limitation

Minerva removed an implant of limitation from my energy field. In my Level Three Soul Detective trainings, students muscle test themselves to find out whether they are carrying any external programs of limitation, whether

---

4   Melchizedek, *The Ancient Secret of the Flower of Life*, 88.

placed there by the Anunnaki to keep us from getting too powerful, by religious institutions to keep us under their control, or by any other outside source. We also check for other kinds of extraterrestrial interference in the system. The results have really surprised me because so far, every single person has had at least one program of limitation, and some have had over a dozen of these programs. What I notice is that whether or not the student or the client or the therapist believes that these implants are real, after doing the protocol I developed to assess for and remove the implants with energy work, the person feels free, light, and shining. People absolutely glow when they can be fully themselves! These implants of limitation act like "hardwired limiting beliefs," which use fear to hold us back. Some examples of the feelings they might convey to the person are:

> It's not safe to be all of who I am.
> Communicating directly with the Divine will get me into
> trouble with the authorities.
> If I reach my full potential, I'll lose my family/loved ones/
> job/income.
> Humans are inferior and limited.
> God is dangerous and vengeful and I need to fear Him.
> I'm sinful, so I don't deserve good things.
> It's not possible.
> I can't.

Prayer for Release of Implants of Limitation

Readers who feel some of these blockage programs sabotaging their goals in life could try getting centered and quiet with whatever method works best for them and then asking their spiritual guidance teams for help with a prayer something like the following:

I call upon help from the beings of Light that guide my incarnation to find and release any implants of limitation that are holding me back from reaching my highest human potential, releasing the limitations in a gentle manner compatible with my body's ability to adjust to a higher degree of sovereignty. I ask for this release only if it is in the highest good for me, for my family, and for all of humanity.

Then watch what happens and see how you feel. If you have several implants, your system may remove them one at a time.

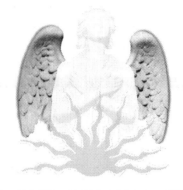

CHAPTER 42

Connecting with Enki/Ea

*W*hether the Sumerian gods are actual beings who walked the Earth, or whether all of the stories on the more than 500,000 cuneiform tablets that have been found are pure mythology, these ancient images form a substrate of emotional templates that give rise to patterns of human behavior, called archetypes in Jungian psychology. We have discussed at length the nature of the Old Testament Lord matching what the Sumerian tablets say about the character of Lord Enlil, and we watched his progression from wielding fear as a control mechanism to giving up and leaving the planet in disgust.

Now we will turn to an in-depth look at the nature of his brother Enki. Long before she ever heard of Soul Detective work, Janet Nestor (author of the Foreword) had a strong intuitive connection to Enki, whom she prefers to call Ea, his original name when he was still on Nibiru. Shamans go into trance and journey into other worlds to gather healing information. I asked Janet to share some of her inner journeys connecting with Ea's essence, especially since he was the father of the first two *Homo sapiens* and thus is in the direct ancestral lineage of all humans. What I noticed the most about her Ea stories was how greatly he loved the humans he helped to create. In the pages below we see his progression from the fear of annihilation of all life on his planet, the motivation to mine gold, to his opening to the golden light of love in his heart. Whether this was actual work with Ea/Enki himself or whether it is transformation in the archetype within Janet, it puts out an uplifting ray of hope into collective consciousness. The material communicated from Ea through Janet includes concrete ways we can ask to have the full potential of our nervous systems activated. The rest of this chapter is Janet speaking.

Janet's Soul Detective Journey

As you read the following record of my Soul Detective Journey, you might ask, "How did your interactions and experiences with Ea facilitate increased mental-emotional-spiritual well-being?" Your second question may be, "Why should I believe this story?" Honestly, I am not sure I believe this story myself, but I am sure of the results of the work. This material goes way outside the box of consensus reality, of what humans usually believe is possible. Whether this whole story is a fantasy my unconscious mind dreamed up to explain why I felt so bad and how I could heal, or whether I tapped into the morphic resonance of Enki/Ea in the collective unconscious, or whether I actually have a soul link to Ea as a parallel life does not matter. What does matter is that the work healed my body and my soul and presents healing opportunities to anyone who reads this account.

My Story

For many years, I was fascinated and almost obsessed with ancient Egypt. When I had the chance to visit the Egyptian exhibit at the 1989 World's Fair, I looked at the artifacts, spent time with the ones that spoke to me, and touched the ones I could. As I walked out the door, I began a stunning journey of healing and insight that would lead me toward unity of body and soul.

A few years later, during my Reiki master teacher training, I journeyed to another time and place. In this experience, a part of me is in a pyramid, sitting at a desk, facing a beautiful, large open area and the inner surface of an outside wall. I am dressed in ancient Egyptian clothing, an oatmeal-colored robe with gold roping at my waist. I am writing on a rectangular tablet and physically and emotionally experiencing a few moments in the life of the Egyptian god Ptah, who I now know is the same person as Enki/Ea. Here is the entry in my journal channeling the feelings of Ptah/Enki/Ea:

> I know I have a lot of work to complete. The weight of the job is heavy on my heart and soul. I want to leave a record, as much information as possible, so important historical, medical, and scientific information is available in the years ahead. The room where I sit is lined with a row of torches, held securely in dark-brown cone-shaped holders. Their fires burn brightly, creating a golden glow all about the rooms. The walls and the floor are a soft, light golden color. I know there are other people in the pyramid, but only Master Charles, my servant, is present. Master Charles has the job of pushing me to write when I am tired and yearn to stop. As he stands by the desk ordering me to continue, I almost hate him. When I can take the weight of my task no longer, I stand up, levitate, and glide toward the wall and float through to the outside world. I fly, invisible, to my statue, and enter it. While a group of people surround the statue, they do not see me float up or notice me enter the statue. However, they know immediately when I am within it and am ready to answer their prayers and their questions. When I am tired of answering prayers and questions, I exit the statue and go back into the pyramid.
>
> I am aware of my thoughts. I am thinking about my wife, Baal. I am aware that we have a son, but neither he nor my wife live with me. They are at their home, and I am alone. I have work to do. My wife, a goddess in Egypt, has her own work to do, and right now work comes first.

As soon as I arrived home, I drew a likeness of Ptah and then wondered about his wife, Baal. I went straight to my computer to check my artwork with historical artifacts and drawings. To my amazement, my drawing was identical to those I found on the Internet. I wondered how this could happen. Even though I experienced myself entering the statue, I did not see it through the eyes of the crowd. This information came from internal awareness.

Soul Origin

During my Level Three Soul Detective training class in 2010, we were each identifying the planet of our soul origin, the location where the soul has spent the most time in its history of incarnations. My planet of soul origin was identified as Nibiru, the home of the Anunnaki.

The following members of my spiritual family are relevant to this story: Yeshua the Christ, Mary Magdalene, Archangel Michael, Archangel Raphael, Enki/Ea, his sister Ninmah, and Enki's son Ningishzidda. All of my interactions with these figures are personally supportive and instructional. My experience is a perfect example of how Soul Detective work helps us uncover our authentic self and heal the impediments blocking our soul's evolution. I hope my story will inspire others to embrace this path, which has corrected feelings of emptiness and underlying anxiety in my life.

Janet's Journal Entries

8-28-09 ~ Archangel Michael

Archangel Michael, when he is "off duty" is dressed casually in his long robe, carrying a shepherd's staff. Today Archangel Michael asked me to hold the staff that he carries everywhere. It is the staff he uses to guard the gateway to heaven. As I held the staff, I could feel the energy expand into a magnificent power. Michael instructed me to see the staff as my spinal column and told me that all of the power of the staff is in my spine, including the gateway to heaven. This is true for all human beings.

2-9-10 ~ Meeting Archangel Raphael

Archangel Raphael teaches me about the "Powers" and the Prince of the Powers: The power of creation. The power of love. The power of knowing. The power of life. The power of healing. The power of safety and security. The power to love and be loved. The power to withstand. The power of empowerment. The power of healthy boldness. All these individual powers are available to each human. The Prince of the Powers and each of these powers, and the others not mentioned, are normal and natural to each of us if we embrace them. We can ask to know them individually.

Raphael looks like a very large man. He appears to be nearly seven feet tall and substantial, an imposing figure. His presence carries respect and strength. He appeared with wings, as if he flew into my view, but he states over and over that they are not really wings. They are the evidence of his vibrational abilities that look like wings and can be used almost like arms that hold and heal. He allows me to be held in that powerful embrace, like a baby in arms, and feel his healing course through my entire body. To be held in Raphael's "wings" is like coming home to rest. We can rest in his energy whenever we need healing. In the center of his chest is a visible heart. It looks like a pink, healthy human heart. It is not beating, but it is there as if to say, "I am all heart, love, and within my heart is healing love."

5-29-10 ~ This morning Christ asked me to call him Yeshua, his given name.

6-29-10 ~ Divine Essence
I have been given the understanding that each of us contains the "essence" we were at birth, and this essence remains present at our core throughout our lifetime. It is the innocence, awareness, and presence of the Divine that always remains. This eternal essence changes everything for each of us. We can rewrite our life story, change perspective, and change the things that hurt or upset us anytime we choose to do so.

1-13-11 ~ Wisdom
Where light is, dark cannot be.

10-5-11 ~ Excerpts from Soul Detective work with Barbara Stone on the life of Ptah
Enki/Ea felt trapped in his job as leader and son of Anu and was afraid to ask for help for fear that asking would create a perception of failure among his people. Barbara and I asked for the veil of darkness to be lifted from Ptah, from all of the Anunnaki, and from the human race. Ea observed the realm known as powers sprinkling sparkling stuff (gold dust) into the atmosphere

of Nibiru to make it stronger, to make the atmospheric shield it now has last longer. The sparkling stuff was infused with a level of love that the minds of the Anunnaki were incapable of understanding. The energy directing that love will continue to direct the work, and this light feels important as part of the shift that is to occur on Earth. We ask for Yeshua to work with Ea to help open his heart to the power of love and to open his mind to deeper understanding of his place and Nibiru's role in the web of the Universe.

10-6-11 ~ Part of an e-mail to Barbara Stone regarding Ea's concept of love

Ea wants you to know how much he loved his family, his planet, humans, and everything, even the smallest of particles, on Earth. He understood love as relationship, responsibility, and doing the leadership job he was needed to do. He did not see himself as a god, but played the role even though it was a great burden to him. He wanted to keep us humans as well and as safe as he could. He has not adjusted to the change of what he learned from the Christ yesterday, but he does appreciate all those many angels and light beings that were with us during our work. He says that a constellation of Anunnaki has been living among humans as humans and that thousands of others all over the world are connecting with their consciousness, like I do.

11-11-11 ~ Unruly Children

Ea was intensely angry with his children at times as some of them were willful, forceful, and had an aggressive feeling that their birthright gave them the right to be non-empathetic, hostile rulers. In general, this willful attitude was true of many of the Anunnaki.

11-12-11~ Ea

As I awake this morning, relaxing in bed, I realize that Ea is fully present, giving me the gift of understanding the magnitude of his physical strength and energy so I might experience this presence for myself in my daily life. He knows I struggle to accept my personal power, and he seeks to help me remedy that limitation. He tells me through a knowing that he has been fully receptive to his education with Christ, which is almost complete.

12-16-11 ~ Allowing Awareness

Today Ea appears huge, omnipotent in his approach. He communicates that Earth is being run by Earthlings up to a point. He says that the Anunnaki influences continue, just as his influence is coming through me right now. He is very large man and I can see why the early humans thought the Anunnaki were gods. I have no words for this experience this morning because his presence is so powerful. He explains he is not the Creator of all, but he, his sister Ninmah, and his brilliant son Ningishzidda, also known as Thoth or Tehuti, are the designers of human beings, giving us inner communication skills, insight, wisdom, and intellectual capacity. Ea says the Anunnaki worshiped the Creator of All and had a very spiritual part to their lives, even though they refused to ask for help. Ea's spiritual attitude is why he took the role of Ptah so seriously and why he, going against his brother Enlil's will, saved Noah and his family during the deluge. Noah was his son, so Noah's children were his grandchildren. In order to save all that had been established on Earth, he says the Ark had a genetics lab that contained the DNA of all life on Earth, including vegetation, fruits and vegetables, and the entire animal kingdom on land, in water, and in the air.

2-21-12 ~ Life Extension (complete autonomic nervous system balance)

Ea showed me that the Anunnaki are fully present in their own bodies by allowing me to experience the feeling through his body. Their feet are much more connected to the earth, so they are constantly being fed by the energy of the Earth. Through this experience, my energy became more grounded and present.

2-23-12 ~ Excerpt from an e-mail to Barbara Stone

Ea said today that the Anunnaki nervous system is much more extensive than ours. The Anunnaki brain stem is used much more than ours and functions as an active part of their brain. He told me that humans can have a nervous system that allows them to use more of their brain. He said all we have to do is ask, and it is provided. But we have to know we can ask. I asked Christ if I could do this. He said yes, and I asked for the upgrade in being able to use more of my brain. My body began to buzz and I could feel a steady surge of energy coming out the ends of my fingers. Ea said the Anunnaki senses are much stronger than ours. They can see better, hear better, and smell better.

The relationship between Ea and Christ: Ea is a fifth-dimension being currently moving to a higher level of consciousness, which is Christ Consciousness (Love Consciousness). The Anunnaki leadership of the world is then moving into a higher level of consciousness...reluctantly. Not all of the Anunnaki agree with the change Ea is making, and Ea is also having second thoughts.

Ea Speaking directly about the long-term relationship with Christ:

It would not have been appropriate to follow the teachings of Christ during his lifetime. We were the rulers of Earth and could not engage at the time. Now we are tired and no longer rulers of Earth as we once were. Now it is appropriate for us to be immersed in the energy of love as he is.

Ea on the Crown Chakra:

Yes, we tried to take care of our own issues. Science and knowledge were our religion. But you forget that we believed and believe our science and our wisdom were brought about by the Creator of All. The Creator of All was honored as the source of all things, including our knowledge and abilities beyond the norm for many civilizations. We are fifth-dimension beings. That means we can think, we have compassion, and we are able to create much of what we want and need with our own abilities. We don't always need to ask for help, and we can do much on our own, and did. You allow the energy of creation to flow through your body, from the crown to the feet and back into the Earth. We stopped that. We are not Earth beings. Yes, shutting off the flow of energy into our crown chakras may have caused us much pain, but we felt we had to. We balance ourselves through the energy of the Earth.

When asked if they drank monatomic gold:

Yes, we drank the monatomic gold. We put it in our water. We wore it as well, but not in the state that you wear it. The gold we wore was absorbed by our skin.

Did Christ drink the monatomic gold?

No. Yeshua always maintained communication with the Creator of All.

Warning about monatomic gold:

The powdered gold is not good for you. We did use that to try to control people. We still do, but not in the way that you may think. Do not drink the white powder gold. It is not good for humans, even those who are close to us in genetics.

Listening Devices

We surgically placed listening devices into many beings, not all of them human beings. We had beams of light that projected sound and language. We were all wired for constant contact with each other.

Our Genetics

Our magic lies within the Earth. We drank other elements too, not just the water gold. Our bodies are not the same as yours. While you have our DNA, our genetics, we did not make you exactly like us. We made you partly like those living beings that were already on Earth. We gave you intelligence, the ability to be conversant, and the ability to think and reason. Those are our gifts to you. We gave you our mind, but most of you have not used it. Our minds are within you, but you must ask us for those skills, and we will open them to you. You must ask. That was the deal we made with the Creator of all. Humans must ask for the gifts.

6-3-2012 ~ Acceptance

I no longer have any qualms about who I am. I accept the spiritual choices that I made before this incarnation. My thoughts are currently filled with Ea's thoughts and his instruction. When I met Yeshua, my thoughts were saturated by his words and his teaching, and the same was true when I met Mary Magdalene and Archangel Michael for the first time. Yeshua, the Christ, Mary Magdalene, and Archangel Michael are now solid, loving members of my spiritual family. At one time I would have felt that communicating with Ea would have meant being disloyal to the Christ, but now I see that the link between these two energies is essential to the spiritual development of the Anunnaki and to the flowering and development of humanity.

6-16-2012 ~ Reluctance and Victory

Ea speaking: Moving to a higher level of consciousness feels like abandoning my people, leaving some behind and turning away from a way of life.

Yeshua speaks: Lord Enki, there has always been violence and jealousy among your people and within the ruling family.

Ea: Yes.

Yeshua: Some have died.

Ea: Yes.

Yeshua: Your people brought violence and war to Earth. Many messengers were sent before me and you ignored them.

Ea: We did not ignore. We did not subscribe.

Yeshua: Yes, you did not subscribe. Is saving your planet and saving some violent people more important than progressing, preferable to making Love your weapon of choice?

Ea: This is the hardest decision I will ever make. How do I make this final step? How do I walk away from all I have ever known? How do I walk away from being the glue in my family? How do I do that?

Yeshua: You are not the glue, Ea. Your love has been the glue. It is time to let go. My love is so great for you that I let go. Can you allow my love to flow through you, into your crown chakra and into the Earth that you love and cherish so much?

Ea: I will die to myself when I do this.

Yeshua: You will not physically die, Ea, you will live, just as we all live from one life to the next as part of the Creator of all. Are you with me, Ea?

Ea: I let go and die to myself. I am free.

For a moment there is a great silence, almost a darkness, when nothing happens. And then I can see the glow as Ea begins to fill with the golden light of Creation love.

Ea: I am changing! I am still breathing.

I see Ea stride around, back and forth, victorious as though the battle is won. There is a cheer from his people and from the Universal beings of Light.

Finally, Ea, together with Christ, is embracing Love as the weapon of choice. Love is growing throughout the world. For Ea and others of his group, Love is now the essence of life, rather than life being the essence of life. They are now acknowledging that long life is not God, Love is God, and they are realizing they can have love, God, and long life simultaneously.

At an advanced Soul Detective class, our group collectively set sacred space and opened a doorway for the Anunnaki who want to accept the love of the Creator of All after more than 500,000 years of living with closed crown chakras. We felt that many, perhaps millions of Anunnaki souls came into our circle of love and accepted the love of Creation, allowing it to flow through their crown chakras and into their hearts. So many of the Anunnaki choosing love as their "weapon of choice" gives the world a better chance to heal from war and find peace.

I'd like to close by sharing this beautiful poem spoken by Ea into my mind. It is meant to teach me who he is as a person, to dispel human fears that he and the Anunnaki are here to harm humanity. These are his exact words, a beautiful love poem to me and to all other human beings living on planet Earth.

Harmony

> I love you.
> You are my friend.
> You are my heartbeat and my heart.
> I'll love you to the end.
>
> Come be with me.
> Walk by my side.
> Hear the wind and the rain with me.
> Our hearts are entwined.
>
> Enjoy life with me.
> I am your friend.
> We are comfortable companions.
> Harmonious soul and mind.

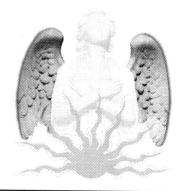

CHAPTER 43

Transforming Fear

he love poem from Ea communicates the love the Father of All Beginnings has for all of creation. I will share some of my own journey from the energies of fear to this intimate connection with the love of the Divine. As a young child, I loved going to my Bible Belt Protestant church and hearing about how much Jesus loved me. When we sang the song "Jesus Loves Me" in Sunday school, I felt the golden light of God's love flowing through my being. I invited Jesus into my heart to be an indwelling spiritual presence to guide every step of my life, and I felt the power and presence of the Divine within my soul.

In my teens I read the Bible through several times. I loved the stories about Jesus in the New Testament, but I hardly recognized the vicious, angry, vengeful God of the Old Testament who was supposed to be the father of Jesus. I asked my mother how God could be so mean. She explained the situation to me in humorous terms that I could understand at the time. She said, "God wasn't a Christian yet." Webster defines the word *testament* as "a covenant between God and man," and so I surmised that the Old Testament God had made a profound shift in his attitude toward humans with the coming of Christ. Logically, it makes no sense that the Creator of All the Universe, the one who set the stars in the sky, lit the sun on fire to warm us, and created all living things on this four-and-a-half-billion-year-old planet would have been such a raging maniac until having a sudden shift two thousand years ago. The idea that the Prime Creator sent his only son to be tortured and killed for my sins felt gruesome and created shame in me for being the cause of the suffering of Christ.

Shame Around Sexuality

As sexual feelings began to blossom within me as a teenager, I felt guilt, because the Bible said that having a lustful thought was just as bad as acting out the thought. My church believed that dancing was immoral because it would create lustful thoughts and lead to fornication. The church also believed that movies, jewelry, short skirts, and short sleeves were all bad, generally for the same reasons of leading to licentious behavior. A woman's beauty was to be on the inside, not on the outside. These rules of how to please God and get to heaven and how to avoid being sent to hell forever after death felt much different from the pure love I felt inside through my direct connection with Jesus.

The Face of God

When I was diagnosed with breast cancer in 1991 and prayed for help, I saw Jesus come and stand before me in my mind's eye. I felt the physical touch of Jesus tapping on my sternum and conveying the complete thought, "I now heal your soul." This event was my first experience with a tapping therapy. Jesus is the face that God wears for me, though others in different traditions may sense the Divine through another face. With that touch of my heart, I felt a deep wound heal in my soul, and I absolutely knew I would survive cancer. How could I not believe in God when I had this direct experience of the touch of the Master healing my heart and my soul?

Writing this book helped me sort out the parts of my belief system that come from the true essence of the Divine and the parts that come from rules to control human behavior to keep order in society. Comparing the information in the Sumerian tablets with the Bible, I conclude that the religion I was taught contained a mixture of New Testament genuine spirituality and Old Testament fear-based rule-keeping.

I truly treasure the pacifist values of my childhood church. Members of our congregation did not ever go to war, for any reason. My father had the courage to stand for his spiritual convictions and refused to fight in World War II, which was a popular war to stop Hitler. Instead, my father spent a year of alternative service as a "smoke jumper," parachuting out of an airplane to fight forest fires out west and then another year as an orderly in a mental hospital in the days before we had chemical restraints. I still believe in my heart of hearts that war and fighting do not solve problems. Even in my Detrimental Energy Protocol, I do not fight the darkness. I make peace with it and encourage the Dark Force Entities to rise to the Light.

Living in Peace

Although the Anunnaki had intelligence and scientific knowledge far surpassing our capabilities, in ancient times they did not seem to have mastered the art of brotherly love and living harmoniously with others. Anunnaki brothers fought viciously over power and territory, an imprint that was handed down to Cain and Abel, the first two *Homo sapiens* brothers, and escalated to Cain murdering Abel. We know that impulse control lessens when a person has been drinking alcohol, and lack of impulse control continues to be a problem for humans, even when they have not been drinking.

The indigenous races on Earth seem to be closer to the life forms that evolved naturally here, and indigenous tribes love, honor, and respect our mother planet. We need more of these values to sustain life on Earth. The white-skinned races, which have more Anunnaki genes, are, in general, more technologically advanced and lacking in concern for living in harmony with our planet. The current level of toxicity put into our environment with all of our sky-based technology exacerbates the upheavals in weather patterns and increases natural disasters as Earth tries to bring herself back into balance.

Religious Challenges

Humans have feared God. It has been bred into us, reinforced over and over in the Old Testament by the vicious acts of Yahweh when his people did not obey orders. Religious fanatics still kill people in the opposing religion, all in the name of the god they worship. The attack on the Twin Towers in New

York City on September 11, 2001 is an example of Muslim religious fanatics doing their religious duty of "jihad," a holy war to wipe out infidels who do not believe in Mohammed. Perhaps the wars between rival gods in the Old Testament, wars between different ideologies that are still going on today, point to Dark Force Entities at work behind the scenes. Look at the ways God's name was used to abuse people in the following case history.

Susannah North Martin

Baptized September 31, 1621, and executed July 19, 1692, in the Salem Witch Trials

After her father died, Charity felt compelled to work on her family tree and search for trapped ancestors. In particular, she had been feeling the call of a great-grandmother many generations back who was executed in the Salem Witch trials, a woman named Susannah North Martin. Charity had read transcripts from the trials and noted how independent and feisty Susannah was throughout the process.

We set sacred space and did a Soul Detective Earthbound Spirit Protocol to find out what had happened from Susannah's viewpoint. Charity channeled the feelings of her ancestor and said that Susannah had been a target all of her life because she spoke out for her rights, a quality not shown by many women in her time. The daughter of the local minister was the ringleader of a group of girls who bullied others. A slave woman from the Caribbean who did voodoo had taken these teenage girls under her wing and done séances with them. When the minister's daughter accused someone of witchcraft, her father backed her up, so everyone was afraid to cross these girls. They sassed Susannah, and she spoke back to them. The minister's daughter pointed her finger at Susannah accusing her of being a witch, and she was brought to trial.

In the Salem trials, the women accused of witchcraft who confessed to the crime had their lives spared, but those who would not confess were executed. Even as the rope was being put around her neck, Susannah affirmed her innocence. Susannah felt anger and rage about what happened to her, feeling her life had been wasted and thrown away. She wanted justice. When she was put to death, she was an old woman of seventy-one who had already lived her life, but some of the other women she witnessed being executed for witchcraft were young and had families who depended on them. She was particularly enraged about all the pain that loss of life and dignity brought to the women killed, as well as their loved ones.

Dark Force Entities

We found five Fallen Angels and two minions at work behind the scenes. We interviewed the highest-ranking Fallen Angel and found his job assignment was to destroy the community by tearing it apart from within and to destroy all belief in God, to destroy the whole idea of God. The United States was founded on freedom of religion, and this Fallen Angel was trying to nip this idea in the bud and make people afraid of God. He worked for the darkness and believed that light was an illusion, there was no light, and there was only darkness. He thought people who follow the light were blind idiots and threatened that anyone who crossed him would be sorry they did. He was angry with Susannah because she had not bowed to him.

We offered this Fallen Angel the chance to get a more powerful job, and he asked, "How much power?" He believed his current boss was extremely powerful and wanted to be sure the new job would be even more powerful than that! We asked Archangel Michael to show him the power of the Light and for other Fallen Angels who had come back to the Brotherhood of Lightworkers to surround him and show the kind of power they had now that they were working for the Light. The Fallen Angel was taken aback and asked, "How can this be? I have only tried to hurt these Angels—why would they come to me?"

When he saw the magnificence of the Light, he got very worried about getting into trouble with his current boss, warning us, "You don't know what he can do. He is very powerful." But he saw that Archangel Michael and his crew were even more powerful than his boss, and he said he wanted to be on the winning side. This angel wanted to be protected by a bubble of angelic light with a ring of angels around him. Archangel Michael and others promptly formed a Bubblemobile of protection around the Fallen Angel, and he felt the Light, a new experience. He was amazed! He asked to be freed from all the cords of deception and lies that had bound him to the dark side. Archangel Michael set him free, and he accepted a new job of working for the Light. He invited the other four Fallen Angels and the two minions who had been involved in the Salem Witch Trials to join him in the Light. They were amazed to see how beautiful this former boss looked in the Light. He told them that, before, he had coerced them into obedience by pressuring them to do things and ordering them around (sounds like Enlil). Now he was inviting them to take the same opportunity he had accepted to come work for the Light. The other four Fallen Angels talked it over and decided to convert, but they wanted the Bubblemobile to come get them so they could have safe passage. They were sure to take their minions with them, too, and all crossed into the Light.

Remorse

Then these former Fallen Angels were filled with remorse at seeing all the damage they had done to humans. The minions said, "We were just doing our jobs." They had been blinded, but now they were seeing the truth. Charity reported that the first Fallen Angel was quite powerful, very high up on the food chain of the dark side. He had been working at destroying people's faith in God on the planet long before Salem. He made people laugh at God and ridicule him, making God into a joke. He was surprised to recognize some of his old colleagues in the Light, those who had converted before he did. He did not know what happened to them, because Satan had told him that they had been removed to the furthest pits of hell for going against him—another lie! He commented, "You have no idea what it's like to see Light when I was only in darkness."

Multiplying the Benefits

We invited any other Fallen Angels who had jobs of making people turn away from God to come get better jobs working for the Light. The leader of the Fallen Angels was inviting all the others he had been responsible for. He told us, "You didn't know how much it put a nail in our coffin every time you chose death rather than to lie, something our boss said humans would never do. It made us fear, a major victory for the Light every time one of you chose truth." He told Susannah, "Your death counted for more than you knew." A convoy of Bubble-mobiles went out into the cosmos to gather other Dark Force Entities who wanted to get on the winning side of the Light!

Susannah

When we came back to Susannah, she was dumbfounded at seeing all the action from the dark side that had gone on behind the scenes. When she was accused of witchcraft, her children all moved away from Salem to escape being accused of practicing witchcraft, too. She understood their attitude and supported their moving to safety, but she also felt abandoned. After she was hanged, since nobody was there to give her a proper burial, her body was just thrown into a ditch. Charity felt that Susannah's spirit was still earthbound and feeling very discarded, cast off, and lonely. We called the spirits of her loved ones to come back, recover her body, and give her a proper burial. She was amazed at how many of them came. They honored her for standing up for truth. They said, "You were never a weak woman, and we are so proud to be your descendants. You took on evil!" Susannah reflected that all the dark side got was her body, not her soul. Then it was time for the whole family to move into the Light.

Susannah requested her own family Bubblemobile, and they all crossed together into the next world. When she got to the Light, she noticed that some of the women who had been executed did not hold on to anger and had already crossed into the Light ahead of her. We multiplied the benefits and asked for any others in the whole universe who had been executed for things they did not do to couple to the healing, leave behind their anger and rage, and come to family reunions with loved ones in the Light.

The Slave Woman

We next focused on the slave woman behind the teenage girls. We started by begging her forgiveness for the way we white people had abused her people, breeding them like animals and separating them from family members to use them for our financial gain. She listened but was not ready to forgive. She told us how lonely she had felt when she was torn away from her entire family and forced to live among strangers for the rest of her life. Her only power was when the teenage girls listened to her stories. We asked her family to come surround her, and they came immediately, fighting to see who would get to hug her first. She could not believe this joyful reunion. She thought she would never see her family again. She had lost her faith in God when her masters tore her away from her family. She told us the slaveholders were also lied to by the darkness, which told them that having slaves would make them powerful. She did not know about the Civil War, so we told her about how it had freed the slaves. She was incredulous and asked, "There was a war fought for my people? Some of the descendants of my masters died in that war for my people? White people were willing to die for my race and set us free? How could I not forgive them? There has to be a God."

She had not wanted to go to heaven when she died because she did not want to be anywhere white people might be, but she changed her mind after learning about the Civil War. She told us that her own people in Africa had captured and sold slaves for money—greed. She said, "The dark continent was dark. We fought among ourselves over power, and that is how the white people got us. Greed and power, that's how the darkness does it." She crossed into the Light and said, "Human beings are not the enemy; the problem is the dark side." She prayed for healing for people of all races and color and noted how good forgiveness felt. She said that any wound can be healed, no matter how old it is, and reflected that she wanted to work for healing in the Light now. Then she went off to a big welcome-home celebration party with her family.

Charity reflected that just like the water poured on the Wicked Witch of the West in *The Wizard of Oz* melted the witch, when we pour the water of Light and love on dark and evil, it just melts away. Evil only looks solid and strong, but it is not nearly as solid and strong as they would like us to believe!

The Minister's Daughter

Next we sent out a search party to bring the minister's daughter into our sacred space. She felt ashamed and humiliated by what she had done, but a part of her did not want to admit that she had done anything wrong. Her former friends no longer wanted to be tied to her. Her father came and told us he was very sorry for the part he had played. He realized that he had betrayed God and was wrong to use God's love as a weapon to destroy people. He talked with his daughter and told her she was just following his instructions from the pulpit. He had been preaching, "There is good and evil, and good should try to destroy evil. Black will always be black." She was just listening to her father, but she felt ashamed of how much she enjoyed the power of being able to target people for death. She did not know how she could ever be forgiven.

Her father said that the bottom emotion behind the trials was pride. "We believed that we were the only ones who knew what God was like. Those who did not believe like us were wrong and evil and needed to be destroyed. We were right and they were wrong. I believed it was my job to destroy anything that was not of God. At the time, I really thought I was doing God's will." He said that the power was not attractive to him; he just wanted to be right. His daughter liked the power. They were deceived and wanted to apologize to all the people whose lives they had destroyed. The minister said, "I don't want to use God as a club anymore. God is not an exclusive club."

The minister and his daughter asked forgiveness of the people they had hurt. They were shocked to see a healing circle form around them of the people they had victimized helping them and sending them love. They realized that this forgiveness is true love. The minister and his daughter wanted to be instruments of good in the future and asked when they could go to the Light. We said, "Right now!"

Multiplying the Benefits

As we multiplied the benefits, Charity saw people coming in from every religion who all thought they were the best and the only right ones. They reflected, "How could we ever think that God, being limitless love, would limit his love to just us?" Some had been blinded by self-righteousness. They realized that all of us are children of God and that God can only love because that is who He is. Love does not beat or exclude; it forgives. The minister reflected that the Fallen Angel had projected his qualities of making people afraid onto God, like the Old Testament vengeful Yahweh. Jesus came to change the system, to put the true face of God on God with his example of forgiveness.

Charity's Reflections

After this work, Charity e-mailed me saying, "I *knew* there was a reason for going into my family tree that was much more than my curiosity. Now I know the reason was Divine, that God truly wants no one to perish in the darkness, but that 'whosoever will' can be brought to the Light. Thank you so much for your healing work with me and for helping me rescue my ancestors and get them to God, and on a much grander scale, helping rescue so many others, especially those who didn't even believe in Light!"

Many Pathways to the Divine

This case shows how dropping our belief that we are the only ones who know truth can open us up to a universal connection with the many faces of God. This change in attitude is the only way this planet can come to world peace. My belief system has changed in the course of six decades of life experience. Now I believe that the Divine communicates to humans in many ways, in many cultures, and that each different pathway to the Light has bits and pieces of absolute truth, which has been filtered in its presentation to the masses for social and political purposes. Just as a diamond has more than one facet, each different faith reflects an aspect of spiritual truth. Also, each faith has some pieces of fear-based propaganda entangled into this spiritual truth. In my previous book, *Invisible Roots: How Healing Past Life Trauma Can Liberate Your Present*, I talk about the process of my mind opening up to the truth of reincarnation, a belief present in many other religious groups such as the Essenes, Chinese Religion, Eckankar, Hare Krishna, Jainism, Scientology, Sikhism, Wicca, and the major world religions of Buddhism and Hinduism. I no longer accept the dualistic Judeo-Christian belief that we each have one life, are judged, and are then sent either to heaven or hell. I now believe that we get many lifetimes to learn the lessons of love and forgiveness and that each action we take has a karmic effect. I also believe Yeshua's radical teaching that "a Guru is not essential to help man reach to the Supreme."[1] In our current times, I feel that each person can access a direct link to spiritual guidance by setting pure intention and listening for "the still small voice of God within." The ego shouts, but Source whispers, and our priests and ministers are not the only ones who have a direct pipeline to the Divine!

The Fifth Sun

The Maya divided history into epochs called Suns. The first Sun ended with the flood, about 11,000 BC. Since then the Suns have lasted about four thousand years each, and the Fourth Sun began around 3800 BC with the beginning of the Sumerian civilization.[2] Mayan Elder Carlos Barrios gives hope for the transition we are now in between the ending of the Fourth Sun and the beginning of the Fifth Sun.

> At sunrise on December 21, 2012, for the first time in 26,000 years the Sun rises to conjunct the intersection of the Milky

---

1 McCannon, *Jesus*, 222.

2 Sitchin, *The Lost Realms*, 33.

Way and the plane of the ecliptic. This cosmic cross is considered to be an embodiment of the Sacred Tree, the Tree of Life, a tree remembered in all the world's spiritual traditions.[3]

He teaches that, in this new era, Earth will be aligning itself with the center of the galaxy, which may open a channel for cosmic energy to flow through and cleanse the planet, raising everyone to a higher level of vibration. Elder Barrios gives a beautiful, hopeful message:

> The greatest wisdom is in simplicity. Love, respect, tolerance, sharing, gratitude, forgiveness. It's not complex or elaborate. The real knowledge is free. It's encoded in your DNA. All you need is within you. Great teachers have said that from the beginning. Find your heart, and you will find your way.[4]

The Truth

If the Sumerian tablets are historically accurate, then the implication is that at least half of the DNA of each person walking and talking on Earth today is from another planet. In essence, we would all be part extraterrestrial, which makes the whole ET subject a bit less frightening. Facing our fears penetrates through the illusions we have believed. Seeing the truth behind the archetypes that have controlled our behavior frees the human heart to fill up with the golden light of the Creator's love.

My prayer is that all of humanity will see and overcome the ways we have been conditioned to fear the gods and the ways the dark forces have infiltrated our systems of worship. May we all take back the power we have given to the Anunnaki war gods and relocate our devotion to the Creator of All—Source energy, the true power in the Universe. May we all renounce greed as a way of life and stop scarcity thinking. May all the Dark Force Entities get better jobs working for the Light, and may we all be set free from the fear that has bound our souls! May we all be set free of the limitations placed on our human

---

3   C. Berrios, Seri Worldwide, online at http://www.seri-worldwide.org/id435.html
4   Ibid.

potential so our minds can expand to our full radiant capacity for intelligence and our hearts can make our decisions based on love. May all civilizations on Earth wake up to the unity of all that is and the realization that we are all passengers on Spaceship Earth and need to honor, love, and care for this beautiful planet on which we live. May we all wake up from the nightmare of fearing the gods, fearing annihilation, and practicing sacrifice of the firstborn to appease the gods. ***I Want This Nightmare to End!***

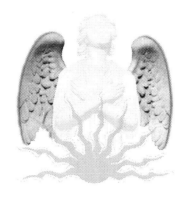

CHAPTER 44

Reflections

The journey with Paula through the nightmare and sorrow of her past has had a profound effect on my life. It triggered past life memories of my being sacrificed thousands of years ago so I could release my anger toward myself and get my power back. I had not wanted to look at this material because it terrified me. When we are afraid, we give our power away to whatever we fear. By facing what has frightened us the most, we call back the energy we lost so we can use it to heal our hearts. Going through Paula's "guided tour of hell" has also given depth and richness to my emotional life. Kahlil Gibran wrote:

> Your joy is your sorrow unmasked.
> And the selfsame well from which your laughter rises was
> oftentimes filled with your tears.
> And how else can it be?

The deeper that sorrow carves into your being, the more joy
you can contain.[1]

This journey has had a profound effect on my life at every level and im-
pelled me to find out how to stop the dark force patterns behind worship of
the darkness and the practice of human sacrifice. As I encountered evidence
that the things I had been taught in my church were not the whole picture,
my first reaction was disbelief. How could the Sumerian account of us being
genetically engineered be true? After disbelief came fear, as I realized that a
serious consideration of the veracity of this information would alienate people
who believed in the Bible as God's complete and impeccable truth. I knew
I would also estrange most of my professional colleagues and the scientific
research community merely by talking about extraterrestrial presence, as the
topic is generally considered "nuts." Who was left? You, the reader, friends,
my family, and Soul Detectives, who all want to know what is really, really
true. Thank you all for your courage to look at new ideas!

Freedom from Religious Dogma

The process of examining my religious beliefs has freed me from fearing going to go to hell if I did not obey church rules. The Sumerian tablets
put the anger and vengeance of the Old Testament Lord into an entirely new
framework for me. Now, rather than fearing the Lord would strike me dead for
disobedience, I have more compassion for Lord Enlil's point of view. He was
feeling the burden of being responsible to get enough gold to save his planet
from dying, along with everyone and everything on it. When things did not run
smoothly, he became infected with Dark Force Entities that made him lash out
like a lunatic and mercilessly destroy not only his people's enemies, but also
his own people.

I have also come to see that the whole idea of sacrifice to the gods was an
imprint that served them. The meat from the burnt offerings of animals fed the
priests and the gods themselves. Now my idea of what my Creator wants from
me is totally different. I think of what I want for my adult children as a model

---

1 Gibran, *The Prophet*, 32.

for what my Heavenly Parents want for me. Do I want my children to suffer so they will need me more? Do I want them to make sacrifices for me? Absolutely not! I want them to have joyful, abundant lives filled with love and peace. I believe my Creator wants the same for me and that the greatest gift I can offer to Spirit is to enjoy fully the precious gift of life given to me, day by day.

I remember a morning in 1989 when I was in prayer and meditation and told God, "I'm tired of carrying around all this psychic and emotional pain. I want *everything healed*!" My Divine Source took me seriously and, one by one, the dysfunctional patterns and the religious dogma that had been controlling my life have come up for examination and healing. I feel more present to my life now. I enjoy both the beauty and the ferocity of nature—the sunlight on tree leaves, the opening of each new daylily bud, and also the intensity of thunder and lightning crashing while Source is watering my garden.

The Joy of Facilitating Healing

Being a vehicle to help others connect with their inner healing resources is an immense spiritual joy. While I loved the emotional connection I had with my clients when I only knew how to do talk therapy, I often felt helpless witnessing their emotional pain and the seemingly insurmountable challenges that many faced. Now that I have healing tools from

I get a vicarious high from watching them grow and heal. Yet, my absolutely greatest joy is watching the Soul Detectives who have trained with me amplify the tools and use them with their own caseloads, making a chain reaction of healing energy that reverberates throughout the universe. We feel we are part of a group called the Intergalactic Federation of Healers working for world and universal peace.

I have seen the progression of issues that arose in the hypnotherapy community with therapists who ask to go to the origins of their patients' symptoms. First past life trauma comes up, then earthbound spirits, Dark Force Entities, and finally, extraterrestrials. Some therapists get stuck along the way and refuse to open to one more area, but the final step of opening to the idea that we may not be alone in the universe expands our ability to heal into other planets, galaxies, and dimensions.

Soul Detective Work

I am amazed by the constant expansion of the breadth of Soul Detective work. My clients seem to bring in the issues that I have just figured out how to deal with. For example, last night I dreamed that a bug had drilled a perfectly straight three-eighth-inch hole in my etheric body starting at my third eye. The hole went through my head and stopped at the back of my skull (a new spin to the term "airhead"). I knew this etheric hole came from an invasive program and was not something I had done to myself. During a Soul Detective session today, a client was working to heal the trauma that his daughter had suffered from having an infection as a baby. I sensed that the infectious agents involved had put holes in the baby's etheric body, which looked like Swiss cheese. We asked Archangel Michael to restore the baby's etheric template to its Divine perfect blueprint. Then, with the permission of the client, we went one step further. We looked at the idea that the infection might have come from a frequency broadcast to the baby girl by a malevolent force that did not want her light to shine in the world. We asked Archangel Michael to block any and all detrimental frequencies broadcast to this child and her whole family.

I perceived a thought coming from Archangel Michael saying, "I've been waiting for you to ask me to do this!" His message is a reminder that because the angels cannot violate the law of free will, we need to ask the angels for what we want. They did not interfere when Lucifer set out with his rebellion, and they do not currently interfere with the actions of the Dark Force Entities unless we request their help. May we all ask to be free from these dark programs, right now! May we also ask that the fallen angels behind the scenes come out of their collective nightmare, find the spark of light in each of their hearts, and convert back to Lightworkers!

Deep healing has come to the wounds in my own soul through this energy healing work, both practicing the methods on myself and being treated by my colleagues. I know I am not done healing yet, because I am still breathing. When I have healed completely, I will be free to go back to the place of my soul's origin. Or, I might stay in this body a few extra decades just to enjoy time with my precious beloved ones and to feel the full expansion of joy that a *Homo sapiens* vehicle can experience!

May we all face our fears, fully connect with the Source of infinite love from which our souls were born, ask to have the golden Light of love fill our energy field, and feel that presence in our hearts, always.

Soul Detective Blessing
from Higher Realms

**A message channeled by Mary Anderson
for all present and future Soul Detectives:**

Beings of Light and lovers of harmony, you are seen, my beloveds.

You are known, and you are held beyond your wildest imagination.

Know this as your truth, my beloveds.

You are here to bring a vibration of light heretofore not seen on planet Earth.

You have been imbued with alchemical powers.

*Your ego is unaware, yet your soul resonates
to the true vibration of pure light.*

Be one with us. Be one with the starlight,

for I am the one who projected that vision to Mary.

It is with protection, unity, and oneness that you move together as one.

Remember this in your forward movement,

that there is strength in the unity that you share.

Your leader, Barbara Stone, has come forward to remind you all

of the innate truth of who you are.

*As you hold your own mantle of remembrance,
you too become a leader of Light.*

May the Light shine in harmony and oneness so that peace may prevail.

*You are blessed. It is with gratitude that I send you forth this evening
with a blessing.*

*Please extend your right hand and know that you are touched
with the essence of starlight.*

APPENDIX

The Formation of Our Solar System

*A*ccording to the clay tablets that the Sumerians painstakingly recorded for us many thousands of years ago to inform us of our ancient origins, no life would be on our planet if Nibiru had not interfaced with Earth long ago. From studying the rate at which galaxies are flying apart from each other, scientists estimate that the universe is about fourteen billion years old and our solar system is approximately four and a half billion years old, a relative newcomer in our galaxy, the Milky Way.

Tiamat and Gold

Astrophysics theorizes that new solar systems are created at the edge of a galaxy and then swirl through the spiral formation of the galaxy toward the black hole in the center of each galaxy. Our galaxy, the Milky Way, is surrounded by clouds of dust, gasses, and dark matter that coalesce and then, through nuclear fusion, ignite a new star. As chunks of matter around our new sun stuck together and were drawn into the orbit of the sun's gravitational pull, the Babylonian Epic of Creation, Enuma Elish, says that the sun, called Apsu, fashioned a huge planet named Tiamat as a spouse for himself. Tiamat was the only planet in our solar system that had gold.

A gift resplendent to his spouse Apsu granted:
A shining metal, the everlasting gold, for her alone
to possess![1]

Gold has amazing properties and has been highly prized throughout recorded history. Why is gold such a big deal? Gold bars and coins represent wealth and financial security. Gold is so soft in its pure metallic form that it can easily be shaped for jewelry and art. It also has great value in electronics. Gold is the most useful metal present on this planet.

> Gold conducts electricity, does not tarnish, is very easy to work, can be drawn into wire, can be hammered into thin sheets, alloys with many other metals, can be melted and cast into highly detailed shapes, has a wonderful color and a brilliant luster.[2]

Of all metals, gold is the least reactive. The reason it never rusts or tarnishes is because it does not react with oxygen. It is also the most electrically conductive and can convey current in temperatures varying from -55° Celsius to + 200° Celsius, which makes it extremely vital in computers and telecommunication equipment. Gold is so malleable that one ounce of it can be drawn into a wire eight kilometers long or hammered into a twelve-meter-square sheet. Gold also reflects infrared rays, making it ideal for firefighters and astronauts. "Gold is also an excellent conductor of thermal energy or heat. It is used to transfer heat away from delicate instruments. For this reason, a 35 percent gold alloy is used in the main engine nozzle of the Space Shuttle, where temperatures can reach 3300° Celsius.[3]

Together Apsu and Tiamat created their children, the other planets, but none of the others got gold. Then Tiamat got tired of having so many children and became grumpy. She raged against her offspring, the other planets. What

---

1 Sitchin, *The Lost Book of Enki*, 46.
2 News and Information About Geology at www.geology.com and http://geology.com/minerals/gold/uses-of-gold.shtml
3 Tellinger, *Slave Species of god*, 113.

science would say is that the orbits of the planets had not yet been firmly established, and Tiamat's huge size in her location between Mars and Jupiter was causing the orbits of the other planets to become unstable. All of our planets rotate counterclockwise around the sun, so none of them could do battle with Tiamat. A planet needed to come in rotating clockwise to intercept Tiamat. The tablets say a cry went out from the council of planets for help, and Nibiru was called in from deep outer space to rush to the rescue. But Nibiru had a condition for going to battle with Tiamat. Nibiru wanted a supreme destiny in our solar system, saying, "Let all the gods agree in council to make me the leader, bow to my command!"[4] Note this characteristic. The spirit of Nibiru itself wanted leadership and power. The council of our solar system agreed and set Nibiru on a circuit toward Tiamat. What science would say is that a huge comet was passing by the sun and became trapped in its magnetic field. Nibiru was pulled into our solar system rotating clockwise around our sun between Mars and Jupiter, which put it on a collision course with Tiamat. The records say that the two planets commenced a Celestial Battle, and Nibiru subdued Tiamat by cleaving her in two, exposing her golden veins.

A large chunk of Tiamat spun off and went into orbit on the other side of Mars to become the planet Earth. To examine the validity of this Sumerian account, look at a globe. Note how land is distributed in a lopsided fashion on our planet. If you look at the globe from the South Pole, you see mostly water, and from the North Pole, mostly land. Likewise, looking at the globe from the side of the Pacific Ocean, you see much more water and less land than when viewing it from the Atlantic Ocean. One can also see evidence supporting the theory of a super-continent named Pangaea in which the continents fit together long ago, then gradually drifted apart in chunks that formed our present continents. On a subsequent pass around our sun, Nibiru shattered the remaining part of Tiamat into the asteroid belt, called "the Hammered Bracelet."[5]

---

4 Sitchin, *The Lost Book of Enki*, 50.
5 Melchizedek, *The Ancient Secret of the Flower of Life*, 81-82.

The Moon

Tiamat's main satellite named Kingu went with the split-off chunk and became our moon. Evidence from physics supports the Sumerian account, because the moons around other planets are considerably smaller in relationship to the planets they orbit. "The physics would not have allowed such a large satellite to form at the point of creation around a planet as small as Earth."[6] The diameter of the moon is one-fourth the diameter of Earth. When we see the moon in the sky, it usually looks as large as the sun, except when it appears larger during a Harvest Moon.

Seeds of Life

Tiamat did not have the elements necessary for life, but Nibiru did. When they collided, some of the elemental building blocks of life got rubbed off on Earth, and life forms began slowly to evolve on our planet. This transmission explains why life would have been so much more developed on Nibiru, because they had a big head start.[7]

Comets

The Celestial battle also produced large chunks of debris that were thrown off their course and forced into a retrograde orbit. "Trembling with fear, they turned their backs about."[8] Thus were born comets, which have retrograde orbits that are greatly elliptical, just like Nibiru. The frozen material in a comet comes to life when the comet nears the Sun, which is why it develops a head and a long tail as part of its mass vaporizes. When Halley's comet passed Earth in 1986, we had the chance to study its movement and its core up close.

Nibiru's Orbit

The orbit of Nibiru is elliptical, like the orbits of comets which come in from deep outer space, circle around the sun, and then to back into space. The orbit of Nibiru passes between Mars and Jupiter at its perigee, its point clos-

---

6   Tellinger, *Slave Species of god*, 85.

7   Sitchin, *When Time Began*.

8   Sitchin, *The Lost Realms*, 34.

est to the sun, and then goes far out into space at its apogee, the point where it turns around and heads back toward the sun. Nibiru's circuit is so large that it needs about 3600 years to complete one pass around the sun. It has an orbit similar to that of comet Hale-Bopp, which has an elliptical cycle of 4000 years.[9]

---

9   Tellinger, *Slave Species of god.*

Bibliography

Alcorn, R. (2011). *Healing Stories: My Journey from Mainstream Psychiatry Toward Spiritual Healing*. Medina, OH: Perception Garden Press.

Baldwin W. (2003). *Healing Lost Souls: Releasing Unwanted Spirits from your Energy Body*. Charlottesville, VA: Hampton Roads.

Bartlett, R. (2007). *Matrix Energetics: The Science and Art of Transformation*. New York: Atria.

Bartlett, R. (2009). *The Matrix Energetics Experience*, audiobook. Louisville, CO: Sounds True.

Bauval, R., and Gilbert, A. (1995). *The Orion Mystery: Unlocking the Secrets of the Pyramids*. New York: Three Rivers Press.

Bliss, J., and E. Bliss. (1985). *Prism: Andrea's World*. New York: Stein and Day.

Bruyere, R. (1994). *Wheels of Light: Chakras, Auras, and the Healing Energy of the Body*. New York: Touchstone.

Cori, P. (2011). *Before We Leave You: Messages from the Great Whales and the Dolphin Beings*. Berkeley, CA: North Atlantic Books.

Crick, F. (1981). *Life Itself: Its Origin and Nature*. New York: Simon & Schuster.

Doreal. (2002). *The Emerald Tablets of Thoth-the-Atlantean*. Nashville, TN: Source Books, Inc.

Fossey, D. (2000). *Gorillas in the Mist*. New York: Mariner Books.

Gibran, K. (1966). *The Prophet*. New York: Alfred A.

Greer, S. (2006). *Hidden Truth: Forbidden Knowledge*. Crozet, VA: Crossing Points.

Hancock, G. (1995). *Fingerprints of the Gods*. New York: Crown Trade Paperbacks.

Hatzfeld, J. (2006). *Machete Season: The Killers in Rwanda Speak*. New York: Picador.

Hawkins, D. (1995). *Power Vs. Force: The Hidden Determinants of Human Behavior*. Sedona, AZ: Veritas.

Hellinger, B. (2001). *Love's Own Truths: Bonding and Balancing in Close Relationships*. Phoenix, AZ: Zeig, Tucker and Theisen.

Herman, J. (1992). *Trauma and Recovery: The Aftermath of Violence—from Domestic Abuse to Political Terror*. New York: Basic Books.

Hoyle, F. (1982). *Evolution from Space*. Berkeley Heights, NJ: Enslow.

Jung, C. (1989). *Memories, Dreams, Reflections*. New York: Vintage Books.

Kardec, A. (1989). *The Spirits' Book*. Albuquerque, NM: Brotherhood of Life.

Karim, I. (2010). *Back to a Future for Mankind: BioGeometry*. Cairo, Egypt: BioGeometry Consulting.

Karjala, L. (2007). *Understanding Trauma and Dissociation: A Guide for Therapists, Patients and Loved Ones*. Atlanta, GA: ThomasMax.

Lampe, S. (2008). *The Christian and Reincarnation*. Ibadan, Nigeria: Millennium Press.

Lewis, C.S. (2001). *The Screwtape Letters*. San Francisco, CA: HarperOne.

Macy, M. (2006). *Spirit Faces: Truth about the Afterlife*. San Francisco, CA: Weiser Books.

McCannon, T. (2010). *Jesus: The Explosive Story of the 30 Lost Years and the Ancient Mystery Religions*. Charlottesville, VA: Hampton Roads.

Melchizedek, D. (1998). *The Ancient Secret of the Flower of Life*, Volume 1. Flagstaff, AZ: Light Technology.

Modi, S. (1997). *Remarkable Healings: A Psychiatrist Discovers Unsuspected Roots of Mental and Physical Illness.* Charlottesville, VA: Hampton Roads.

Osborne, H. (1968). *South American Mythology.* Feltham, Middlesex, UK: Hamlyn Publishing Group.

Osho. (2007). *A Cup of Tea: Letters Written by Osho to Disciples and Friends.* New Delhi, India: Adarsh Printers.

Prophet, E. C. (1994). *The Lost Teachings of Jesus,* Book 1. Corwin Springs, MT: Summit University Press.

Putnam, F. (1989). *Diagnosis and Treatment of Multiple Personality Disorder.* New York: Guilford Press.

Sitchin, Z. (1980). *The Stairway to Heaven: Book II of the Earth Chronicles.* New York: Harper.

Sitchin, Z. (1985). *The Wars of Gods and Men: Book III of the Earth Chronicles.* New York: Harper.

Sitchin, Z. (1990). *The Lost Realms: Book IV of the Earth Chronicles.* New York: Avon.

Sitchin, Z. (1993). *When Time Began: Book V of the Earth Chronicles.* New York: Harper.

Sitchin, Z. (1998). *The Cosmic Code: Book VI of the Earth Chronicles.* Rochester, VT: Bear and Co.

Sitchin, Z. (2002). *The Lost Book of Enki.* Rochester, VT: Bear and Co.

Sitchin, Z. (2007). *Twelfth Planet: Book I of the Earth Chronicles.* New York: Harper.

Sitchin, Z. (2008). *The End of Days: Armageddon and Prophecies of the Return: Book VII of the Earth Chronicles.* New York: Harper.

Sitchin, Z. (2010). *There Were Giants upon the Earth: Gods, Demigods, and Human Ancestry: The Evidence of Alien DNA.* Rochester, VT: Bear & Co.

Stapleton, R.C. (1977). *The Experience of Inner Healing*. Waco, TX: Word Books.

Stone, B. (2008). *Invisible Roots: How Healing Past Life Trauma Can Liberate Your Present*. Santa Rosa, CA: Energy Psychology Press.

Swanson, C. (2009). *Life Force, the Scientific Basis: Volume II of the Synchronized Universe*. Tucson, AZ: Poseidia Press.

Tellinger, M. (2005). *Slave Species of god*. Johannesburg, South Africa: Music Masters Close Corporation.

Thomas, J. (2010). *Day Breaks Over Dharamsala: A Memoir of Life Lost and Found*. Friday Harbor, WA: Nutshell Books.

The Holy Bible, New International Version. (1978). Grand Rapids, MI: Zondervan Bible Publishers.

Tolle, E. (1999). *Practicing the Power of Now: Essential Teachings, Meditations, and Exercises from The Power of Now*. Novato, CA: New World Library.

Urantia Foundation Staff. (2008). *The Urantia Book*. Chicago, IL: Urantia Foundation.

Virtue, D. (1997). *Angel Therapy: Healing Messages for Every Area of Your Life*. Carlsbad, CA: Hay House.

Von Däniken, E. (1999). *Chariots of the Gods: Unsolved Mysteries of the Past*. New York: Berkley Books.

Walthers, L. (2010). *Life in Nature Revealed: Real Photographs of Faeries, Gnomes, and Elves*. Bloomington, IN: Author House.

Webber, C. S., and W. D. Webber. (1994). *A Rustle of Angels: Stories about Angels in Real Life and Scripture*. Carmel, NY: Guideposts.

Wolffe, B. (1981). *Henry VI*. London, UK: Methuen.

Index

About the Author

arbara Stone is a workshop presenter, public speaker, bilingual psychotherapist in private practice, and a Professor at Energy Medicine University, a distance learning program. She is a licensed independent social worker in the state of Ohio and a Diplomate in Comprehensive Energy Psychology. The topic of healing is very close to her heart, as her first book, *Cancer as Initiation: Surviving the Fire*, is the autobiographical account of her holistic approach to recovery from a diagnosis of breast cancer in 1991. Her second book, *Invisible Roots*, shows how past life trauma and earthbound spirit attachments may underlie many emotional problems that feel "stuck" and presents Soul Detective Protocols she developed to resolve these issues using energy therapies to help earthbound spirits heal and cross into the Light. Dr. Stone is also a musician, potter, gardener, grandmother, and holds a doctorate in clinical psychology from Pacifica Graduate Institute in Carpinteria, California.